FURTHER CONTRIBUTIONS TO THE

THEORY AND TECHNIQUE OF PSYCHO-ANALYSIS

BY

SÁNDOR FERENCZI, M.D.

COMPILED BY

JOHN RICKMAN, M.A., M.D.

AUTHORIZED TRANSLATION BY

JANE ISABEL SUTTIE, M.A., M.B., CH.B.

AND OTHERS

MARESFIELD REPRINTS

LONDON

Reprinted 1980, with permission of
Hogarth Press Limited, by
H. Karnac (Books) Limited,
58 Gloucester Road,
London S.W. 7
England

ISBN 0 9507146 1 5

MANUFACTURED IN THE UNITED STATES OF AMERICA

COMPILER'S NOTE TO FIRST EDITION

Dr. Ferenczi possesses so remarkable an imaginative quality that we feel justified in including a great number of short contributions, some only a few lines long, in a volume that contains some of the most important contributions to psycho-analysis that have been made in the past decade. The reader is urged to bear in mind that the papers are not in chronological order, and that each one should be placed in its 'period' before being read; as an aid to this the date has been printed at the top of every sheet in this case as in Freud's *Collected Papers*.

The understanding of psycho-analytical literature may be compared to that of a mathematical science such as physics. Some things are comprehended in a flash, others only after long rumination, when in order to bring about understanding elaborate mental adjustments have to be made; in mathematical science these are almost entirely intellectual, in psycho-analysis almost entirely emotional, but in both the adaptation is an *unconscious process.*

J. R.

21st August 1926.

FURTHER NOTE

The completion of the Bibliography of Ferenczi's writings is the only addition to this book since its first appearance. The material for this addition has been kindly supplied by his literary executor, Dr. Michael Balint.

Ferenczi died in 1933.

November 1949.

AUTHOR'S PREFACE

The courtesy of the Institute of Psycho-Analysis enables me to publish a second collection of my psycho-analytical writings in English; the first appeared in 1916 in the splendid translation of my honoured friend, Dr. Ernest Jones, under the title, *Contributions to Psycho-Analysis* (Boston: Badger and Co., reappearing in several new editions under the title *Sex and Psycho-analysis*).

The present collection in no way gives a systematic survey of the development of psycho-analysis in the intervening years, but only the disjointed papers which represent the author's personal contribution to this development. Even in their diversity of form, perhaps in their very medley, I believe these papers give a true picture of the manifold interests which continually occupy the physician practising psycho-analysis, and which bring him into touch with the most varied fields of the natural and mental sciences. The personal inclinations of the author inevitably find expression; the outlook is predominantly that of the medical rather than that of the abstract sciences, and there gradually emerges a sort of psycho-analytical theory of one of the important manifestations of instinct—'Genitality'. The theories of 'genitality' have been collected under the title, *An Attempt to formulate a Genital Theory*, which appeared in German in 1924; an English translation will shortly be published.

The experiences collected in the course of my practice

of psycho-analysis become grouped under two heads. One of these tends to shed some analytical light derived from experience upon certain normal and pathological psychic phenomena which have not been fully explained previously, and attempts to explain the symptoms of hysteria, tic, etc. A somewhat larger work falling under this heading has already appeared in English in the 'Nervous and Mental Disease Monograph Series' as the theoretical part of an analytic research into General Paralysis of the Insane.

The other focus of interest in my work lies in the field of technique; my attempt to speed up the analytic technique by so-called 'active' measures belongs to this category. I mention this particularly, because an erroneous opinion repeatedly crops up that the classical Freudian technique was to be replaced by something new in my *Active Technique*. It will not escape the attentive reader that there can be no question of that, and that my technical innovations should only be applied occasionally as adjuvants in reinforcing the Freudian method. Inasmuch as I have overworked this measure occasionally, following one of Rank's suggestions (the setting of a limit to the duration of the analysis), I must on empirical grounds reduce its value to its legitimate measure (see *Contra-indications of the Active Technique*). For the rest I hold fast to the critical views expressed in the brochure on the *Development of the Psycho-Analytic Technique* (Nervous and Mental Disease Monograph Series) on certain deficiencies in the application of the conventional method, but I take exception to the one-sidedness of the *Birth-Theory* of the neuroses and the much-overdone *Birth-Technique*.

It gives me great pleasure to lay my work once more before Anglo-Saxon readers, particularly because I have found that with their broad-mindedness they often strive to view such opinions as mine quite without prejudice, whereas elsewhere these are turned down *a limine* on account of their novelty or their boldness.

I owe many thanks to the translator of most of this work—Dr. Jane Suttie—who has not flinched from the toil of following the train of my thought with so much understanding, and my special thanks are due to my colleague, Dr. John Rickman, without whose valuable assistance this collection might not have appeared at all.

S. FERENCZI.

BUDAPEST, 21*st August* 1926.

TABLE OF CONTENTS

PAGE

COMPILER'S NOTE 5

AUTHOR'S PREFACE 7

NOSOLOGY

1. The Analytic Conception of the Psycho-Neuroses. [1908] 15
2. Actual- and Psycho-Neuroses in the Light of Freud's Investigations and Psycho-Analysis. [1908] . 30
3. Suggestion and Psycho-Analysis. [1912] . . 55
4. On Forced Phantasies. [1924] . . . 68
5. Disease- or Patho-Neuroses. [1916/17] . . 78
6. The Phenomena of Hysterical Materialization. [1919] 89
7. 'Materialization' in Globus Hystericus. [1923] . 104
8. Psychogenic Anomalies of Voice Production. [1915] 105
9. An Attempted Explanation of some Hysterical Stigmata. [1919] 110
10. The Psycho-Analysis of a Case of Hysterical Hypochondria. [1919] 118
11. Two Types of War Neuroses. [1916/17] . . 124
12. Psycho-Analytical Observations on Tic. [1921] . 142
13. Sunday Neuroses. [1919] 174

TECHNIQUE

14. On the Technique of Psycho-Analysis. [1919] . 177
15. Technical Difficulties in the Analysis of a Case of Hysteria. [1919] 189
16. The Further Development of an Active Therapy in Psycho-Analysis. [1920] 198

PAGE

17. Contra-indications to the 'Active' Psycho-Analytical Technique. [1925] 217
18. Thinking and Muscle Innervation. [1919] . . 230
19. Discontinuous Analysis. [1914] 233
20. On Influencing of the Patient in Psycho-Analysis. [1919] 235
21. Attention during the Narration of Dreams. [1923] . 238
22. Restlessness towards the End of the Hour of Analysis. [1915] 238
23. Sensations of Giddiness at the End of the Psycho-Analytic Session [1914] 239
24. A Transitory Symptom: the Position during Treatment. [1913] 242
25. The Compulsion to Symmetrical Touching. [1916/17] 242
26. The Psychic Consequences of a 'Castration' in Childhood. [1916/17] 244
27. On Falling Asleep during Analysis. [1914] . . 249
28. Silence is Golden. [1916/17] . . . 250
29. Talkativeness. [1915] 252

SEXUAL THEORY

30. The Scientific Significance of Freud's *Three Essays on the Theory of Sexuality*. [1915] . . . 253
31. Composite Formations of Erotic and Character Traits. [1916/17] 257
32. Psycho-Analysis of Sexual Habits. [1925] . . 259
33. Pollution without Dream Orgasm and Dream Orgasm without Pollution. [1916/17] . . . 297
34. The Dream of the Occlusive Pessary. [1915] . 304
35. Washing-Compulsion and Masturbation. [1923] . 311
36. Paræsthesias of the Genital Regions in Impotence. [1913] 312
37. Shuddering at Scratching on Glass, etc. [1923] . 313
38. Infantile Ideas about the Female Genital Organs. [1913] 314
39. Ptyalism in an Oral-erotic. [1923] . . . 315
40. Embarrassed Hands. [1914] 315

PAGE
41. Rubbing the Eyes as a Substitute for Onanism. [1914] 317
42. An 'Anal Hollow-penis' in Woman. [1923] . 317
43. Micturition as a Sedative. [1915] . . . 317
44. Dread of Cigar and Cigarette Smoking. [1914] . 318
45. Obsessional Etymologizing. [1913] . . . 318
46. Cornelia, the Mother of the Gracchi. [1919] . 318

FROM THE NURSERY—SHORT PAPERS

47. The 'Grandfather Complex'. [1913] . . 323
48. Flatus as an Adult Prerogative. [1913] . . 325
49. Childish Ideas of Digestion. [1913] . . . 325
50. Disgust for Breakfast. [1919] . . . 326
51. The Cause of Reserve in a Child. [1913] . . 327
52. Two Typical Fæcal and Anal Symptoms. [1915] . 327
53. Nakedness as a Means for Inspiring Terror. [1919] . 329

DREAMS, ETC.

54. The Psycho-Analysis of Wit and the Comical. [1911] 332
55. Interchange of Affect in Dreams. [1916/17] . 345
56. Dreams of the Unsuspecting. [1916/17] . . 346
57. To Whom does one Relate one's Dreams? [1913] . 349
58. The Dream of the 'Clever Baby'. [1923] . . 349
59. A Striking Picture of the 'Unconscious'. [1912] . 350
60. Pompadour Phantasies. [1915] . . . 351

SYMBOLISM—SHORT PAPERS

61. The Symbolism of the Bridge. [1921] . . 352
62. Bridge Symbolism and the Don Juan Legend. [1921] 356
63. Significant Variants of the Shoe as a Vagina Symbol. [1916/17] 358
64. The Symbolism of Bed-Linen. [1913] . . 359
65. The Kite as a Symbol of Erection. [1913] . . 359
66. On the Symbolism of the Head of Medusa. [1923] . 360
67. The Fan as a Genital Symbol. [1915] . . 361
68. Vermin as a Symbol of Pregnancy. [1914] . . 361

PAGE

69. Pecunia Olet. [1916/17] 362
70. An Anal-erotic Proverb. [1915] . . . 365
71. Spectrophobia. [1915] 365
72. The Psychic Effect of the Sunbath. [1914] . . 365

APPLIED PSYCHO-ANALYSIS

73. The Problem of Acceptance of Unpleasant Ideas—Advances in Knowledge of the Sense of Reality. [1926] 366
74. The Psyche as an Inhibiting Organ. [1922] . 379
75. Concerning the Psychogenesis of Mechanism. [1919] 383
76. Supplement to 'The Psychogenesis of Mechanism'. [1920] 393
77. The Analysis of Comparisons. [1915] . . 397
78. On Supposed Mistakes. [1915] . . . 407
79. The 'Forgetting' of a Symptom and its Explanation in a Dream. [1914] 412
80. The 'Family Romance' of a Lowered Social Position. [1922] 413
81. Mental Disturbance as a Result of Social Advancement. [1922] 417
82. The Sons of the 'Tailor'. [1923] . . . 418
83. 'Nonum Prematur in Annum'. [1915]. . . 419
84. Stage-fright and Narcissistic Self-observation. [1923] . 421
85. Hebbel's Explanation of 'déjà vu'. [1915] . . 422
86. Polycratism. [1915] 423

MEDICAL JURISPRUDENCE AND RELIGION

87. A Lecture for Judges and Barristers. [1913]. . 424
88. Psycho-Analysis and Criminology. [1919] . . 434
89. Belief, Disbelief and Conviction. [1913] . . 437
90. Obsessional Neurosis and Piety. [1914] . . 450

A BIBLIOGRAPHY OF FERENCZI'S WRITINGS TO END OF 1933 451

INDEX 470

NOSOLOGY

I

THE ANALYTIC CONCEPTION OF THE PSYCHO-NEUROSES [1]

THERE are many ways in which the flattering request of the Medical Association, that I should deliver a lecture reviewing the progress in the study of the neuroses, might be treated. I might discuss various functional neuroses seriatim and mention the novelties that have appeared among the individual kinds of neuroses in the course of the last few years. On a little reflection I rejected this plan, because if I mentioned merely the names of all the disease-phenomena nowadays included under the heading 'functional neurosis' it would create such a chaos of new Græco-Latin words that I should only increase the confusion reigning at present where the neuroses are concerned. I shall therefore try to carry out my task in a different way. Instead of going into details I shall review matters individually and give the general impression which a nerve specialist acquires of the present state of his department of medicine.

One of the wittiest of German writers, Georg Christian Lichtenberg, once asked the paradoxical question why did it never strike researchers that discoveries could be made not only with a magnifying glass but also, perhaps, with a diminishing lens? He obviously meant that the increasing search for details in which science gets tied up and loses its perspective over things as a whole might from time to time be given up for the consideration, individually and from a distance, of the results already achieved. He means,

[1] From a series of lectures delivered in 1908 to the Budapest Medical Association. Published in *Populäre Vorträge über Psychoanalyse*.

therefore, approximately the same thing that Herbert Spencer mentions as the necessary phase in all natural evolution, namely, that differentiation should occasionally be freed from the work of correlation and integration.

When, therefore, I consider the various neuroses through a diminishing lens, their multiplicity reduces itself to a twofold division that cannot be further integrated.

One kind of neurosis is, though it does not leave the mental life untouched (there is, indeed, no illness without psychic participation), mainly confined to the somatic domain. Another great group of the neuroses on the other hand, though not wholly without concomitant bodily phenomena, manifests itself chiefly in psychic changes—indeed, owes its origin exclusively to psychic shocks.

You will, perhaps, be surprised that such a dualistic division of diseases is possible to-day in this age of monism. I hasten also to add here that this nosological dualism agrees quite well with the agnostic monism of the philosophers, since the latter—as its name indicates—only postulates the uniform conformity to law throughout the whole of nature, but at the same time is frank enough to allow that we can say nothing about the nature of this conformity. In my opinion the monistic conception is in the meantime only a philosophic declaration of faith or an ideal that one would fain approach, but which is still so remote from the confines of our present knowledge that we are as yet unable to make practical use of its teachings. It is useless to attempt to palliate facts; as things stand to-day we can analyse one set of phenomena only physically and another set only psychologically. Psycho-physical parallelism, too, is certainly a possible but really very improbable philosophic theorem by which we need not let ourselves be misled in our observations. In a word, we call it disingenuous when—as is at present customary—psychic happenings are defined by anatomical and physiological conceptions, for the truth is that we know nothing of either the physiological side of psychic life or of the anatomical substratum of its mechanism. The most we learnt in this respect from natural science is the fact of cerebral localization of sensory functions and the recognition of individual co-ordinating centres for movements. Flechsig, indeed, attempted to construct a modern phrenology on the basis of the chronological sequence of the embryonic brain tissues, but the whole complicated system of the three to four dozen psychic centres and their projection and association fibres which he assumed is only an extremely unstable even if ingenious theoretical edifice about which the clinician need not greatly trouble himself.

So far, too, all search for the anatomical brain changes accompanying mental disease has remained quite fruitless, as has also the endeavour to correlate the pathological-anatomical findings with the mental symptoms noted during life for the purpose of drawing conclusions about the psychic functions of individual parts of the brain. Neither in mania nor in melancholia, in paranoia, hysteria nor in obsessional neurosis were any changes found on microscopical examination of the brain; in other diseases such as paralysis, alcoholism, and senile dementia, changes were certainly found, but the relation of the brain lesion to the psychic symptoms could not be stated, so that we may confidently say that we can to-day as little speak of a pathological anatomy of the psychoses and psycho-neuroses as of the material correlation of mental functioning in general.

Our learned men, even if they allow that they do not yet know the functional mechanism of 'thinking matter', show an extraordinary resistance against acknowledging their ignorance as regards the pathology of this matter. If it is a fallacy to speak of 'molecular movements' of the brain cells instead simply of feeling, thinking, and willing, then it is no less disingenuous to throw anatomical, physiological, physical, and chemical expressions about when describing the so-called functional psychoses and neuroses. Our learned men seem to be of the opinion that a *docta ignorantia* is more supportable than an *indocta ignorantia*, that, therefore, the naïve acknowledgement of our ignorance is more shameful than a lack of knowledge that cloaks itself in scientific language.

Let us suppose, however, that man at last manages to

observe directly in himself the brain changes occurring parallel with his own sensations; the twofold division of the phenomenal series, the separation of what is observed from the exterior, and what is seen inwardly would nevertheless persist. Even the most accurate description of the movements of the brain molecules would not render introspective psychology superfluous.

For the understanding of the healthy and diseased mind, therefore, analysis of direct inner perception remains the chief source of psychological knowledge; indeed, it has more prospect of permanence than the purely materialistic point of view. It has been our experience that a few unforeseen discoveries have been able to shake physics to its foundations, while the principles of introspection always remain the same.

I could not spare you this philosophical excursion, although it constantly reminds me of another witty saying of the above-mentioned Lichtenberg, that one can as easily do oneself an injury with philosophy as with a sharp razor blade if one does not proceed with the utmost care. I, therefore, lay this dangerous weapon aside and confine myself to repeating once more that the dualistic division of the neuroses is, according to the present position of our knowledge, fully justified.

Amongst the organic neuroses, or, as I should like to call them, the physio-neuroses, we reckon, for instance, chorea, myxœdema, Basedow's disease, neurasthenia and the anxiety neuroses in Freud's sense and other conditions in which the cause of the disease is sought for or has already been found in disturbances of metabolism and such like. In my lecture to-day I should like to direct your attention exclusively towards the other great group of neuroses—to the psycho-neuroses—those neuroses whose causation, pathological nature, and symptomatology are at present open only to an introspective psychical scrutiny, and particularly to hysteria and obsessional neurosis. I would remark here at once that the psycho-neuroses cannot be sharply distinguished either from 'normal' mental functioning or from the functional psychoses; it is mainly practical considerations that compel the doctor to treat normality, psycho-neurosis, and psychosis as separate chapters in psychology. From the scientific point of view there is no fundamental difference between the outbursts of passion in the ' normal ' person, the attacks of the hysteric, and the ravings of the insane.

The ' psycho-genetic ' view of the psychoses and neuroses is of primeval antiquity.

The dominance of the materialistic and mechanistic point of view in the nineteenth century first misled psychologists and psycho-pathologists to renounce the naïve but honest introspective psychology and to imitate the experimental methods so successful in the natural sciences. Finally, it went so far that doctors and natural philosophers handed over as though unworthy of their consideration the great and little mental problems of humanity to the writers of *belles lettres*, and confined themselves more and more to the task of the registration of the physiology of the senses. Since Fechner and Wundt, hardly anyone has animated the dead matter of experimental psychology with an in any way informative idea. Freud's exertions have succeeded recently in joining up the broken threads connecting scientific psychology and daily life, and in making a scientific field that had long lain fallow fruitful once more.

I have already had an opportunity of telling you, honoured colleagues, about the evolution of Freud's theory and method—about psycho-analysis. This time I shall indicate the advances that the study of the psycho-neuroses owes to psycho-analysis.

This new psychology starts from a theory of instinct. The controller-in-chief of all our actions and thoughts is the ' pleasure-principle ', the endeavour to escape if possible from unpleasant situations, the desire to obtain the greatest possible gratification with the smallest possible effort.

No person, however, can exist for himself alone, but must adapt himself to a complicated, almost unmodifiable *milieu*. Already in early childhood he must learn to renounce a great part of his natural impulses; when he is grown up, culture requires of him that he should even regard self-sacrifice for the community as something beautiful, good, and worth striving for. The greatest sacrifice the individual has to make in the interests of society, however, is in regard to his sexual desires. All educational factors work towards the suppression of these desires, and most people adapt themselves to these requirements without any particular injury.

Psycho-analysis proceeded to show that this adaptation occurred with the help of a peculiar psychic mechanism, the essential feature of which is that the unfulfillable wishes, and the ideas, memories, and thought-processes belonging thereto, are submerged in the unconscious. To put it more simply: one 'forgets' these wishes and all the thoughts associated with them. This forgetting, however, does not mean the complete destruction of those tendencies and ideational groups; the forgotten complexes continue to exist below the threshold of consciousness: they preserve their potential power and can in suitable circumstances appear again. The healthy person protects himself successfully against the return of these wishes and the sudden appearance of the objects of desire by erecting moral ramparts round these 'repressed complexes'. Feelings of shame and disgust conceal from him all his life the fact that he still really cherishes those despised, disgusting, shameful things as wish-ideas. Things happen in this way, however, only with healthy people; but where, owing to some peculiarity of temperament or to too great a strain on those protective ramparts, the psychic mechanism of repression fails, a 'return of the repressed material' occurs, and with it the formation of symptoms of disease.

The question is often asked why psycho-analysis ascribes so great a part in the ætiology of the psycho-neuroses precisely to sexual repression. But those who ask this forget that since the beginning of time 'hunger and love' have ruled the world, that the impulses for self- and race-preservation are equally powerful instincts in every living creature. Were there a society in which the taking of food was as shameful a manifestation of life as coitus is with us, that is to say, something that one must indeed do but about which one may not speak, of which one may scarcely think, and were the manner of eating there as sternly restricted as sexual gratification is with us, then perhaps the repression of the instinct of self-preservation would play there the chief part in the ætiology of the psycho-neuroses. The predominance of sexuality in the origination of mental disease is therefore in great part due to social causes.

These are of course entirely novel views, standing in the utmost conceivable contrast to everything that has been so far taught by a neurology dealing with anatomical and physiological conceptions. Claude Bernard, indeed, clearly said that when new facts contradicted old theories it was the theories that had to go. It is quite possible, too, that this new libido theory of the neuroses is not the last word that can be said about the neuroses; such a 'last word' is unknown to science. It is my conviction, however, that at the present time there is no theory better adapted to the facts and everything associated with them than the psycho-analytic one.

How then does psycho-analysis classify the psycho-neuroses? What is the basis upon which it constructs its nosology? The answer is simple: it distinguishes the disease groups according to the special way in which the 'complexes' that have been warded off and have returned from repression manifest themselves as symptoms of disease. The patient suffering from obsessional neurosis knows how to displace the affective value of the complex ideas upon other but more harmless thoughts. In this way apparently quite meaningless obsessional ideas are formed that constantly obtrude themselves.

The hysteric goes still further; he can suffer amongst his thoughts not even these harmless substitutes for the repressed instinctive impulses, and creates a symbol for them in his physical body. He therefore represents by means of motor and sensory symptoms both the desires that are unable to become conscious as well as the defence set up against them. Hysterical anæsthesias, pains, paralyses, and spasms are nothing but symbols of repressed thoughts.

There are other forms of defence against unpleasant ideational complexes. In paranoia, for instance, the patient simply sets the ideas that have become insupportable free from his 'ego' and projects them upon other people.

The boundary between 'ego' and external world can be displaced; the tendency to attribute unpleasant ideas to others is often seen, even in healthy people. The paranoiac does the same, but of course to a far greater extent. Instead of acknowledging certain forms of love and hate in himself, he allows himself to consider that these feelings and thoughts, which are insupportable for his self-regard, are whispered in his ear by invisible spirits, or he reads them in the countenances or the movements of his fellow-men.

We find a fourth form of self-defence against the complexes referred to in dementia præcox. Since the fundamental work of Jung and Abraham, we know that people who suffer from this trouble do not *dement* in the sense that they are incapable of logical thought, but that they withdraw their libido so completely from the external world that, so to say, it ceases to exist for them.

The dement transfers the whole of the interest and the affective cathexis that he withdraws from the external world to himself; hence his childish ideas of megalomania, his infantile habits, the revival of auto-erotic forms of gratification, the recklessness in regard to cultural requirements, particularly his utter disregard and carelessness of the external world.

All the kinds of flight from unpleasant ideas referred to are found also in 'normal' people. The bodily manifestations of 'normal' emotional outbursts have much in common with hysteria; a lover can transfer his love affect to every object, to every person who has an associative connection with the real object of his feelings, and this has no more meaning than an obsessional neurotic displacement of affect; does not the distrustful and the jealous person often simply project the idea of his own good-for-nothingness or unlovableness upon others? and if anyone has been deceived in people, does he not become an egoist, a person turned in upon himself who observes, without sharing, the labour and toil of others, whose sole interest is in his own well-being, his own bodily and mental gratification?

The famous saying of Brücke the physiologist, 'disease is only life under changed conditions', applies also, therefore, to the psycho-neuroses. Functional psychoses and psycho-neuroses are distinguished from normal mental activity only by a matter of degrees.

A few words now about the ætiology of these neuroses. No amount of brain anatomy could dissuade novelists, who view life naïvely but with sharp eyes, from the idea that mental excitement of itself was capable of occasioning a mental illness. While we doctors were thrashing the empty straw of physiological catchwords, Ibsen in his 'Lady from the Sea' had made an almost faultless psycho-analysis, by which he exposed the origin of an obsessional idea in a psychic conflict. Johann Arany's[1] 'Die Frau Agnes', who constantly washes her white linen cloth in the stream, suffers from dementia præcox, and her stereotypy in the ballad tragedy finds the same explanation as has been given at the Zürich clinic for the stereotyped actions of many mental patients. Lady Macbeth's washing obsession has become much more plausible since we have convinced ourselves that our neurotics would also fain wipe away the moral stains from their consciences by the same obsessional actions. Formerly the man of science often made merry over the naïveté of the novelist-poet who, when puzzled for an ending, simply made his hero mad, and now to our shame we have to acknowledge that it was not the scholars but the naïve poets who were right. Psycho-analysis showed us that an individual who finds no way out of his mental conflicts takes refuge in a neurosis or a psychosis. In view of the short-sightedness of the professional wiseacres who might overlook this, one is tempted to agree once more with

[1] A noted Hungarian epic poet and ballad writer.

Lichtenberg who in this connection declared ' professional people often do not know what is best '.

Before psycho-analysis the question of the ætiology of functional mental disease was considered to be answered by the catchword ' hereditary stigma '. But just as it was premature and of no avail to force the solution of the problem of the neuroses by means of cerebral anatomy, physics, and chemistry, so also it was very premature to invoke hereditary disposition in explanation of the ætiology of the neuroses before the possibilities of the post-natal influences leading to disease had been exhausted. It is, of course, unquestioned that heredity plays an important part in the origin of mental disease. But as yet we know absolutely nothing about these temperamental factors,[1] so that to trace the neuroses to ' degeneration ' is equivalent to a confession of complete ignorance as to their pathology and of helplessness as to their therapy. According to the psycho-analytic view, no one is completely secure against a too powerful or too prolonged emotional strain or shock, the only significance of temperament being that the individual who is severely taxed from birth is damaged by lesser, and the more robustly constituted by greater shocks. Of course psycho-analysis recognizes the possibility that inherited factors can also influence the particular form of neurosis. Freud compares the inheritance of the neuroses with that of tuberculosis. Just as in inherited tuberculosis, a thorough examination often shows that one has to deal with an infection acquired in childhood from a diseased environment and not merely with a congenital organic weakness; in the same way, in the case of children of neurotic parents, we must, along with heredity, attribute great importance also to the abnormal mental impressions to which they have been exposed since earliest childhood. Every boy and every girl longs to be father or mother respectively, and we need not be surprised if the children appropriate not only the real or supposed advantages of their parents but also their peculiarities and neurotic symptoms.

[1] This sentence, thanks to psycho-analytic researches, does not hold good any longer to-day. (Note added when correcting the [German] proofs.)—S. F.

That psycho-neurosis is more frequent among women is comprehensible when we consider the difference in degree of the cultural pressure that weighs upon the two sexes. Much is permitted to men in youth that is denied to women not only in reality but also in fantasy. Marriage, too, knows two moralities, of which one applies to the husband and the other to the wife. Society punishes sexual lapses much more strictly in women than in men. The periodic pulsations in feminine sexuality (puberty, the menses, pregnancies and parturitions, the climacterium) require a much more powerful repression on the woman's part than is necessary for the man. All this increases the incidence of the psycho-neuroses among them. Women are in overwhelmingly the greater number, especially among the hysterics, while men take refuge rather in obsessional neuroses. As regards paranoia and dementia, there are no reliable data as to how they are divided according to sex; my own personal impression is that paranoia finds its victims more among men and dementia more among women.

In what I have said I have given you a sketch—very rough and primitive, to be sure—of the psycho-analytic theory of the neuroses. I am aware, however, that as practitioners you expect from me some orientation towards therapeutic procedures hitherto in use, and at least some suggestions about analytic therapy.

This is really not so much a matter of course. 'Why does one not demand', asks Dietl, 'of the astronomer that he should change day into night, of the meteorologist cold winter into hot summer, of the chemist water into wine?' and with what right does one demand precisely of the doctor that he should concern himself with the linking-up of the causes of the intricate processes of life and should change the diseased condition of the most complicated of nature's creatures—of man—into health? Happily scientific brooding over this question only came about when medical treatment had been at work already for thousands of years and could point to really significant successes. After all, 'healing is the oldest handicraft and the youngest science' (Nussbaum). Were it otherwise, and had we to base our attempts at treatment not on a rough empiricism but on logical deduction, we would not even now be so daring as merely to attempt the difficult task of healing. In the therapy of the psycho-neuroses also, action far outstripped thought. After what has been mentioned above we are still only at the beginning of the road in progress along which we hope to win a more definite idea of the nature of the neuroses, and yet already the books concerned with their therapy are sufficient to fill a library. How then does the neurologist, who is also at home with psycho-analysis, stand in regard to the matter of therapy? Biegansky's book *Logik in der Heilkunde* (Logic in Medical Science), to which, of course, every special branch of medicine must submit, sets up as the therapeutic signpost the not quite new but undoubtedly correct principle that a method of treatment is only right in so far as it persecutes the noxious and encourages the beneficial symptoms. This is the idea of pathological teleology; it rests on the basis of a theory of purpose according to which only some of the symptoms are considered noxious, while others are the expression of an automatic repairing and compensatory tendency. It is, therefore, not reasonable to want blindly to 'cure' the symptoms of the disease. We are only fitted for our task when we endeavour to assist, so far as in us lies, the diseased organism's attempts at self-cure.

It is to be assumed that the hitherto purely empiric therapy of the neuroses achieved success in those cases in which the doctor, even if not fully consciously, succeeded in imitating the automatic healing tendencies of nature. The symptoms, too, of the psycho-neuroses are often 'teleologically' understandable. The patient who displaces unpleasant ideas, converts them into bodily symptoms, projects them into the external world or withdraws himself from them into his 'ego', strives in this way for a state of mental peace and insensibility. In paranoia and dementia the escape from painful stimulation is so completely successful that, according to our present experience, these two afflictions are therapeutically quite inaccessible. The distrust of the insane, the lack of interest of the dement, rendered any influencing of the mental condition impossible. In hysteria and obsessional neurosis, however, pre-analytic therapy, too, had many, even if mostly impermanent, successes to record. Many patients became well when they were removed out of their surroundings to another *milieu*, but they mostly relapsed again when they had to return to the old environment. In many cases it was possible more or less to achieve a success by improving nutrition and strengthening the physical condition. But even in these cases it was constantly to be feared that if later for any reason the organic powers of resistance were again lowered, the mental disease, the seeds of which had not been eradicated, would burst forth afresh. Also, we only understand the usually ephemeral success of change of surroundings since psycho-analysis has been able to establish that the repressed pathogenic ideas of the neurotic usually refer to individuals of his nearest environment, and that the doctor is only imitating the patient's instinctive aversion to his complexes when he removes him from his home, in which the pathogenic ideational groups can get no peace.

Amongst the various methods of psycho-therapy the worst proceeding is the so-called 'encouraging' and 'explanatory' one. We tell the patient in vain that his trouble is not 'organic', that he is not but only feels as if he were ill; we explain in vain that he only needs to make use of his will—we only deepen the patient's despair by all this. If we smile at Münchhausen mendaciously relating that he drew himself and his horse out of the swamp by his own hair, we should not require of the neurotic that he should 'pull himself together'. Dubois's moralizing procedure merits the same criticism. I will only touch briefly here on the question of hypnosis and suggestion, and remark forthwith that some successes are to be achieved by these means. Charcot already explained that hypnosis is a kind of artificial hysteria, and psycho-analysis further supported this by confirming that suggestion, whether employed during hypnosis or in the waking state, merely suppresses the symptoms, *i.e.* it employs the method in which the hysteric failed in his wish for self-cure. The ideational group occasioning the disease remains untouched by the treatment in the unconscious of the neurotic whose symptoms we strangled by hypnotism. Indeed in a certain sense it is enlarged, that is, the hitherto existing symptoms are now joined by a new one that can certainly for a time prevent the expression of pre-existing symptoms. When the force of the suggested prohibition weakens (and for this it suffices that the patient leave the doctor's environment), the symptoms may immediately manifest themselves again. I regard hypnosis and suggestion as usually safe and harmless methods of treatment, but as holding out little promise of success, and their employment, moreover, is much circumscribed by the fact that only quite a small number of people can really be hypnotized.

Sanatorium treatment combines the advantages of change of surroundings with those of suggestion. The chief means of sanatorium treatment is the pleasant, impressive appearance, the amiability or severity of the doctor. Women particularly show an exalted enthusiasm for the person of the sanatorium doctor, and for love of him can even suppress their hysterical moods. Once they have reached home again, however, the spell soon vanishes. The habit of living in sanatoria can itself become a kind of disease that might be called *sanatorium-disease*; many people are by it completely estranged from their homes and occupations.

Occupational therapy, physical and mental work, is an approved method of treating the psycho-neuroses; it also assists a flight from the tormenting mental conflicts. Unfortunately in the severe cases the patient is usually incapable of directing to more useful ends the energy that he squanders upon his symptoms.

Electricity, massage, baths, etc., are only vehicles for suggestion, and only deserve mention as such in the therapy of the psycho-neuroses.

Anti-neurotic medicaments fall into two groups. The narcotics (bromides, opium, etc.) stun the patient for a time, and with the mental alertness diminishes also for a period the force with which the symptoms are manifested. If the patient becomes habituated to them, or if they are stopped, the symptoms return. In principle, then, one cannot approve of the dealing out of drugs, even if one is sometimes compelled to have recourse to them. The so-called specific cures for the neuroses are mostly completely inactive drugs, or at best they act by suggestion.

If we glance over the methods and means of treatment so far discussed, we do actually see that those that have some effect are those that succeed in strengthening the tendency to self-cure, the repression. This effect, however, cannot be permanent, because the conflict giving rise to the disease remains unresolved concealed in the unconscious, and as soon as external circumstances become less favourable makes itself felt again.

Psycho-analysis, on the contrary, is a proceeding that seeks to cure neurotic conflict not by a fresh displacement or temporary repression, but radically. It endeavours not to tie up psychic wounds but to lay them bare, to render them conscious. Of course, not without 're-educating' the patient, and accustoming him to endure the painful ideas instead of fleeing from them to disease. This psychic method of treatment is in many cases successful. It certainly usually takes many months to get there, even if the doctor occupies himself with the patient daily for an hour. The interpretation of the ideas cropping up in 'free association', the analysis of dreams and of the symptoms themselves, gradually makes the patient intimate with the hitherto unconscious part of his ideational life, with, so to say, his second 'ego', which so long as it was not under the control of consciousness was able to disturb the mental functions.

The fullest possible knowledge of one's self attained by analysis is what makes it possible to render the disease-causing complexes innocuous, that is, to subject them to the control of reason.

The laying bare of the buried layers of the mind not only increased the understanding of the pathological nature of the psycho-neuroses; not only opened up new passable roads to treatment, but made the prophylaxis of these afflictions more hopeful. What had hitherto been scribbled about prophylaxis for the neuroses could have no more meaning in our ignorance of the real pathogenesis of these troubles than the ordinance of the village magistrate that the casks were to be filled with water three days before every conflagration. Real prophylaxis for the psycho-neuroses is only to be hoped for from a change in educational methods, and in social arrangements that will confine repression to the unavoidable minimum.

All the facts and theories with which I have acquainted you in the present lecture are still subjects of fierce controversy amongst the learned men, and then really only the theoretical conclusions—for the opponents of Freud's psychology mostly confine themselves to announcing the improbability of his statements: as a rule they do not undertake the irksome task of inquiring into their actuality.

Psycho-analysis occupies itself with excavating hidden archaic memorials in the depths of the mind; from them it deciphers the hieroglyphs of the neuroses. Only those have the right to sit in judgement on those researches who learn to read the hieroglyphs, certainly not those who base their opinions on prejudices or on judgements of moral values.

II

ACTUAL- AND PSYCHO-NEUROSES IN THE LIGHT OF FREUD'S INVESTIGATIONS AND PSYCHO-ANALYSIS [1]

On the occasion of the third Hungarian Psychiatric Congress in Budapest I delivered several years ago a lecture

[1] A lecture delivered at the 'Budapester Kgl. Gesellschaft der Aerzte', 1908. Printed in the *Wiener Klinischen Rundschau*, Nr. 48-51, 1908, and reprinted in *Populäre Vorträge über Psychoanalyse*.

on 'neurasthenia', in which I asked for the correct nosological classification of this far too varied clinical picture, this cloak for so many wrong or wanting diagnoses. And although I was in the right when I maintained that real exhaustion neurasthenia is to be sharply distinguished from all other nervous states, amongst others from those only explicable on psychiatric grounds, nevertheless I made a mistake difficult to remedy when I left out of account Professor Freud's investigations of the neuroses. This omission was all the greater as I was acquainted with Freud's work. Already in 1893 I had read the paper he wrote, along with Breuer, concerning the psychic mechanism of hysterical symptoms, and, later, another independent paper in which he discusses infantile sexual dreams as the causes or starting-points for the psycho-neuroses. To-day, when I have convinced myself in so many cases of the correctness of Freud's theories, I may well ask myself why did I reject them so rashly at that time, why did they from the first seem to me improbable and artificial, and particularly, why did the assumption of a purely sexual pathogenesis of the neuroses rouse such a strong aversion in me that I did not even honour it with a closer scrutiny? In excuse I must at any rate mention that by far the greater number of men of my profession, amongst them men of the eminence of Kraepelin and Aschaffenburg, take up a similar standpoint even to-day in opposition to Freud. The few, however, who nevertheless did attempt later to solve the peculiar problems of the neuroses by means of Freud's laborious methods, became enthusiastic followers of the hitherto quite unnoticed movement.

However tempting it would be, nevertheless I cannot undertake to recount the history of the development of Freud's line of thought, and to relate how Breuer and Freud discovered in the peculiarities, which might have been regarded simply as accidents, of a case of hysteria psychic manifestations of general validity destined to play a part of inestimable importance in the future development of normal and pathological psychology. Here, too, I must deny myself accompanying Freud any further, who henceforth paces solitary the laborious way by which he attained his present standpoint. I content myself with elucidating, in so far as it is possible in a lecture, the main points of his theory and their significance by examples taken from life.

One of the fundamental principles of the new teaching is that sexuality plays a specific part in the neuroses, that most neuroses are at bottom nothing else than screen-symptoms of an abnormal *vita sexualis*, and that these abnormalities and the manifestations of disease in the neuroses are only rendered comprehensible and, on the basis of this comprehension, accessible to treatment, by being unmasked.

As the first group of the neuroses Freud distinguishes that nervous condition in which any actual irregularity in the physiology of the sexual function acts as the cause of disease without the assistance of psychological factors. Two diseased conditions belong to this group to which Freud gives the name of 'actual-neuroses', but which in contrast to the psycho-neuroses might also be called physio-neuroses. These are neurasthenia in the narrower sense, and a sharply circumscribed group of symptoms entitled anxiety-neuroses.

If we separate out from the cases of illness hitherto designated as neurasthenia everything that should be relegated to other, more natural nosological classifications, there remain behind a well-characterized group in which there predominate, pressure in the head, spinal irritation, constipation, paræsthesias, diminished potency, and from the effect of these conditions, a depression of spirits. Freud found excessive masturbation to be the causal factor of neurasthenic neurosis in this narrower sense. To forestall the immediate objection of banality, I emphasize that we are dealing here with an excessive onanism mostly continued long after puberty, therefore not merely with the ordinary onanism of childhood. The latter is, according to my experience, so widely distributed that I am more inclined to doubt an individual's normality from an entire absence of auto-erotic antecedents.

The estimation of the ætiological significance of onanism is constantly fluctuating; at the crest of the wave it is assumed to be the cause of tabes, in the trough to be completely innocuous. I agree with those who estimate the significance of onanism neither too high nor too low, and can confirm from my own observations that in neurasthenia, in Freud's sense, excessive self-gratification is never absent and is a sufficient explanation for the signs of the disease.

Here I must at once say that this directly neurasthenic effect of masturbation is not so damaging as is the mental distress that is its consequence. People suffer unspeakably from the consciousness of the supposed harmfulness and immorality of these acts of onanism. Most frequently they endeavour to suppress this passion, but while they are escaping the Charybdis of neurasthenia they may suffer shipwreck on the Scylla of an anxiety-neurosis or of a psycho-neurosis.

Masturbation is a pathogenic factor because it endeavours to lower the organism's sexual tension by means of worthless surrogates, or, as Freud says, by an inadequate discharge. This form of gratification, when excessive, exhausts the neuro-psychic sources of energy. Normal intercourse is a complicated but nevertheless reflex process, the reflex arcs passing mainly only through the spinal cord and the subcortical centres, although the higher psychical centres also play a part. In masturbation, on the contrary, where the external stimuli are so meagre, the erection and ejaculation centres borrow chiefly from phantasy (from a source of psychic energy therefore) the degree of tension needed to set the reflex mechanism going. It is comprehensible that such a willed gratification requires a greater consumption of energy than the almost unconscious act of coitus.

In the second form of actual-neurosis, the anxiety-neurosis of Freud, we find the following symptom-complex: general irritability, which shows itself mostly in sleeplessness and auditory hyperæsthesia; a peculiar chronic anxious expectation, for instance, persistent anxiety about one's own health or safety as well as about that of one's relations; anxiety attacks with cardiac or respiratory difficulties, with vasomotor and secretory disturbances that make the patient dread cardiac failure and cerebral hæmorrhage. The anxiety attacks may be rudimentary in form—attacks of sweating, palpitations, sudden attacks of hunger, or diarrhœa. Sometimes they may be manifested only in anxiety-dreams and night terrors. Fits of giddiness often play a great part in anxiety-neurosis; they may be so serious that they interfere more or less with the patient's liberty of movement. The great majority of agoraphobias are really the remote results of such attacks of giddiness; the patient is afraid to go about, that is, he dreads that he may be surprised by an anxiety attack on the open street. The phobia is like a protective measure against the anxiety, but the anxiety itself is a manifestation explicable on purely physiological lines and psychologically not further analysable.

The much misused name of hysteria or neurasthenia could easily be applied to all these anxiety symptoms and symptom-complexes had Freud not succeeded in demonstrating their ætiological unity. Anxiety-neuroses occur whenever sexual libido is separated in any way from the psyche. It is one of the most important of Freud's discoveries that this keeping of the psyche apart from the libido makes itself felt subjectively as anxiety, and therefore sexual excitement that is withheld from orgasm evokes physiological effects, the psychological correlate of which is anxiety. In this respect anxiety-neurosis stands in diametrical opposition to masturbatory neurasthenia, where we are dealing with an excessive demand upon psychic cathexis for a process that would naturally evolve automatically. By means of a comparison borrowed from physics we could draw an analogy between neurotic anxiety, the transformation of pleasure into anxiety on exclusion of the psychical, with the transformation of electricity into heat on the narrowing of its channel. In any case Freud is not pledged to a physical but to a chemical explanation of the actual-neuroses; he regards them as a chronic intoxication by sexual substances.

Virginal anxiety is one of the best known forms of anxiety-neurosis described by Freud. It arises from the fact that the unprepared psyche cannot associate itself with the libido on the occasion of the first sexual experiences. Very often anxiety-neurosis is a result of frustrated excitement, which frequently occurs in the case of engaged couples. Severer forms of anxiety-neurosis are caused in men by coitus interruptus and in women by the absence of orgasm due to ejaculatio præcox, which, in the man, again, is mostly the result of masturbation. Considering the tremendous prevalence of premature seminal discharge it is not to be wondered at that the combination, neurasthenic husband and nervously anxious wife, is so extraordinarily frequent. Besides the constant coincidence of one of these troubles with anxiety-neurosis, therapeutic success also vouches for Freud's accuracy when he declared the specific cause of anxiety-neurosis to be the separation of libido from the psyche. For if the hurtful conditions or disturbances are corrected the symptoms of anxiety-neurosis vanish too. The cure for virginal anxiety is habituation, that for the other anxiety-neuroses is abstention from unsuitable forms of gratification; the wife's anxiety very often disappears if the husband's potency is increased. Even the severest cases of these neuroses, in which every known sedative has failed, recover if the sexual difficulties are dealt with. This discovery of Freud's therefore not only extends our insight into the genesis of many nervous conditions, it also puts us in a position to base a rational and effective therapy upon this insight.

The second, more difficult chapter of the Freudian theory, his conception of the psycho-neuroses, discards the chemico-mechanistic and anatomico-physiological basis; Freud can explain them only psychologically.

He considers two diseased conditions, hysteria and obsessional neurosis, as belonging to this group.

The obsessional neuroses are nowadays mostly ranked among the 'neurasthenias'; on the other hand it has long been known of hysteria that it is a psychogenic neurosis the symptoms of which are caused by psychological automatisms.

But however much they have increased neurological knowledge in this connection, by observations and experiments, writers have nevertheless not succeeded in reviewing the varying clinical aspects of hysteria from one uniform point of view. Nor could they explain what it was that in one patient determined this and in another that group or series of hysterical symptoms. So long, however, as this could not be done, every case of hysteria like the sphinx merely asked questions that were unanswerable. While, however, the sphinx gazes with inflexible calm into infinity, hysteria is never done distorting her face—as though she meant to mock our ignorance—into remarkable and always unexpected grimaces. This illness finally becomes a torment, not only for the sufferer, but for the doctor and those of the environment as well. The doctor soon wearies of changing and combining medicaments and Spa treatments, he gives up the ephemeral successes of suggestion and longingly awaits the summer when hysterical patients can be sent away—the farther the better—into the country. But even if they return improved, on the first occasion of any serious psychic excitement a relapse indubitably takes place. This goes on for years and decennia until no practical doctor any longer believes in the benign course of hysteria so esteemed in the text-books. In these circumstances Freud's evangel of the discovery of the real key to hysteria proclaims a veritable release for doctors and patients.

Breuer was the first who succeeded in tracing the disease manifestations of a hysterical patient to psychic traumata, to psychic shocks of which the patient had no memory but the memory pictures of which together with the corresponding affect lurked in the unconscious and, enclosed in the mind like a foreign body, evoked permanent or recurrent states of excitement in the neuro-psychic domain. Breuer and Freud succeeded in many cases of hysteria in showing by means of hypnotic hyperamnesia that the disease manifestations were really the symbols for such latent memories. If on waking the patient was consciously reminded of the antecedents thus discovered, the immediate result was an affective outburst, after the full discharge of which, however, the symptoms vanished. According to Breuer and Freud's original idea the locking up of affect was due to the subject being prevented at the moment of psychic shock from reacting by an adequate motor discharge in speech, gesture, mimicry, tears, laughter, or the movements expressive of anger or hate, or by dispersing these feelings along ideational associative paths. The feelings belonging to the unconscious memory thus left undischarged in the psyche were then able to radiate into the bodily sphere, to 'convert' themselves into hysterical symptoms. The treatment—called 'catharsis' by these authors—afforded the patient opportunity to recapture what he had lost, to 'abreact' the undischarged feelings, whereupon the pathogenic influences of the now conscious and effect-free memory ceased.

From this seed sprang psycho-analysis, the Freudian method of psychic investigation. This procedure renounces hypnotism and is employed with the patient in the waking state. This renders it applicable to a larger number of patients, and at the same time disposes of the objection that the results achieved by the analysis depend upon suggestion.

In explaining the meaning of this proceeding we may start with Freud's view of forgetting.

Freud made the remarkable discovery that not all forgetting is due to the natural fading of memory-traces with time, but that we are unable to recall many impressions only because a critical factor in the mind, a censorship, succeeds in suppressing below the conscious threshold the idea that is irksome or insupportable to consciousness. This defensive proceeding Freud calls repression and adduces proof that many normal and morbid psychic processes are comprehensible only on the assumption of this mechanism. Nevertheless, repression as well as the permanent suppression of unpleasant memories is hardly ever completely successful; the struggle between the repressed thought-complexes endeavouring to reproduce themselves and the censorship repressing them, usually ends in a compromise; the complex as such remains forgotten (unconscious), but is replaced in consciousness by some superficial association or other. As such substitutes or symbols for complexes Freud instanced free ideas, that is, the thoughts which irrupting into logical thought series suddenly crop up in consciousness apparently quite disconnectedly. For instance, experiences of childhood are almost completely forgotten. If one wishes to recall them ridiculously trivial, unimportant, and innocuous matters recur to one. We should be unable to say why our memory should have been burdened with them had Freud not successfully shown that these memories are 'screen memories' for much more significant and usually not in the least innocuous childish impressions. Hidden complexes, besides screen memories, may be suspected, too, behind apparently insignificant disturbances of speech and movement (slips of the tongue, clumsiness, mislaying things), as well as behind certain stereotyped playful meaningless movements (Freud's 'symptomatic acts').

Jung has shown experimentally that in so-called free association to stimulus words every 'disturbed' reaction (prolongation of the reaction time, 'indirect' or otherwise remarkable reaction words, forgetting the reaction word on reproducing the test, etc.) proves on closer analysis to be constellated by a 'complex'. On observing the reactions simultaneously with the variations in intensity of a weak galvanic current led through the body, Jung found every time at the 'complex reactions' a rise in the curve which had to be interpreted as indicating a variation in electrical resistance caused by the liberation of affect. Jung now starts his analyses with the stimulus words of the complex reactions thus found and shows that the ideas associated with such words lead easily and rapidly to pathogenic groups of thought.

It is a difficult task to describe the real technique of Freud's method. In the narrow space of this lecture I must confine myself to sketchy indications.

The patient to be analysed is instructed that he must relate without any exercise of judgement, as though observing his own thoughts quite objectively, everything that occurs to him, however senseless or ridiculous, whether pleasant or unpleasant. The kind of intellectual effort thus exerted is the opposite of the usual way of thinking which simply discards as ' of no value ', or as ' disturbing ', and does not further pursue, thoughts not related precisely to the goal-idea predominating at the moment. Analysis, however, lays the emphasis precisely upon what consciousness is inclined to ward off. Hence the patient is required to communicate everything that comes into his mind when his attention is directed precisely upon these ideas. The association of ideas is usually at first superficial, deals with events and impressions of the day. Soon, however, ideas of older memory-traces come to hand—screen memories—which on further analysis bring to light, to the astonishment of the patient himself, old and very significant but none the less up till now quite ' forgotten ' experiences that perhaps elucidate current hitherto inexplicable psychic processes. One of Freud's fundamental principles is that accident occurs as little in psychic life as in the physical world. In the psyche, too, everything is determined, only previous to psycho-analytic knowledge most of the determinants were hidden in an inaccessible deeper stratum of the psyche, in the unconscious. Our main task in psycho-analysis is to make the patient conscious of his thoughts and feeling impulses, the unpleasant and therefore rejected ones as well, and to make him acknowledge to himself the usually unconscious motives for his actions. Analysis, which is a sort of scientific confession, demands from the doctor much tact and psychological understanding; it can only be learnt by long practice. It is a study that is never completed; each case requires as it were an individual technique that takes into consideration the degree of the patient's culture, his intellect, and psychic sensibility. One has to feel one's way forward, give up a line perhaps that has proved misleading, search instead for fresh indications amongst the patient's ideas, and adapt the form and speed of the analysis to the actual disposition of the person to be treated. At the same time one must never adopt a moralizing attitude, but in accordance with the fundamental principle of ethical determinism understand and forgive all things.

An excellent approach to the unmasking of unconscious thoughts and memories is by way of the dream. Freud's most important work is precisely the foundation of a scientific interpretation of dreams, the principal sentence in which is 'The dream is invariably the more or less disguised fulfilment of a repressed wish'. The interpretation of a dream consists in the analysis of the dream content; it is a difficult task that one must learn and practise for oneself; without it, however, no psycho-analysis is conceivable. The dream always exposes a larger extent of the unconscious than do the waking ideas, because the upsurging wishes and the latent thoughts striving to reproduce themselves are much less sharply supervised by the repressing forces of the psyche during sleep than by day.

During the analysis one must—as already said—also analyse all 'accidental' actions, slips of memory, clumsinesses on the part of the patient, every unmotivated mimic movement of expression and gesture just exactly as the 'free coming' ideas. To complete and control the analysis one can perhaps from time to time carry out Jung's association experiment and even carry the analysis on from the stimulus and reaction words.[1]

If analysis is employed in the manner indicated with a person suffering from hysteria, and is continued for a considerable period or several months, then gradually, little by little, thoughts and memories that have been repressed and are connected with the symptoms, come into consciousness. Once the analysis is finished and the patient's whole psychic development can be reviewed it becomes evident that the hysterical symptoms, too, were nothing else than symbol-complexes that had no meaning in themselves, but became comprehensible when it became possible to release from repression and bring into consciousness the hidden ideational complexes with which they were connected—often only by a thin thread of associa-

[1] This technical artifice, however, has already in many cases proved disturbing, so that it is better given up. (Note on correcting the [German] proofs.)—S. F.

tions. The remarkable and satisfactory result of a complete analysis of all the symptoms—often, however, only after a fresh flare up of the illness—is the gradual but final cure of the hysterical signs of disease.

To obtain these unexpected glimpses into pathological psychic processes, Freud, quite apart from his analytic studies of nervous patients, had also to work out a great deal of normal psychology for himself. Above all, emphasis must be laid on his *Interpretation of Dreams*, a book in which for the first time the sense of the confused nocturnal hallucinations called dreams, which were held to be meaningless, was successfully deciphered. He next wrote the *Psychopathology of Everyday Life*, in which all the small hitherto almost unnoticed apraxes of normal people are explained on the basis of the mechanism of repression. Freud also made the first successful attempt to depict a form of æsthetic production and of æsthetic enjoyment, namely, wit and the comical, as the achievement of unconscious and preconscious tendencies and working methods, and to bring them into line with dream work, thus rendering them more comprehensible. Finally, he also gave us the outline for a future normal psychology and psychogenesis that will do justice to all this newly acquired knowledge, and undoubtedly points to a happy turn in the development of this discipline which had strayed somewhat into by-paths. I must, unfortunately, deny myself taking up all this in detail and must confine myself here to the communication of facts that are directly connected with the pathology and therapy of the neuroses. I would, however, stress that the study of Freud's writings is the indispensable pre-condition of any success in psycho-analytic work.

The psycho-analysis of psycho-neurotics led Freud to the significant and extraordinary conclusion that the repressed complexes lying at the root of the symptoms are always of a sexual character; or, to speak more accurately, that unconscious sexual factors are never absent, nay, usually play the leading part in cases of psycho-neuroses. The apparent strangeness of this fact disappears, however, when one considers that the sexual instinct is one of the most powerful instincts in all living creatures and urges imperatively to action, and that, on the other hand, in human beings from the earliest childhood all cultural forces work for the repression of this instinct. The ethical ideas attained during education by precept and example, conscience, decency, honour, consideration for those belonging to one and for society, as well also as the commands, threats, and punishments of ecclesiastical and civil authority, that is to say, an inner and an external compulsion, erect in the mind a powerful censorship against the unbridled activity of the sexual instincts, even indeed against the inner acknowledegment of them. The conflict is therefore unavoidable, and may end either in the victory of uncontrolled sexuality (' perversities ') or in its complete suppression; most frequently, however, a compromise occurs by which the sexual desires can be at the same time consciously denied and unconsciously acknowledged. Hysteria is a form of unsuccessful repression. Here consciousness succeeds in keeping the ' impure ' thought-complex at a distance, but the affective energy of what is repressed nevertheless finds ways and means of becoming active: it radiates into the bodily sphere and becomes converted into hysterical symptoms. What individual factors determine the localization of the symptoms to this or that organ is explicable after analysis by the associative connection (in thought) of the organ concerned or of its function with the complex; probably, however, ' bodily predisposition ' (Freud), that is, a special suitability or tendency of the organ concerned to combine with the excitation masses liberated from the repressed material, also plays a part.

On the basis of numerous psycho-analyses of hysterics I can confirm that Freud is right in every point, and that his method is the only one of those as yet known that adequately explains this hitherto problematical disease. I will now adduce a few examples.

A seventeen-year-old lad visited my consulting-room with the complaint of suffering from salivation and of being constantly forced to spit. I was able to assure myself that he was telling the truth; his mouth was always full of saliva and he ejected incredible quantities of it. Neither the anamnesis nor the physical examination threw any light on this condition, and in consideration of the numerous hysterical 'stigmata' present I had to assume that the symptom was functional in nature, hysterical. Instead, however, of contenting myself with this diagnostic position and the employment of suggestive measures, I advised psycho-analysis. The first surprising result of this was the observation that the secretion of saliva was much increased in the presence of women. To the question why he had not mentioned this before he replied that he had thought it a matter of no importance. The negation of their significance is a well-tried and often successful means of turning the attention from unattractive thoughts. Later the patient remembered that he had noticed the flow of saliva in a popular museum of anatomy when he was looking at wax modellings of female genitals with and without sexual diseases. He had also at that time felt unwell and had had to go home and wash his hands. (Combination of hysteria with an obsessive action.) He could not say why he did it. Later, however, he recollected that while in the museum the memory of his first and only coitus, and of the feelings of pain and disgust associated with this experience, had occurred to him. The explanation of this exaggerated disgust at female genitalia, however, only came towards the end of the treatment, when it appeared that he had as a six-year-old boy practised cunnilingus with several girls of about the same age and amongst them with his own sister; the thought association, genitals—cunnilingus—mouth, made the hysterical salivation comprehensible. From the moment when he perceived that the child persisting in his unconscious desired now as formerly the repetition of this unseemly activity, which was so forcibly rejected by his consciousness, when, that is, his 'complex' became conscious for him, the symptom ceased and did not recur. Apart from the therapeutic success, I owe to this analysis a much deeper insight into the genesis of this case of disease than I would formerly have held possible.

A nineteen-year-old girl who was always extraordinarily

bashful with men, and avoided them whenever she possibly could, lost her hysterical paræsthesias concomitantly with the progressive recalling of memories of passive sexual experiences in childhood that had reference to the bodily parts affected with the abnormal sensations, and with the recognition of the actual unconscious phantasies that were associated with these concealed memories. A seemingly quite innocuous dream afforded a peculiar explanation of the pains she felt in her back. She dreamt she had fallen into a river. On being questioned she related that the river had looked exactly like a little stream with which she was acquainted in upper Hungary, called the Ondova. The resemblance, however, of this name to the Hungarian word for semen, 'ondo', is so striking that I found myself compelled to explore her knowledge in this respect. It then turned out indeed that the patient was possessed of lay knowledge about seminal discharge. As, however, it proved on this occasion that she suffered from a white discharge that could be traced to her earlier onanist practices, and as, further, she shared the widely spread belief that spermatorrhea and onanism can occasion diseases of the spinal cord, she had besides the desire to masturbate to repress also the idea that she was suffering from tabes. The pains in the back were only the conversion symbols of this repression. To anyone who is in some degree familiar with the technique of dream work, discovered by Freud, and of its relation to the mechanism of wit, this interpretation will seem neither too witty nor forced.

Behind the symptoms (singultus, globus, tremor) of another young hysteric I could demonstrate the repressed memories of an exhibitionist, probably seen in childhood, and of two sexual experiences at puberty, as well as the equally repressed phantasies associated with them.

You will ask me how I could speak to young girls about 'such things'. Freud himself, however, has already given the answer in the counter-question, How do doctors permit themselves, when necessary, directly to inspect and touch the sexual organs about which the analyst only speaks? You will all probably admit that it would be senseless to forgo the necessary gynæcological examination of young girls out of consideration for their feelings of modesty. It would be by no means a negligible error, however, to refuse the exploration and treatment of psycho-sexual conditions for the same reason. That the analysis must be conducted tactfully and considerately goes without saying; this is, of course, requisite in all medical procedures without exception. The possibility of working mischief through ignorance and malevolence is not confined to psycho-analysis; it can be done in operative gynæcology too. To the doctor who permits himself to make genital examinations, but condemns psycho-analysis as indecent, following Freud we quote Goethe's saying: 'Du darfst es nicht vor keuschen Ohren nennen, was keusche Herzen nicht entbehren koennen' ('Thou mayst not say in modest ears what modest hearts cannot forgo').

I could give examples *ad libitum*. A forty-year-old hysteric who periodically felt a bitter taste in her mouth remembered in the course of the analysis that she had felt the same bitter taste when she did not, as was her custom, give her mortally ill brother his quinine herself but let it be given by a nurse, in consequence of which the wafer disintegrated in his mouth and caused the sick man to have a very bitter taste. (Hysterical identification, Freud.) I further discovered that the patient as a child had been excessively cherished and unduly tenderly embraced by her father; the bitter taste symbolized also the bitter taste of these kisses, as her father was a very heavy smoker. When we also take into consideration that the patient has to endure many 'bitternesses' from her now nearly ninety-year-old but dreadfully strict father, then we have in this case a characteristic example of the over-determination of a neurotic symptom; one morbid manifestation represents here several repressed complexes.

I had great difficulties with this patient with the transference. On the journey from the symbols of disease to the repressed material which patients must accomplish during analysis, they usually make a last effort to avoid an insight into their unconscious. This they do by transferring on to the doctor all their affects (hate, love) magnified by the unconscious. Nevertheless the transference can be dissolved by the tactful and understanding prosecution of the analysis—nay, may even be rendered of service to the analysis.

Hysterical fits, convulsive attacks, and fainting fits occur, as the analyses show, when an external stimulus is so intimately associated with the repressed material that consciousness cannot escape from its reproduction in any other way than by handing itself over completely to the unconscious. If the mind, therefore, is powerfully affected at its hysterogenic points of contact the result may be loss of consciousness. This is 'the overpowering by the unconscious' (Freud); the convulsions, the movements of expression occurring in the attacks, are symbols and concomitant manifestations of unconscious phantasies. Here is an example.

A fifteen-year-old apprentice locksmith suffered for three weeks from attacks of loss of consciousness with tonic-clonic convulsions; the attacks ended with the patient thrusting out his tongue three or four times. The first attack occurred after his fellow-apprentices had tied his arms and legs together; this is a rough but in many localities very popular sport and consists in someone who is not as yet acquainted with this amusement having his hands tied together below his bent knees. A pole is then slipped through the space between his knees and elbows, and the individual, who is thus rendered quite helpless, is spun round the pole. From the tremendous fright that the victim of this torture suffers (I went through it once as a child) I should formerly simply have declared the illness to have been a traumatic hysteria; since Freud's work, however, I am aware that even in neuroses consequent upon shock there is also usually a predisposition based upon the earlier history to be discovered. Accordingly I attempted an analysis. It soon appeared that the lad some three months previously had fallen into a cess-pit of stinking, filthy water, when some of the disgusting fluid had got into his mouth. At the time he had felt sick, and the reproduction of this experience determined, too, a severe fit during the analysis. A still severer attack was preceded by the memory of the following experience from his thirteenth year. He was playing with his barefoot companions on the grass and the game was 'blind man's buff'; his eyes were blindfolded and the others were allowed to fool him with a stick. One of his playmates had the horrible idea of smearing the stick that was held out to him with excrement. He clutched hold and the unexpected sensation of humidity and the laughter of the others caused him immediately to snatch away the cloth from his eyes, but, unfortunately, he could not avoid noticing the smell and taste of the filthy stuff as he did so. The case was only completely cleared up when the analysis showed that as quite a young child he had, besides other sexual practices, attempted mutual coprophagia with his little friends and that when his mother kissed him he had always to contend with the thought that the same thing could be tried with her too. The fact, too, that his latest big fright (on the occasion of his fellow-apprentices' jest) was followed by the involuntary passage of urine and fæces probably roused in the lad all these long, insufferable, and therefore repressed wishes and memories, from the reproduction of which he was compelled to escape into unconsciousness, though not without indicating by movements of the tongue the content of the phantasies that were incapable of becoming conscious. For a time I could promptly bring on an attack if I had occasion to refer to either of the two excretory functions. It was only after prolonged pedagogic efforts that I got him to understand that to think evil and to do evil is not the same thing, and that he might think out these childish phantasies to their conclusion without any conscientious fears. Finally, I rendered conscious for the lad a marked masochistic component-instinct which was associated with anal-erotism; upon this the attacks ceased once for all. Such cases support Jung's assumption, who regards analysis as a dynamic treatment that accustoms the patient to acknowledge freely to himself the ideas and wishes displeasing to consciousness.

If a thorough analysis is possible, then 'perverse'

childish memories and just such unconscious phantasies are always to be obtained in each individual case of hysteria. The manifestly precarious sexuality of hysterics works itself off in the repressed perverse thoughts and their conversion symptoms; treatment results not only in the cessation of the formation and persistence of symptoms but also in the capacity for normal sexual life. Those to whom this last is denied by external circumstances must simply after the conclusion of the analysis 'sublimate' their libido, that is, divert it consciously to asexual ends.

Obsessional neurosis (obsessional ideas, obsessional acts) is, according to Freud, the second great group of the psycho-neuroses. In obsessed people certain ideational groups, which have apparently no connection with any other thought cycles, force themselves unmotivated into consciousness. The patient is fully aware of the illogical, morbid nature of his obsession, but seeks in vain to rid himself of it. Or else he is compelled constantly to repeat a co-ordinated but, as he quite well knows, absolutely purposeless and senseless movement which not even his utmost efforts can suppress. Formerly our endeavours to explain and cure such cases were failures. The latest edition of Oppenheim's text-book to which I have access still mentions obsessional neurosis as a disease the prognosis of which is 'serious or at least doubtful'. According to my present experience it is from the start impossible to obtain permanent cures without Freudian psycho-analysis, that is, without the recognition of the genesis and meaning of these symptoms. The bizarre manifestations of this disease were only rendered comprehensible by 'the dissection of the mind'. It turned out that the obsessional idea is only apparently so utterly senseless, but proves to be quite significant when analysis demonstrates its certainly quite superficial associative connection with repressed psychic formations. The difference between hysteria and obsessional neurosis is that in the hysteric the affective energy of repressed ideational complexes becomes converted into bodily symptoms; the obsessional neurotic, on the other hand, rids himself of the consciousness of painful ideas by withdrawing their affects from them and displacing it upon other but innocuous ideas, associatively connected with the original ones. Freud calls this peculiar process of displacement of affect, *substitution* (displacement). We learn that the persistently obtruding irksome idea is an innocent whipping-boy, while the real 'guilty' ideas remain undisturbed in the unconscious deprived of their affects. The psychic balance is displaced until it is possible to discover the hidden thought-complex and to trace the displaced affect to its source. The path to it is psycho-analysis. At the end of the treatment the patient has complete insight into the shady side of his moral and æsthetic psychic life, but he is rid of the obsessional idea.

What it is that determines that one individual should indicate his hidden complexes by a bodily and another by a psychic symbol is not yet decided. From analogy with the bodily predisposition in hysteria one might perhaps invoke a psychic predisposition, that is, psychic-constitutional factors to explain obsessional thoughts. 'Family analysis', that is, the psychic examination of several nervous members of the same family, will perhaps decide this question.

By means of analysis Freud succeeded in showing that the real source of the ideas of temptation so prevalent, especially in women (the fear they will kill their children, that they will have to jump out of the window, etc.), is usually dissatisfaction with marriage and the fear of thoughts of sexual temptation.

A young patient of Freud's who was constantly tormented by the fear of being unable to control her urine in company and had therefore to live in complete retirement learnt during the analysis that she was really afraid of her own sexual wishes and ideas, amongst which the memory of an incident when orgasm and the need to urinate had occurred simultaneously played a part.

One of my patients, a highly gifted young man, was compelled to brood constantly on life and death, on the problem of the human organism, and lost all pleasure in life and work in so doing. The analysis showed clearly that as a little child he had manifested sexual curiosity about his mother's genitals and permitted himself to wish for the death of his severe father (Oedipus-complex, Freud). Hence the complete withdrawal from everything sensual and the philosophic brooding mania.

A remarkable disinclination for reading or even merely touching books was the complaint of an elderly spinster (a working woman) who although beautiful, much sought after and poor, yet refused marriage. The result of the analysis was the discovery of the following facts. When she was eight years old a thirteen-year-old boy had practised actual coitus with her; this, however, she had completely forgotten during the 'period of successful defence' until in her sixteenth year after reading a book about 'Jack the Ripper' she on one occasion in a dream (?) remembered the childish incident, and for a time was constantly tormented by the thought that her future husband would discover her shame on the wedding night and kill her. In spite of her fear she entertained ideas of suicide, although certainly of an unusual kind: she proposed to get married so that her husband would discover her lapse and kill her. This wish, therefore, she could acknowledge to herself by laying the affect upon the dying and not upon the sexuality. The shifting of the phobia from the 'penny-dreadful' to all printed matter indicated a further stage of the displacement and may be regarded as a protective measure in Freud's sense against the emergence into consciousness of the anxiety-causing wish and its immediate derivatives.

One of my patients' idiosyncrasy against fat meat and all salted food proved to be a symbol of his repressed homosexual tendencies. When still a child he was forced by an older corpulent boy to endure coitus per os (fat meat = penis, salty taste = semen). In all neurotics I have been able, after Freud, to demonstrate in an unusual degree the permanent bisexuality of all human beings which was discovered by Fliess. How much of this is to be traced to constitutional factors and how much to infantile experiences, remains in the meantime undecided.[1]

[1] A number of cases here called obsessional neurosis would to-day have to be treated under the heading of 'anxiety hysteria'. (Note added in 1919.)

Obsessional movements and obsessional acts are, as Freud correctly stated, protective measures against the reproduction of obsessional ideas and disguised manifestations of onanist tendencies. The work of displacement which, as we saw in one of our cases, occurs also in the domain of conscious thoughts finally succeeds in forcing the affect from the psychic into the bodily sphere and thus by very circuitous ways attaining to the same thing as does hysterical conversion without any such effort. We must therefore note that behind every obsessional action there is concealed an obsessional idea, which in turn represents an incompatible unconscious idea. Obsessional washing, for instance, is a quite illogical but effective means for mitigating painful obsessional thoughts whose complexes bear witness to the individual's moral 'impurity'. Other acts, too, of an obsessional character (counting, the reading of street placards, the maintenance of a certain rhythm in walking, etc.), serve to divert the attention from painful (hyper-significant) thoughts. A patient of Freud's had to pick up and read every scrap of paper on the ground and put it in her pocket; this obsession had developed secondarily from obsessional thoughts that had reference to a secret interchange of love letters. Superstitious fear compelled an otherwise very enlightened young man whom I analysed to put money on all conceivable occasions into the collecting-box of a temple. By means of these sacrificial offerings this economically disposed patient did penance for his unconscious evil thoughts towards his parents, but also at the same time for the long-forgotten trick of having at one time thrown stones instead of money into similar boxes. I discovered a remarkable instance of *conscious* displacement of the obsessional thought in a patient who having been forced into a marriage against her will by parental authority had constantly to brood over her unhappiness. A friend counselled her to think rather about something else, something harmless, for instance, about words and letters. From that moment she brooded persistently on the marvel that sounds and words have meaning and can communicate thoughts.

Freud at first concluded from the extraordinary frequency of infantile psycho-sexual traumata among his patients that the psycho-neuroses occur only after such abnormal experiences in childhood. But later he had to acknowledge that analysis of healthy people often revealed severe psychic traumata in childhood which nevertheless were followed by no pathogenic after-effects at all. On the other hand he found many neurotic illnesses determined by quite insignificant and apparently harmless sexual impressions. Besides the symptom-forming powers of infantile experiences Freud had also therefore to call in the constitutional factor to his assistance, only that in place of the far too general and hence uninformative idea of 'disposition' of 'degeneration' he put that of an abnormal sexual constitution with a tendency to repressive mechanisms. Nor did Freud recoil from the difficult task of revising the whole developmental history of sexuality. This he did in his *Drei Abhandlungen zur Sexualtheorie*.[1] Here he showed that sexual pleasure in the wider sense is wholly inseparable from life, and accompanies man from the moment of conception till his death. In sucklings and quite young children, for instance, libidinal tendencies play a much larger part than we have hitherto cared to believe; indeed precisely this age-period, the period of infantile perversion, in which the clearly bisexual libido is not yet bound up with the activity of any one organ, when as yet no shame, no incest boundary narrows the selection of sexual aims and sexual objects, is pre-eminently adapted for the reception of impressions and for the fixation of tendencies which education can sublimate for a time, but which obtrude themselves forcibly at the later organic impulse of puberty and require so powerful a repression that less robust constitutions cannot achieve it without a neurotic illness. It is evident that a sexual pedagogy that does not take these facts into consideration must be described as useless.

Neurasthenia, anxiety, hysteria, and obsessional neurosis hardly ever appear separately; life usually offers a mixture

[1] [Translation by A. A. Brill, *Three Contributions to the Theory of Sex*. Mental and Nervous Disease Monograph Series, No. 7, and in *Gesammelte Schriften*. Bd. V.]

of their symptoms. Where, however, the signs of disease are mixed we can with certainty deduce the corresponding 'ætiological blending' (Freud). Whosoever has masturbated for a long period and suddenly abstains will be found to be suffering from neurasthenic paræsthesias and anxiety states simultaneously. If a woman with an abnormal sexual development begins to feel 'forbidden' sexual impulses she will repress them and become simultaneously anxious and hysterical. Masculine psycho-sexual impotence is also a mixture of actual- and psycho-neurosis. It goes without saying that in such cases analysis only resolves the psychogenic symptoms, while the physiologically determined ones are left as an insoluble remainder and are only to be influenced by the corresponding sexual-hygienic measures.

I will not conceal the fact that some of my analyses have failed. But this occurred only in cases where I did not observe the conditions for a hopeful analysis indicated by Freud, or where the indispensable patience was lacking either in myself or the patient. I have on occasion broken off the treatment because I saw that in the given circumstances it was better for the patient to suffer from repressions than to obtain clear insight into the reality. For such cases the treatment advocated by Ibsen's Dr. Relling for unhappy people of 'bolstering up the living lie' is more suitable.

I can only touch here on the delightful fact that the scientific application of psycho-analysis has proved to be fruitful also as regards psychiatry. Freud obtained the proof that paranoic or insane ideas are only unconscious thought complexes projected into the external world; Jung's excellent monograph makes the whole symptomatology of dementia præcox comprehensible by means of the psychology of complexes, and Otto Gross attributes great importance to Freud's idiogenic factors in manic-depressive insanity too.

A few words more about the ætiology of the neuroses. It has become a catchword that Freud derives the neuroses exclusively from sexual traumatic origins. This is not the case. As mentioned above, he grants the proper significance to constitutional factors. I must further add that according to him non-sexual psychic shocks (accidents, fright, tragic events) can also contribute by their traumatic power to a neurosis or even indeed occasion one. In any case Freud considers the sexual factors as 'specific' causes of the neuroses, not only because they are always to be demonstrated in every case, very often without the assistance of other causes, but chiefly because they determine qualitatively the symptoms of the illness. And—last, not least—he points to the results of analytic therapy, which cures the neurotic symptom by bringing to light the pathogenic sexual factors, and by overcoming them re-establishes the balance of the sexual life and of sexual feeling.

I am prepared for Freud's sexual theory of the neuroses meeting with the greatest resistance from you too. I should indeed have to doubt the correctness of Freud's teaching if the censorship against sexual matters were only to be demonstrable in nervous patients and no trace of such a defence were discoverable in healthy people, for instance amongst healthy doctors. We all harbour in our unconscious a crowd of repressed sexual ideas and tendencies, and the aversion to the open discussion of sexual problems is a reaction formation to prevent their coming into consciousness. Self-analysis taught me, too, that I had formerly been so bitterly opposed to the examination of Freud's discoveries for similar reasons. I can, however, assure you that the instruction which I owe to the unprejudiced investigation of sexual psychic processes amply repays the effort that the overcoming of the antipathy against these things cost me. Unfortunately this insight does not recompense me for the years during which I took the field against the problems of functional nervous diseases armed only with the old blunt weapons of the pathology of the nerves.

It was the practical neurologist in me that spoke when I laid so much stress here on the pathological importance of the new teaching. Considered from a higher, more general point of view we must estimate it as a far greater gain that with the help of Freud's teachings we have been able to see further into the functioning of psychic mechanisms and into the economy of the forces actuating it.

III

SUGGESTION AND PSYCHO-ANALYSIS[1]

MANY people from lack of information regard psycho-analysis as a therapy that acts 'suggestively'. But those also who have perhaps read something of analytic literature are inclined if they have no experience of their own to refer to the scientific and therapeutic results of analysis, on superficial grounds, as 'suggestive'. On the other hand, whoever is engaged, as I am myself, in practice with the analysis of mind, perceives a great difference between the two methods of research and healing which are distinguished as analysis and suggestion. I should now like to say something about these differences.

It is perhaps excusable if I make the concession to my feelings by beginning with the enlightenment of the uninformed, that is, of those still impartial; and of only after this attempting to disarm the objections, which will have become clamant, of the second group.

To define the meaning of the word 'suggestion' is perhaps difficult, but everyone knows what the word implies; it is the deliberate smuggling of sensations, feelings, thoughts, and decisions of the will into another person's psychic world, and this in such a way that the person influenced cannot of himself modify or correct the suggested thoughts, feelings, and impulses. Put briefly, suggestion is the forcing upon, or the unquestioning acceptance of, a foreign psychic influence. The setting aside of all criticism is therefore the pre-condition for successful suggestion; by what means, however, can this

[1] A lecture delivered at the 'Free School for Social Sciences' in Budapest, 1912, and published in *Populäre Voträge über Psychoanalyse*.

be achieved? On the one hand by impressiveness, by intimidation, on the other by bribery, by means of friendly, kindly talk. Elsewhere I endeavoured to show that suggestion reduces people precisely to the level of a helpless child incapable of contradicting or of independent thought, whereby the suggester forces himself upon the medium's will with paternal authority, or insinuates himself into his mind with maternal tenderness. And what is it that the hypnotist or the suggester requires of his medium? No less than that he shall not feel, know, and wish what he would naturally be compelled to know, feel, and wish. He is not to feel the tormenting physical or mental pain, the obsessional ideas from which he suffers; they must no longer oppress his consciousness; he is no longer to pursue unattainable or absurd goals. Or perhaps he is to know, feel, and wish what something in him rebels against; he must work, concentrate his attention, carry out projects, be able to forgive, love, and hate even when external and inner reasons have paralysed those capacities. The hypnotist says to the hysterical paralytic as Jesus once said: Arise and walk—and the patient must get up and walk; to the woman in child-bed he says: Thou shalt bring forth painlessly—and the miracle happens.

As we see, it makes no difference to hypnotism and suggestion whether they abolish an organic pain, a real knowledge, and a motivated act of will or an 'unreal' so-called imaginary symptom of disease.

Hypnotic or suggestive methods of cure would be splendid, fairy-tale miracles, if there were not so many drawbacks to their application.

The first and greatest drawback is that not everyone can be influenced by suggestion. The more independent, mature, psychically developed humanity becomes, the fewer people there are whom the medical miracle-workers can tame into obedient little children.

The second fault lies in the fact that even if an individual owing to a relative weakness, ultimately to a narrowing of consciousness, becomes suggestible, the effect is only temporary, lasts only so long as the suggesting authority or the confidence placed in it remains unshaken. And the reverse can appear really very rapidly. You may perhaps not consider it important, but from the point of view of the person treated by suggestion it is also to be regarded as a drawback that either hypnotism or suggestion artificially encourages the narrowing of consciousness, and therefore, as regards inner and outer perceptions, is an education in blindness. Whosoever trusts the hypnotizing doctor blindly will presently also believe in the miracle-working Virgin of Lourdes and the woman quack of Ó-Buda.[1]

Psycho-analysis, on the contrary, stands upon the firm foundation of the strict determinism of psychic happenings. Above all it drops the assumption according to which so-called 'imaginary illnesses' are unfounded, akin to simulation or absurd. Formerly so long as I was still unacquainted with psycho-analysis, patients often nonplussed me when I wanted to suggest something to them. When I said to the patient who was incapable of systematic effort: 'There is nothing the matter with you, my friend, pull yourself together, you have only to use your will!' he would reply: 'That is exactly my complaint, I have no will! Day and night I say to myself, you must, you must—and yet I can't. I have come precisely in order that you should teach me how to will.' In such cases it makes little or no impression upon the sufferer—for that he does suffer is surely beyond question—for the doctor in perhaps raised tones or with a still severer, sterner, or more self-complacent visage to shout at him once more: 'Yes, you must use your will-power.' The sick man returns home sad and disillusioned, goes to another doctor, and when he has disillusioned himself with them all he despairs or he falls into the hands of the quacks. I know a case where a famous doctor to whom a young woman tormented by obsessional ideas had confidently gone sent her home with the diagnosis that there was nothing wrong with her. The patient went straight home and hanged herself.

Can we declare that what has tormented so many people for decennia, on account of which they neglect their business,

[1] Suburb of Budapest.

their families, and from which they finally free themselves by self-inflicted death, is not a deadly ailment? Is there not a deal of truth in the satirical remark of a patient who answered the doctor's soothing assurance that he was only imagining it all with the question: 'Why don't *you* imagine something, doctor?'

Now psycho-analysis has discovered that in this matter it was not the medical hypnotists but the patients who were right. The imaginary sick man, the person without a will, is really ill, only he is mistaken as to the real reason for his sufferings. The anxiety of the hypochondriac who constantly observes his heart-action and sees death threatening at every moment is 'baseless': but it is not to be denied that there is a hidden wound in his mind, some real anxiety, or one as powerful as a reality, from which the hypochondriac fear constantly derives fresh sustenance. The sufferer from hysterical agoraphobia who dare not walk a step in the street has in reality quite healthy organs, his brain, his spinal cord, and his peripheral nerve trunks are in order; he has healthy muscles, bones, and joints. But this does not mean that there is nothing whatever the matter with him! Psycho-analysis searches for and finds, though with much trouble and patience, the forgotten psychic wounds that have become unconscious, whose caricatured, deformed manifestation the agoraphobia is. Thus while hypnotism and suggestion either simply deny the evil or endeavour to bury it more deeply, but really leave it to smoulder in the depths of the mind like the glow under ashes, analysis hunts energetically for the cause of the illness, digs the fire, as it were, out of the ashes and extinguishes it on its hearth.

And what are these furnaces? Apparently long-forgotten but really still living memories, wishes, self-accusations, severe injuries to self-consciousness or to self-conceit about which people will not render themselves an account, preferring illness rather than release from them; mainly, however, they are unresolved conflicts encouraged by individual propensity or provoked by external experiences, between the two most important human instincts, those of self- and of race-preservation.

You might ask what use is it to anyone if, after prolonged searching, he finally does discover what is really the matter with him?

Were it not wiser to leave him his obsessional ideas or his hysterical paralysis, in which he has instinctively taken refuge, rather than compel him pitilessly to lay bare well-hidden æsthetic and ethical defects of his mind?

Experience teaches that this is not the case. For a real evil can be dealt with somehow; indeed, in many instances it does not have even the significance ascribed to it. The persons who played a part in the repressed ideational groups are perhaps long since dead, or have lost all significance for the patient, and yet these thought-complexes can occasion years of mental suffering to anyone who for the sake of sparing his sensibility selects the way of repression, of self-deceit, of concealment from himself, instead of the painful way of release by psychic awareness.

The drama that is so affectingly unrolled in Ibsen's 'The Lady from the Sea' is repeated not infrequently in our analyses. The heroine of the piece is a woman who although possessed of every outward reason for happiness is tormented by severe obsessive feelings. The sea, and the sea alone, enthrals her whole feeling world; all the tenderness of her environment, of her family, rebounds from her ineffectually. Her troubled husband, a doctor, takes the field armed with all the weapons of his learning in order to bring about the recovery of his wife's emotional life; tranquillity, amusement, distraction of every kind is tried, but all in vain. Finally by what one might almost call a kind of psycho-analytic interrogatory he comes to the conviction that there is a background of reality to his wife's imaginary illness. Her peace of mind is destroyed by the memory of an adventurer, a dashing sailor to whom as quite a young girl she had pledged herself. Unconsciously she is for ever tormenting herself with the thought that she does not really love her husband, that she has become his wife merely from interested motives, that her heart still belongs to the adventurer. At the end of the drama this one-time lover really returns and claims his right. At first the husband wants to protect his wife from him by force, but on reflection he soon sees that the four walls within which he meant to imprison his wife could certainly keep her body captive, but never her feelings; he therefore gives his wife back her right to self-determination, he leaves her free to choose between him and the adventurer. On the instant that the woman has her free choice she again chooses her husband; and this independent decision frees her finally from the torment of always having to think only of the sea which was, after all, only the symbol of her connection with the sailor and a substitutive idea for the repressed idea that it was not love but merely interest that bound her to her husband.

It is easy for the poet to reanimate departed forms and let them vanish again at will; it is not possible of course to do this in psycho-analysis. But phantasy released from its fetters by analysis can also conjure up in wonderfully vivid and active fashion the memories of long ago, and then it often occurs, as in 'The Lady from the Sea', that the unconscious worry or idea that occasions so much suffering to the patient can only disturb their peace of mind so long as it is concealed in the unconscious, while in the ghost-banishing light of complete consciousness it vanishes of itself.

But also when it appears on analysis that the existence of the dreaded but repressed idea is justified, that it is still adapted to cause present conflicts, even then it is more advantageous to present the sheer truth to the patient.

There are of course real evils that can be remedied; but what if one denies them to oneself? Recognition of the evil is the precondition of its remedy. If a 'Lady from the Sea' who has freedom of choice feels that she does not love her husband, well, then, let her leave him. Then she can always consider whether she should follow the adventurer or whether it would not be more sensible to belong to neither the worthy but unloved, nor to the attractive but undependable, but apart from both to set herself new aims and to look for compensation in a new life.

This, however, would afford the example for a third possibility, namely, that even after analysis the conflict should prove insoluble. One might think that in that case a senseless obsessional idea, for instance a love amounting to monomania for the sea, is more supportable than an understanding of the inexorable truth. But that is not so. A leading characteristic of neurotic symptoms is the impossibility of relieving them and the indestructibility that this entails. Round the complex hidden in the unconscious fresh quantities of energy are constantly collecting as in the lap of an apparently extinct volcano, and whenever the pressure rises above a certain point there is always another outburst. On the contrary, however, whatever we consciously consider and feel in all its depths undergoes in the mind a process of discharge, of being used up; it loses in feeling value. 'Associative dispersal' of feeling-tension follows on the heels of complete understanding. Grief also has two forms of manifestation, one normal and one pathological. In the first the initial psychic paralysis is soon followed by philosophical resignation; the cares and duties of the future soon allow the instinct of self-preservation to come into play. When, however, years and decennia pass without remission of the grief we can be certain that the mourner is not weeping for only the lost one or his memories, but that concealed in the unconscious earlier depressing motives are using the opportunity of the actual incident to make themselves felt.

Analysis changes pathological grief into physiological grief, and thereby makes it accessible to the healing influences of time and life upon the feelings, just as the antique work of art whelmed in the earth remains intact only so long as it remains there as soon as it is brought to light rain, ice, snow, and sunshine begin their disintegrating work upon it. Suggestion, therefore, is a palliative treatment, analysis desires to be called a 'causal process of healing'. The suggester behaves like the hygienist who, warring against alcoholism and tuberculosis, preaches everlastingly only about abstinence and disinfection; analysis, however, resembles rather the sociologist who seeks for the social evils that are the real origins of drunkenness and tuberculosis and does battle with these fundamental causes.

As I have already said, there have been people who declared that analysis itself is nothing else than a form of suggestion. The analyst was much preoccupied with his patient, he 'put it to him' that the symptoms were caused by this or that and the suggestion had a curative effect. Generally the same critics say in one breath that the statements of fact of psycho-analysis are untrue and that these particular facts have been known for a long time already; that analysis is either ineffectual or also harmful, and that it only cures by suggestion.

According to the dialectical principle that the onus of proof lies with the maker of the assertion, I ought not to concern myself with these objections as they are thrown out everywhere merely hypothetically and as empty statements and do not rest upon the personal experience of the critic. As, however, these objections are so frequently repeated and may produce an impression on this account, I shall adduce a few facts contra-indicating that suggestion in the ordinary sense of the word could play a considerable or indeed the chief part in analysis.

As I said, in suggestion the patient's belief is the precondition of success. Now in analytic treatment we begin by explaining to the patient that the utmost scepticism on his part is permitted, nay necessary. We permit him to control all our statements; he may laugh at us, scold us, and criticize whenever anything we say seems to him incredible, laughable, or unfounded. I cannot say that at the beginning of the treatment patients make much use of this permission; on the contrary they show a great propensity to take all our statements for revelation. In such cases we recognize the suppressed scepticism even from slight mistakes, slips of the tongue on patient's part, and compel him to acknowledge this disbelief to himself and to us. Many a patient is seized after the very first explanations with an extraordinarily strong tendency to proselytize; he preaches constantly and everywhere about psycho-analysis, can talk about absolutely nothing else and always wants to gain new adherents. To such people we must then ourselves prove that all this ado only serves to shout down certain of their own doubts. In a word, in contrast to the suggester who desires only that the patient should believe him, we are constantly on our guard that the patient should believe nothing of which he has not convinced himself.

The suggester wishes to impress the patient. He adopts the self-satisfied expression of scientific and moral authority, of altruistic benevolence, and looks upon his patients in this way, giving them tranquillizing explanations or issuing commands to them. He even wishes to impress them with his outward appearance, with the size of his beard and with his ceremonial garb.

How otherwise the psycho-analysts: they compel the patient to tell them everything that comes into his head, not to put anything aside, not even what he thinks might affect the doctor disagreeably or insultingly. In this way, therefore, everything comes to light, whatever is hidden away of suspicion, detraction, scorn, hate, wrath, and sensibility, without which humanity never manages along even where in general sympathetic feelings predominate. The impressive appearance of the suggesting doctor, the benevolence or sternness that he displays, repels these negative affects *in statu nascendi*. Could there, however, be a less fertile ground for the evocation of suggestion than a relationship in which the person treated is at liberty to entertain himself in every conceivable way at his doctor's expense, to disparage him—if it occurs to him—and to humiliate him? I may remark here at once that many patients gladly avail themselves of this opportunity of getting rid of all the hate and defiance they have cherished and repressed within themselves from childhood against all authority. They observe the doctor with a keen eye; his exterior, his features, his dress, his walk—all are criticized; ideas occur to them in which he is suspected of various misdeeds, and his integrity is questioned. The analysing doctor, however, who understands his business will not defend himself against such ideas, but will quietly wait till the patient comes to see for himself that his aggressiveness is really directed against quite other people who are much more significant for him, and that he is only 'transferring' his unfounded or hair-raisingly exaggerated accusations to the doctor.

During treatment by suggestion and hypnosis the doctor as far as possible says only pleasant things to the patient. He denies that the latter is ill at all, comforts him, wants to inculcate into him strength and self-confidence, in a word he suggests to the patient only beneficial things, and this is so agreeable to the latter that he is really able out of gratitude to forgo the manifestation of his symptoms for a while. In contrast to this the analyst must constantly tell his patient unpleasant truths to his face. He reveals to him the shady side of his character, of his æsthetic nature, of his intellect, and deflates his swollen self-conceit to the level of reality. If the patient fights tooth and nail against so unpleasant an insight, the analyst takes care not to talk him over, and finally even concedes the possibility of an error on his side. Only when the patient of himself brings up memories and ideas that strengthen the analyst's suspicions, that is to say, after the patient's self-conviction, can one count on an advance in analytic knowledge and also upon an improvement in the condition.

If anyone wants to call this kind of careful enlightenment suggestion, there is of course no objection to be made to such nomenclature, only we must define the idea of suggestion entirely differently, and also subsume under this idea a logical conviction based on inductive proof. By this means, however, both the word as well as the objection would lose their meaning.

The suggester has other weapons besides impressiveness at his command: as regards the patient he can simulate interest and selflessness. This naturally heightens in the utmost degree the esteem and sometimes the passion which the person of the neurologist who practises suggestion calls forth.

A similar inclination to unquestioning submission on the part of the patient certainly manifests itself also in analysis, and in so far the presence of suggestive factors in analysis also must be acknowledged; but this 'suggestion' in analysis is only a transitional stage, and no patient can analytically be held to be cured who has not sobered down out of this condition. Care is also taken that during the analysis enthusiasm for the doctor does not 'go sky high'. The analyst does not spare with his pruning-knife this sympathetic emotion either, which the hypnotist so zealously cherishes. The liking confessed to by the patient, however, could not be more insulted than when instead of returning it we explain it as scientifically and therapeutically a significant symptom. And truly this pathological love vanishes just as does pathological grief; by the end of the analysis the transference to the doctor loses all its charm.

The suggester begins by promising the patient a cure. The skilful analyst does not do this. From the start of the treatment he mentions only the possibility of a cure, at most its probability; he cannot do otherwise, for the exact nature of the trouble, its extent, the inhibitions due to the patient's personality, only come to light during the course of the analysis, and only then does it gradually become clear whether and in how far it is possible to combat the patient's affective and intellectual resistances. If, however, the patient recovers in spite of all this, then only someone who either does not know what analysis is or who has mistaken ideas about psycho-analytic technique can speak of it as being the result of suggestion.

The analysing doctor must keep strict watch that he is not content with a success due to suggestion. It often happens that the patient appears with a radiant countenance and announces the gospel of his cure; thereupon it is the unpleasant duty of the doctor to draw his attention to the indications to the contrary. But further discussion is altogether impossible with anyone who would still call such a procedure 'suggestion'.

Historically, at the beginning of its evolution, psycho-analysis was combined with hypnotism, but has long since emancipated itself from the latter. The discoverers of the method at first made use of the convenient sharpening of memory in hypnosis in order to recall hidden memory traces. It was soon evident, however, that stimulation of the analysis by suggestion, even if it in many cases facilitated the beginning of the treatment, only made the end of it and the breaking down of the transference to the doctor all the more difficult. I am borne out by the opinion of all competent analysts when I say that analysis carried out by means of the help of hypnosis is an inferior surrogate to real analysis without hypnosis. It is necessary to lay stress on this, as many people hold the mistaken view that even to-day analysis, as in Breuer's time, is nothing else than the recalling of memories and the abreacting of affects in the hypnotic state. There is no question of this; on the contrary, the patient must be awake in order that his intellectual and affective resistances may display themselves in their entirety and be overcome.

In what I have said I have only wanted to show that not only is analysis not any kind of suggestion but a constant battle against suggestive influences, and that the technique of analysis uses more protective measures against blind belief and unquestioning submission than any methods of teaching and enlightenment that have ever been used in the nursery, the university, or the consulting-room.

The great dislike for this method in official circles shows that suggestive influences play no great part in psycho-analysis.

Even if analysts did not fight against suggestion, and the patient's inner resistances did not create any counterpoise to suggestive influence, the general attitude of a considerable section of the medical profession would suffice to undermine the credulity of our patients. In this respect more than is absolutely necessary often takes place. If when an analysed patient by chance gets another doctor's opinion of psycho-analysis—and we are acquainted with the tendency of neurotics to consult doctors—he goes home heavily burdened with all sorts of misgivings about our methods of treatment. It is not so bad if he is only told that analysis 'is a clever man's colossal mistake', and it is still bearable when analysis is curtly dismissed as 'phantasy', or 'of a literary interest', by doctors who have not the faintest inkling of what it is about. But it also happens, thanks to the benevolence of many colleagues, that the patient's suspicions are roused as to the trustworthiness of the analyst.

Of course these well-meaning informers do not realize that in the analysis the patient really tells the doctor everything, and that precisely this compulsion to relate every thought takes away from the sting of the counter-suggestion that might shake the patient's confidence. The 'clever man' referred to above declares that to-day analysis is an operation in which members of families and doctors are constantly spitting into the 'field of operation'.

There is therefore no question of suggestion in analysis, but on the contrary of the free expression of those powerful resistances that originate partly in the pain it gives the patient to put up with unpleasant truths and partly in the great distrust that the rejection of psycho-analysis by doctors of good repute and official positions must rouse in him. And if it is nevertheless possible under conditions of such difficulty to cure patients or permanently to ameliorate tormenting mental states by means of psycho-analysis, then this is wholly and solely due to the merit of the method, and only the uninformed can ascribe it to 'suggestion'.

There are two philosophies that in our day wrestle with one another at the bedside of the neurotic; they have taken each other's measure for a long time with hostile eyes not only in medicine but also in society. The object of the one is to cure by hushing up, cloaking, repressing; its means are: a pretence of sympathy in the priestly manner and maintenance of the worship of authority. The other roots out 'the living lie' wherever it is to be found, does not abuse authority, and the goal of its endeavour is to let the light of consciousness penetrate to the deepest instinctive springs of thought and feeling; it recoils from no painful, unpleasant, or disgusting knowledge if by this means it can penetrate to the sources of the evil. Were psycho-analysis to succeed in releasing an individual's thought and feeling from every fetter, it may safely be left to his reason to bring his personal interests and desires into harmony with those of society.

Man, the healthy as well as the sick, is ripe to do battle with his hidden evils, and it is exaggerated anxiety to want to treat him like a child with reassuring suggestion, instead of strengthening him for life with the occasionally bitter but always wholesome pill of the truth.

IV

ON FORCED PHANTASIES[1]

Activity in the Association-technique

In my paper delivered at the Hague Congress[2] on the 'active' psycho-analytic technique, I put forward the view that one is sometimes in a position when one must issue orders and prohibitions to the patient regarding certain actions for the purpose of disturbing the habitual (pathological) pathways of discharge of excitations out of the psychical, and that the new distribution of psychical tension resulting from this interference makes possible the activation of material till then lying hidden in the unconscious and allows it to become manifest in the associations. Every now and then I observe in this connection that this activity can be extended to influencing the material of associations. If, for example, one observes signs that a patient is 'misusing the freedom of associations' and one calls his attention to this, or if one suddenly interrupts the flow of words of the analysand and harks back to something brought forward

[1] A lecture to the Hungarian Psycho-Analytical Society in May 1923. Published in *Zeitschrift für Psychoanalyse*, 1924, x. 6-16. [Translated by John Rickman.]

[2] The Sixth International Psycho-Analytical Congress, 1920. 'Further Developments of "Active" Technique.'

earlier, from which the patient with his logorrhœa seeks to fly by means of 'talking past the point', we sin apparently against the 'fundamental rule', but we remain true to another and even more important regulation of psycho-analysis, which is that the chief duty of the analyst is to unmask the resistances of the patient. We may not make any exceptions to this rule in those cases in which the resistance employs the fundamental rule of associations to frustrate the objects of the treatment.

Still more rarely, as I said at the Hague, have I found it necessary to extend the prohibition even to the patient's phantasy-activities. Occasionally I tell patients whose symptoms consist in habitual day-dreaming forcibly to interrupt these phantasies and to exert all their force in seeking out those psychical impressions which have been avoided through fear (phobically), and which have switched the patients over on to the tracks of pathological phantasy. Such influence I thought and still regard as invulnerable to the reproach that one is mixing the method of free-association with the procedures of suggestion; our intervention here consists only of an *inhibition*, a shutting off of certain paths of association, while the products of the analysand himself, which take its place, provide ideas without our having awakened them in him.

Since then I perceived that it would be an exaggeration and a pedantry to introduce this limitation into all cases; indeed, I had to acknowledge that we had never actually followed this injunction literally. When we interpret the patient's free associations, and that we do countless times in every analytical hour, we continually deflect his associations and rouse in him expected ideas, we smooth the way so that the connections between his thoughts so far as their content is concerned are, therefore, to a high degree active; meanwhile we impart to him at the same time association-prohibitions. The difference between this and the ordinary suggestion simply consists in this, that we do not deem the interpretations we offer to be irrefutable utterances, but regard their validity to be dependent on whether they can be verified by material brought forward from memory or by means of repetition of earlier situations. Under such conditions, as Freud has established long since, ' suggestibility ', that is, the uncritical acceptance of the propositions of the analyst by the analysand, is in no way strong; on the contrary, as a rule the first reaction to an interpretation is resistance in the form of a more or less brusque repudiation, and only much later can we put the confirmatory material to use. Another difference between us and the omnipotent suggestionist is that we ourselves retain a grain of scepticism about our own interpretations and must be ever ready to modify them or withdraw them completely, even when the patient has begun to accept our mistaken or our incomplete interpretations.

Once this is grasped, the principal objection to the somewhat energetic application of the prohibition of associations in analysis falls to the ground, but naturally it is only applied in cases in which without it the work either does not proceed at all or only crawls along slowly.

I turn next to a type of person who both in analysis and life is particularly poor in phantasy, if not actually without them, on whom the most impressive experiences leave no apparent trace. Such persons are able to reproduce in memory situations which according to our reckoning must necessarily rouse the intense affects of anxiety (Angst), revenge, erotic excitement, and so forth, which call for discharge through the pathways of deeds, volition, phantasies, or at least external and internal means of expression, but these people show no trace either of feeling such reactions or of expressing them. Supported by the preconceived opinion that in these cases such conduct is due to repression of psychical material and suppression of affect, I now have no hesitation in forcing the patients to recover the adequate reactions, and if they still persist in saying that they have no ideas, I commission them to discover such reactions in phantasy. To the objection that I am then generally met with that such phantasies are quite ' artificial ', ' unnatural ', quite foreign to their nature, illogical, and the rest (by which the patient puts aside every responsibility), I am accustomed to retort that he does not have to tell the truth (actuality), but all that comes to his mind without regard for objective reality, and that certainly he is not required to acknowledge these phantasies as completely spontaneous performances. With his intellectual resistance disarmed in such a fashion the patient then tries, usually only very warily, to depict the situation in question, halting and breaking off at every feature, which requires a continuous pressure on the part of the analyst. In the course of time, however, the patient becomes more courageous, his 'fabricated' experiences in phantasy more varied, animated, and full of impressions, so that finally he can no longer regard them in a cool objective way—the phantasy 'transfixes' him. I have found several times that such a 'discovered' phantasy returned in an experience of almost hallucinatory distinctness with the most unmistakable signs of anxiety, rage, or erotic excitement according to the context. The analytical value of such 'forced phantasies', as I would like to call them, is unquestionable. Especially do they furnish a proof that the patient is generally speaking capable of such psychical productions of which he thought himself free, so that they give us a grasp of deeper research into unconscious repression.

In special cases, if the patient in spite of the utmost pressure will produce nothing, I do not stop at laying before him wellnigh directly what he probably ought to have felt in the given situation, or thought or phantasied; and when he finally agrees with my suggestion I naturally lay less weight on the main plot furnished by myself than on the added details supplied by the analysand.

This kind of surprise attack, in spite of the intense strength of the experience of the 'forced phantasy' produced in the hour, tends to mobilize everything (till the next hour) to the undoing as far as possible of its *power of conviction*, and the patient must live through the same or a similar phantasy several times till a modicum of insight remains. In other cases, however, scenes that were unexpected by physician and patient alike are produced or reproduced, which leave an indelible impression on the mind of the patient and the analytic work advances with a bound. If, however, we started our conjectures on the wrong track and furnished the patient with ideas and emotions in continuation of the ideas which we had roused, and if these ideas and emotions contradict those forced up by us, we must freely confess our mistake, although it is not to be excluded that the later analytic material will prove our conjecture to have been right.

The phantasies which I have thus been constrained to force up fall for the most part into three groups: these are (1) positive and negative phantasies of the transference, (2) phantasies recollecting infancy, (3) onanistic phantasies.

I wish to bring to your notice examples from the analytic material of the past few weeks.

A man who was by no means poor in phantasy life, but was strongly inhibited in his own expression of feeling on account of preconceived notions (ideals), was somewhat harshly reminded by his analyst, to whom he had transferred much friendliness and tenderness, towards the end of the analysis of the aimlessness of his attitude towards it, and at the same time a time limit was set at which he must break off whether he was cured or not. Instead of the expected reaction of anger and revenge, which I wanted to provoke as a repetition of deeply repressed infantile mental processes, there followed several hours that were tedious and without tone or activity, but were also completely free from both affect and from phantasies coloured by it. I put it to him that he must hate me for what had happened, and that it would be unnatural that he should not notice anything. But he repeated unblenchingly that he was only grateful to me, that he only felt friendliness towards me, and so on. I pressed him nevertheless to concoct something aggressive against me. Finally, after the customary attempts at defence and repudiation came timorous, then more vigorous phantasies of aggression, the latter accompanied by signs of obvious anxiety (cold sweats). At last he got to beating phantasies of hallucinatory vividness, then the phantasy that he gouged out my eyes which promptly switched over into a sexual scene in which I played the rôle of a woman. During the phantasying the patient had a manifest erection. The further course of his analysis maintained the language of these enforced phantasies which had enabled him to experience with the person of the analyst practically all of the situations of the 'complete Oedipus complex', and enabled the analyst to reconstruct the early infantile developmental history of the libido of the patient.

A patient asserts that she does not know the commonest obscene designation for the genitals and genital processes. I have no ground for doubting her sincerity, but must point out to her that she certainly knew these words in her childhood, had then repressed them, and later on account of repression had let them slip by unnoticed at the moment of hearing them. At the same time I bade her mention to me the words or sounds which came to her mind when thinking of the female genital. About ten words came first, all having the correct initial letter, then a word containing the first, followed by a word containing the second syllable of the desired expression. In similar fragmentary fashion she told me the obscene word for the male member and for sexual intercourse. In this enforced neologising repressed word memories made their appearance in the same way that knowledge kept secret from consciousness emerges in the surprise attack method in the association experiment.

This case reminds me of another in which the patient brought me an experience of being seduced (which in all probability really happened), but with innumerable variations in order at the same time to confuse both me and herself and to obscure reality. I had again and again to constrain her to 'fabricate' such a scene, and thus new details were established with certainty. I had then to correlate the points that were thus established, first with her general behaviour immediately after the occurrence already mentioned (in her ninth year), during which for months together she suffered from the obsessing idea that she would have to marry someone with a different religious belief from her own, and secondly, with her conduct immediately before her marriage, where she paraded a shocking naïveté, and with the events of the bridal night, during which the absence of difficulty in initiation surprised the bridegroom. The very first of the phantasies indicated above led gradually to establishing the fact of the event, which the patient under the stress of circumstantial evidence had to admit. She employed the general uncertainty of the experience as a last weapon of defence (*i.e.* a kind of scepticism) and finally resorted to the philosophical question on the evidential value of sensory impressions (metaphysical mania). 'Indeed one cannot say definitely', she imagined, 'whether the stool standing there is really a stool.' I replied that by giving expression to that idea she had raised the certainty of that memory to the level of a direct sensory experience, and with that degree of certainty we could both rest content.

Another patient suffered from an unbearable 'feeling of tension' in the genitals which often lasted for hours, during which time she was incapable of work and thought; she had to lie down and remain motionless till either the condition passed off or else passed over into sleep, which happened not infrequently—the states never ended with orgastic sensations. When the analysis brought sufficient material concerning the objects of her infantile fixation, and these had come out clearly in repetition in the transference to the analyst, I had to communicate to her the well-founded conjecture that she phantasied in these states unconsciously a (presumably aggressive) sexual act, and indeed with her father, or his surrogate the physician. She remained undiscerning, whereupon I did not hesitate to charge her at the next 'state of tension' to turn her attention consciously to the phantasy I had pointed out. After overcoming the greatest resistance she confessed to me later that she had experienced a phantasy of sexual intercourse, though not an aggressive one, and at the end of it had felt an irresistible impulse to make a few onanistic movements with the pelvis, whereupon the tension suddenly ceased with the feeling of orgastic ease. This then was repeated several times. The analysis showed clearly that the patient entertained the hope unconsciously that the analyst would on hearing the account of these phantasies give effect to them. However, the physician contented himself with making this wish clear to her and searching for the roots in her previous history. From then onwards the phantasy changed: she would then be a man with a conspicuous male member; she made me, however, into a woman. The analyst had then to make clear to her that by so doing she was only repeating the way in which as a child she had reacted to her father's disdain by identification with him (masculine attitude), in order to make herself independent of the favour of her father; this attitude of obstinacy characterized her entire emotional life towards men. There were other variations: phantasies of being teased by a man (with manifest urethral-erotic content), then phantasies of sexual occurrences with her older brother (whom on account of his strength she pretended to love less than the younger brother). Finally she had the quite normal feminine onanistic phantasies, full of resignation, which were surely in continuation of the original loving attitude to the father.

She only brought the smallest part of the phantasies spontaneously; for the most part I had, on the basis of her dreams and the associations she gave in the hour, to provide the direction in which she ought to force her unconscious experiences. A 'period of prohibition' must, however, in every complete analysis follow this 'period of injunctions', that is to say, one must bring the patient to the point of tolerating the phantasies without onanistic discharge, and thereby make conscious the feelings of distress and painful affects related to them (longing, rage, revenge, etc.) without converting them into hysterical 'feelings of tension'.

With the foregoing examples I hope I have illustrated sufficiently the way in which I am able to make use of 'forced phantasies'. My task is now to say something on the indications and contra-indications for this technical stroke. As with 'active' interventions generally, these tasks in phantasying are justified practically always only in the period of detaching, *i.e.* at the end of the treatment. One must add, to be sure, that such detaching never occurs without painful 'deprivations' [Versagungen—frustations], that is, without the activity of the physician. So much for the question of the time when it is suitable to apply this technique. As to what phantasies to put to the patient, one cannot in general say; that must be decided by the analytic material as a whole. Freud's aphorism that progress in the analytic technique is to be expected from an extension of our analytical knowledge applies here also. It is necessary to have much experience of 'not-active' analyses and not-forced phantasies before one may allow oneself such interferences, which are always risky, with the spontaneity of the associations of the patient. If the phantasy-suggestion is tried in the wrong direction (which occurs in those most practised in it occasionally) it may unnecessarily protract, though it is intended to shorten, the treatment.

I owe to these researches into the unconscious phantasy life of patients an insight not only into the mode of origin of particular phantasies (in respect to their content) but also—as an incidental gain—an insight into the cause of the animation and torpidity of phantasy life generally. Among other things I made the discovery that the animation of the phantasy stands in direct relation to those childhood's experiences which we call infantile sexual traumata. The greater number of the patients whose phantasy activity I had to rouse and push forward artificially in the manner alluded to belonged to those classes of society or families with whom the comings and goings of the children from earliest infancy onwards were strongly controlled, the so-called childish naughtiness was hindered from the very first, and naughtiness was broken off before it had come to full bloom, and where the children lacked every opportunity to observe, much less to experience, in their surroundings anything sexual. They are such *well-brought-up* children that their infantile-sexual instinctual impulses simply *have not the opportunity to get anchored in the world of reality*. Such an anchoring, in other words a piece of real experience, appears to be a pre-condition for later freedom in phantasy and the psychical potency connected with it, while the infantile phantasies of the too-well-brought-up child fall into repression—the 'primal repression'—before they ever reach consciousness. We may say in other words that a certain amount of infantile sexual experience (that is to say, a little 'sexual traumatism') not only does not damage but actually promotes the later normality, particularly the normal activity of phantasy. This fact—which corresponds in detail to the comparison Freud made of the consequences of upbringing 'on the ground floor and on the first storey'[1]—leads us to place a lessened value on infantile traumata. Originally these were thought to be the origin of hysteria; later Freud himself stripped them of a great part of their significance in that he discovered that the pathological element lay not in real infantile experiences but in unconscious phantasies. Now we find that a great part of the real experiences of childhood actually offers a certain defence against abnormality in the directions of development. Nevertheless the 'actual experience' ought not to exceed a certain optimum; too much, too early, or too strong may bring about repression and with it a poverty of phantasy.

Viewed from the standpoint of the development of the ego, we are able to trace the poverty of phantasy of the too-well-brought-up child (and his tendency to psychical impotence) to this, that children who really have experienced nothing wilt hopelessly in the ever anti-sexual atmosphere of educational ideals, while the others never let themselves become so completely overpowered by education that on its cessation at puberty they do not trace the regressive path to the abandoned objects and aims of infantile sexuality, but can accomplish the precondition of psycho-sexual normality.

[1] In Freud's *Introductory Lectures on Psycho-Analysis*. (London: Allen and Unwin and The Institute of Psycho-Analysis, and *Gesammelte Schriften*, Bd. VII.)

V

DISEASE- OR PATHO-NEUROSES[1]

A STUDENT, aged twenty-two, came to see me complaining that he was much bothered by 'sadistic' (in part, masochistic) phantasies. He also informed me that recently he had had a testicle removed because of tubercular degeneration. Months later he came again and asked me whether, on the advice of a surgeon, he should permit the second testicle, now also diseased, to be removed. It struck me that the patient's mood was not, as one might have expected, depressed, but peculiarly excited, almost elevated. His request that I should give him psychoanalytic treatment after the operation—'since, after removal of the organic libido, the pathological displacements in the mind can be resolved more easily and with less disturbance'—seemed incongruous with the tragedy of the situation. He had conceived the idea after reading some psychoanalytical literature. I had to leave the decision about the operation to the surgeon, and could hold out no hopes of psychotherapy proving advantageous. The castration was carried out within the next few days.

A short time after I received a despairing letter from the patient's father, in which he informed me of so striking a change in his son's character and demeanour as to waken the suspicion of mental disorder. He was behaving oddly, neglecting his studies as well as his music, which till then he had keenly pursued, he was unpunctual, did not wish to see his parents; to explain his conduct he referred to his being in love with a girl, the daughter of a respected townsman of his city.

I had the opportunity of seeing the young man twice after these events. On the first occasion indications of erotomania and insane ideas of reference were prominent. Every girl was in love with him (he saw this from various

[1] *Zeitschrift*, 1916–17, Bd. IV. S. 219.

little indications). But everyone looked at his genitals, many made remarks about them; indeed, he challenged a young man to a duel for this reason. (These facts were vouched for by his father.) He would soon show people that he was a man! He used his knowledge of psycho-analytical literature to put the blame of his illness on to other people, particularly his parents. 'Mother is unconsciously in love with me, therefore she behaves so oddly towards me.' He even initiated his mother into this secret, to her no small alarm. At this time the patient, as sometimes occurs in paraphrenia, had a sort of awareness of the alteration that had occurred in himself. Not only had other people changed, but he also had become different. His love for the girl had not the same strength that it had, but he would put the matter right by 'self-analysis'.

A few weeks later I saw him for the last time. The condition had meantime progressed rapidly and, unnoticed only by the patient himself, was clearly approaching the condition which is the nucleus of every paranoic breakdown, *i.e.* homosexuality. He felt himself 'influenced' by men. It was this influence that had altered his feelings towards the girl he loved. Like most paraphrenics, he imagined the influence to be due to 'thought-transference'. He did not at first express it clearly in words, but soon let it be guessed that the whole world suspected him of homosexuality. He recounted in detail the scene when he finally lost his self-control. He was travelling in a railway carriage; opposite him sat a funny little man who looked at him scornfully, as though to say 'I could have intercourse with you'. The idea that even the emasculate little man took him for a woman excited him greatly, and for the first time he had the revengeful thought 'I can still have intercourse with *you*'. In spite of this he left the train in a sort of flight at the next station, even abandoning his luggage, which was lost for some considerable time. (I would here remark that from the interpretation of dreams we know 'luggage' to be a genital symbol, so that in this instance the losing of the luggage can be interpreted as an allusion to the castration.)

Soon afterwards the patient had to be taken to an institution, so that I do not know much about his further career. I hear that he is becoming steadily more demented. But even what little we do know about this case is important enough to occupy us more particularly.

The first thing that strikes one is the pointedness with which, in the patient's insane ideas, the homosexual basis of the mental disorder—usually only to be arrived at by means of interpretation—becomes apparent. Nevertheless, similar cases have already been published by myself and Morichau-Beauchant (Poitiers). The paranoiac, starting with quite confused insane ideas of reference and accusation, can finally become conscious also, amongst other things, of his own homosexuality, although only in the form of an unjust accusation; just as the obsessional neurotic, whose illness expresses itself in senseless obsessions, may in time disclose the whole real mental background of his illness—but in the form of a compulsive ceremonial, that is, in a form unrecognized by his ego.

One is aware of a deeper problem in this case, however, when one comes to consider whether the mental disorder, the paranoia, was determined traumatically by the castration. Castration, 'emasculation', is certainly well-adapted to induce phantasies of femininity, or to revive such from the repressed bisexual memories of childhood which find expression in the insane ideas.

Moreover, in this respect the case is not an isolated one. Several years ago I published a paper on 'Irritation of the anal erotogenic zone as a determining cause of paranoia'.[1] It was the case of a man who developed persecution mania after undergoing an operation on the rectum. The interference with the rectum was well-adapted to excite or revive phantasies of having suffered a homosexual assault.

The original psycho-analytical traumatic theory of the neuroses has maintained itself till the present day. It was not set aside, but supplemented, by Freud's theory of the sexual constitution and of its predisposing significance for

[1] Centralblatt für Psychoanalyse, Jahrg. I., 1910–11.

the development of the neuroses; so that in principle we have nothing to object to in the possibility of a traumatic paranoia in which, in spite of a normal sexual constitution, certain experiences supply the impetus for the development of this psycho-neurosis.

Considered from the standpoint of Freud's teaching of the sexual constitution, paranoia is a narcissistic neuro-psychosis. People fall ill of it when their sexual development has suffered a disturbance at the transition stage from narcissism to object-love, so that they remain with a tendency to regress to the homosexual stage, that is, to a form of object-love which is nearer to narcissism.

In his essay on narcissism[1] Freud mentions among others my suggestion that the peculiar changes in the love-life of those physically sick (the withdrawal of object-libido and the concentration of all egoistic as well as libidinal interests in the ego) support the view that, concealed behind the object-love of the normal adult, a great part of the earlier narcissism continues to exist, only waiting for the opportunity to make itself felt. A bodily illness or injury can therefore quite well result in regression to a so-called traumatic narcissism, and even to its neurotic variants.

Observations about behaviour of the libido in those physically ill have meanwhile become somewhat more numerous, and I take this opportunity of discussing those neuroses that supervene upon organic illness or injury, which I shall call disease- or patho-neuroses.

It appears that in very many cases the libido that is withdrawn from the outer world is directed, not towards the whole ego, but chiefly to the diseased or injured organ, and evokes symptoms at the injured or diseased area that must be referred to a local increase of libido.

People who have a hollow tooth or toothache are not only capable—as is comprehensible—of withdrawing their whole interest from the outer world and directing it to the painful place, but they employ that place also for a peculiar

[1] [*Gesammelte Schriften*, Bd. VI.; *Sammlung kleiner Schriften zur Neurosenlehre*, 4te Folge; *Collected Papers*, vol. iv.]

pleasure-gratification that one cannot describe otherwise than as libidinal. They suck and pull at the diseased tooth with the tongue, they poke about in the hollow tooth with instruments, and themselves acknowledge that these manipulations are accompanied by markedly pleasurable feelings. One can only say that in consequence of stimuli set up by the disease a bodily region has here—as in hysteria on the basis of a special disposition—taken on *genital qualities*, that is, has become 'genitalized'. On the basis of a case that I analysed I am able to state that these dental paræsthesias can result in marked oral-erotic and cannibalistic phantasies mentally, that is, can affect the psycho-sexual attitude correspondingly. As Freud informed me, long-continued dental treatment, dental regulation, etc., may be followed by a similar excitation of oral erotism.

A man who had stomach trouble, and whose whole interest was absorbed by his digestion, made the characteristic remark that 'the whole world tastes bad'; it seemed as if his whole libido was centred round his stomach. Perhaps it will some day be possible to trace specific character-changes in organic illnesses to reaction-formations in the ego against such displacements of the libido. Sufferers from indigestion are said to be 'choleric', 'snappy'; one speaks of a 'phthisicus salax,' etc.

I know from children's physicians that after whooping-cough attacks of nervous coughing may persist for years, in spite of recovery from the infective process; I should explain this little hysterical symptom also as being due to the displacement of libido on to an organ that had been diseased.

The reanimation of anal erotism, usually in neurotic garb, following a bowel complaint, is an occurrence frequently observed in analysis.

These examples could certainly be multiplied, but they suffice for our consideration. We learn from them that organic illness can result not only in a narcissistic, but eventually, preserving the libidinal object-relation, in a 'transference-neurotic' (hysterical) disturbance of the libido. I should call this condition patho-hysteria (disease-hysteria), as contrasted with Freud's sexual neurosis, in which the disturbance of libido is the primary, the organic disturbance of function the secondary thing (hysterical blindness, nervous asthma).

The distinction of these conditions from hypochondria, Freud's third 'actual neurosis', is more difficult. The difference is chiefly that in hypochondria demonstrable changes in the organ are lacking and generally have never been present at all.

A traumatic neurosis is the result of a powerful mental and physical shock *without* considerable bodily injury. Combined in the symptomatology of it are narcissistic regression (setting free of a part of the object-cathexes) with conversion- or anxiety-hysterical symptoms, which, as is well known, we regard as belonging to the transference-neuroses.[1]

Under what circumstances, however, will the illness or injury be followed by a far-reaching regression into narcissism and evoke a 'disease-narcissism' or a true narcissistic neurosis? I think this might be determined by three conditions: (1) if the constitutional narcissism—even if it be only latent—was already too powerful before the injury, so that the slightest harm to any part of the body affects the ego as a whole; (2) if the trauma endangers life or is thought to do so, that is to say, threatens existence (the ego) in general; (3) if one can imagine the formation of a *narcissistic regression or neurosis of this kind as a result of an injury to a part of the body especially powerfully charged with libido, with which the ego as a whole easily identifies itself.* I shall here consider only this last eventuality.

We know that the distribution of libido throughout the body is not equal, that there are erotogenic zones where the libidinal energies are at a high tension, as though concentrated, while this is much less so in other parts of the body. It is to be assumed at the outset that injury or disease in these zones is much more likely to be accompanied by far-reaching disturbances of libido than similar occurrences elsewhere in the body.

[1] Cf. 'Über zwei Typen der Kriegsneurose'. ('On Two Types of War Neurosis.' Chapter XI. of this book.)

During my short experience for a few months in hospital as ophthalmologist I was able to observe that psychoses supervening upon eye operations are not rare; this fact, moreover, is also emphasized in the text-books of ophthalmology. Now the eye is one of the bodily organs most powerfully charged with libido, as is shown not only by psycho-analysis of the neuroses, but also by the wealth of folklore relating to the value of the eye. It is comprehensible that the loss of an eye or the risk of this should sympathetically involve the whole ego, or give rise to a narcissistic disease-neurosis.

In the neurological division of a military hospital of which I had charge during the war, only one patient in the course of a whole year was transferred from the surgical side for observation of his mental condition. He was a man of about thirty years of age whose lower jaw had been almost entirely blown away by a shell. His face was horribly deformed by the injury. The only striking thing about his behaviour, however, was his naïve narcissism. He requested that the nursing sister should manicure him thoroughly every day; he would not eat the hospital food, since much finer fare was due to him, and he reiterated these and similar requests unceasingly, after the fashion of querulants—a case, therefore, of true 'disease-narcissism'. Only after prolonged observation was it possible to establish that beside these seemingly harmless symptoms there were also present indications of persecution-mania.

Just as I was writing this paper I read a notice of a work by v. Wagner on the mental conditions following upon severe face-wounds. The author finds that after such injuries the mood is much more deeply depressed than after no matter what dreadful wounds in other bodily parts. All the wounded declared that they would far rather have lost an arm or a leg. It was also noteworthy how often those suffering from face-wounds looked at themselves in the mirror.

Now one cannot exactly describe the face as an erotogenic zone; but as the seat of a very significant component-impulse, of normal exhibitionism, it has—as the most noticeable uncovered part of the body—an important sexual rôle. It is quite conceivable that the mutilation of so important a part of the body could lead without any peculiarly powerful predisposition to a narcissistic regression. I was able to observe a case of temporary emotional stupor resembling paraphrenia in a beautiful young girl after an operation on her face.

The identification of the whole ego with parts of the face is common to all mankind. It seems quite probable to me that the displacement of libidinal impulses 'from below upwards' (Freud) that occurs during the period of sublimation, secondarily 'genitalizes'—probably with the help of the rich vascular innervation—the sexual rôle of the body which is at first merely exhibitionistic. (By genitalization of a part of the body I understand, with Freud, a periodically heightened hyperæmia, œdema, and turgescence accompanied by corresponding nervous excitation.)

As is known, the other pole of the body, the anus and the rectum, retains a great part of its erotogenicity throughout life. The case I mentioned above of an irritation of the anal region as the inciting agent of a paranoia indicates that the path to disease-narcissism and its neurotic variants is accessible from this side also.

The status of the genitals amongst the erotogenic zones is a quite peculiar one. We know from Freud that they very early take over the primacy of all the erotogenic zones, so that the erotogenic function of all the other zones is circumscribed in favour of the genital zone. One must further add that this primacy also expresses itself by every excitation of an erotogenic zone immediately affecting the genital region sympathetically; so that as the central erotic organ the genital is related to the other zones as the brain is to the organs of sense. The evolution of an organ of this kind, which includes all the other erotisms, might in general be the pre-condition of the narcissistic stage of sexuality postulated by Freud. We can assume with certainty that throughout life the most intimate relations exist between the genitals and the narcissistic ego (Freud); indeed, that the nucleus round which the whole narcissistic ego-formation crystallizes is probably the genitals. The widespread identification of the ego with the genitals in dreams, in neuroses, in folklore, and in wit serves as a psychological confirmation of this assumption.

After all this, it would not be surprising if it proved that diseases or injuries of the genitals are peculiarly adapted to evoke a regression to disease-narcissism. Here I will first refer to the so-called puerperal psychoses that are certainly not to be traced to 'infection' or to ordinary 'excitement', but to the unavoidable injury to the central erotogenic zone at parturition. As is known, a great number of these psychoses belong to the group of paraphrenias (dementia præcox). Other diseases of the genitals, gonorrhœa, syphilis, etc., can, especially in men, evoke profound alterations in mood and sympathetically involve the entire ego. The exaggerated statement of an Italian gynæcologist that all mental illnesses in women are to be traced to diseases of the genitals and adnexæ is an unjustified generalization from the possibility of a genital pathoneurosis. The painful pleasure associated with an organ of excretion (here the vagina) is in part carried over on to the excreted product (the child). It thus becomes explicable that so many mothers actually prefer the 'child of their pain'. Freud drew my attention to this analogy.

It may be granted that a lesion of the genitals or of any other of the erotogenic zones indicated may just as well have as a consequence an hysterical (that is, a non-narcissistic) neurosis, but *cæteris paribus* these regions are more apt than others to react narcissistically to disease or injury. We therefore believe ourselves justified, in the case of paranoia following upon castration mentioned in the introduction, in attributing to an injury of the genital zone not merely the significance of an ordinary precipitating cause but a specific ætiological significance.

Besides the considerations that have been adduced, which are in part theoretical, a very frequent psychiatric observation supports this last statement. Patients suffering from paraphrenia (dementia præcox) very often complain of peculiar sensations in particular parts of the body: for instance, their nose is crooked, the position of their eyes is changed, their bodies deformed, etc., although the most minute examination of the part concerned can establish no objective change.

Now it cannot be accidental that these hypochondriacal sensations so often manifest themselves in the face, or the eyes, and not infrequently in the genitals—in the very parts of the body the narcissistic significance of which we have just emphasized. Still more striking is it that paraphrenics so often mutilate themselves in their erotogenic zones; castrate themselves, put out their eyes, etc., or request the physician to undertake a plastic operation on their face or nose.

Now we know from Freud that in paraphrenia such striking symptoms subserve the tendencies to self-cure, and we must therefore assume in these cases of self-blinding and self-castration too that the patient wishes by means of this brutal measure to rid himself of hypochondriac-narcissistic paræsthesias such as were mentioned above. At all events the fact that a pure psychogenic paraphrenia is able to evoke such paræsthesias in the erotogenic zones, and that the patient reacts by having recourse to self-injury, clearly indicates the possibility that this process may also be reversible, that therefore a traumatic or pathological disturbance of these narcissistically-significant parts of the body can attract a narcissistic patho-neurosis to themselves sooner than one to other parts.

Such a reciprocity of central and peripheral excitations is known to us in other directions. For instance, a skin wound can itch, but a purely central itch can lead to scratching; in other words to an inflicting of skin wounds on the itching surface and give rise, therefore, to a kind of self-injury.

In what way a bodily injury or a disturbance of an organ by disease can alter the distribution of libido is still quite incomprehensible; for the present we must content ourselves with the statement of the fact.

When a dog, however, licks his injured paw tenderly

for hours on end it is an unjustified rationalization to assume that he intends this to be a medical treatment, the disinfection of his wound or some such thing. Much more plausible is the presumption that an increased amount of his libido has been directed to the injured limb, so that he regards it with a tenderness otherwise reserved only for his genitals.

After all this, it is not improbable not only that the white blood-corpuscles collect together by 'chemitaxis' at the injured or diseased parts of the body in order to develop their reparatory functions, but also that a greater amount of libido derived from the remaining organ-cathexis is concentrated there. Perhaps indeed this heightening of libido has its share in the healing processes set up. 'The wound closes rapidly with a voluptuous titillation' (Mörike).

But if the ego defends itself against this localized increase of libido by means of a repression, then an hysterical, or, if there is complete identification, a narcissistic patho-neurosis, or possibly a simple disease-narcissism, may be the result of the injury or illness.

It is to be expected that further examination of these processes will throw some light on a few still very obscure problems of sexual theory, particularly those of masochism and feminine genitality.

The seat of masochistic activity, whatever complicated and sublimated forms it may later assume, is, according to Freud, originally always the cutaneous envelope of the body. It seems that unavoidable skin injuries cause in everyone localized traumatic increases of libido which—at first purely auto-erotic—can later in corresponding circumstances become the nucleus of a real masochism.[1] So much at least can be asserted, that in masochism increases of libido supervene at injured parts of the body in a manner similar to that which has happened, as we conclude, in the cases mentioned above of disease- or patho-neuroses.

[1] I know verbally from Freud that masochism is always to be referred to a castration threat, and I suppose that owing to this a second, now neurotic, process leads to a repression of the normal sexual impulse and to the regressive, although already genitalized, reanimation of the skin masochism referred to above, that is, of the *primal* type of masochism.

As for feminine genitality, we know from Freud that the genital function of the woman, at first quite virile and active, associated with the clitoris, gives place only after puberty to a feminine, passive (vaginal) one. The pre-condition of the first completely feminine sexual enjoyment seems to be a bodily injury, the tearing of the hymen and the powerful dilatation of the vagina by the penis. I surmise that this injury, which originally caused no sexual enjoyment but only pain, brings with it secondarily the displacement of the libido to the injured vagina, after the fashion of the patho-neuroses—just as the cherry that has been pecked by a bird sweetens and ripens the sooner.

It is true that this displacement of libido from the clitoris (activity) to the vagina (passivity) has become organized in the course of phylogenesis and also occurs more or less without any trauma. In one of the types of love-life described by Freud, the woman who hates her first conqueror and can only love the second, there seems to be still preserved the original two phases of the process that leads to feminine (passive) sexuality, namely, the primary hate reaction against the bodily injury, and the secondary displacement of libido to the injured part of the body, to the instrument that caused the wound, and to the bearer of this weapon.

VI

THE PHENOMENA OF HYSTERICAL MATERIALIZATION [1]

Thoughts on the Conception of Hysterical Conversion and Symbolism

"You have travelled the way from worm to human being and much in you is still worm" (Nietzsche, *Also sprach Zarathrustra*).

Freud's psycho-analytic researches showed the symptoms of conversion hysteria to be representations of unconscious

[1] [Published in 'Hysterie und Pathoneurosen'.]

phantasies in bodily terms. For instance, an hysterical paralysis of the arm can signify—by a negative representation—an intended aggressive activity, a wrestling of opposing emotions; a localized anæsthesia or hyperæsthesia, the unconsciously retained and elaborated memory of a sexual contact at that place. Psycho-analysis has also given us unexpected explanations concerning the nature of the forces at work in the formation of hysterical symptoms; it shows us in each individual case that in the symptomatology of these neuroses erotic and egoistic impulses come to expression either alternately or, most often, in compromise-formations. Finally Freud's latest decisive researches concerning the choice of neurosis have revealed in addition the genetic point of fixation in the history of the development of the libido which conditions the disposition to hysteria. He found the disposing factor to be a disturbance of the normal sexual development at the stage when complete primacy of the genital zone had already been reached. Those thus disposed react to an erotic conflict brought about by a psychic trauma by the repression of the genital impulses and eventually by the displacement of these impulses on to apparently indifferent parts of the body. I should like to express it thus: conversion hysteria genitalizes those parts of the body at which the symptoms are manifested. In an attempt to reconstruct the developmental stages of the ego, I was able to point out that the disposition to hysterogenesis presupposes also a fixation of the reality-sense at a given period of development at which the organism does not yet endeavour to adapt to reality by a modification of the external world, but by that of its own body—by magic gestures; and the hysterical language of gesture may indicate a regression to this stage.

No clear-minded person will deny that these formulations impart a wealth of knowledge about the hysterical neuroses of which pre-analytic neurology had not the remotest conception. Nevertheless, I believe that in spite of all our satisfaction with what has been achieved, it is more to the purpose to indicate the lacunæ in our knowledge of these matters. The 'mysterious leap from mental to bodily ' (Freud), for instance, in the symptoms of conversion hysteria is still a problem.

In attempting to deal with this problem various points of attack can be selected, thus amongst others the peculiarities of the innervation conditioning the formation of many conversion symptoms.

The capacity possessed by hysterics of interrupting or disturbing the normal afference of sensory and efference of motor innervation as regards consciousness is shown in hysterical paralysis, convulsions, anæsthesia, and paræsthesia. But, apart from these changes in the discharge of excitation occurring in the psychic sphere, we know of hysterical symptoms the production of which demands a decided increase of innervation, which the normal neuro-psychic apparatus is incapable of manifesting. The unconscious will of the hysteric brings about motor manifestations, changes in the circulation of the blood, in glandular function and in the nourishment of the tissues, such as the conscious will of the non-hysteric cannot achieve. The smooth musculature of the alimentary canal, of the bronchi, the tear and sweat glands, the nasal erectile tissue, etc., are at the disposition of the hysteric; he can bring about individual innervations, for instance, of the musculature of the eyes and Adam's apple, that are impossible for healthy persons; his capacity for manifesting local hæmorrhages, blisters, and cutaneous and mucous swellings, though certainly rarer, is also well known.

We do not forget, however, that it is not only hysteria which is capable of such achievements, but that it is also possible to evoke similar manifestations by hypnotism and suggestion to which the normal person also is more or less accessible. There are, too, people otherwise normal who make a habit of a few such super-achievements in childhood, for instance, the individual control of muscles which ordinarily contract symmetrically, the voluntary control of the cardiac, gastric, and intestinal functions, of the muscles of the iris, etc., which they finally display as though endowed with some special gift. A great part of the education of a child consists of breaking away from such tricks and acquiring others. In any case, however, the education of a child presupposes a psychic control of certain organ-activities which later apparently occur 'automatically' or as 'reflexes', but which are really command-automatisms active since childhood; for example, the regular functioning of the sphincter and expulsive muscles of the bowel and bladder, going to sleep and awakening at regular intervals of time, etc. An increase of capacity due to affects which can influence the most varied circulatory and excretory processes is equally well known.

If we confine ourselves first of all to the increased capacity employed in the formation of hysterical symptoms, it will be advisable to select a definite group among the almost inexhaustible and complex possibilities that exist. For this purpose I shall select hysterical symptoms in the digestive tract, of which we have a fairly complete series at our disposal.

One of the commonest hysterical manifestations is the symptom of globus hystericus, that peculiar condition of spasm of the œsophageal musculature that along with another œsophageal symptom, the loss of the swallowing reflex, is often reckoned among the stigmata of this neurosis. A special investigation which I undertook showed that this anæsthesia of the gullet and the œsophageal region could be traced to a reaction to unconscious fellatio, cunnilingual, coprophagic phantasies, etc., which owed their origin to the genitalization of those areas of mucous membrane. While these phantasies find their negative expression in anæsthesia, globus hystericus, as one can convince oneself in all cases subjected to psycho-analysis, represents the same phantasies in a positive sense. The patients themselves speak of a lump that stuck in their throats, and we have every reason to believe that the corresponding contractions of the circular and longitudinal musculature of the œsophagus produce not only the paræsthesia of a foreign body, but that a kind of foreign body, a lump, really is brought about. On analysis the lump certainly appears as a quite peculiar and not harmless foreign body, but one with an erotic significance.

In not a few cases this 'lump' moves rhythmically up and down and this movement corresponds to unconscious representations of genital processes.

For a great number of patients who suffer from neurotic distaste for food, tendency to vomit, and other stomach disturbances, eating (the passage of a foreign body through the narrow tube of the œsophagus) signifies, unconsciously, genital incursions similar to those which are phantasied even without any external provocation by people who suffer from a globus condition. Since the date of Pavloff's researches on mental influence over the digestive juices, no one will marvel that such phantasies may be followed by every degree of decreased or increased stomach secretion, of hyperacidity and anacidity.

Those 'infantile sexual theories' (Freud) by which getting children depends on the incorporation of a substance by way of the mouth are the foundation of the process by which the unconscious can bring about an imaginary pregnancy through similar feats on the part of the stomach, bowel, and belly musculature, or even by means of air-swallowing.

The occurrence of intractable sickness in real pregnancy (vomitus gravidarum) which has already been given so many toxicological explanations is still more comprehensible to the psycho-analyst. Psycho-analytic experience has compelled me to a different kind of interpretation of this symptom. One is dealing here with a defence or rejection tendency, directed against what is unconsciously felt as a foreign body in the uterus—the fœtus—but displaced according to the approved pattern 'from below upwards' and carried out in regard to the stomach contents. Only in the second half of the pregnancy, when the movements of the child no longer permit even the hysteric to deny the genital localization of the changes and sensations, does the inclination to vomit cease, that is, the ego of the hysteric acquiesces and adapts itself to irrefutable reality and gives up the phantasied 'stomach-child'.

It is well known that emotions affect bowel peristalsis, that anxiety and fear can be followed by diarrhœa, and anxious expectation by spasm of the sphincter and constipation. It was reserved for Freud, however, and his psycho-analysis to demonstrate how extensively these influences act throughout life, and what a special part in this is played by ideational complexes and instincts.

An experienced Viennese physician, Prof. Singer, long ago recognized that the large bowel has only a slight significance as an organ of digestion, and that it is essentially anal in character and controls the function of excretion. Psycho-analysis can confirm this observation and supplement it in a few points. Our neurotics, especially the hysterics, show us clearly that any point in the large bowel can act as a sphincter, and that besides the '*en bloc*' innervation that propels the fæcal column, it is capable of finely graduated and localized contractions, making it possible to retain a fæcal mass or a gas-bubble at some place or other and compress, so to say, shape it; this may be accompanied by painful paræsthesias. The notions that specially influence these innervations belong, extraordinary to relate, to a complex ruled by ideas of possession, retention, and unwillingness to give up. We find on analysis in innumerable cases that the neurotic from whom a prize or something of worth has been taken against his will, piles up a possession in his bowel for a considerable period as a substitute; that he announces his intention of communicating long-withheld confessions by an unusually copious stool; that he is annoyed for days with 'suppressed wind' that can only be passed after the resistance to the analyst has been given up, when there is no longer anything standing in the way of the intention to make him a present. Such symptoms of anal inhibition or looseness by preference accompany the conflicts that are aroused by the necessity of paying a fee to the analyst, who is in other respects regarded as quite a friendly person.

In one case I was able to study the hysterogenic rôle of the rectum and anus for months on end. A patient who had been an elderly bachelor and then married in order to please his father came for treatment for psychic impotence; he suffered from time to time from a peculiar constipation. He was acutely aware, even painfully so, that the fæcal mass was accumulating in the rectum, but he was incapable of voiding it; even if defæcation occurred any feeling of relief was lacking. Analysis showed that this symptom always appeared when he had come into conflict with a masculine personality who in any way impressed him. It proved ultimately to be an expression of his unconscious homosexuality. Just on the occasions when he wanted to make a determined stand against someone, he was prevented by an unconscious homosexual phantasy and with the help of the contractile rectal walls was compelled to mould for himself a male organ—the member of the consciously hated opponent—from the plastic material of the ever-present rectal contents that would not remove itself from the rectum till the conflict was solved in some fashion or other. He gradually learnt the psycho-analytic method of solving it, that is, insight into the conflict described.

Now what is in common among all the symptoms of the series mentioned? Evidently the physical representation of an unconscious sexual wish as discovered by Freud. But the mode of this representation must be more fully inquired into.

When in a case of globus hystericus the unconscious wish for fellatio causes a lump in the throat, when in real or imaginary pregnancy the hysteric makes a 'stomach-child' out of the contents and wall of the stomach, when the unconscious homosexual moulds the rectum and its contents to a body of definite size and shape, we are dealing with processes that do not correspond in nature with any of the 'faulty perceptions' known to us. We cannot call them hallucinations. An hallucination results when an affect-laden thought-complex is denied a progressive path to consciousness by the censorship, and when the excitation proceeding from it, taking a backward—regressive—path, re-excites the raw material of the thought-complexes that is stored up in memory and makes it conscious as an actual perception.[1] Motor processes which, as we have seen,

[1] For this conception of hallucination see the chapter 'Regression' in Freud's *Traumdeutung*, Vierte Auflage, S. 420; *Gesammelte Schriften*, Bd. II., S. 453.

play so large a part in the formation of hysterical conversion symptoms are on the other hand essentially different from hallucinations. The contraction of the gastric or intestinal wall in globus, in hysterical vomiting, or in constipation, is certainly not ' imaginary ' but real.

Neither can we speak here of an illusion in the sense hitherto customary. An illusion is a sensory misinterpretation or distortion of a real external or internal stimulus. The subject of an illusion is passive, while on the other hand the hysteric himself creates the stimulus, to which he can then give an illusory misinterpretation. A special name is therefore required for the type of hysterical symptom-formation described, as well as for this psycho-analytic phenomenon in general. It might be called a *materialization phenomenon*, since its essence consists in the realization of a wish, as though by magic, out of the material in the body at its disposal and—even if in primitive fashion—by a plastic representation, just as an artist moulds the material of his conception or as the occultists imagine the ' apport ' or the ' materialization ' of objects at the mere wish of a medium.[1]

Here I must at once remark that this process occurs not only in hysteria, where it is a morbid process of comparatively little significance, but also in many affective states in normal people. A great many of the so-called expressional movements that accompany the emotions of the human mind—blushing, pallor, fainting, anxiety, laughter, crying, etc.—evidently ' represent ' important happenings in the career of the individual and of humanity, and are therefore ' materializations ' of a similar kind.

Now how can this phenomenon be interpolated into the series of psychic processes already known to us, and how is its mechanism to be conceived of? The comparison that strikes one at once is the analogy with dream-hallucination, as we know it since Freud's researches into dreams. In dreams wishes are represented as fulfilled, yet this

[1] In the opinion of many investigators a great number at least of the instances of occult materialization is of the nature of hysterical self-deception. Owing to lack of experience in this matter I cannot express any opinion upon it.

wish-fulfilment is purely hallucinatory; motility is paralysed in sleep. In the phenomenon of materialization, on the other hand, one is dealing with an apparently still more far-reaching regression; the unconscious wish, incapable of becoming conscious, does not content itself here with a sensory excitation of the psychic organ of perception, but leaps across to unconscious motility. This signifies a topographical regression to a depth in the psychic apparatus at which states of excitation are no longer disposed of by means of a mental cathexis—even if only hallucinatorily—but simply by a motor discharge.

Chronologically this region of the mind corresponds to a very primitive onto- and phylogenetic stage of development, in which adaptation was not yet achieved by a modification of the outer world but by modifications of the individual's own body. In discussions about questions of evolution we are in the habit of calling this primitive stage, with Freud, the autoplastic in contradistinction to the later alloplastic one.

We should have to conceive the psychic processes here as simplified in *form* to the level of a physiological reflex.[1]

If, therefore, the reflex process is considered not only as a prototype but as a preliminary stage of the psychic process, a stage to which indeed the highest psychic elaboration always remains inclined to regress, then the puzzling leap from mental to bodily in the conversion symptom and the reflex wish-fulfilling phenomenon of materialization become less amazing. It is simply regression to the ' protopsyche '.

Those primitive vital processes which hysteria seems to fall back upon consist of bodily changes which are quite natural and habitual, although when they are psychogenic they impress one as supernormal. The movement of the smooth muscle fibres of the vascular walls, the functioning of glands, the entire process of tissue nourishment, are regulated infra-psychically. In hysteria all these physio-

[1] This threefold conception of regression is also based on Freud's *Traumdeutung* [translation, ' The Interpretation of Dreams ", by A. A. Brill] in the place quoted above.

logical mechanisms are at the disposal of unconscious wish-impulses so that, by a complete reversal of the normal path of excitation, a purely psychic process can come to expression in a physiological bodily change.

Freud in his *Traumdeutung*[1]—in the chapter on the psychology of dream-processes—propounds the question of what changes in the psychic apparatus make the formation of the dream-hallucination possible. He finds the solution to this problem on the one hand in the peculiar character of the discharge of psychic excitation in the unconscious, and on the other in the favourable nature of the changes that accompany the sleeping condition. The 'free flowing-over of intensities' from one psychic element to another permits of a peculiarly intensive excitation of more distant parts of the psychic system, amongst others of the psychic sensory-organ, the perceptual surface level of consciousness. Besides this positive factor, the sleeping condition creates also a 'negative' one, in that the condition of aloofness from actual sense-stimuli allows, as it were, an empty space to come into existence at the sensitive end of the apparatus, so that as a result of the falling away of competing external stimuli the inner excitation attains an excessive sensorial value. In psychotic hallucination Freud assumes a still greater intensity of the 'positive factor', so that the hallucination is maintained in spite of the waking condition, that is, in spite of the competition of external stimuli.

How then are we to conceive of the conditions of excitation on the appearance of a conversion symptom? In my paper on hysterical stigmata (p. 110), I had to describe hysterical anæsthesia as a permanent change at the sensitive end of the Ψ-system, which like the sleeping condition favours the appearance of hallucinations and illusions. Now in those cases, therefore, in which a conversion symptom is superimposed upon an anæsthetic area—a very frequent occurrence, by the way—one may assume similarly that symptom-formation is facilitated by the disappearance of conscious sensory stimuli.

In all other cases the source of energy which, for

[1] *Traumdeutung*, Kap. VII.

instance, brings about a materialization must be looked for in a positive factor.

The monotony with which genital processes, and no others, recur in the psycho-analytic interpretation of hysterical symptoms proves that the active force in conversion springs from a genital instinctual source. We are dealing here, therefore, with an irruption into the higher psychic layers of gross genital forces, and it is these that make it possible for positive powers of such an extraordinary kind to be manifested.

Perhaps the most significant result of organic evolution, aiming as it does at division of labour, was that it achieved the differentiation of particular systems of organs, whose duty on the one hand was the control and distribution of stimuli (psychic apparatus), and on the other of special organs (genitals) whose duty was to discharge periodically the accumulation of sexual excitation in the organism. The organ of distribution and control of stimuli becomes ever more intimately associated with the instinct of self-preservation, and in its highest development becomes the organ for thought and for testing reality. The genital, on the contrary, even in the adult, preserves its primitive character as an organ of discharge; it becomes by the coalescence of all erotisms the central erotic organ (cf. p. 85). The full development of this polar contrast allows of thought being relatively independent of the pleasure principle and of a capacity for genital sexual satisfaction undisturbed by thought.

Hysteria, however, appears to be a relapse to that primitive condition in which this division has not yet been achieved, and signifies an irruption of genital instinctual impulses into the intellectual sphere or, alternatively, a defence-reaction to this irruption. We may therefore conceive of the origin of an hysterical symptom thus: An over-powerful genital impulse wants to press forward into consciousness. The ego perceives the nature and strength of this impulse as a danger, and represses it into the unconscious. Upon the failure of this attempted solution follows a further forcing back of the disturbing quantities of energy, even to the psychic sensory organ (hallucination) or to involuntary motility in the widest sense (materialization). On the way, however, this instinctual energy would come into most intimate contact with the higher psychic layers and be subjected to their selective elaboration. It has ceased to be a simple quantity, has become qualitatively graduated and thus a symbolic means of expression for complicated mental contents. This conception, perhaps, offers us a clue to that primal riddle of hysteria, 'the leap from psychic to bodily'. We can at least conceive how a psychic formation—a thought—can attain the power that enables it to set gross organic quantities in motion; this force was lent it from the organism's most important reservoir of energy, that of genital sexuality. On the other hand it also becomes more comprehensible how physiological processes can achieve in the hysterical symptom a representation of complicated psychic processes, and a finely graduated adaptation to their changing complexities. What we have to do with here is the production of an *hysterical idiom*, a peculiar symbolic language composed of hallucinations and materializations.

Looking at it as a whole we can conceive the psychic apparatus of the hysteric as a clockwork with its mechanism reversed. Normally, the function of the clock-hands that conscientiously register the processes going on in the inner wheel-work is performed by thought. In hysteria the clock-hands are taken possession of by a masterful apprentice and compelled to forcible movements otherwise foreign to them; the movements of the hands then set the inner mechanism going.

The symbolism of hysterical conversion-phenomena next comes under consideration as a further starting-point for investigation.

Freud pointed out that the symbolic mode of expression is not peculiar to the language of dreams, but belongs to all forms of activity in which the unconscious takes part. Most remarkable of all, however, is the complete correspondence between the symbolism of dreams and of hysteria.

All dream symbolism proves on interpretation to be

sexual symbolism, just as, without exception, the bodily representations of conversion hysteria demand a sexual-symbolic interpretation. Indeed, the organs and bodily parts that generally represent the genitals symbolically in dreams are those usually employed by hysteria also for the representation of genital phantasies.

Here are a few examples: a dream of dental irritation symbolizes onanistic phantasies; in a case of hysteria that I analysed, the same phantasies manifested themselves in the waking state by dental paræsthesias. In a dream which I recently had to interpret an object was thrust into the neck of a girl as a result of which she died; the previous history of the case shows the dream as a symbolic representation of illegitimate coitus, pregnancy and secret abortion which endangered the patient's life. Here is the same displacement from below upwards, the same use of the throat and œsophagus in lieu of the genitals, as in cases of globus hystericus. In dreams the nose often stands for the male member; in several cases of hysteria in men I was able to prove that congestion of the turbinates represented unconscious libidinal phantasies, the erectile tissue of the genitals themselves remaining unexcitable. (Incidentally this connection between the nose and sexuality was discovered by Fliess prior to the inauguration of psycho-analysis.) Pregnancy in dreams is not infrequently symbolically represented by 'over-eating oneself', or by vomiting, just as we have been able to show in the case of hysterical vomiting. Defæcation in dreams sometimes signifies a present, not infrequently the wish to give some one a child. We have already mentioned that in hysteria the same bowel symptom can have a similar significance; and so on.

This far-reaching correspondence leads us to the supposition that in hysteria there comes to the fore a part of the organic basis upon which psychic symbolism in general is built.

Since the publication of Freud's *Drei Abhandlungen zur Sexualtheorie*[1] it is not difficult to recognize the organs upon

[1] [Translation, *Three Contributions to the Theory of Sex*, by A. A. Brill.]

which the sexuality of the genitals is symbolically displaced as the most important localizations of the preliminary stages of genitality—the erotogenic zones of the body. The path of development of auto-erotism via narcissism to the genital phase and therewith to object-love is in dreams as in hysteria pursued backwards from the genital phase. Here, too, we find a regression, in consequence of which instead of the genitals these preliminary stages and their sites of localization are charged with excitation.

According to this the 'displacement from below upwards', so characteristic of hysteria, would only be the reverse of the displacement from above downwards to which the genital zone owes its primacy and the complete development of which leads to the polarity between sexual function and intellectual activity referred to above.

Of course I do not mean that in hysteria genitality is simply resolved into its raw material; on the contrary, I believe that those preliminary stages serve only as guiding zones for the excitation, but that this excitation itself preserves its genital character in kind and intensity even after the displacement. One might therefore say that in hysterical conversion the earlier auto-erotisms are charged with genital sexuality, that is, erotogenic zones and component impulses are *genitalized*.[1] This genital quality shows itself in the tendency to turgescence and œdema of the tissues (Freud), compelling friction and thus the removal of the irritation.

The original theory of conversion considered the hysterical conversion symptom to be due to the abreaction of strangulated affects. This 'strangulation', by its nature unknown, proved later to be in every case 'repression'. To complete this it must be added that this repression always concerns the libidinal and particularly the genito-sexual impulses, and that every hysterical symptom, considered from whatever aspect, is always to be recognized as

[1] 'Hysteria is the negative of perversion', runs one of Freud's axioms. In actual fact, too, one never finds pure auto-erotism in the perversions of adults, but here also genitalization of previously overcome infantile preliminary stages.

a heterotype genital function. The ancients were, therefore, right when they said of hysteria: Uterus loquitur!

. . . .

I cannot conclude this train of thought without referring to some points for research that forced themselves upon me in the course of this investigation, as, indeed, they have done on many similar occasions.

In hysterical symptoms we see—to our no small amazement—that organs of vital importance subordinate themselves entirely to the pleasure principle, regardless of their own particular function in utility. The stomach and the bowel play puppet-games with their own walls and contents, instead of digesting and excreting their contents; the skin is no longer the protective cover of the body which by its sensitiveness gives warning of unusual impressions; it behaves like a genuine sexual organ, contact with which is, of course, not consciously perceived but unconsciously provides gratification. The musculature, instead of as usual assisting in the maintenance of life by purposively co-ordinated activities, exhausts itself in dramatic representations of the pleasurable situations of phantasy. And there is no organ nor any part of the body that is proof against being employed for such pleasure purposes. Now I do not believe that we are dealing here with processes that hold good for hysteria only and are otherwise meaningless or generally absent. Certain processes in normal sleep indicate that phantastic materialization-phenomena are also possible in people who are not neurotic. I have in mind the peculiar hyperactivity in the process of pollutions.

Presumably, however, these pleasure-trends of the bodily organs do not cease entirely by day, and it would require a special 'physiology of pleasure' to understand their entire significance. Hitherto the science of vital processes has been exclusively a physiology of utility, and has been concerned only with the functions of organs that are of utility in the preservation of life.

No wonder that even the best and most exhaustive text-books of human and animal physiology leave us in the lurch when we require of them particulars about coitus.

They can tell us nothing, either of the extraordinary peculiarities of this deeply rooted reflex mechanism, or of its onto- and phylogenetic significance. And yet I believe this problem is of crucial significance for biology, and I await signal advances in that science from its solution.

At the same time even the propounding of these problems shows us that, contrary to the current view, according to which biological research is the pre-condition of psychological advance, psycho-analysis leads us to biological problems that could not be formulated from the other side.

Another problem hitherto considered only from the psychological side, that of artistic endowment, is in hysteria illuminated to some extent from its organic side. Hysteria is, as Freud says, a caricature of art. Hysterical 'materializations', however, show us the organism in its entire plasticity, indeed in its preparedness for art. It might prove that the purely 'autoplastic' tricks of the hysteric are prototypes, not only for the bodily performances of 'artists' and actors, but also for the work of those creative artists who no longer manipulate their own bodies but material from the external world.

VII

'MATERIALIZATION' IN GLOBUS HYSTERICUS[1]

As an example of hysterical 'materialization' (by which process an idea actually becomes true in the flesh) I mentioned in my work on this topic globus hystericus, and put forward the opinion that it deals with not only a paræsthesia but an actual materialization. I now read in Bernheim's book, *Hypnotism*, *Suggestion*, *Psycho-*

[1] *Zeitschrift*, 1923, ix. 68. [Translated by Olive Edmonds.]

therapy, on page 33, the following: 'When I was a pupil of M. Sédillot, that eminent master was called on to examine a patient who could not swallow any solid food. He felt in the upper part of the œsophagus, behind the thyroid cartilage, an obstruction at which level the alimentary bolus was retained, not regurgitated. On introducing his finger as deeply as possible across the pharynx, M. Sédillot felt a tumour which he described as a fibrous polypus projecting in the area of the œsophagus. Two distinguished surgeons touched it after him, and ascertained without hesitation the existence of a tumour such as the master had described. Œsophagotomy was performed; no malformation existed at this level.'

VIII

PSYCHOGENIC ANOMALIES OF VOICE PRODUCTION[1]

I. In 1910 a young man came to me accompanied by his mother; he wished to be cured of his impotence. Even at the first examination I recognized his condition as a combination of neurosis and paranoia. In the course of an analysis carried on tentatively for a time his peculiar megalomania became more and more apparent. He had the feeling and the certain conviction that he was possessed of supernatural (magical) power that compelled other people (especially men) to look round at him whenever he looked at them. He discovered this for the first time when at the theatre he looked fixedly through his opera glasses at the actors on the stage, whereupon they had at once to look in the direction where he sat in the audience. Later he became aware of his miraculous power over several other men, which alarmed him excessively, and

[1] *Zeitschrift*, 1915, Bd. III. 24.

finally compelled him to give up all social intercourse and to settle down with his long-widowed mother in a remote dwelling; he gave up his profession (although he had already progressed far in it) entirely. The neurotic element in his condition was the anxiety he endured when he noticed his own magical powers, especially when the magic extended to inanimate objects; 'for'—so he said—'if the inorganic world also obeys my will, the whole world can be destroyed through me'. To prevent this, he had—when standing in front of people whom he wished to spare—to shut his eyes. Even after only a few hours of analysis, I was able to recognize as the true kernel of his megalomania his enormous self-satisfaction (nowadays we would call it narcissism) and the homosexuality associated with it. The unconscious wish to please the whole world, particularly men, returned from repression as on the one hand an hysterical phobia, and on the other as an omnipotence phantasy. When the talk got on to homosexual love, he told me spontaneously about his homosexual love affairs in the secondary school, where he thoroughly enjoyed the girl's part that was given him by the professors and his school companions. He was given a girl's name, and fun was made of his blushes at unseemly conversations and of his girlish soprano. 'These things are all over long ago! I don't bother about men any more, I should like to have sexual intercourse only with women, but I cannot manage it.' In arranging the occurrence of the facts in their chronological order we showed conclusively that the appearance of the insane idea synchronized with the cessation of love relations with men. The occasion for this change, however, was a change of dwelling-place and therefore, too, of school companions. From his native city, where everyone knew him and where he was quite happy amongst his teasing comrades in spite of the apparent annoyance, he went to a larger, quite strange town, where he sought in vain for a substitute for the 'consideration' he had lost. He did not take the real content of his wishes into consideration, however; instead he believed himself quite free from his (previously quite apparent) homosexuality—as a result of which there presently appeared the symptom already described, dread of being observed and the idea of magical omnipotence. It is evident that the case offers nothing remarkable from the standpoint of psycho-analytic teaching about paranoia, as it only substantiates the view hitherto held by us of the pathogenesis of paranoia, and particularly of its genetic association with narcissism and homosexuality. The reason why I nevertheless report it is because of a peculiar symptom that the patient manifested. He had *two voices*: a high soprano voice and a fairly normal baritone voice. The larynx showed no abnormalities externally or internally; it was here only a matter of 'nervous disturbance', as one would say in circles where such fine-sounding names are taken for explanations. It was only on psycho-analysis of this case that it was shown that here one was dealing neither with 'subcortical' nor 'cortical' disturbances of innervation, nor with a developmental anomaly of the larynx, but with a psychogenic disturbance of the voice. It soon struck me that the patient only used his baritone voice when he was earnestly and objectively absorbed in something; as soon, however—in the transference—as he unconsciously wished to coquette with me or please me, so that he was more concerned with the effect of than with the content of his talk, he spoke with the feminine voice. As he only seldom succeeded in emancipating himself from the desire to please, his 'usual' voice was the feminine one. This voice, however, was no normal soprano, but a falsetto of which he was not a little conceited. He once sang me a little song in falsetto, and he liked to use this voice in laughing. He could always alter the voice register voluntarily, but evidently felt more at home in the falsetto. As distinct from the sudden 'break' of voice that occurs so frequently at puberty in men, and which is actually due to a disturbance in innervation, a lack of skill in the control of the rapidly growing larynx, our patient could speak for hours in one of the two voices without ever a 'break' in a sentence or on a word.

II. The other patient, a seventeen-year-old lad, was also brought to me by his mother (1914), with the complaint that he had an insufferable voice which the laryngologists had said was due to nervousness. As a further disturbance an exaggerated fear of mice was mentioned. In private he also acknowledged the unreliability of his potency; he could only practise coitus subsequently upon fellatio. This patient also had *two voices*, that is, he spoke constantly in a rather hoarse falsetto, and only on my asking whether he could not speak in any other way did he let go in so deep a *bass* that I was properly startled. This voice of his rang full and sonorous and was in keeping, too, with the fairly powerfully developed thyroid cartilage and the prominent *pomum adami*. Evidently this was his natural voice. The psychological examination of the case, for which I had only two hours at my disposal, yielded the following: the father (as in the first case) played no part; he was alive, it is true, but was intellectually quite inferior, while the mother was the real head of the family. In a study of homo-eroticism I drew attention to how greatly this family constellation favours homo-erotic fixations. It was the same, too, in this case. Although now seventeen years of age, the patient, who was otherwise quite accessible to normal sexual impulses, could not even yet free himself from the erotic attractions of his own sex. (As a boy he practised mutual masturbation for a long time with a relative of the same age, and he still had phantasies at times of himself in the passive sexual part, with a 'smart lieutenant of Hussars'.) At the same time he was not at all insensitive to the female sex, only his wish representations in this respect were accompanied by hypochondriac ideas, which—strikingly enough—did not hamper his homo-erotic desires very much. Hypothetically I could solve this contradiction by assuming an unconscious incestuous mother-fixation. A talk with the latter showed me that she must have been the real originator of the boy's sexual hypochondria. It was she who frequently corrected the boy, *when he began to use his bass voice.* She often said to him, '*I cannot endure that voice; you must learn to leave it off*'.

In my opinion we have to do here with one of those numerous cases that I am in the habit of calling *Dialogues of the Unconscious*, where namely, the unconscious of two people completely understand themselves and each other, without the remotest conception of this on the part of the consciousness of either. The mother must unconsciously have taken the bass voice quite correctly as a sign of dawning manhood, and also have interpreted the incestuous tendency directed against her. The boy, on the other hand, had unconsciously taken up her 'antipathy' to this voice as a prohibition of his incestuous desires, as a better defence against which he mobilized hypochondriacally rationalized ideas against heterosexuality in general, which then resulted in disturbances of potency. The patient, therefore, was already a fully developed man, but *for love of his mother* he still maintained his girlishness and the corresponding voice register. A little light on the early history of this case is obtained from the account of long-continued bed-wettings (that were directly derived from nocturnal pollutions); one can consider these as vestiges of forgotten infantile onanism. The mice phobia was probably the hysterical sign of resisted phallic phantasies.

The marked resemblance of the two cases in particular points seems to suggest that there is something typical here that will certainly be observed in numerous boys if one pays proper attention to anomalies of voice production and to delay in the change of voice. These cases seem to be due to that homo-erotic neurosis that I have contrasted as *compulsive homo-eroticism* with real 'inversion'.[1] This type of boy seems also to supply the largest contingent of *lady imitators*, who delight the audiences of our variety theatres with the abrupt transitions of their soprano and bass voices.

[1] Ferenczi, Zur Nosologie der männlichen Homoerotik. [Translated in *Contributions to Psycho-Analysis*, chap. xii.]

IX

AN ATTEMPTED EXPLANATION OF SOME HYSTERICAL STIGMATA[1]

THE word 'stigma' is historically of clerical origin and formerly indicated the amazing fact that the wound-marks of the Christ were transferred to believers by the efficacy of fervent prayer. At the period of witch trials insensitiveness to contact with red-hot iron was held to be a stigma of guilt. One-time witches are to-day called hysterics, and certain permanent symptoms that recur in them with great regularity are described as hysterical stigmata.

A striking difference between psycho-analysts and other neurologists in regard to the estimation of stigmata is already evident on the first examination of a case of hysteria. The psycho-analyst is content with a physical examination sufficient to exclude the possibility of confusion with an organic nervous disease, and hastens to consider the psychic peculiarities of the case only by the help of which he can make an accurate diagnosis. The non-analyst hardly lets the patient finish speaking, is glad when he has done with his complaints which tell the doctor nothing, so that the organic examination can begin. He dwells on this with great satisfaction even after the exclusion of organic complications, and rejoices if in the end he can demonstrate the hysterical stigmata demanded by pathology, the reduction of touch- or pain-sensibility, absence of reflex winking on touching the conjunctiva or cornea, the concentric contraction of the field of vision, the absence of gum or throat reflexes, the sensation of a lump in the throat (globus), the hypersensitiveness of the lower abdomen (ovaries), etc.

With the single exception of Janet's clever experiments on hysterical hemi-anæsthesia, our understanding of hysteria, not to speak of therapeutic results, has been little advanced by diligent researches in these matters. Nevertheless, they

[1] [Published in *Hysterie und Pathoneurosen*.]

remain the most important components in clinical histories of hysterics and, by their quantitative and graphic representation, lend these the appearance of exactitude.[1]

I had long had no doubt that these symptoms of hysteria, in cases in which they are particularly strongly marked, must be referred to psycho-analysis for explanation.

Until now I have been able to fathom analytically only a few cases of *hysterical disturbance of skin sensibility*; in what follows I wish to discuss one such case dating from 1909.

A young man of twenty-two came to me with the complaint that he was ' very nervous ' and suffered from terrifying dream-hallucinations. It then appeared that he was married, but ' because he is so frightened at night ' was not sleeping with his wife but in the next room on the floor beside his mother's bed. The nightmare, whose return had alarmed him for the last seven or eight months, and which he could not relate without horror, ran the first time as follows: ' I wakened ', he said, ' about one o'clock in the night, had to clutch my neck with my hand and shouted : there is a mouse on me, it is running into my mouth. My mother woke, lit a light, petted and soothed me. I could not, however, go to sleep till my mother took me into her bed.'

After Freud's explanations of infantile anxiety, probably no psycho-analyst will doubt that we are dealing here with an anxiety hysteria in the form of *pavor nocturnus*, and that the patient has discovered the most efficient method for its cure—the return to the loving mother.

The supplement to this account of this dream is, however, of interest: ' When my mother struck a light I saw that instead of the much-feared mouse I had *my own left hand* in my mouth, and I was endeavouring with all my strength to pull it out with my right hand.'

It thus became clear that in this dream the left hand played a peculiar part, the part of a mouse; he wanted to catch or chase away with his right hand, this hand that felt

[1] Neither can I say anything better of a similar paper of my own in which I pointed out certain differences between organic and hysterical anæsthesia. (Published in 1900 in *Gyogyaszat* and in the *Pester Med.-Chir. Presse.*)

around at his neck, but the 'mouse' ran into his open mouth and threatened to suffocate him.

What sexual scenes are represented symbolically in this dream is of less interest than the remarkable division of rôles between the right and left hands, which vividly recalls the case of an hysterical patient of Freud's, who in the attack lifted her skirts with the one hand and endeavoured to arrange them decently with the other.

It must be emphasized that the patient had already wakened and shouted in a suffocated voice for light, but that his left hand was still sticking in his mouth without his being able to distinguish it from a mouse. I correlated this condition of things with *hysterical anæsthesia of the left side of the body*, even if I must own that I was unable to examine the skin sensibility with the requisite exactitude. Even a very superficial examination of this dream showed that the patient, who was attached to his mother by an infantile fixation, was here realizing sexual intercourse displaced 'from below upwards' (from the 'Oedipus phantasy'), in which the left hand represented the masculine, the mouth the feminine genital, while the right, and so to say more decent, hand was at the service of the stirring defence tendencies and wanted to chase away the criminal 'mouse'. All this was rendered possible only by the loss of conscious sensibility in the left hand and its becoming the battleground of repressed tendencies.

As a contrast I mention a second case of hysterical hemianæsthesia that I was able to observe in my division for soldiers suffering from nervous conditions. The notes about the case are as follows:

X. Y., an artillery team driver, admitted 6th February 1916. The patient was on active service for fourteen months and was lightly wounded on the left temple (scar visible). After six weeks in hospital he returned to duty, but a little while later a grenade fell about thirty paces to the left of him and he was knocked down by the air concussion from the explosive and struck by fragments of earth. He served for a time longer, but later became 'confused', 'giddy', and as he drank a good deal he was sent to the rear with the diagnosis of 'alcoholism'. At his unit depôt he had a scene with his superior artilleryman, who (as he recounted during analysis after overcoming powerful resistances) beguiled him into his room and chastized him with a riding whip. He kept the disgrace a secret, and as he felt ill he let himself be taken to the military hospital. For a time the half of his body that had received the blows was almost completely paralysed. On transfer to another hospital, when he was already making attempts to walk, a tremor developed in the musculature of the left half of the body. His chief complaint is the disturbance of gait caused by the tremor.

On examination: the patient is quite quiet in the resting posture; on walking there is tremor of the left half of the body. He supports himself really only on the right leg and on a stick. The left upper and lower extremities take no part in locomotion and are pushed rigidly forward, the shoulder in advance. No indications of organic disease are obtainable. Besides the dysbasia described, the following functional disturbances are present: marked temperamental excitability, hypersensitiveness to noise, sleeplessness, and a *complete analgesia and anæsthesia of the left side of the body*.

If a pin is stuck deeply into his skin from behind on the left without his noticing it, he does not react in the least; if, however, one approaches his left side from in front with a needle, so that he can see it, he performs violent flight and defence movements in spite of the analgesia and anæsthesia being present also in front. He catches hold of the approaching hand, clasps it convulsively, and declares that at a threatened touch he feels a shudder in the anæsthetic half of the body which compels him to these irrepressible actions of defence. If his eyes are bandaged he proves to be just as analgesic and anæsthetic on the left in front as behind. This 'shuddering' is therefore a purely psychic phenomenon, a feeling and not a sensation; it recalls the feeling that healthy people have when a ticklish part of the body is threatened with a touch.[1]

[1] I am collecting material for a psychological explanation of the feeling of ticklishness which is supported by Freud's theory of the pleasure of wit.

H

The reader will have already guessed that the exclusion of the sensibility of the left half of the body from consciousness subserved a tendency to repression. The loss of touch sensations facilitated the suppression of the memory of those dramatic experiences which, in the course of the war, were associated with the left side, the last of these, the punishment by a superior, having started the symptoms. I must add that the patient, who was generally considered wild and who submitted with difficulty to hospital discipline, had made not the least resistance—inexplicably to himself—on the occasion of that maltreatment. He behaved towards the sergeant as he did formerly as a child to his, at that time, superior, his father. He did not feel, in order that he should not have to hit back, and for the same reason he wants to prevent every approach to the injured part of his body.

If we compare these two cases of hemi-anæsthesia, we can perhaps from the contrast of the traumatic hemi-anæsthesia with the hemi-anæsthetic stigmata guess at the characteristics of the latter. Common to both cases is the exclusion from consciousness of touch stimulation, along with the preservation of the other psychic uses of this stimulus. We saw in the anxiety hysteric that the insensibility of one half of the body was used to employ the unconscious sensations elicited by contracts and altered positions of this half of the body for the 'materialization' of the Oedipus phantasy.

In the case of the traumatic hemi-anæsthesia I must, on the grounds of other experiences in war neuroses, as well as from observations of the disturbance of libido in bodily injuries in general, equally assume a libidinal employment of the repressed touch sensations which are incapable of becoming conscious.[1]

In any case, in both instances we are dealing with the same inaccessibility of the ideational arc of one half of the body to new associations that Freud, as early as 1893, recognized as the basis of hysterical *paralyses*.[2]

[1] See the chapters on 'Pathoneuroses' and 'Materialization

[2] *Archives de Neurologie*, 1893.

In the second of these cases, the association inaccessibility arises from the fact that the idea of the insensitive parts of the body 'is connected with the memory, laden with undischarged affects, of a trauma ',[1] while in the first case, in which the loss of sensation had to be denoted as a stigma, there was no traumatic happening the memory of which would have been associated with the left side.

One distinction between 'stigmatic' and traumatic hemi-anæsthesia can be drawn according to the part played in them by 'physical predisposition'. In the traumatic case no such predisposition existed; it was brought about only by the shock experience. In the case of anæsthetic stigma, on the contrary, such a predisposition seems to have existed from the very first, a purely physiological disposition of the affected parts of the body to relinquish their conscious excitation and sensational stimuli to the unconscious libidinal impulses. We might also say that the anæsthesia is of ideational origin in the traumatic case, but in the stigmatic, though psychogenic, it is not ideational in origin. One half of the body is insensitive following upon the trauma *because* it has suffered an injury, while it is so with the stigma *in order that* it shall be adapted for the representation of unconscious phantasies, and that 'the right hand shall not know what the left hand doeth'.

I derive support for this conception from the consideration of the difference between right and left. It struck me that in general the hemi-anæsthetic stigma occurs more frequently on the left than on the right; this is emphasized, too, in a few text-books. I recalled that *the left half of the body is* à priori *more accessible to unconscious impulses than the right*, which, in consequence of the more powerful attention-excitation of this more active and more skilful half of the body, is better protected against influences from the unconscious. It is possible that—in right-handed people—the sensational sphere for the left side shows from the first a certain predisposition for unconscious impulses, so that it is more easily robbed of its normal

[1] Breuer-Freud, *Studien über Hysterie*, 3. Aufl., 1916. *Gesammelte Schriften*, Bd. I.

functions and placed at the service of unconscious libidinal phantasies.

But even if we disregard this—at any time very inconstant—preference of the hemi-anæsthetic stigma for the left side, so much at any rate remains of this line of thought that in stigmatic hemi-anæsthesia we are dealing with a division of the cutaneous envelope between the two conflicting forces (consciousness and unconsciousness, the ego and the libido).

A vista opens here for the understanding of another hysterical stigma: *the concentric narrowing of the field of vision*. What we said of the difference between right and left holds in an increased degree for the difference between central and peripheral vision. Central vision, owing to its manner of functioning, is certainly more intimately associated with conscious attention, while the periphery of the field of vision is more remote from consciousness and is the scene of indistinct sensations. It needs only another step to rid these sensations entirely of conscious excitation and to let them become the raw material of unconscious libidinal phantasies. Thus Janet's comparison, according to which the hysteric suffers from 'a narrowing of the field of consciousness', is justified at least in this sense.

The insensibility of the conjunctiva and cornea in hysterics might find its explanation in an intimate association with the narrowing of the field of vision. It is possible that it is the expression of the same repression of optical sensations; we are accustomed in hysteria to find that the anæsthesia is not defined according to anatomical function but according to the idea of the organ [entertained by the individual]. Another point must be taken into consideration here. The cornea is normally the most sensitive part of the whole body, so that the reaction to corneal injury, weeping, has become the means of expression for psychic pain in general. It may be that the failure of this reaction in hysterics is associated with the suppression of feeling impulses.

The hysterical anæsthesia of the throat is used, as I have been able to observe in many cases of analysis, for the representation, by swallowing movements, of genital phantasies. It is comprehensible that the genital excitement which is displaced from ' below upwards ' does not let this source of stimulation, so similar to itself, escape. In *hyperæsthesia of the throat* we are dealing with the reaction formation against the same perverse phantasies, while the *globus hystericus* can be regarded as a ' materialization ' of such wishes along with their defence tendencies. Wherein lies the special tendency of the œsophagus for stigma formation is, however, inexplicable.

While fully conscious of the insufficiency of this material, I must sum up my impression of the manner of origin of hysterical stigmata in the following sentences: hysterical stigmata signify the localization of converted excitement masses at parts of the body which, in consequence of their peculiar suitability for physical predisposition, are easily placed at the disposition of unconscious impulses, so that they become ' banal ' companion manifestations of other hysterical symptoms ideational in origin.

As there is no explanation so far of hysterical stigmata, I must meantime make shift with this attempt at one, till I am aware of a better.

In no case, however, can I accept Babinski's ' explanation ', according to which stigmata (like hysterical symptoms in general) are only *pithiatisms* suggested by the doctor. The real kernel of this peculiarly primitive view is that, as a matter of fact, many patients knew nothing of the existence of their stigmata before they were demonstrated to them by the doctor. Of course they *were* present nevertheless, and this can only be denied by those entangled in the old error of equating what is conscious with the psychical in general.

To try to explain hysteria by suggestion, and suggestion by hysteria, without analysing these manifestations individually for themselves is, moreover, a very common logical error.

X

THE PSYCHO-ANALYSIS OF A CASE OF HYSTERICAL HYPOCHONDRIA[1]

In consequence of the wearisome and slow progress of its method of cure psycho-analytic technique entails the blurring of the general impression of a case, and the individual factors of its complicated connections force themselves on the attention only intermittently.

In what follows I shall communicate a case whose cure was very rapid and whose clinical picture, both in form and content very varied and interesting, unfolded itself dramatically, almost without interruption, like a series of cinematograph pictures.

The patient, a pretty young foreigner, was brought to me for treatment by her relatives, after various other methods of cure had been tried. She made a very unfavourable impression. Her most prominent symptom was a very marked *anxiety*. Without being exactly agoraphobic, she had for months been unable to exist without being accompanied at every moment; if she were left alone, the most intense attacks of anxiety occurred, even at night she had to waken her husband or whoever happened to be sleeping with her and tell them about her ideas and feelings of anxiety for hours on end. Her complaints were of hypochondriacal bodily sensations and the fear of death associated with them. She felt something in her throat, 'points' were coming out of her scalp (these sensations compelled her constantly to touch her throat and the skin of her face); her ears were lengthening, her head was splitting in front; her heart was palpitating, etc. In each such sensation, for whose occurrence she was constantly looking, she saw an indication of her approaching death; she had thoughts too of suicide. Her father had died of arterio-sclerosis and that now seemed imminent to her; she would also

[1] Published in *Hysterie und Pathoneurosen*.

(like her father) become insane, and would have to die in the asylum. She at once constructed a new symptom out of the fact that at the first examination I explored her throat for possible anæsthesia or hyperæsthesia. She had constantly to stand in front of the mirror and look for changes in her tongue. The first interviews passed in continuous, monotonous complaints about these sensations, and the symptoms seemed to me to be of an unmodifiable, hypochondriacal, insane type, especially as a few such cases were still fresh in my memory.

After some time she seemed to have exhausted herself somewhat, probably because I never tried either to soothe or otherwise influence her, but let her run on with her complaints undisturbed. Slight signs of transference, too, showed themselves; she felt quieter after the interview, awaited the beginning of the next hour with impatience, etc. She grasped very quickly how to 'associate freely', but the associations changed over at the very first attempt into insanely passionate and theatrical behaviour. 'I am N. N.—manufacturer.' (Here she gave her father's name, with visibly heightened self-consciousness.) She then behaved as though she were actually her father giving orders in the yard and shops, swore (pretty roughly and shamelessly too, as is customary in that district); then repeated scenes enacted by her father when he was insane, before he was confined in an asylum. At the end of the hour, however, she was quite well orientated, said good-bye nicely, and let herself be accompanied quietly home.

She began the ensuing hour with the continuation of the above scene; she repeated over and over again: 'I am N. N. I have a penis'. Between whiles she related an infantile scene in which an ugly nurse threatened her with an enema syringe because she would not defæcate spontaneously. The hours that now followed were taken up alternately with the hypochondriacal complaints, her father's insane episodes, and soon with passionate transference phantasies. She demanded—in down-right peasant speech—to be sexually satisfied, and rated at her husband who could not do it properly (which, however, did not agree with the truth). Her husband then told me that from this time the patient did actually ask to be sexually satisfied, while she had previously refused it for a considerable period.

After these unburdenings her manic exaltation quietened down and we were able to study the previous history of the case. She related the exciting causes of the illness. The war had broken out, her husband had been called up, she had had to replace him in the business; she could not do this properly, however, as she had constantly to think about her elder daughter (about six years old), and had the idea that something might happen to her at home, so she had constantly to run home to see about it. This elder daughter was born with rickets and a sacro-meningocele which was operated on, so that the little creature lived but her lower extremities and bladder were incurably paralysed. She could only crawl about on all fours, and on account of the incontinence must be changed 'about a hundred times a day'. 'It makes no difference, however, I love her a thousand times more than the second (the healthy!) daughter'. This was confirmed, too, by all those about her; the patient petted this sick child at the expense of the second, healthy one; she would not admit that one should be unhappy about the sick child—'she is so good, so clever, has such a pretty face'.

It was quite soon apparent to me that this was a tremendous effort of repression on the part of the patient; that in reality she yearned unconsciously for the death of her unfortunate child, and was not capable of the increased efforts demanded of her by the war, because of this previous burden. She therefore took refuge in illness.

After careful preparation I explained this conception of her illness to her, whereupon—after vain attempts to precipitate herself once more into insanity or into the transference passion—she gradually managed to let herself become conscious to a certain extent of the great pain and shame which the crippled condition of her child caused her.

I now had recourse to one of the methods of 'active

technique'.[1] I sent the patient home for a day, in order that she should have the opportunity of reviving, with the help of her newly won insight, the feelings which her children inspired in her. While at home she devoted herself again passionately to the love and care of the sick child, and then said triumphantly at the next interview: 'You see it is none of it true! I do love only my eldest girl!' and so on. But even in the same interview she had to admit the contrary with bitter tears; corresponding with her impulsively passionate nature there occurred to her sudden compulsive thoughts in which she strangled or hanged this child, or cursed it 'God's lightning strike you'. (This curse was familiar to her from the folklore of her home.)

The remainder of the treatment progressed on the lines of the transference love. The patient showed herself seriously wounded at the purely medical handling of her repeated love declarations, involuntarily indicating her unusually powerful narcissism. We lost a few hours owing to the resistance evoked by this hurt to her conceit and self-love, but this afforded us the opportunity for the reproduction of similar 'insults' of which she had experienced an unusual number. I was able to show her that each time one of her numerous sisters had become engaged (she was the youngest), she felt herself injured by the neglect of her person. Her jealousy and revengefulness went so far that out of sheer envy she reported a relative whom she caught with a young man. In spite of her apparent reserve and her introspection she was very self-conscious, and had a high opinion of her own physical and intellectual qualities. To protect herself from the risk of too painful disillusionments she preferred to stand obstinately aside where any competition with other girls was concerned. Now, too, I understood the extraordinary phantasy to which she gave expression in one of her pseudo-insane attacks; she again represented herself to be her (insane) father, and declared that *she wished to have sexual intercourse with herself*.

[1] See page 189 in this book: 'Technical Difficulties in the Analysis of a Case of Hysteria'.

Her child's illness influenced her so powerfully only because of her—quite comprehensible—*identification* with her; she herself had formerly at one time had to endure some painful violations of her own bodily integrity. She too came into the world with a physical disability; she squinted, and had in her youth to undergo an operation of which she had stood in the utmost terror, and almost went insane at the thought that she might go blind. Moreover, on account of this squint she had been in her childhood the object of her playfellows' scorn.

We also gradually achieved the interpretation of the individual hypochondriacal sensations. The feeling in her throat was the substitute for the wish that her beautiful alto voice should be heard and admired. The 'points' that 'came out' of her scalp were little vermin, that were once—to her great humiliation—discovered on her head; the 'elongation of the ears' referred to the fact that at school she was once called a 'donkey' by the teacher, and so on.

The most remote covering memory to which we could penetrate was a mutual exhibitionism that had occurred between her and a boy of her own age in the attic of her home, and I do not doubt that behind this scene lie the most powerful impressions affecting the patient. It was probably the *penis jealousy* implanted at that time that rendered her capable of the remarkably successful identification with her father in her attacks of delirium. ('I have a penis', etc.) Finally, the congenital abnormality of her eldest child need not be considered so much the cause of her illness as the fact that she had given birth, not to a boy, but to two girls (creatures without a penis, that could not—like boys—urinate properly). Hence the unconscious horror of her daughter's incontinence. It seems, moreover, that the illness of her first-born began to affect her more powerfully when the second child also proved to be a girl.

The patient returned from a second visit home quite changed. She was reconciled to the idea that she preferred the younger child and that she wished for the death of the sick daughter; she ceased to wail about her hypochondriacal sensations, and occupied herself with planning to return home soon for good. Behind this sudden improvement I discovered the resistance to the cessation of treatment. From the analysis of her dreams I had to conclude that she had a paranoid distrust of her doctor's integrity; she believed that I wanted to prolong the treatment in order to get more money from her. From this point of vantage I tried to find the approach to her anal erotism associated with her narcissism (*cf.* her infantile fear of the enema syringe), but I only partially succeeded. The patient preferred to keep a part of her neurotic peculiarities, and went home practically cured.[1]

Apart from the unusually rapid course of this illness, the epicrisis of this case presents much of interest. We are dealing here with a mixture of purely hypochondriacal and hysterical symptoms, and at the beginning of the analysis the clinical picture of the illness merged into schizophrenia, while towards the end it showed indications, however slight, of paranoia.

The mechanism of individual hypochondriac paræsthesias is noteworthy. They were based originally on her narcissistic preference for her own body, but then became—something after the fashion of a 'physical predisposition'—the means of expression of hysterical processes (ideational in origin), for instance, the feeling of the elongation of her ears became the memorial of a psychic trauma.

In this way one observes problems—still unsolved—

[1] Here are a few more details: the compulsive sensation, *my head is splitting open in front*, was the expression of a pregnancy wish displaced 'upwards'. She wished for new children (boys) in place of those she already had (the sick child and the other girl). She was in the habit of repeating constantly, 'There is nothing new again'—pointing to her forehead; this also belonged to the pregnancy complex. The patient had aborted twice—not altogether accidentally—and unconsciously regretted it. The *palpitation* was the memory of libidinal feelings on meeting sympathetic young men who seemed potent to her. (To be potent meant for her, ability to beget *boys* and *healthy* children in general.) The '*points*' that came out were over-determined. They meant not only vermin but (as so often) little children also. Here are two characteristic dreams: 1. *She sees bags hanging up* (*money bags ?*). (Interpretation: If she realizes that she wishes to hang her child she will be able to save further fees.) 2. *One of her sisters is dancing a cake walk*; *her father is there too.* (Reproduction of her bridal night, when her pleasure was spoiled by the thought that her father was in an institution.)

of the organic basis of conversion hysteria and hypochondria. It seems as though the same stagnation of organ libido [1]—according to the patient's sexual constitution—can have either a purely hypochondriacal or conversion hysteria 'superstructure'. In our case we were dealing apparently with the combination of both possibilities, and the hysterical side of the neurosis rendered possible the transference and the psycho-analytic discharge of the hypochondriacal sensations. Where this possibility of discharge does not exist the hypochondriac remains inaccessible and fastens—often insanely—on the sensation and observation of his paræsthesia.

Pure hypochondria is incurable; only where—as here—transference neurotic components are present, can one attempt psycho-therapeutic influence with any hope of success.

XI

TWO TYPES OF WAR NEUROSES [2]

It is very far from my intention to say anything final about the important subject of war neuroses after studying them for so comparatively short a time. I have been in charge of the section for nervous diseases in this hospital for only two months, and have had about two hundred cases under observation. This number is too great, the time for observation has been too short; psycho-analysis has taught us that progress is to be expected not from the statistical turnover of many, but from the intensive exploration of individual cases. These are, therefore, only preliminary communications, and merely reproduce a psycho-analyst's impressions on observing war neuroses in the mass.

[1] See the article 'Über Pathoneurosen'. ['Concerning Pathoneuroses', Chap. V.]

[2] *Zeitschrift*, 1916–17 Bd. IV. 131. [Based on a paper given at a Scientific Congress of Hospital Physicians.]

The first impression that the ward full of war neurotics made on me was one of bewilderment, and if you glance at the groups of patients standing, sitting, and lying about before you you would probably share this impression. You see here about fifty patients, who almost all give the impression of being seriously ill, if not of being crippled. Many are incapable of moving about; for most of them the attempt to move causes such violent tremors of knees and feet that my voice cannot be heard above the noise of their shoes upon the floor.

In most of the cases, as I said, the tremor affects only the feet, but there are a few in whom—as you see—every intended movement is accompanied by tremor of the whole body musculature. The gait of the trembler is most remarkable; he gives the impression of spastic paresis; but the varying mixture of tremor, rigidity, and weakness occasions quite peculiar gaits, possibly only to be reproduced by cinematography. Most of the patients say they became ill after a shell explosion in their neighbourhood, a fairly large minority blame severe and sudden chill (a plunge into ice-cold water, getting wet in the open) as a cause of their illness, the remainder experienced accidents of other kinds, or fell ill apparently merely from over-exertion in the field. Those who were concussed by a shell explosion speak of the 'air pressure' that knocked them down; others were partly buried by masses of earth thrown up by the exploding shells.

This correspondence of the symptoms and causes of disease in so many patients would probably have suggested to everyone an organic injury to the brain or spinal cord. I too had at first the impression that this peculiar symptom-complex, hitherto unknown to pathology, would be referable to some organic change in the central nervous system, to a central paralysis and irritation which had hitherto never been observed, because concussions such as soldiers are exposed to in this war had not occurred in peace time. I did not dismiss this possibility for a long time, not even when I was able to convince myself by the examination of individual cases that the symptoms never wanting in central organic lesions, and particularly the signs of a lesion of the pyramidal tract (spastic knee jerks, Babinski's sign, ankle-clonus), are not here distinguishable.[1] I had finally, however, to acknowledge to myself that not only the absence of these characteristics but the general picture of the individual cases, especially the extraordinarily variable and unusual disturbances of innervation, were powerful arguments against an organic, even if only a 'molecular' or 'micro-organic' change in the nervous reticulum.

The impression of peculiarity and oddness cleared up only after I had more closely examined a smaller group of patients in whom not the whole body, but only individual parts of it, seemed affected by the disease. The correct nosological classification of the whole disease group is possible only after an understanding of these *mono-symptomatic* cases.

Here you see two patients. In both—besides the not very marked disturbance of gait (the description of which I pass over meantime)—the constant oscillating tremor *of the head*, caused by the alternating rhythmic contraction of the neck muscles, is very striking. This third patient keeps his *right arm contracted at an obtuse angle* at the elbow joint; this limb is apparently incapable of active movement, any attempt at active or passive movement sets up the most violent tremor in the arm muscles and at the same time an increased pulse rate. Pain sensibility is lowered in the arm; the hand is cyanotic. There is no trace of paresis in either the facial musculature or in the lower extremities. If the patient makes a *great* effort, he can alter the rigid position to some extent, but this is accompanied by violent tremors. Very similar is the case of this other patient, only that *his right arm seems contracted at an acute angle at the elbow, and the upper arm adducted spastically against the thorax.* In another patient the morbid symptom shows itself in the region of the shoulder. You observe the *left shoulder permanently raised*, as well as the tic-like twitching of this shoulder from time to time.

[1] I entirely disregard cases in which the clinical picture was complicated by any symptoms of an organic lesion.

Yonder is a patient sitting perfectly quiet; on his being asked to get up, violent clonic twitchings develop in his *left foot*—and only in the left one. When he is stripped, the only indication of disease is a *permanent cramp in the musculature of the left calf*, like a persistent contraction. The clonic twitchings, which, however, have not the character of a typical ankle-clonus, occur only on attempting to change the position of the foot actively or passively—getting up. The other symptoms of a pyramidal lesion are also lacking. The duration of the cramp could be observed for weeks; a (waking) remission was never observed. This other patient has contractures and tremors of *both right extremities*, the left half of the body is spared.

The exact anamneses of these cases and their relation to the individual symptoms permit their being recognized now more correctly as 'functional', as *psycho-neuroses*. Let us ask this man with the *one-sided contracture* (of the left half of the body) how he came by his injury; he will tell us that a shell landed *on his left* and exploded, so that he was struck on the left side by the 'air pressure'. Had the air blast really caused an organic change in the soldier's brain, it would (if we disregard the occurrence of contre-coup) have affected the left cerebral hemisphere at the least more powerfully, but then the symptoms must certainly have been more marked on the contra-lateral (right) side, which has entirely escaped. The assumption that we are dealing with a psychogenic condition, with the traumatic fixation of the psychic accent on one part of the body, that is, with hysteria, is much more plausible.

This plausibility becomes a certainty when we take into account the anamneses of all the cases just presented. The man whose right arm is contracted at an obtuse angle was concussed by the shell just as he was sliding *his rifle into the 'stand easy' position*. This position corresponds exactly with that imitated by the contracture. The other one who has his shoulder pressed to his side and the elbow fixed at an acute angle perpetuates in the same way the situation in which he was caught by the explosion; he was lying down at the time *with the rifle at his shoulder, and taking aim*

—for this he had to press his arm to his side and bend the elbow at an acute angle. In these cases central organic lesions as results of commotion are to be excluded. It is inconceivable that in comparatively so many cases a cerebral lesion could affect the centres for just those muscles that were in action at the moment of the trauma. Much more probable is the assumption that in these cases *we are dealing with a fixation of the innervation predominating at the moment of the concussion (of the shock)*. The patient with the one-sided contraction persistently maintains the innervation—probably to be interpreted as a flight reflex—of the half of the body that was first endangered. Both the others show perseveration in the position of the arms that immediately preceded the concussion (' stand easy ' position, firing position). In support of the correctness of this conception I can adduce a well-known fact from everyday life and a less familiar one from psycho-analysis. In a sudden fright one can often notice that one's feet become ' rooted ' in the position accidentally assumed at the moment, that indeed the last innervation of the whole body—the arms, the facial muscles—remains rigidly fixed for quite a while. Actors know this ' gesture of expression ', and employ it successfully for the representation of the emotion of fear.

There is, however, a less well-known variant of these gestures of expression. We know from Breuer and Freud that the essence of hysterical manifestations of excitement or paralysis consists in the conversion of an affect into a bodily innervation. Psycho-analysis can trace every such case of *conversion hysteria* back to one or more affective experiences that themselves remain unconscious or forgotten (or, as we say to-day, repressed), but their energy is lent to certain bodily processes associated in thought with these experiences, which project into the present like memorial stones of deeply buried reminiscences as rigid and unchangeable as such a memorial. This is not the place to discuss the conditions which are necessary in addition to the psychic trauma described before the symptomatic picture of a conversion hysteria can occur (sexual constitution); it suffices to remark here that the cases of *war neuroses* just presented are, from their anamneses, to be considered as *conversion hysterias* in the sense of Breuer and Freud. The sudden affect that could not be psychically controlled (the shock) causes the *trauma*; it is the innervations dominant at the moment of trauma that become permanently retained as morbid symptoms and indicate that undischarged parts of the affective impulses are still active in the unconscious. In other words, such a patient has not yet recovered from the shock even though he does not consciously think of it any longer, he may indeed at times be cheerful and good-tempered, as though his soul were in nowise tormented by any such terrible memory.

After these considerations it no longer surprised me, nor will it surprise you, that the other 'mono-symptomatic' cases shown here became comprehensible on a more thorough inquiry into their anamneses. This soldier with the permanent contracture of the left calf recounts how he was cautiously descending a steep mountain in Serbia, and, while *stretching his left foot downwards* to find a support, was concussed by an explosion and rolled down. Here, too, therefore, there is a 'petrifaction' due to shock, in the attitude that had just been adopted. Of the two patients with tremor of the head, one tells us that at the critical moment he struck his head against the wall of the shelter, the other that as he heard the characteristic whistle of the approaching shell he 'ducked'. The patient with the constant twitching of the left shoulder *was slightly wounded* at the explosion on the now 'spasmophil' *part of the body* (the scar is visible).

I obtained the first of these anamnestic data from the patients without their significance for the symptom formation being known either to me or to them, so that suggestive questions on my part were excluded. Later, certainly, I purposely drew the patients' attention to the circumstances of their concussion, without indicating, however, what meaning I attributed to their replies.

I expect that you will raise objections to this attempted explanation. You will say, the patient could not have noted the actual situation so clearly at the critical moment; these anamnestic data, therefore, are perhaps only subsequent attempts at explanation by the patient himself which we have simply 'swallowed'.

My reply is as follows: the soldier was certainly fully conscious immediately *before* the concussion; he may also have been aware of the approaching danger (this is acknowledged by many who remained well in spite of the proximity of the explosion). He may then have lost consciousness at the moment of the concussion, and later even have developed a retrograde amnesia; the memory trace of the situation before the concussion once made might—from the unconscious—influence the symptom formation. The suspicion of being 'misled' by the patient, and the distrust of his statements, were the causes of the profound ignorance prevailing until recently among doctors concerning all matters pertaining to the psychology of the neuroses. Only since Breuer, and more particularly Freud, began *to listen to* nervous patients was access discovered to the secret mechanism of their symptoms. Even in case the patients had subsequently invented the situation present at the concussion, this 'invention' may have been determined by the memory traces of the real circumstances which have become unconscious.

The possibility in these cases that, besides the trauma, any other 'bodily predisposition' acted as a disposing cause could only be excluded by a systematic psycho-analysis of each individual. It is quite possible that at the moment of concussion the active innervation in and for itself forms a 'predisposing factor', a 'bodily predisposition', and brings about the fixation of the affective excitement (which, on account of its strength, we must consider incapable of becoming conscious) to just that part of the body then being innervated. Such 'displacements of affect' on to an indifferent but, just at the critical moment, accessible bodily innervation are well known to us from the psycho-analyses of conversion hysteria.

Unfortunately I am not in a position to support these

particular points by the psycho-analyses of the different patients concerned. I must confine myself, therefore, to grouping these 'mono-symptomatic' war neuroses with *conversion hysteria* purely on the grounds of the anamnestic data.

Let us now turn to the second and, as you see, much larger group of patients, those with *generalized tremors* and *disturbances of gait*. Here, too, if we wish to understand the complete picture we must start from the specialized symptom, *the disturbance of gait*. Look, for instance, at this quietly recumbent patient; as soon as he attempts to rise his lower limbs begin to tremble at the ankle and knee joints; the tremor increases more and more, its excursions become continuously greater till finally the static balance of the body is so disturbed that the patient would fall if he were not caught; if he sits or lies down the tremor ceases at once of itself. (I repeat, signs of organic illness are completely lacking.) This other patient can walk supported on two sticks, but his gait is uncertain, and we hear a reduplicated sound when he puts down his right foot; his right heel touches the floor twice at each step before he has the confidence to support himself on it completely. A third has a wide-based gait like a tabetic, the fourth one beside him walks as though he were completely ataxic—and yet in a recumbent posture they show no trace of a real ataxy, much less can any disease of the spinal cord be demonstrated. The gait of two of the patients shown here can only be described as a 'thrusting gait', they lift the leg without flexing the knee and let it come down with a loud noise. This man here is probably the most severely affected; on his attempting to walk the intention tremor passes into a generalized spasm of the entire body musculature, at the acme of which the patient's consciousness is disturbed.

This last symptom warns us to bestow more attention upon the manifestations accompanying the disturbance of gait. On attempting to walk or to walk without support, all these patients without exception suffer from palpitations and increased pulse rate, most of them sweat profusely, especially at the arm-pits, also on the forehead, and the facies denote anxiety. Thus if we watch them more closely we see that besides the disturbances of gait other permanent symptoms are present as well. There is hyperæsthesia of almost all the senses;[1] hearing is especially affected in most of the cases, but the eyes are also hypersensitive. As a result of this hyperacusis and photophobia they are very timid; most of them complain of very light sleep that is disturbed by anxious, terrifying dreams. The dreams for the most part repeat the dangerous situation experienced in the battlefield. Almost all of them complain as well about their quite inhibited or much reduced sexual libido and potency.

Before we decide how to classify these symptoms for diagnosis we must here, as previously for the 'monosymptomatic' cases, consider the anamneses more closely. Most of the patients say they were affected by a 'shell explosion', some that they were also covered with earth. They lost consciousness immediately, and only came to themselves again in a hospital behind the line. Then they were completely 'paralysed' for days, mostly weeks on end—a few for one or two months. *The tremor appeared on the first attempts at walking*, after the power of movement in bed had been established for a long time, and apparently no further paralysis had occurred. In a few cases the soldier continued on duty after the shell explosion and fell ill later in consequence of a quite negligible—purely psychic—shock. This volunteer, for instance, was sent out on advance guard at night after a shell concussion; on the way he stumbled over a ditch, got a fright, and only fell ill after this experience. Still more striking is the 'summation of the causes of illness' in those very frequent cases in whose anamnesis the cause of the illness is to be discovered in general, not in the shell explosion but in terrible experiences of other kinds, indeed in the superhuman effort and deprivation and the constant anxious tension of the war. Almost as frequent as shell con-

[1] The sensitiveness to touch is sometimes so great that the examination of the patella reflex elicits the most violent defence reactions.

cussions are the accounts in the anamneses of sudden or frequently repeated, sometimes insupportably prolonged, chills (a plunge into ice-cold water especially on crossing rivers in winter, rain storms and snowfalls when camping in the open). Twelve soldiers from the same regiment were admitted to our hospital on one day all presenting the symptoms previously described as incapacity to walk; all of them fell ill from the same cause, a river crossing after marching all day in snow and rain. In these cases, too, the present condition was preceded by a 'period of paralysis' that passed fairly quickly, to make way, *on the first attempt at walking*, for the present state of things.

I probably do not need to repeat that here, too, I have sought carefully—and without result—for organic symptoms.

In many of these cases of chill one learns that the condition was improving spontaneously until they began to be treated for their supposed 'rheumatism' with hot baths, or were sent for after-treatment to one of our natural hot springs (Trencsén-Teplitz, Pöstyén), where they relapsed.

Let us sum up what has been said; soldiers fall ill after a sudden concussion or after repeated smaller or greater concussions. On loss of consciousness (not always present) there follows a stage resembling paralysis, which passes off spontaneously after a longer or shorter period to give place on the first attempts at walking, or, on certain therapeutic efforts, to a chronic condition. This last is composed of certain general phenomena and of a disturbance of gait without any organic basis. There is a distinct relation between the disturbances of innervation on attempting to walk and the general phenomena, in that the latter are increased by the attempt to walk, are partly indeed only brought about by them. Certain permanent symptoms also occur, of which hyperæsthesia of all the senses is the most prominent.

Now from psycho-analysis we know a condition in which the attempt to perform certain actions evokes generalized phenomena. This is Freud's *anxiety hysteria*, which is characterized in many cases by this, that the attempt *to change one's place*, the attempted innervation of standing or walking, is associated with an acute *anxiety* that compels the patients to avoid certain attempts at movement and to modify their whole manner of life accordingly. These avoidances have been known to neurologists for a long time as *phobias*, but have never been understood. The disturbance of innervation was called *astasia* (incapacity to stand), or *abasia* (incapacity to walk), and the various avoidances were named according to certain inessential superficialities (agoraphobia, claustrophobia, topophobia, etc.).

It was psycho-analysis that first threw any light on this peculiar morbid condition. It appeared that these patients had repressed into the unconscious the affective reactions to certain *psychic traumata*, for the most part experiences that were adapted to diminish their *self-confidence*, and that these continued from the unconscious to influence their activities, and on any threat of repetition of the pathogenic experience led to a development of anxiety. The patient then learns to escape these anxiety states by avoiding every activity that would in any way lead to the repetition of the pathogenic situation. *Astasia-abasia* is only the highest stage of development of this system of avoidances; it prevents all locomotion in general in order all the more surely to avoid one definite situation. I can only mention here that the root of every neurotic dread is a sexual one (Freud), and also that there is a constitutional predisposition for topophobia (Abraham).

Now the 'general' symptoms also correspond completely with the clinical picture of *anxiety*. I have said that for our patients every attempt to overcome the apparent paralysis and to move about may induce palpitations, increased pulse rate, sweating, grimaces, even a condition similar to a fainting fit. This picture corresponds in every feature with that sudden development of anxiety, as well known to us in daily life as it is in the histories of patients suffering from *anxiety neurosis*. The hyperæsthesia of all the senses, which was described as a permanent symptom, and the disturbance of sleep by anxiety dreams, corresponds to the constant 'anxious expectation' from which the anxiety neurotic suffers. The disturbance of the sexual libido and potency can assuredly be considered as neurotic.

I believe that after all this we have the right to regard every case belonging to this group of war neuroses as an *anxiety hysteria*, and to consider the motor disturbance as an expression of phobia that serves the purpose of preventing an outbreak of anxiety. In particular, then, we can give the name of '*hysterical astasia-abasia*' to most of the cases here shown; for the case, where as you see there exists a complete inability for *sitting*, we should have to coin the term '*hysterical anhedria*'.

We shall now endeavour to picture to ourselves how the concussions, on which stress is laid in the anamneses, were able to cause such types of illness. This attempt can only have a very partial success, systematic psycho-analysis, as mentioned, not being available. Nevertheless, daily intercourse with the patients and brief psycho-analytic interrogatories of a few of them procured me some material that I can employ meanwhile in answering this question.

It struck me that many of the anxiety-smitten soldiers had obtained high distinctions for previous services, and for gallantry against the enemy. To the question whether they had been frightened, previous to this, they usually answered that neither now nor previously had they felt any alarm. On the contrary, some of them told me, 'I was always the first to volunteer when there was something dangerous on.' I can only tell you a little about the cases that I analysed rather more thoroughly. A Hungarian peasant, orphaned of his father at a very early age, had very soon to do the work of the 'grown ups' on the farm. For reasons that it was no longer possible to examine analytically, he became very ambitious, wanted to do everything just as well as the grown ups, and was very touchy if any fault was found with his work, or—as often happened—any one actually made fun of him. Later he had to put up many a fight with his neighbours and also with the local *gendarmerie*; ultimately he 'was afraid of no one', as he put it himself. He had a shell concussion and a fall from a great height on the field of battle, since when he has a tremulous gait (and a conversion symptom as well, cramp in the calf), is emotional, weeps easily, but has occasionally outbursts of rage—for instance, when he learnt that he must remain under treatment for a further period. The other one, whose case I was able to go into more closely, was a Hungarian Jew engineer; he had always been very assiduous at school, had great schemes in his head (discoveries, acquisition of riches, etc.); previously religious, he gradually came to getting along without God, and was also in the process of breaking off his engagement of six years' standing to a girl because he had come to the decision that he was no longer bound by a promise given in early youth, adherence to which would imperil his career. He entered the war as a volunteer and remembers the details of his falling ill quite well. His company on one occasion was exposed to severe shelling; when he heard the whistling of the shell that fell beside him, he vowed to himself to marry his bride if nothing happened to him, and he also muttered a Hebrew prayer (' Schema Israel '). He recovered his senses after being stunned for a short time, but soon noticed that he had become incapable of walking. As a matter of fact his gait is peculiar, he takes quite short steps (without any tremor), supports himself on a stick, is constantly alarmed lest he fall, and therefore whenever possible leans against the wall or a piece of furniture. He has also become rather dejected, is uncommonly modest, his voice is low, his speech short-winded and hurried, his handwriting almost illegible. He has half-heartedly resumed relations with his bride, but (since he has been rather better) he has once more given up his relations to God.

It is not difficult to recognize in these two cases the conditions under which, as previously said, an anxiety hysteria accompanied by phobia may develop. Both these patients have carried their estimation, perhaps their over-estimation, of self pretty far. The encounter with an overwhelming force, the blast of air from the shell, that hurled them to the ground as of no account may well have shaken their *self-love* to its foundations. The result of such a psychic shock may quite well have been a *neurotic regression*, that is, the relapse into a phylo- and ontogenetic stage of development long outgrown. (Such a regression is never lacking in the symptomatology of the neuroses, as apparently outgrown phases never quite lose their power of attraction and on the occurrence of a more favourable opportunity always reassert themselves). Now the stage to which these two neurotics regressed seems to be the infantile stage of the first year of life, a time when they could not yet either walk or stand properly. We know that this stage has a phylogenetic model; the upright gait being after all a fairly late achievement of our ancestors among the mammalia.

It is not absolutely necessary to suppose that the self-love of all these war neurotics was so greatly exaggerated as this. A correspondingly severe trauma can, in so-called normal people, have an equally shattering effect upon their self-confidence and make them so timid that even the attempt to sit, to stand, or to walk—as for the child just learning to walk—is accompanied by an outburst of anxiety. (I was strengthened in my assumption by the naïve remark of one of my nurses at the morning round: 'Why, doctor, he walks just like a child learning to walk'.) Besides this regressive trait that fetters the patients to their bed or diminishes their freedom of movement, there may also be at work in many, perhaps in all, of the cases the 'secondary' function of the neurosis. It is comprehensible that the prospect of being sent back after convalescence to active duty, where things have already gone so badly with them, acts as a deterrent for these patients, more or less unconsciously preventing recovery.

Let us consider a few more of the symptoms described. The most striking of all is certainly the *tremor*, which in most of the cases entirely dominates the clinical picture. The disturbances of gait just discussed are almost always brought about by a slow tremor of the lower limbs. The regressive trait is unmistakable in the symptom of tremulousness. In the case of these neurotics an extremity provided with manifold innervations and with complicated co-ordinated movements becomes on intended effort an aimlessly tremulous prolongation of the body, unavailable for any better performance. For the prototype of this reaction we must look—ontogenetically—to the earliest childhood, phylogenetically, far back in the animal ancestral series where the life-habit did not yet react to stimuli by changes of relation to the external world (flight, approach), but only by changes of the body itself. I think, too, that in these 'neurotic' tremors we are dealing with the same disturbance of innervation with which we are acquainted in everyday life, the trembling due to anxiety—perhaps rather to fear. Every innervation of muscle can be hindered or prevented by the inhibiting innervation of the antagonists. If this innervation of agonists and antagonists synchronizes, the result is spastic rigidity; should it occur in a rhythmic alternation, the limb affected will be tremulous. In our cases we find all possible combinations of spasticity and tremor. In this way is brought about the peculiar disturbance of gait in which, in spite of every effort to walk, no change of place is effected, and which might best be described as an 'inability to stir' (*nicht vom Fleck kommen*, *piétiner sur place*). This disturbance of co-ordination at the same time becomes a defence formation that will protect the patient from the re-experiencing of the alarm. It may be mentioned here that this combination of disturbance of gait with tremor is absent in the ordinary astasia-abasia with which we are acquainted in peace time practice, where topophobic manifestations are occasioned simply by conditions of weakness, by feelings of giddiness, etc.

The other striking persistent symptom of these war neuroses is the more or less marked *hyperæsthesia of all the senses*, photophobia, hyperacusis, and the dread of passive contact. (This last is not usually associated with hyperæsthesia of the skin—skin sensation may even be lowered or lacking; it is only a matter of over-powerful defence reactions against being touched.) We must adopt the following assumption of Freud in explanation of this symptom. If one is prepared for a shock, for the approach of a danger, then the attention excitations mobilized by the expectation are able to localize the stimulus of the shock and to prevent the development of those remote effects which we see in the *traumatic neuroses*. Another means of localizing the effects of shock is—according to Freud—a severe, actual, physical injury proportionate to the psychic shock occurring with the traumatic incident. In the cases here shown of traumatic *anxiety hysteria* none of these conditions are fulfilled; we are dealing with a sudden, mostly unexpected shock without a serious bodily injury. But even in the cases in which the approach of the danger was noticed, the expectation excitation may not have been proportionate to the actual stimulus force of the shock and so was unable to prevent the discharge of the excitement along abnormal channels. It is probable that consciousness generally shuts itself off automatically at first from such too-powerful stimuli. We may take it for granted that after the trauma a certain discrepancy exists between consciousness that has been relatively protected from the shock and the rest of the neuro-psychic apparatus. An equalization is here only possible when consciousness too becomes aware of the source of pain; this is then achieved by a certain 'traumatophilic' attitude—the hyperæsthesia of the senses which in small doses gradually allows just so much anxious expectation and shock to reach consciousness as was spared to it at the time of the shock. In the constantly repeated little traumata, in each expectation of contact, in each little sudden noise or light, we should—following Freud's assumption—see a tendency towards recovery, a tendency to the equalizing of a disturbance in the distribution of tension throughout the organism.

Freud interprets in the same way the anxiety dreams of traumatic neurotics in which disasters that have occurred at one time are constantly lived over again. Here the psyche does not even wait for an external stimulus in order to react to it exaggeratedly, but creates for itself the image at which it can then become alarmed. This unpleasant symptom too, therefore, subserves the effort at self-healing.

As a crude example of traumatophilic hypersensitiveness, I show you this shell-shocked man whose whole body—

as you see—is in a state of constant muscular restlessness without his being able to carry out any intended movements. His eyes are so hypersensitive that in order to avoid the light of day they are constantly kept rolled upwards; at short intervals—once or twice a second—he turns the eyes downwards far enough to let him obtain a fleeting glimpse of his surroundings, otherwise the pupils are hidden behind the rapidly blinking upper lids. His auditory hyperæsthesia is—if possible—still greater; it reminds one of the hyperacusis of acute mania. He simply cannot exist by day in the general ward on account of the noise, and we had to let him sleep alone in the attendant's room. It was very remarkable that the patient at once requested to be allowed to sleep at night in the general ward. Asked for the reason of his request he immediately replied: 'I certainly do start up often at night in the general ward, but it is worse sleeping alone; *I can't get to sleep at all in the absolute quiet, because I always have to listen so carefully to hear whether there really is not some sound to be heard.*' This case confirms the hypothesis suggested above that the repeated affects of alarm and the heightening of the acuity of the senses are things that the traumatic neurotics themselves seek out and maintain involuntarily, because they subserve an effort at healing.

In spite of all its tragedy this behaviour of the traumatic neurotic recalls the situation of the hotel guest startled out of his sweetest slumbers by his next-door neighbour, who when undressing had flung one shoe against the communicating door. After vainly endeavouring to fall asleep again, he had to implore his restless neighbour to hurl the second shoe against the door in order that he might get to sleep. Many people behave similarly—as Abraham first pointed out—who were victims of sexual assaults in their childhood. Later they have the compulsion to expose themselves anew to similar experiences as though they were trying to control the originally unconscious and uncomprehended experience by a subsequent conscious one.

It is not impossible that the results achieved by many neurologists from treating war neuroses by painful electrical stimuli are due to the fact that these painful sensations satisfy the patients' unconscious traumatophilia.

Freud's theory that in the neuroses we are dealing, not with disturbances of the balance of energies in the ordinary sense but with a disturbance particularly of the libidinal energies was rejected by many with the argument that an ordinary trauma 'which certainly causes no sexual disturbance' may evoke a neurosis. Now we see that a shock that in itself can certainly not be called sexual—the explosion of a bomb—results in many cases in *the loss of libido sexualis and in sexual impotence.* It is therefore not impossible that ordinary shocks, too, may lead to the neuroses by way of a *sexual disturbance.* The apparently least important symptom of traumatic neurosis, namely impotence, may also on a closer examination of the pathology of that condition come to be more highly considered. For us psycho-analysts the assumption serves, as a preliminary explanation, that we are dealing in these traumata with an *ego-injury*, *an injury to self-love*, *to narcissism*, the natural result of which is the retraction of the range of the 'object cathexis of the libido', that is the cessation of the capacity to love anyone else than oneself.

I do not think that I have awakened in you the expectation of hearing from me an explanation of the psychopathological processes of the traumatic or war neuroses. My object is achieved if I have succeeded in showing you that the clinical pictures presented to you really do belong to those two disease groups that psycho-analysis designates by the names of *anxiety hysteria and conversion hysteria.* I am also not in a position to explain in detail why in one case a state of *anxiety*, in another a *conversion*, and in a third a mixture of both was developed. I have, however, I believe, shown this much, that in these neuroses, too, psychoanalytic research indicates at least the path by which the explanation must be sought, while the rest of neurology exhausts itself in description and nomenclature.

XII

PSYCHO-ANALYTICAL OBSERVATIONS ON TIC [1]

I

Psycho-analysis has done very little so far towards investigating that very common neurotic symptom which, following French nomenclature, goes under the general term of *tic* or *tic convulsif*.[2] In the notes appended to the account of 'Technical Difficulties in the Analysis of Hysteria'[3] in a case I had for treatment, I gave a short digression on this subject and expressed the opinion that many tics may turn out to be stereotyped equivalents of onanism, and that the remarkable connection of tics with coprolalia, when all motor expression is suppressed, might be nothing else than the uttered expression of the same erotic emotion usually abreacted in symbolic movements. On the same occasion I drew attention to the close relation between stereotypies and symptomatic acts (in sickness and in health) on the one hand and the tics, or rather onanism, on the other. For instance, in the case cited above, these muscular actions and skin irritations carried out apparently without thought and believed to be without meaning were able to seize the whole of the genital libido; they were at times accompanied by regular orgasm.

When I incidentally discussed the meaning and significance of tic with Prof. Freud he mentioned that apparently there was an organic factor in the question. In the course of this paper I may be able to show in what sense this view proved to be right.

This is about all the information I was able to gather from psycho-analytical sources about the tics, nor can I say

[1] Translated by Sybil C. Porter in *The International Journal of Psycho-Analysis*, 1921, vol. ii. p. 1.

[2] See J. Sadger, 'Ein Beitrag zum Verständnis des Tic'. *Int. Zeitschrift f. Psychoanalyse*, 1914, Bd. II. S. 354.

[3] *Hysterie und Pathoneurosen*, 6 [this Vol., Chap. XV.].

that since then I have been able to learn anything fresh either from direct observation or from the analysis of 'passing' tics, in spite of the frequency of their appearance in neurotic cases. In the majority of cases one can carry the analysis to a close, and even heal a psycho-neurosis, without being obliged to pay much heed to this symptom. On occasions one was led to inquire which psychical situation favoured the appearance of such a tic (*e.g.* a grimace, a twitch of the shoulders or of the head, etc.). Here and there one can also touch upon the meaning, the sense, of the symptom. One patient of mine continually shook her head vigorously as though saying "No" when carrying out a purely conventional gesture such as taking leave of or greeting anyone. I noticed the movement occurred more frequently and more violently whenever the patient desired to show more feeling, as for instance friendliness, than she really felt, and I was obliged to tell her that the shaking of her head was intended to give the lie to the friendly manner or gesture.

I have never so far had a patient who came for analysis for the express purpose of curing a tic; the minor tics I have had under observation during my analytical practice were so little trouble to the patients that they never complained of them; in each case I had to draw attention to the symptom myself. Naturally under these circumstances all motive was lacking for deeper research and, as stated above, the patients left the treatment with it unaltered.

Now we know this never occurs in the usual analysis of hysteria or obsessional neurosis. The most insignificant symptom can be proved before the end of the analysis to be part of the complicated structure of the neurosis and even to be supported by more than one determining factor. This peculiarity of tic in itself points to the suggestion that the disturbance in question is in some way differently orientated from other features of a transference neurosis, so that the usual reciprocal action of symptoms does not apply to it. The circumstance of tic being peculiar among neurotic phenomena gives strong support to the idea of Freud regarding the heterogeneous (organic) nature of this symptom.

I was helped in the next step forward by a quite different set of data. A patient (an obstinate onanist) practically never ceased to carry out certain stereotyped actions during analysis. He kept on smoothing his coat to his figure, frequently several times to the minute; in between he assured himself of the smoothness of his skin by stroking his chin, or he gazed with satisfaction at his shoes, which were always shining and polished. His entire mental attitude, his self-sufficiency, his affected speech couched in balanced phrases to which he was his own most delighted listener, marked him out as a narcissist contentedly in love with himself, who—impotent with women—found his most apposite method of gratification in onanism. He came for treatment only at the request of a relative and fled from it in haste at the first difficulties.

Although our acquaintanceship was so short it made a decided impression on me. I began to occupy myself with the question of whether the different orientation of the tics mentioned above originated in their being in fact signs of narcissistic disorder that are at the most attached to the symptoms of transference neurosis, but are not capable of fusing with them. I am not taking into account the opinion expressed by many authors that there is a marked distinction between a stereotypy and a tic. In a tic I have seen and continue to see nothing but a stereotypy performed with lightning rapidity, in an abbreviated way, and often only symbolically indicated. The following observations will reveal tics as the derivatives of stereotypies.

At all events I began to watch *tiqueurs* that I met in everyday life, in consultation, or in treatment, with regard to their narcissism. I recalled several pronounced cases I had seen medically before I practised psycho-analysis and was quite astounded at the amount of confirmatory evidence that literally poured from these sources. One of the first cases I now encountered was a young man who had a repeated twitching of the face and neck muscles. I watched him from a neighbouring table in a restaurant and observed how he behaved. Every few moments he gave a little cough and fidgeted with his cuffs till they were absolutely in order with the links turned outwards. He corrected the sit of his stiff collar with his hand or by means of a movement of the head or else he made a series of those movements usual with *tiqueurs* as though he would free his body from the irksomeness of his clothing. In fact he never ceased, although unconsciously, to devote the greater part of his attention *to his own body* or to his clothes, even while he was consciously occupied in quite other directions, such as eating, or reading the paper. I took him for a man possessed of pronounced *hypersensibility and unable to endure a physical stimulus without a defence reaction*. This conjecture was confirmed when I saw to my surprise this young man, who in other respects was well brought up and accustomed to move in good social circles, draw out a small hand-mirror immediately after the meal and in front of those present proceed to clear the remains of food from his teeth with a toothpick and this all the time with the aid of the little glass; he never paused until he had cleaned all his well-kept teeth and he was then visibly satisfied.

Now we all know that remains of food sticking between the teeth can at times be very disturbing, but such a thorough, unpostponable cleansing of all the thirty-two teeth demands a more precise explanation. I recalled to mind a similar view I expressed on a previous occasion [1] on the conditions of genesis of pathoneuroses, that is to say of 'narcissistic disease'. The three conditions there put forward under which the *fixation of libido on single organs* can occur are: (1) Danger to life or menace of a trauma; (2) Injury of a part of the body already heavily charged with libido (an erotogenic zone); (3) *Constitutional narcissism when the smallest injury to a part of the body strikes the whole ego*. This latter eventuality fitted in very well with the idea that the over-sensitiveness of tic patients, their incapacity to endure an ordinary stimulus without defence, may also be the motive of their motor expressions, *i.e.* of the tics and the stereotypies themselves; while the hyperæsthesia, which can be either local or general, might be only the expression of narcissism, the strong attachment of

[1] *Hysterie und Pathoneurosen*, S. 9 [see p. 83].

the libido to the subject himself, his body or to a part of his body, *i.e.* 'the damming-up of organ libido'. In this sense Freud's view of the 'organic' nature of tic comes to its own, even if it must be left an open question whether the libido is bound to the organ itself or to its psychical representative.

After attention had been drawn to the narcissistic-organic nature of the tics I recalled several severe cases of tic that, following the example of Gilles de la Tourette,[1] one usually designates as *maladie des tics.*

These are progressive muscular convulsions affecting practically the entire body which combine later with echolalia and coprolalia and can result in dementia. The frequent complication of tics with a typically narcissistic psychosis certainly did not pronounce against the hypothesis that also the motor phenomena of less severe cases of illness of convulsive movement that do not result in dementia owe their origin to narcissistic fixation. The last severe case of tic that I met with was that of a young man who was completely incapacitated in consequence of his psychic over-sensitiveness and shot himself as the result of an imagined injury to his honour.

In the majority of text-books on Psychiatry tic is scheduled as a 'symptom of degeneration', as a sign—often the familiar first sign—of a psychopathic constitution. We are aware that, comparatively speaking, a great number of paranoiacs and schizophrenics suffer from tic. All this appeared to me to support the suggestion that these psychoses and tic have the same root. The theory proved to stand on a yet firmer basis when I came to compare the principal symptoms of tic with the knowledge gained of catatonia from psychiatry and in particular from psycho-analysis.

The tendency to echolalia and echopraxias, to stereotypies, grimacing movements, and mannerisms, is common to both conditions. Psycho-analytical experience with

[1] Gilles de la Tourette, 'Etudes sur une affection nerveuse, caractérisée par l'incoordination motrice, et accompagnée d'écholalie et coprolalie', *Arch. de Neurologie*, 1885.

catatonic patients led me some time ago to suspect that the extraordinary behaviour and attitudes were adopted in defence against local (organic) damming-up of libido. A very intelligent catatonic patient who possessed insight to a remarkable degree even told me he was obliged to carry out a certain gymnastic movement continuously in order to break down 'the erection of the intestine'.[1] In the case of another catatonic patient I could also interpret the occasional rigidity of one or the other extremity, which was connected with a sensation of enormous extension, as a displaced erection, *i.e.* as the expression of abnormal localized organic libido. Federn groups all catatonic symptoms collectively as 'organic intoxication'.[2] All this fits in with the hypothesis of a common constitutional basis of tic and catatonia and explains the broad similarity of their symptoms. At any rate one is tempted to draw an analogy between the principal symptoms of catatonia—negativism and rigidity—with the immediate defence against all external stimuli by means of convulsive movement in tic, and to presume that when in the 'maladie de Gilles de la Tourette' tics are converted into catatonia it is merely a question of perpetuating and generalizing a partial defence-innervation appearing in tic only paroxysmally. Tonic rigidity would prove to be a summation of numberless clonic defensive convulsions, in which case catatonia would be merely the climax of cataclonia (tic).

I must not leave the subject without reference in this connection to the well-known fact that tics very often appear as the result of physical illness or traumata *in loco morbi*, *i.e.* twitching of the lids after a cure for blepharitis or conjunctivitis, tic of the nose after catarrh, particular movements of the extremities after painful inflammation. I must bring this circumstance into connection with the theory that a pathoneurotic increase of libido tends to attach itself to the seat of a pathological somatic alteration

[1] 'Some Clinical Observations on Paranoia and Paraphrenia', *Contributions to Psycho-Analysis*, 1916, by the author.

[2] Quoted from Nunberg's paper, 'Über den katatonischen Anfall', *Int. Zeitschrift f. Psychoanalyse*, 1920, Bd. V.

(or to its psychic equivalent).[1] The hyperæsthesia of tic patients which is frequently only local could in these cases be traced back to 'traumatic' displacement of libido and, as stated above, the motor expression of tic arises from defence reactions against the stimulation of such parts of the body.

As a further support of the assumption that tic has something to do with narcissism I quote the therapeutic successes attained by a certain method of treating tic. This treatment consists of systematic innervation exercises with enforced quiescence of the twitching part; the success is still more marked if the patient controls himself by looking in a mirror meanwhile. The authors explain that the control by the sense of sight facilitates the graduation of the inhibition innervation necessary to the treatment; it appeared to me, however, that beyond this (or perhaps as the greater factor) the distortion of face and body observed in the mirror would have a deterrent effect on narcissists and function as a powerful encouragement of the healing tendencies.

II

I am well aware of the weak points in the arguments I have advanced. The hypothesis, constructed rather speculatively, for my own use so to speak, on the basis of very meagre observations, would not have been made public but for the fact that its plausibility received essential support from a quite unexpected quarter. For this help I am indebted to the perusal of a book on the tics, of particularly valuable and conclusive content, in which the whole of the literature on the subject is worked up: *Tic, its Nature and Treatment*, by Dr. Henry Meige and Dr. E. Feindel.[2] I should like to connect my further remarks to the contents of this book.

Owing to the particular nature of psycho-analysis, physicians who devote themselves to its practice get few opportunities of observing certain forms of nervous dis-

[1] *Hysterie und Pathoneurosen*, S. 7.

[2] German translation by O. Giese.

orders such as 'organic' neuroses (M. Basedowii) which require physical treatment in the first instance, as well as the psychoses the treatment of which is only possible in asylums, and the many varieties of 'common nervousness' which on account of its insignificance is not made the subject of detailed psychotherapy.

For such cases one has to rely on the observations of others and upon literary communications, which, although not of the same value as one's own observation, at least has this advantage that one is spared the accusation of biased and prejudiced observation, that one has 'suggested' to the patient or been 'suggested' to. Meige and Feindel knew hardly anything of the Breuer-Freudian Catharsis; at any rate these names are missing from the index of authors in their book. It is true that *Studies on Hysteria* is referred to in one place, but this appears to be an interpolation of the translator who wished 'to draw attention to several German writers whom the French authors had overlooked'. Also the translation dates from the early days of psycho-analytical development (1903), so that the far-reaching concurrence of opinions in the work with those of the latest discoveries of psycho-analysis is in itself a criterion of an objective argument.

I will quote Trousseau's short but classic description of tic: 'Painless tic consists of momentary twitching of lightning rapidity confined as a rule to a small group of muscles, usually those of the face, though the muscles of the neck, the trunk, the limbs can also be affected . . . With one patient there may occur blinking of the lids, a twitch of the cheeks, the nostrils, or the lips, that makes one think he is pulling faces; with another the head nods or there is a sudden and repeated twist of the neck, with a third a shrug of the shoulders, a spasmodic movement of the stomach muscles or of the diaphragm; in short it is an unceasing series of bizarre movements that defy description. In some cases the tic is accompanied by a cry or by a more or less loud vocal sound. The tic may consist entirely of this very characteristic larynx- or diaphragm-chorea. There also occurs a very strange propensity to reiterate a cry or a word, and the patient will even utter words in a loud voice which he would rather keep back.'[1]

Grasset gives the following account of a patient, a characteristic picture of the manner in which tic can get displaced from one part of the body to another. 'A young girl had tics of the mouth and eyes as a child, at fifteen for several months she stuck her right leg out in front, later this leg became lame, then for several months a whistle took the place of the motor disturbances. For a year she would utter a loud cry from time to time: 'Ah'. At eighteen years appeared nodding movements, backward jerks of the head, shrugs of the right shoulder, etc.'[2]

These tic displacements often come about in the same manner as compulsive actions which displace the actual and original on to the most distant, only to return in the end to the repressed by a byway. A patient of Meige and Feindel[3] named these secondary tics 'Paratics' and recognized clearly that they were in character defence-mechanisms against the primary tics, converted in their turn into tics.

The starting point of a tic may be a hypochondrical self-observation. 'One day I felt . . . a crack in the neck', recounted a patient of Meige and Feindel, 'at first I thought something had broken. To make sure I repeated the movement once, twice, three times without noticing the crack. I varied it in a thousand ways and repeated it more and more violently. At last I felt my crack again and this gave me real pleasure . . . however the pleasure was soon disturbed by the fear that I had caused some injury.' 'Even to-day . . . I cannot withstand the desire to reproduce the crack and I cannot overcome the feeling of unrest directly I have succeeded.'[4] The nature of these sensations, now pleasurable, now anxious, allows us to tabulate them confidently as pathological expressions of the patient's sexuality and of hypochondriacal narcissism in particular. We have here the unusual case of the patient

[1] Quoted from Meige and Feindel, *op. cit.* pp. 29 and 30.

[2] *Idem, op. cit.* p. 143.

[3] *Idem, op. cit.* p. 8.

[4] *Idem, op. cit.*

remaining aware of the sensory motive for his stereotyped movement. As we shall see, in the majority of cases the motive becomes an unconscious reminiscence of the real sensation.—Charcot, Brissaud, Meige, and Feindel are among the few neurologists who did not disdain to listen if the patient recounted the history of the origin of his trouble. Meige and Feindel say: 'Only the patient can answer the question of the genesis of his illness (tic) when he harks back to the experiences, often long past, which first gave rise to his motor reactions.' With this view in sight, the authors encouraged their patients (although only with the help of the conscious mind) to reproduce those experiences which were to blame for the first appearances of their convulsive actions. We see that the path to the discovery of the unconscious and to its investigation by psycho-analysis would have been also possible from this point. They found physical traumata to be often a final explanation: an abscess in the gum was the cause of an inveterate grimace, an operation on the nose a motive for a later wrinkling up of the nose, etc. These authors come near to Charcot's view, according to whom tic is 'only a physical illness in appearance and is actually in reality psychical' . . . 'the direct product of psychosis . . . a form of hereditary psychosis'.[1]

Meige and Feindel have also very much to tell us regarding the character traits of tic patients which we should call 'narcissistic'. For example, they quote the confession of one patient: 'I must admit that I am full of self-love and am particularly sensitive to praise or blame. I watch for any words of praise and suffer cruelly from indifference or derision . . . hardest to bear is the thought that I behave in a ridiculous manner and that everyone laughs at me.'[2] 'When I meet people on the street or in an omnibus I fancy they regard me with a peculiar look of scorn or pity which makes me feel either ashamed or angry.' Or 'Two persons live in me: one with tic and one without.

[1] Some disadvantages of this conception lie in the fact that Charcot and his followers often class the tics and obsessions under one heading.

[2] M. and F., *op. cit.* p. 20.

The first is the son of the second, a worthless child who gives his father much trouble. The father should punish his son, but he is generally unable to do so; he therefore remains a slave to the whims of his own creation.'

Such confessions show tic patients as of a mentally infantile character, narcissistically fixated, from which the healthily developed part of the personality can with difficulty free itself. The predominance of the pleasure-principle (corresponding to narcissism) can be seen from the following pronouncements: 'I only do well what pleases me, that which bores me I either do badly or not at all.' 'If he has an idea, he must give himself up to it absolutely. He listens to others unwillingly.' Further remarks of Meige and Feindel on the infantilism of tic patients run as follows: 'The mental condition of tic patients is at a lower age level than it should actually be.' 'Every tic patient has the mind of a child' (p. 88). 'Tic is mental infantilism.' 'Tic patients are big, badly brought-up children accustomed to give way to their moods and who have never learned to discipline their wills' (p. 89). 'A nineteen-year old *tiqueur* had to be put to bed by "Mama" and cared for like a baby.'[1] He also showed physical signs of infantilism. The incapacity to keep back a thought is purely a psychic pendant to the incapacity to endure a sense stimulus without an immediate defence reaction. Speech is the motor reaction to abreact the preconscious (in thought) psychic tension. In this sense we are in agreement with Charcot's view of the existence of a purely psychic tic. The proofs continue to increase that go to show that it is the narcissistic over-sensitiveness in *tiqueurs* which results in the incapacity for motor and psychic self-control. This view gives an explanation of the fact that in tic the apparently heterogeneous symptoms of motor twitching and coprolalia come to be fused in the same illness. Further character traits of tic patients, easily understood from this standpoint, and

[1] Idiots (who have not emerged from infancy nor therefore from narcissism) very often suffer from tics and stereotypies. Noir compares the balancing and rotating of the head in idiots with 'a kind of rocking that quiets the patient and helps him to sleep, and which he much likes' . . . 'it has a similar action to the actual rocking of a little child'. M. and F., *op. cit.* p. 273.

described by the authors, are: the ease with which they are excited or tired, aprosexia, rambling and flight of ideas, the tendency to inordinate desire (alcoholism), incapacity to endure physical pain or strain. All these traits can be explained in accordance with our views without our being arbitrary if in the case of tic patients we think of the tendency to abreact as being heightened and the capacity for psychic retention lowered as the result of enhanced or fixated narcissism, corresponding to Breuer's bi-partition of psychical functioning activities into abreaction and retention. Abreaction is a more archaic method of relieving accrued stimulation; it approximates more closely to the physiological reflex than does the still primitive method of control, *e.g.* repression. It is characteristic of animals and children. It is not by chance that the authors state, simply from communications from their patients and from their own conclusions, without any idea of the deeper meaning, that tic patients are often 'like children', that they feel themselves young, are unable to govern their emotions, that traits of character seen frequently 'in badly brought up children and eradicated in normal persons of adult age by reason and reflection persist in tic patients in spite of increasing years, and that to such a degree that in many characteristics they appear to be nothing but big children.'[1]

Their 'need of contradiction and opposition' is worthy of special notice, not only on account of the psychical analogy to motor defence reactions in tic patients but because it is also calculated to throw light upon much of the negativism in schizophrenia. We know through psycho-analysis that in paraphrenia the patient withdraws his libido from the outside world to concentrate it on himself; every outside stimulus, whether it be physiological or psychical, disturbs his new state, and he is therefore prepared to withdraw himself from such stimuli by active flight or to ward them off by motor reaction or negativism. But we will subject this question of motor expression to a more penetrating inquiry.

One may confidently assume that of a series of tics or

[1] *Idem, op. cit.* p. 15.

stereotypies, the secondary if not the chief function is to direct attention and feeling from time to time towards particular parts of the body, as for instance the aforementioned stroking of the waist, pulling at or settling the clothing, stretching the neck, extending the breasts (in women), licking and biting the lips and also to some extent grimacing and distorting the face, sucking the teeth, etc. These may be cases in which tic is the outcome of constitutional narcissism, when the inevitable, common outer stimulus calls up the motor symptom. In contradistinction to this there exist cases which one could call pathoneurotic tics, arising from an organ pathologically and traumatically altered by an abnormal libido charge. Our authorities furnish several good examples:

'A girl presses her head on to her shoulder to allay the pain from an abscess in a tooth, an action called forth by a genuine cause, a wholly intentional muscular reaction that has undoubtedly been actuated through the activity of the cerebral cortex. The patient desires to allay the pain by pressing and warming her cheek. The abscess continues, the gesture is repeated with diminishing intention, then more from habit and at last automatically. Still there is reason and purpose in the act; up to the present nothing abnormal has occurred. Now, however, the abscess is healed and the pain ceases, but the girl continues to rest her head on her shoulder every few moments. What is now the reason for the movement? What is the purpose? Both have disappeared. What is then this systematic process originally intentional and co-ordinated and now repeated automatically without reason or purpose? It is tic.' [1] Naturally some part of the authors' explanation remains to be criticized. As they know nothing of the unconscious mind, they hold that tics, in opposition to a conscious act of will, arise without any participation of the mind, and as they are unaware of the possibility of a fixation of memory by a trauma and the tendency to reproduction from the unconscious they hold the actions of a *tiqueur* to be senseless and without purpose.

[1] M. and F., *op. cit.* p. 55. See also the designation of tic: 'memory-spasms'.

Obviously to a psycho-analyst the analogy of the origin of tic and the origin of a hysterical conversion-symptom in the acceptation of Breuer and Freud is at once apparent. Common to both is the possibility of retrogression to a perhaps already forgotten trauma, the affect of which was incompletely abreacted at the traumatic moment: there are also, however, not inessential differences between the two. In hysteria the physical symptom is only the symbol of a mental shock with the emotion suppressed and the memory of it repressed. In actual tic the organic injury is the only trauma, which is, it appears, no less qualified to leave behind pathogenic memories than is the mental conflict of hysteria. (At any rate the relative independence of tic from actual pathological alteration and its dependence on memories would go to show that the 'lasting change' that remains behind after trauma lies not in the periphery, in the organ itself, but in the psychical representative of the organ.) Hysteria is a transference neurosis in which the libidinal relation to the object (person) is repressed and appears as a conversion-symptom, as it were an auto-erotic symbolization in the body of the patient himself.[1] In tic, on the contrary, it would seem that no relation to the object is hidden behind the symptom; in this case the memory of the organic trauma itself acts pathogenically.

This differentiation obliges us to introduce a complication into the scheme put forward by Freud on the building up of the 'psychical systems'. The psychical systems consist of simple reflex arcs in the form of unconscious, preconscious, and conscious memory-systems (M-systems) interpolated between the afferent (sensory) and the efferent (motor) apparatus. Now Freud himself already accepts a plurality of such M-systems that are orientated according to the different principles of temporal, formal, or affective association, or association of content. What I should like to introduce here is the acceptance of a particular M-system, that one would have to call the 'ego-memory-system', to which fell the task of continually registering the subject's

[1] Compare 'Hysterische Materialisationsphänomene', in *Hysterie und Pathoneurosen*, by the author [p. 89 of this volume].

own physical or mental processes. It is self-evident that this system would have a stronger development in a constitutional narcissist than in persons of completely developed object-love, but an unexpectedly powerful trauma can have the result in tic, as in traumatic neurosis, of an over-strong memory fixation on the attitude of the body at the moment of experiencing the trauma, and that to such a degree as to provoke a perpetual or paroxysmatic reproduction of the attitude. The increased tendency of tic patients to self-observation, to attention to their endosomatic and endopsychical sensations, is also remarked on by Meige and Feindel.[1] The 'ego-memory system', as well as the system of memory for things, belongs in part to the unconscious and in part extends into the preconscious or into consciousness. To explain the symptom formation in tic one must suppose a conflict inside the ego (between the ego-nucleus and narcissism), and a process analogous to repression.[2]

We must regard the symptoms of traumatic neurosis as a mixture of narcissistic phenomena and phenomena of conversion hysteria, and we agree with Freud that they consist in essence of incompletely mastered shock affect, repressed and carried over, abreacted little by little; in addition they show a marked similarity to the 'pathoneurotic' tics. I should like, however, also to call particular attention to a remarkable resemblance between the two. Practically all students of the war neuroses agree that neuroses occur almost only after shock *without* severe physical injuries (wounds). Shock complicated by wounds is provided with a corresponding

[1] M and F., *op. cit.* pp. 5 and 6. Compare also *Psycho-Analysis and the War Neuroses*, 1921 (International Psycho-Analytical Library, No. 2), see also *Two Types of War Neuroses* [p. 124 of this volume]. The mental difference between the manner in which an hysteric and a narcissist register the memory of the same experience reminds us of an anecdote of two sick nurses who were on duty with the same patient on alternate nights. The one reported early in the morning to the doctor, that the patient had slept badly, had been restless, had asked for water so and so many times, etc. The other received the doctor with the words: 'Doctor, I have had such a bad night!'—The tendency to auto-symbolism is also occasioned by narcissism (Silberer).

[2] We have also met with cases of conflict between ego and libido, inside the ego and inside the libido.

discharge for the shock affect and a favourable path for the distribution of the libido in the organism. This led Freud to form the hypothesis that the addition of severe physical wounds (*e.g.* a fracture) must expedite the cure of traumatic symptoms. Compare with this the following case-history.[1] 'Young M . . . ., who suffered from tic of the face and head, fractured the lower part of the thigh; during the time that his leg was set the tics ceased entirely.' The authors consider that this is owing to the attention being diverted; according to our opinion it is due to the diversion of the libido as well. Both views are compatible with the fact that tics can give way before 'important business' and before 'occupation with things of profound interest'.[2]

That tics cease entirely during sleep is intelligible from the absolute supremacy of the narcissistic sleep wish and the complete emptying of all other systems of the charge, but it is inessential for the resolution of the question of whether tics are psychogenic or somatogenic. The fact that concurrent illnesses, pregnancy and parturition, increase tics is evidently no argument against their narcissistic genesis.

III

I should now like to subject the chief phenomena of tics—the motor symptom and the dyspraxias (echolalia, coprolalia, imitation mania)—to a somewhat more searching inquiry, relying on the few observations of my own and the wider information of Meige and Feindel.

These authors desire to confine the designation 'tic' to those conditions which show two essential elements: the psychic and the motor (that is the psycho-motor). There is no objection to this restriction of the conception of 'tic', but we consider it would promote the better understanding of the matter if one did not restrict oneself solely to the typical conditions, but also reckoned the purely psychical and even sensory disturbances as of this illness when they correspond essentially to typical cases. We have already mentioned that sensory disturbances are of importance as

[1] M. and F., *op. cit.* p. 111.

[2] *Idem, op. cit.* p. 12.

motives for tic-like twitchings and actions. We must now provide ourselves with a clear understanding of the nature of this operation. I will here refer to an important work by Freud on 'Repression' [also translated in *Collected Papers*, vol. iv. p. 84-98] where he states as follows: 'When an external stimulus becomes internal, for instance, through harassing and destroying an organ, so that there results a fresh source of continuous excitement and increase of tension, . . . it acquires . . . a far-reaching similarity to an instinct. We know that this condition is experienced in pain.'

What is here mentioned of actual pain must be extended in the case of tic to the memory of pain. That is to say, in over-sensitive persons (of narcissistic constitution) on the injury of a part of the body heavily charged with libido (erotogenic zone) or by other still unknown situations a depot of instinctive stimulus forms in the 'ego-memory system' (or in a special organ-memory system) from which unpleasurable excitation will flow to the internal perception even after the disappearance of all results of the external injuries. A particular method of relieving this excitation is by a direct outflow into motility. Which muscles are put into motion, and the particular actions that are carried out, is naturally not a matter of chance. If one takes the very instructive cases of pathoneurotic tic as prototypes of all other kinds, one may assume that the *tiqueur* will invariably carry out such actions (or their symbolic rudiments) that were for him the most suitable in warding off or easing the suffering at the time when the external disturbance was an actual fact. We see, therefore, in this form of tic a new instinct as it were *in statu nascendi* that furnishes us with a complete confirmation of all that which Freud teaches in general on the origin of instincts. According to Freud every instinct is an inherited organized adaptation-reaction to an external stimulus which later without external cause or upon an insignificant external signal is set in motion from within.

There is a variety of methods by which an individual can ward off suffering. The simplest is to withdraw oneself from the stimulus; this corresponds to a series of tics which merit the designation of flight-reflexes. One recognizes the general negativism of catatonia as the climax of this form of reaction. A more complicated tic repeats an active defence against a disturbing external stimulus; a third form is directed against the person of the patient. As example of this latter form I mention the widespread scratching tic and the tic when the patient inflicts pain on himself which reaches its climax in the tendency to self-mutilation in schizophrenia.

A very instructive case is reported in the monograph by Meige and Feindel: 'The patient could not keep a pencil or a wooden penholder longer than twenty-four hours without gnawing it from one end to the other. The same thing happened with the handles of sticks and umbrellas; he destroyed an extraordinary amount of them. To help him out of this predicament he was seized with the idea of having metal penholders and sticks with silver knobs. The result was most disastrous; he bit at them all the more and as he could not destroy the iron and silver he very soon broke all his teeth. A small abscess then started and the incentive produced by the pain became the source of a fresh mischief. He acquired the habit of loosening his teeth with his fingers, the penholders, or the stick; he had to have all the incisors taken out one by one, then the eye-teeth, and at last the front molars. Then he had a set of teeth made which proved a fresh pretext for tic! With his lips and tongue he continuously shifted the plate about, pushed it back and forth, to the right and left, turned it round in his mouth at the risk of swallowing it.'

His own account was: 'At times I am seized with the desire to take the plate out . . . I look for the smallest pretext to be alone for a moment only, then I take the plate out and push it in again at once; my desire is satisfied.'

'He had also a tormenting scratching-tic. On every opportunity he felt his face with his hand, or scratched with his fingers at his nose, the corner of his eye, his ear, his cheek, etc. At one moment he would stroke his hair hastily with his hand and at the next he would twist, pull, and tear his moustache that at times looked as if it had been cut with scissors.'

The following is a case of Dubois' : 'A girl of twenty years would thrust at her breast with her elbow, the forearm bent back against her upper-arm; she thrust from fifteen to twenty times a minute and continued until her elbow had struck the whalebone of her stays sharply. This violent thrust was accompanied by a little cry. The patient seemed only to derive satisfaction from her tic when she had carried out this last thrust.'

I shall refer later to the connection of similar symptoms with onanism. Here I will touch on the analogy of the third kind of tic, *i.e.* the motor discharge (' turning against one's own person ', Freud), with a method of reaction that occurs in certain lower animals, which possess the capacity for ' Autotomia '. If a part of their body is painfully stimulated they let the part concerned ' fall ' in the true sense of the word by severing it from the rest of their body by the help of certain specialized muscular actions; others (like certain worms) even fall into several small pieces (they ' burst asunder ', as it were, from fury). Even the biting off of a painful limb is said to occur. A similar tendency for freeing oneself from a part of the body which causes pain is demonstrated in the normal ' scratch-reflex ', where the desire to scratch away the stimulated part is clearly indicated, in the tendencies to self-mutilation in catatonia and in the like tendencies symbolically represented in the automatic actions of many tic patients, only that in the last mentioned the struggle is not in opposition to an actual disturbing stimulus, but against a detached instinctive stimulus in the ' ego-M-system ' (organ-M-system). As I have mentioned in my introduction and laid stress on in previous writings,[1] I believe that at least a portion of this enhanced stimulus can be traced back to the local increase of libido accompanying the injury (or connected to the corresponding spheres of sensation). (The psycho-analyst will without hesitation connect the active defence reaction with sadism and the self-injury with masochism; in

[1] *Hysterie und Pathoneurosen* [p. 81 of this book].

autotomia we see an archaic prototype of the components of the masochistic instinct.) As is well known, when the intensification of libido increases beyond the power of the ego-nucleus to control it, pain is produced; unbearable libido is converted into fear. Meige and Feindel describe as a cardinal symptom of tic-like convulsions that their active or passive suppression calls up reactions of fear, and that after the cessation of any prevention or hindering the actions are spasmodically carried out with every sign of pleasure.

The inclination to shake off a stimulus by means of a muscular convulsion or the incapacity to brook any hindering of a motor (or affective) discharge one can, for descriptive purposes, compare with a certain temperament that is known in scientific circles as the 'motor type'.[1]

The tic patient reacts with over-emphasis for the reason that he is already burdened with an inner instinctual stimulus. It is not impossible that something similar is also the case in one sense or another with the above-mentioned 'temperament'. At any rate we must reckon the tics as belonging to those cases, whose motility and affectivity are governed, not as is normal by the preconscious, but by undesired and partly unconscious (and as we suggest 'organ-erotic') instinctual forces, and that to a degree otherwise only known to occur in psychoses. We have thus one more factor making probable the common (narcissistic) basis of tics and the majority of the psychoses.

The tic malady attacks children as a rule in the sexual latency period, when the tendency for other psycho-motor disturbances (*e.g.* chorea) also occurs. It can have various outcomes, apart from remissions, remaining stationary or degenerating into the symptom-complex described by Gilles de la Tourette. To judge by a case that I was able to investigate psycho-analytically, the motor over-sensitiveness can be compensated for in later years by an over-strong inhibition; such as in neurotics who are conspicuous for

[1] The uncontrollable urge to dance at the sound of rhythmical music (Magic Flute !) presents an intuitive picture of the manner in which a sensory, in this case an acoustic, increase of stimulus is relieved by an immediate motor discharge.

their excessive caution, exactness and ponderous form of gait and movement.[1]

The authors state that there are also attitude-tics, that is no longer the lightning-like clonic convulsions but tonic rigidity in particular attitudes of the head of a limb. There is no doubt that these cases are transitional between cataclonic and catatonic innervation. Meige and Feindel themselves say explicitly: These phenomena (tonic or attitude tic) approximate nearer to the catatonic attitudes, the pathogenesis of which shows many points of contact with that of attitude-tic! (Meige and Feindel, p. 136.) This is a characteristic example: S. had a 'Torticollis' (attitude-tic) towards the left. He set up a considerable muscular resistance to every effort one made to bend his head towards the right. But if one talked to him and occupied his attention during the experiment little by little his head would become quite free and one could turn it in any direction without using any force (Meige and Feindel, p. 136).

Towards the end of the book it appears that one of the authors (H. Meige) even recognized the essential equality of catatonia and tic. He mentioned his idea in a paper read before the International Medical Congress at Madrid in 1903. ('L'aptitude catatonique et l'aptitude échopraxique des tiqueurs.') The translator refers to the contents of this paper as follows: 'If one examines a number of tic patients the following conclusions are arrived at which are not without interest for the pathogenesis of the trouble . . . Many tic patients incline in the most extraordinary manner to retain positions that their limbs adopt or in which they are placed. It is therefore a question of catatonia. At times this is so strong as to impede an examination of the tendon-reflexes and in several cases to simulate a failure of the knee-jerk. The question has in reality to do with an exaggerated muscular tension, an enhanced muscle tone. If one asks these patients suddenly to relax a muscle, they often only succeed in doing so after

[1] On this 'action-anxiety' see 'On Obscene Words', *Contributions to Psycho-Analysis*.

rather a long while. Further one often notices that tic patients have a tendency to repeat passive movements of their limbs in an exaggerated manner. For instance if one moves their arms several times in succession one can observe that the movement will be persisted in for a longer period. Besides the symptom of catatonia these patients give evidence also of echopraxia to a decidedly greater degree than normal persons.' (Meige and Feindel, p. 386.)

We here have the opportunity to refer to the fourth kind of motor reaction which occurs in a similar way in tic and catatonia, namely, flexibilitas cerea. 'Waxen flexibility' consists in the patient passively allowing his limbs to be placed in every sort of position without the smallest muscular resistance and this position is retained for some time. This symptom, as is well known, also occurs in deep hypnosis.

In another paper [1] in which I dealt with the explanation of psycho-analytical pliability in hypnosis, I traced the weak-willed pliability to the motives of anxiety and love. In 'father-hypnosis' the subject performs all that one asks him to do, as by that means he hopes to escape from the danger threatened by the dreaded hypnotist; in 'mother-hypnosis' he does everything to ensure to himself the love of the hypnotist. If one looks to the animal world for analogies to these methods of adaptation, the pretence of death in certain animals on threatened danger strikes one at once and also that method of adaptation called mimicry. The 'waxen pliability', the catalepsy of catatonia (and the hint of this in tic patients) may be interpreted as bearing a similar meaning. To the man suffering from catatonia everything is of equal value; his interest and libido are concentrated on his own ego; he only desires that the outside world shall leave him in peace. In spite of complete automatic subordination to every opposing will, inwardly he is actually independent of his disturbers; it matters not to him whether his body adopts one position or another, therefore why should he not continue in the physical attitude he has passively accepted? Flight, opposition,

[1] 'Introjection and Transference', *Contributions to Psycho-Analysis*, 1916.

and turning against oneself are methods of reaction which nevertheless bear witness of a fairly strong emotional relation to the exterior world. Only in catalepsy docs the patient acquire that degree of fakir-like concentration on the inner ego when even his own body appears as something foreign to his ego and is perceived as a part of the environment, whose fate leaves its owner absolutely cold. Catalepsy and mimicry therefore would be regressions to a much earlier primitive method of adaptation of the organism, an auto-plastic adaptation (adaptation by means of alteration in the organism itself), while flight and defence aim at an alteration in the environment (allo-plastic adaptation).[1]

According to the description in Kraepelin's *Text-book of Psychiatry* catatonia is often a remarkable mixture of symptoms of imperative automatism and negativism as well as of (tic-like) movements; this would suggest that different methods of motor tension reactions can be present in one and the same case. (Of the stereotyped movements of catatonic patients, which we should describe as tic-like, Kraepelin mentions the following: 'Pulling faces, twisting and dislocating the limbs, jumping up and down, turning somersaults, rolling about, clapping the hands, running about, climbing and skipping, uttering senseless sounds and noises.' Kraepelin, *Text-book of Psychiatry*, 6th edition, Book I.)

In an endeavour to explain echopraxia and echolalia in dements and tic patients one must take into consideration the more subtle processes of ego-psychology to which Freud has drawn our attention.[2] 'The development of the ego consists in a separation from primary narcissism and engenders an intensive struggle to regain this. The separation comes about by means of an enforced displacement of libido on to an ego-ideal, and satisfaction comes from fulfilment of the ideal.'

Now the fact that the dement and the *tiqueur* both possess such a strong tendency to imitate everyone in word

[1] See 'Hysterische Materialisationsphänomene' in *Hysterie und Pathoneurosen*, S. 24 [and p. 97 of this book].

[2] Freud, *Gesammelte Schriften*, Bd. VI., S. 184.

and action, taking them as it were for an object of identification and ideal, seems to be in opposition to the assertion that they have regressed to the stage of primary narcissism or have never advanced beyond it. This opposition is, however, only apparent. Like other blatant symptoms of schizophrenia, these exaggerated expressions of the identification-tendency serve the purpose of concealing the lack of real interests; they act, as Freud would express it, in the struggle for healing, the struggle to regain the lost ego-ideal. But the indifference with which every action, every form of speech, is simply imitated, stamps these identification-displacements as a caricature of the normal search for an ideal; they often operate in an ironical sense.[1]

Meige and Feindel describe cases where even complicated tic ceremonials have been assumed *en bloc*. They emphasize in particular that many *tiqueurs* possess the nature of actors and display the inclination to copy every acquaintance. One of their patients assumed as a child the eye-winking of a policeman, who appeared to him as especially imposing. These people are as a matter of fact always on the watch to see how an imposing person 'clears his throat and spits'. As is generally known, with children tics tend to be contagious.

The antithesis that have been proved in the motor behaviour of patients suffering from catatonia and catalonia are known not to be confined to muscular actions; they have a complete parallel in the speech of these patients. In schizophrenic catatonia absolute mutism alternates with uncontrollable compulsion to talk and with echolalia; the first is the pendant to tonic muscular rigidity, the second to an uncontrollable motor tic, and the third to echokinesis. So-called coprolalia gives a particularly clear demonstration of the close connection of disturbances of speech and movement. Patients who suffer from it feel compelled to utter aloud without adequate reason words and sentences of erotic, principally anal-erotic, content (curses, obscene words, etc.). This symptom is particularly pronounced

[1] It is well known that imitation is a favourite method of irony; the feeling of annoyance at being copied shows that the action does not fail in its purpose.

when the patient tries to suppress a motor tic.[1] The 'detached instinctual energy' mentioned above, finds an outlet to the 'ideational motor', the action of speech, when the discharge by mobility is denied it. I should like to connect the fact that it is just speech of an erotic, and above all 'organ-erotic' (perverse), nature that finds expression with the so-called 'organ-speech' (Freud) of narcissistic psychotics. (In the content of the expressions of schizophrenics references to bodily organs and bodily innervations are often very prominent.)

IV

Although the observations of the authors are of such value to us, the theoretical conclusions that they deduce from them profit us but little. For the most part their explanations are confined to tracing the symptoms to certain near causes (occasions) or to predisposition or degeneration. Where the patient can offer no explanation for the tic, they regard it as 'senseless and without purpose'. They forsake the psychological path too soon and lose themselves in physiological speculations. At last they get so far as to accept Brissaud's theory of 'hypertrophy of the functioning centre in the brain' (inborn or acquired by constant use), and this they regard as the 'central organ of the tic function' in tic patients. Their therapy also is based upon 'causing this hypertrophy to recede by a treatment of quiescence'. Meige and Feindel speak of 'congenital anomaly' of 'deficient and faulty development of the cortical association paths and subcortical anastomoses'; of 'molecular teratological misconceptions, which our anatomical knowledge unfortunately does not permit of our recognizing'. Grasset[2] differentiates between the bulbar-spinal 'polygonal' and mental tics, in the proper sense of the word. The former Meige and Feindel exclude, with right, from the series of

[1] On the method of converting repressed actions into thought and speech stimuli see 'Technical Difficulties in the Analysis of a Case of Hysteria', page 189.

[2] *Anatomie clinique des centres nerveux*, Paris, 1900.

tics and assign it a place among the 'cramps'; 'mental' tics are those that owe their origin to conscious psychic motor force; Grasset terms 'polygonal' tics all those to which we should ascribe unconscious psychic motives. On the basis of a cortical mechanism constructed after the well-known Aphasia scheme, which he calls the 'cortex polygon', he attributes all unconscious and automatic functioning to the functioning of the polygon. 'One dreams with the polygon', 'People in a state of abstraction act with the polygon', etc. Finally Meige and Feindel come to a decision on the following definition of tic: 'It is not sufficient that a gesture is inappropriate at the moment it occurs; on the contrary it must be certain that at the moment of its being performed it is not in connection with any idea to which it could owe its origin. . . . If beyond this the action is characterized by too frequent repetition, by constant lack of purpose, by violent urge, difficulty in suppression, and resulting satisfaction, then it is tic.' In one place only they say: 'We here find ourselves on the dangerous territory of the subconscious' and are on their guard against entering this much feared domain.

We cannot, however, reproach them for this, as at that time the doctrine of unconscious mental functions was yet in its infancy. Besides, even to-day after nearly three decades of psycho-analytic work, the scientists of their country lack the courage to tread the path which makes discovery in this 'dangerous territory' possible. Meige and Feindel have the merit, which is not to be undervalued, of being the first to attempt a psycho-genetic theory of traumatic tic, even if it is incomplete.

As these authors relied upon the conscious expressions and accounts of their patients and had no method at their disposal for arriving at the meaning of what the patients said, sexuality finds no place in their explanations. What a wealth of erotic material—concealed it is true—the histories of the patients contained extracts from the detailed anamnesia of a tic patient of Meige and Feindel will illustrate.

The same tic patient who was mentioned before as having nearly all his teeth removed also suffered from an 'attitude tic': he was obliged to hold his chin high. The idea occurred to him to press his chin on to the head of his walking stick; he then varied it so that he 'stuck the stick between his suit and his buttoned-up overcoat, in such a way that the head of the stick appeared in the opening of his collar, and on this his chin found its support. Later, without the stick, his head always needed a support or else it oscillated to and fro without it. At last he was obliged to rest his nose on the back of the chair if he wished to read quietly. His own account will illustrate the further ceremonials he was obliged to carry out.

'To start with I wore a collar of medium height but too tight to get my chin into it. Then I unbuttoned my shirt and let my chin slide into the open collar, strongly bending my head at the same time. For several days the effect of this was satisfying, but the unbuttoned collar did not offer enough resistance. So I bought much higher collars, real cravats into which I forced my chin till I could turn it neither to the right nor to the left. This was perfect,—but only for a short time. However stiff the collars might be they always gave way at last and after a few hours presented a miserable appearance.

'I had to discover something else and the following absurd idea occurred to me: I fastened a thread to the buttons of my braces, carried it under my waistcoat and finished off the upper end with a small ivory stud which I took between my teeth. The length of the thread was so arranged that I had to bow my head to reach the stud. A splendid trick!—but only for a short time, for not only was this position as uncomfortable as it was ridiculous, but also by the continuous pulling my trousers took on a really grotesque and very embarrassing shape. I had to give up this beautiful idea. However I have always preserved a predilection for this device, and even to-day it often happens on the street that I take the collar of my coat or overcoat between my teeth and so walk along. I have bitten up the border of more than one lapel in that way. At home I do differently: I quickly remove the cravat, unbutton the collar of my shirt and bite into that.' In consequence of the raised chin he could no longer see his feet when walking. 'So I have to be careful when walking, as I cannot see where I step. I know quite well that in order to remove this discomfort I have only to bend down my eyes or my head, but that is just what I cannot do.'

The patient still has: 'a certain aversion to looking down', and is also inconvenienced by a 'shoulder-crack', 'analogous to the subluxation of the thumb at will, or the peculiar noises that many people can produce to amuse others.' He also produced it as a 'small society talent'. So long as he was in the society of others, he suppressed his abnormalities, because they made him feel awkward, but 'as soon as he was alone he let himself go to his heart's content.' 'All his tics were let loose, it was an absolute wallow in absurd antics, a motor debauch which eased the patient. He then returned and resumed the interrupted conversation.'

His sleeping ceremonials were still more grotesque. 'The rubbing of his head on the pillow drove him desperate, he turned himself in every direction to avoid this, . . . at last he selected a remarkable attitude which seemed the most efficacious in obviating his tic: he lay on his side quite at the edge of the bed and let his head hang over.'

Before we go into the psycho-analytic meaning of the patient's history we must unfortunately express a doubt whether in this case we are dealing with an actual tic or with a severe obsessional neurosis. The distinction between the ceremonial of an obsessional neurotic, the pedantry and peculiarities of less severe forms of catatonia and the means for defence against a tormenting tic is difficult to determine in many cases, and this can often only be done after analysis of several weeks or even longer.[1] Also for a long while 'tic' was used in France as a dumping ground for heterogeneous neurotic conditions, like the 'vapeurs' at the beginning of last century or 'psychasthenia' to-day. This doubt prohibits us from making use of the abundant symbolization of the penis, of onanism, and of castration which appear in the history of this patient, for the purpose

[1] On this difficulty of differentiating see further note.

of generalizing about the pathogenesis of tics (head, nose, relaxation of the neck muscles, stiff collars, cravat, walking-stick, the stick put between the trousers and the mouth, the knob of the stick in the mouth, the symbolism of irritating teeth, tooth extractions, letting the head hang, etc.). Fortunately in this respect we are not dependent upon a single example. A case that I have closely investigated by analysis[1] showed me quite clearly that onanistic activities, and genital ones altogether, and erotic excitation of the genitals can be transferred to parts of the body or skin, otherwise not specially erotogenic, in the form of stereotyped movements. The connection between repressed onanism and onychohyperæsthesia, onychophagia, sensitiveness of the hair, and the tic-like tugging and tearing of the hair is generally known. Not long ago I was able to break a young man of the worrying habit of biting his nails by a single discussion of his onanistic tendencies.[2] The greater amount of the tics concerns the head and the parts of the face which are particularly favourite spots for symbolical representations of the genital processes.

Meige and Feindel allude to the relationship of the 'occupations cramps' to the tics. These cramps as well as the 'occupation delirium' of alcoholism, are in reality substitutes for onanism, as Tausk has pointed out. The peculiar *gêne* that urges *tiqueurs* to hide or mask their distortions reminds one forcibly of the way in which children are wont to conceal their 'Sucking or pleasure-sucking', described by the pediatrist Lindner of Budapest in 1879. 'Monasterism' also, the tendency to work off one's feelings in seclusion, may originate in onanism.[3]

In this connection we return to the observations of

[1] *Hysterie und Pathoneurosen*, 'Technical Difficulties', etc.

[2] A keen-sighted Hungarian surgeon, Prof. Kovacs, used to draw the attention of his audiences to the symptom of biting the nails and said these were people who were unable to let prominent parts of the body alone.

[3] The word 'tic' is according to Meige and Feindel an 'onomatopoetikon'. It is like a short sound. *Zucken, Ticken, Tic* in German ; *tic, tiquer, ticqué* in French ; *tug, tick* in English ; *ticchio* in Italian ; *tico* in Spanish, all have the same root and the same onomatopoetical origin (M. and F., *op. cit.*, p. 29). We must remember in this connection that in consequence of a peculiar and general acoustic synæsthesia the palpitation of the erection of the clitoris is described by the majority of women as 'klopfen' (knocking).

Gowers and Bernhardt that tics often increase in power at the time of early puberty, pregnancy and childbed, at the time therefore of increased stimulation of the genital systems. Finally if we take into consideration the coprolalia, streaming into anal-erotic obscenities, paraded by many tic patients [1] and their tendency to enuresis (nocturna and diurna) to which Oppenheim draws attention, we cannot avoid the impression that the significant 'displacement from below upwards' so strongly emphasized in neurotics as well as in normal sexual development plays no inessential part in the formation of tic.

One can link up this fact with the possibility of tracing back the origin of tic to an increase of narcissism (which has been a prominent feature of our considerations so far) in the following manner: In the case of 'pathoneurotic tic' the injured or stimulated part of the body (or its psychic representative) is charged with excessive interest and libido. The quantity of energy required for this is drawn from the greatest libido reservoir, the genital sexuality, and this must of necessity be accompanied by a decrease of potency in the normal genital sensations. This results in a displacement of not only a certain quantity of energy from below upwards but also a displacement of quality (innervation-character), hence the 'genitalization' of the parts attacked by tic (excitability, tendency to rhythmical rubbing, in many cases definite orgasm). In cases of tic of 'constitutional narcissists' the primacy of the genital zone generally appears to be not quite firmly established, so that even ordinary stimuli or unavoidable disturbances result in a similar displacement. Onanism would thus still be a half-narcissistic sexual activity from which the transition to normal satisfaction in a foreign object would be just as possible as also the regression to auto-erotism.

I will here touch upon some reflections that I shall refer to later in another connection. To me genital sexuality

[1] There are also otherwise healthy people who are impelled to speak their thoughts at once, *e.g.* murmur when reading or talk to themselves. According to Stricker every thought is accompanied by a slight innervation of the motor organ of speech.

appears as the sum of auto-erotism displaced upon the genitalia, which in this ' displacement downwards ' carries with it not only its qualities but the ' innervation-characters ' in addition (' Amphimyxis of Auto-erotism '). The chief quantity of genitality is furnished by urethral and anal-erotism. In pathological ' displacement upwards ' genitality appears to some extent to divide itself up into its component parts, which must lead to the strengthening of certain urethral- or anal-erotic features. The strengthening concerns not only the organ-erotism itself, but also its derivatives, the so-called anal- or urethral-character traits. As urethral characteristics I mention (in tic and catatonia) the incapacity to endure strain, the urge to discharge at once every increased stimulus, every affect, by a motor-reaction and uncontrollable speech impulses. The following are probably anal characteristics: the tendency to rigidity, negativism, and muteness, viz. the ' phonator ' tics.

I also draw attention to what Sadger terms ' muscle-erotism ' and the constitutional reinforcement of the pleasure of movement (which Abraham has pointed out), which can fundamentally encourage the appearance of motor phenomena in tic and in catatonia.

V

It cannot but occur to me that the ' genitalization of auto-erotism ', to the consequences of which I attribute the motor expressions of tic and catatonia, I have already described in earlier works as the origin of the hysterical ' materialisation phenomena ' (in conversion hysteria). I cannot shirk this knotty problem any longer, but must endeavour to substantiate the differences that in spite of many similarities divide these conditions from each other. I have already mentioned the essential difference between an hysterical conversion symptom and the localized physical symptom of a narcissistic neurosis (tic, catatonia). In hysteria, which is a transference neurosis, the repressed pathogenic material belongs to the memory-traces in the unconscious for things that refer to the libido objects (persons). In consequence of the incessant reciprocal associative linking-up of the memory-systems of 'the thing' and of 'the ego' (body), the pathogenic psychic material of the hysteric can use the associated physical memory material as a means of expression. That is the explanation of the so-called 'physical approach' which Breuer and Freud remarked on in reference to the very first analysed cases of hysteria. In the celebrated case of the patient 'Anna' the hysterical paralysis of the arm was traced back to the fact that in a most critical moment when contending tendencies came into conflict her arm was inadvertently left hanging over the back of the chair and had 'gone to sleep'. In similar manner a tear that obscured her sight was the cause of macropsia which developed later. The accidental catarrh of a patient of Freud's (Dora) was the finely graduated means of expressing the most complicated love emotions under the mask of a 'nervous cough'. Thus in conversion-hysteria the object memories repressed by psychic energy are used to reinforce and finally to 'materialise' the ego (body) memories associated with them. This is the mechanism of the 'leap from the mental to the physical' in the formation of hysterical symptoms.

In tic, on the contrary, traumatic ego (body) memory forces itself spontaneously to the fore on every occasion that offers. One could say that tic and catatonia are in reality ego-hysterias. Or expressed in the terminology of the libido theory: the hysterical conversion-symptoms are expressions of (genital) object love, clothed in the form of auto-erotism, while the tics and catatonias are auto-erotism which has to some extent adopted genital qualities.[1]

Finally we must also compare the motor expressions of

[1] See in this connection the following passage from the important work of Nunberg on the catatonic attack (*Internationale Zeitschrift für Psycho-analyse*, 1920, Bd. V., S. 49). 'In conclusion I should like to refer to the many singularly striking similarities between catatonic and hysteric attacks, as, for instance, the "dramatization" and *Angst*. There is, however, this difference between them, namely, that while in Hysteria we are concerned with a Libido-charge of an object, in Catatonia a Libido-charge of an organ takes place.'

Also, the perversions of adults are of course 'genitalized' auto-erotism (Perversion is indeed the 'Positive of Hysteria').

obsessive actions. We know through Freud, that these actions are psychic protective measures with the object of guarding against the return of certain painful thoughts; they are actually physical 'displacement substitutes' for compulsive thoughts.

Obsessive actions are chiefly differentiated from the tics and stereotypies by their greater complexity; they are real actions that aim at the alteration of the external world (chiefly in an ambivalent sense) and in which narcissism plays no part or else a subordinate one.

A differential diagnosis of these motor symptoms is often only possible after prolonged psycho-analysis.

XIII

SUNDAY NEUROSES[1]

We know from psychiatry of illnesses that display a marked periodicity; it will suffice to recall periodic mania and melancholia. We know, too, since Freud established it psycho-analytically, that psycho-neurotics—so many of whom, as is well known, suffer from repressed memories—cheerfully celebrate the anniversary or the time of year of certain experiences significant for them by an exacerbation of their symptoms. But as far as I am aware no one has yet described neuroses the oscillation of whose symptoms were dependent on the particular day of the week.

And yet I think I can assert the existence of this peculiar periodicity. I treated several neurotics the history of whose illness, recounted spontaneously or reproduced during the analysis, contained the information that certain nervous conditions had developed—mostly in youth—on a certain day of the week, and had then regularly recurred.

Most of them experienced these periodical returns of the disturbances on *Sundays*. They were mostly *headaches*

[1] *Zeitschrift*, 1919, Bd. V. 46.

or *stomach disturbances* that were wont to appear on this day without any particular cause, and often utterly spoilt the young people's one free day of the week. I probably do not need to state that I did not neglect the possibility of other rational causes. The patients themselves, too, endeavoured —apparently successfully—to hit on a reasonable explanation for this peculiar periodic regularity of their condition, and wanted to connect it with the dietetic peculiarities of the Sunday. One sleeps longer than usual on a Sunday, therefore one has a headache, said some; one eats so much and so well on Sundays, and therefore one upsets one's stomach so easily, said the others. Nor do I wish to deny the activity of this purely somatic factor in evoking the Sunday periodicity.

Many things, however, indicate that these physiological factors do not exhaust the facts of the case. The headache, for instance, occurred also when the duration of sleep on Sunday did not differ from that on the other days of the week, and the stomach troubles appeared when the environment and the patients themselves were forewarned, and the diet for the day prophylactically restricted.

In one of the cases that was known to me the little boy had rigors and vomited every Friday evening. (He was a Jewish boy for whom the 'Sabbath rest' began on Friday evening.) He and the whole family referred the condition to the eating of fish, for hardly a Friday evening passed without a dish of fish. It availed nothing, however, if he denied himself the enjoyment of this dish; the disturbances appeared afterwards just as they had previously; this time they were, perhaps, traced to an idiosyncracy for the sight of the dangerous food.

The psychological factor that I should like to consider as an adjuvant factor, or sometimes even as the sole cause, in explaining the certainty of the chronological return of the symptoms, is given in the circumstances that, apart from longer sleep and better meals, characterize Sunday.

Sunday is the holiday of present-day civilized humanity. But one is mistaken if one thinks that a holiday is only significant as a day of physical and psychic rest; for the recuperation that it usually affords us the factor of mood is of great importance. It is not only that on this day we are our own masters and feel ourselves free from all the fetters that the duties and compulsions of circumstances impose upon us; there occurs in us—parallel with this—a kind of inner liberation also. We have heard from Freud that the inner powers that direct our thinking and acting in logically, ethically, and æsthetically unobjectionable ways only reproduce instinctively what was once forced upon mankind by external necessity. What wonder than if on remission of the actual external pressure a part of the otherwise already permanently repressed instincts are set free. The remission of the external censorship involves the inner one, too, sympathetically.

For those not concerned it is always remarkable to observe how the level of a group of people alters on festive occasions. 'On the mountain pastures there is no sin', says the Styrian, meaning that on a Sunday excursion to the mountain pastures everything is permissible, adults behave like children, but the children get out of all bounds and not infrequently are quite carried away and play pranks that then provoke punishment from those in authority and put an abrupt and sad end to the previous exaggerated gaiety. It is not always so, for the adults are on such occasions amazingly long-suffering, as though they felt themselves bound by a secret and unspoken convention that guaranteed the guilty ones a temporary security from punishment.

But it is not given to everyone to vent their holiday wantonness so freely and naturally. The neurotically disposed will be inclined just on such occasions to a reversal of affect, either because he has much too dangerous impulses to control which he must guard closely, particularly when tempted by the bad example of others; or because his hypersensitive conscience will not overlook even little omissions. Beyond the untimely depression of these 'spoil sports', however, their repressed impulses as well as the self-punishment fantasies mobilized against them, which have been activated by the holiday, may be manifested in little hysterical symptoms. And I must also qualify as such the Sunday headaches and stomach manifestations mentioned above; the 'long sleep', the 'over-eating', etc., are only circumstances of which this little neurosis makes use, and with which it conceals its true motivation.

XIV

ON THE TECHNIQUE OF PSYCHO-ANALYSIS[1]

I. Abuse of Free Association

The whole method rests on Freud's 'fundamental rule of psycho-analysis', on the patient's duty to relate everything that occurs to him in the course of the analytical hour. Under no circumstances may an exception be made to this rule, and everything that the patient—from whatever motive—endeavours to withhold, must be unrelentingly brought to light. It may happen, however, that when the patient has with no little pains been educated up to literal acquiescence in this rule that his resistances take possession of it and endeavour to defeat the doctor with his own weapon.

Obsessional neurotics sometimes have recourse to the evasion of relating *only* senseless associations, as though deliberately misunderstanding the doctor's request that they should recount everything, senseless things as well. If they are let alone and not interrupted, in the hope that in time they will weary of the proceeding, this expectation is often disappointed, until one is convinced that they are unconsciously displaying a tendency to reduce their doctor's request to an absurdity. With this kind of superficial association they usually deliver an unbroken series of word associations, the selection of which, of course, betrays the unconscious material which the patient wishes to avoid. It

[1] *Zeitschrift*, 1919, Bd. V. 181. A paper read before the Hungarian Psycho-Analytical Society ('Freud Society') in Budapest.

is quite impossible, however, to achieve a thorough analysis of any particular ideas, for if by chance certain striking concealed traits are pointed out, instead of simply accepting or rejecting the interpretation—one is merely presented with more 'senseless' material.

There is nothing for it but to make the patient aware of his tenacious behaviour, whereupon he will not fail to remark triumphantly, 'I am only doing as you asked, I am telling you all the nonsense that occurs to me'. At the same time he may perhaps make the suggestion that the strict adherence to the 'fundamental rule' might be relaxed, the conversations be systematically arranged, definite questions be put to him, and the forgotten material searched for methodically or even by means of hypnosis. The reply to these objections is not difficult: the patient, it is true, is asked to say everything, even the senseless things, that occurs to him, but certainly not to repeat only meaningless or disconnected words. This behaviour contradicts—so we explain to him—just that rule of psycho-analysis that forbids any critical choice of ideas. The quick-witted patient will thereupon retort that he cannot help it if only nonsense occurs to him, and propounds perhaps the illogical question whether from now on he should withhold all the nonsense. One must not get annoyed, otherwise the patient would have attained his object, but must keep him to the continuation of the work. Experience shows that the admonition not to misuse free association usually has the result that from then on it is no longer only nonsense that occurs to the patient.

It is only in the rarest cases that a single explanation of this matter suffices; if the patient again becomes resistant to the doctor or the treatment, he starts the meaningless associations again, he even puts the difficult question of what he should do when not even entire words but only inarticulate sounds, animal noises, or instead of words, melodies, occur to him? He is requested to repeat such sounds and tunes confidently, like everything else, but he is told of the bad intention that is concealed behind his apprehension.

Another well-known manifestation of the 'association resistance' is that 'absolutely nothing occurs' to the patient. The possibility of this can be granted without further discussion. But if the patient is silent for a more prolonged period, it usually signifies that he is withholding something. A patient's sudden silence must therefore always be interpreted as a *passagère symptom*.

A long silence is often due to the fact that the request to relate *everything* has not yet been taken literally. If the patient is asked after a considerable pause what was in his mind during the silence, he will perhaps reply that he had *only* contemplated an object in the room, had a sensation or a paræsthesia in this or that part of the body, etc. There is often nothing for it but to explain all over again to the patient that he must relate everything that goes on inside him, sensations, therefore, as well as thoughts, feelings, and impulses. But as this enumeration can never be complete, the patient will always—when he relapses into a resistance—discover fresh possibilities for rationalizing his silence and secretiveness. Many, for instance, say they withhold something because they had had no clear thoughts but only indistinct confused sensations. Of course this is a proof that, in spite of the request to the contrary, they are still subjecting their ideas to criticism.

If explanations have no result, it must be assumed that the patient wants to beguile one into detailed instructions and explanations and in this manner to obstruct the work. In such cases it is best to encounter the patient's silence with silence. It may happen that the greater part of the hour passes without the doctor or the patient having said a single word. The patient finds it very difficult to endure the doctor's silence; he gets the impression that the doctor is annoyed with him, that is, he projects his own bad conscience on to the doctor, and this finally decides him to give in and renounce his negativism.

One must not let oneself be misled even when one or other patient should threaten to go to sleep from sheer boredom; in a few instances the patient actually has fallen asleep for a short time, but I had to conclude from their speedy awakening that the preconscious had kept a grip of the situation even during sleep. The danger that the patient may sleep away the whole hour does not therefore arise.[1]

Many a patient makes the objection to free association that too much occurs to him at once and he does not know what to relate first of all. Should one allow him to determine the sequence himself he will perhaps reply that he cannot decide to give one or other idea the preference. In such a case I had to have recourse to letting the patient relate everything in the sequence in which it had occurred to him. He replied that in that case he was afraid lest while he followed out the first thought of the series he would forget the others. I soothed him with the hint that everything of importance—even if for the moment it seems to be forgotten—will come to the surface later of itself.[2]

Little peculiarities, too, in the manner of associating have their significance. So long as the patient introduces every idea with the phrase, 'I think that', he shows that he is inserting a critical examination between the perception and the communication of the idea. Many prefer to cloak unpleasant ideas in the form of a projection upon the doctor, by saying perhaps, 'You are thinking that I mean that . . .', or 'Of course you will interpret that to mean . . .'. To the request to omit any criticism, many reply, 'criticism is ultimately also an idea', which one must

[1] The fact that the doctor at many interviews pays little heed to the patient's associations and only pricks up his ears at certain statements also belongs to the chapter 'on counter-transference'; dozing may happen in these circumstances. Subsequent scrutiny mostly shows that we were reacting unconsciously to the emptiness and worthlessness of the associations just presented by the withdrawal of conscious excitation; at the first idea of the patient's that in any way concerns the treatment we brighten up again. The danger, therefore, of the doctor falling asleep and leaving the patient unobserved is not great. (I owe the full confirmation of this observation to a verbal discussion of the subject with Prof. Freud.)

[2] It is probably hardly necessary to state expressly that the psycho-analyst must avoid any untruth in relation to his patient; this holds, of course, equally in respect of matters concerning either the doctor's methods or person. The psycho-analyst should be like Epaminondas, of whom Cornelius Nepos tells that he 'nec ioco quidem mentiretur'. Of course the doctor may and must withhold a part of the truth at first, for instance, what the patient is not yet prepared for; that is, he must himself determine the speed of initiation.

acknowledge without further debate, but not without drawing attention to the fact that if the fundamental rule were strictly kept to it could not happen that the common communication of the criticism should precede or indeed replace that of the idea itself.

In one case I was forced, in direct contradiction to the psycho-analytic rule, to insist that the patient should always complete any sentence he had begun. For I noticed that whenever a sentence took an unpleasant turn he never completed it, but switched off in the middle with a 'by the way' on to something unimportant and beside the mark. It had to be explained to him that the fundamental rule did not, it is true, demand the *thinking* out of an idea, but certainly the complete *utterance* of what had been thought. He required many admonitions, however, before he learnt this.

Quite intelligent and otherwise sensible patients sometimes try to reduce the methods of free association to absurdity by putting the question, 'What, though, if it occurred to them to get up suddenly and run away, or to maltreat the doctor physically, to kill him, to smash a piece of furniture, etc.?' If one then explains that they were not told to *do* everything that occurred to them but only to *say* it, they usually reply that they are afraid they could not distinguish so sharply between thinking and doing. We can reassure these over-anxious folk that this fear is only a reminiscence of childhood when they actually were not yet capable of such a differentiation.

In rare cases patients are overwhelmed by an impulse, so that instead of continuing to associate they begin to *act* their psychic content. Not only do they produce 'transitory symptoms' instead of ideas, but while fully conscious they carry out complicated activities, entire scenes, of whose transference or reconstruction nature they have not the least conception. Thus one patient at certain exciting moments in the analysis jumped up suddenly off the sofa, walked up and down the room and ejaculated abusive words. The historical basis for the movements as well as for the abusive words was then revealed by the analysis.

An hysterical patient of the infantile type surprised me after I had succeeded in weaning her temporarily of her childish seduction artifices (constant imploring contemplation of the doctor, striking or exhibitionist apparel) by an unexpected direct attack; she jumped up, demanded to be kissed, and finally came actually to grips. It goes without saying, of course, that the doctor must not lose his attitude of benevolent patience even in the face of such occurrences. He must point out over and over again the transference nature of such actions, towards which he must conduct himself quite passively. An indignant moral rebuff is as out of place in such cases as would be the agreement to any of the demands. Such a reception, it will be found, rapidly exhausts the patient's inclination for assault, and the disturbance—that is to be interpreted psycho-analytically in any case—soon settles itself.

In a paper 'Über obscöne Wörte',[1] I have already insisted that one must not spare patients the effort of overcoming the resistance to saying certain words. Easing of the difficulty, as by permitting certain communications to be set down in writing, contradict the purposes of the treatment, which consist essentially in the patient's mastering his inner resistances by continuous and progressive practice. When, too, the patient is endeavouring to remember something of which the doctor is quite aware, he must not just be helped out at once; otherwise the possibly valuable substitute ideas will be lost.

Of course this withholding of help on the doctor's part cannot be absolute. If for the moment one is less concerned about exercising the patient's psychic powers than with hastening certain understandings, then one simply puts into words the ideas one supposes him to have, but which he lacks the courage to utter, and thus obtains a confession from him. The doctor's position in psychoanalytic treatment recalls in many ways that of the obstetrician, who also has to conduct himself as passively as possible, to content himself with the post of onlooker at

[1] ['On Obscene Words', translated in *Contributions to Psycho-Analysis*, chap. iv., first published in *Centralblatt*, Bd. I. 390.]

a natural proceeding, but who must be at hand at the critical moment with the forceps in order to complete the act of parturition that is not progressing spontaneously.

II. Patient's Questions—Decisions during Treatment

I made it a rule, whenever a patient asks me a question or requests some information, to reply with a counter interrogation of how he came to hit on that question. If I simply answered him, then the impulse from which the question sprang would be satisfied by the reply; by the method indicated, however, the patient's interest is directed to the sources of his curiosity, and when his questions are treated analytically he almost always forgets to repeat the original enquiries, thus showing that as a matter of fact they were unimportant and only significant as a means of expression for the unconscious.

The situation becomes particularly difficult, however, when the patient appeals to one, not with some question or other, but with the request that some matter of personal significance, such as the choice between two alternatives, be decided for him. The doctor's endeavour must always be to postpone decisions till the patient is enabled, by a growing self-reliance due to the treatment, to deal with matters himself. It is well, therefore, not to accept too easily the patient's stressing of the urgency for an immediate decision, but to consider also the possibility that such apparently very real questions have perhaps been pushed into the foreground unconsciously by the patient, whereby he is either clothing the analytic material in the garb of a problem, or his resistance has taken this means of interrupting the progress of the analysis. In one patient's case this last manœuvre was so typical that I had to explain to her, in the military phraseology in vogue at the time, that when she could find no other way out, she flung problems at me like gas-shells, in order to confuse me. Of course a patient may really on occasion have to decide an important matter without delay during treatment; but it is as well if on these occasions, too, the doctor plays as little as possible the part of spiritual guide, after the fashion of a *directeur de conscience*, contenting himself with that of analytic *confesseur* who illuminates every motive, those, too, of which the patient is unconscious, as clearly as may be from every side, but who gives no direction about any decisions and actions. As far as this is concerned, psycho-analysis is diametrically opposed to every psychotherapy as yet practised, to suggestion as to treatment by persuasion.

In two circumstances the psycho-analyst is in the position of interfering uncompromisingly in the patient's career. First, when he is convinced that the patient's vital interests really demand an immediate decision of which he is as yet incapable by himself; in this case, however, the doctor must be aware that he is no longer dealing as a psycho-analyst, indeed that certain difficulties in the prosecution of the treatment may arise from his interference; for instance, an undesirable strengthening of the transference relation. Secondly, the analyst can, and must from time to time, practise 'active therapy' in so far as he forces the patient to overcome the phobia-like incapability of coming to a decision. By the change in the affective excitations that this overcoming will occasion he hopes to obtain access to as yet inaccessible unconscious material.

III. 'For Example' in Analysis

If a patient presents one with some generalization, whether it be a manner of speaking or an abstract statement, he should always be asked what occurs to him in connection with that generalization. This question has become so fluent with me that it occurs almost automatically as soon as the patient begins to speak in too general terms. The tendency to pass from the general to the more and more particular dominates the whole of psycho-analysis; it is this alone that leads to the fullest possible reconstruction of the patient's life history, to the filling in of his neurotic anamnesias. It is therefore wrong, following the patient's inclination for generalization, to co-ordinate one's observations about him too soon under any general thesis. In real psycho-analysis there is little room for moral or philosophical generalizations; it is an uninterrupted sequence of concrete facts.

A young patient gave me the confirmation in a dream that the phrase 'for example' is really the proper technical method for guiding the analysis from the remote and unessential directly to the imminent and essential.

She dreamt: '*I have toothache and a swollen cheek; I know that it can only get better if Mr. X.* (*formerly engaged to me*) *rubs it; for this, however, I must get a lady's permission. She really gives me permission, and Mr. X. rubs my cheek with his hand; at this a tooth jumps out as though it had just grown and as though it had been the cause of the pain*'.

Second dream fragment: '*My mother asks me what happens at psycho-analysis. I tell her: one lies down and must say everything that passes through one's head. But what passes through one's head? she asks again. All sorts of thoughts, even the most incredible ones. What, for example? For example, that one has dreamt that the doctor has kissed one and* . . . this sentence remained unfinished and I woke'.

I shall not enter into the details of the interpretation, and need only remark that we are dealing here with a dream whose second part *interprets* the first. The interpretation is set about quite methodically. The mother, who evidently takes the place of the analyst, is not satisfied with the generalizations by means of which the dreamer attempts to get herself out of the affair, and will not be content till, in reply to the question, 'what, *for example*?' occurs to her, the latter concedes the only correct sexual interpretation of the dream.

What I maintained, therefore, in a paper on 'The Analysis of Comparisons',[1] namely, that just the most

[1] See my paper 'Technical Difficulties', etc., p. 189. *Zeitschrift*, V. Nr. 1 (included in the author's book, *Hysterie und Pathoneurosen*, Intern. Ps.-A. Verlag 1919) and Freud's lecture to the fifth International Psycho-analytical Congress in Budapest, 'Wege der psychoanalytischen Therapie' (*Zeitschrift*, V. 2, 1919).

significant material is concealed behind comparisons apparently thrown out in passing, holds good also for ideas that the patients evolve in reply to the question, 'what, for example?'.

IV. The Control of the Counter-Transference

Psycho-analysis—to which, generally speaking, the task of exposing mysticism seems to have fallen—succeeded in laying bare the simple, one might say naïve, rule of thumb that lies at the bottom of even the most complicated medical diplomacy. It discovered the transference to the doctor to be the effective agent in all medical suggestion, and showed that such a transference ultimately only repeats the infantile-erotic relationship to the parents, to the indulgent mother or to the stern father, and that it depends upon the patient's experience of life or his constitutional tendency whether or how far he is susceptible to the one or the other kind of suggestion.[1]

Psycho-analysis thus discovered that nervous patients are like children and wish to be treated as such. Doctors with a gift of intuition knew this even before us, at least they behaved as though they knew it. The vogue of many a 'downright' or 'kindly' sanatorium doctor is to be explained in this way.

The psycho-analyst, however, may no longer be gentle and sympathetic or downright and hard according to inclination and wait till the patient's soul moulds itself to the doctor's character; he must understand how to *graduate* his sympathy. Indeed he may not even yield inwardly to his own affects; to be influenced by affects, not to mention passions, creates an atmosphere unfavourable for the taking up and proper handling of analytic data. As the doctor, however, is always a human being and as such liable to moods, sympathies and antipathies, as well as impulses—without such susceptibilities he would of course have no understanding for the patient's psychic conflicts—he has

[1] ['Introjection und Übertragung' (*Jahrbuch für Psychoanalyse*, Bd. I. 1919.) Translated in *Contributions to Psycho-Analysis*, chap. ii.]

constantly to perform a double task during the analysis: on the one hand, he must observe the patient, scrutinize what he relates, and construct his unconscious from his information and his behaviour; on the other hand, he must at the same time consistently control his own attitude towards the patient, and when necessary correct it; this is the mastery of the *counter-transference* (Freud).

The pre-condition for this is of course the analysis of the doctor himself; but even the analysed individual is not so independent of peculiarities of character and actual variations of mood as to render the supervision of the counter-transference superfluous.

It is difficult to generalize about the way in which the control of the counter-transference should interfere; there are too many possibilities. To give some conception of it, it would probably be best to adduce some examples from actual experience.

At the beginning of psycho-analytic medical activities one naturally suspects least of all the danger that threatens from *this* side. One is in the blissful mood into which a first acquaintance with the unconscious transports one, the doctor's enthusiasm transfers itself to the patient, and the psycho-analyst owes surprising cures to this happy self-assurance. There is no doubt that these results are only in a small degree due to analysis, but are for the most part purely suggestive, that is, are the results of the transference. In the elevated mood of the honeymoon months of analysis, one is miles from considering, let alone mastering, the counter-transference. One yields to every affect that the doctor-patient relationship may evoke, is moved by the patient's sad experiences, probably, too, by his phantasies, and is indignant with all those who wish him ill. In a word, one makes all their interests one's own, and is surprised when one or other patient in whom our behaviour may have raised irrational hopes suddenly breaks out in passionate demands. Women demand that the doctor shall marry them, men that he shall support them, and they construct arguments for the justification of their claims out of his utterances. Naturally one gets out of these difficulties easily enough during the analysis; one falls back upon their transference nature and employs them as material for further elaboration. In this way, however, one gets an insight into the cases of non-analytic or 'wild' analytic therapy that eventuates in accusations or legal proceedings against the doctor. The patients are simply unmasking the doctor's unconscious. The enthusiastic doctor who wants to 'sweep away' his patient in his zeal to cure and elucidate the case does not observe the little and big indications of fixation to the patient, male or female, but they are only too well aware of it, and interpret the underlying tendency quite correctly without guessing that the doctor himself was ignorant of it. In such arraignments, therefore, both the opposing parties, remarkably enough, are right. The doctor can swear that he—consciously—intended nothing but the patient's cure; but the patient is also right, for the doctor has unconsciously made himself his patient's patron or knight and allowed this to be remarked by various indications.

Psycho-analytic discussion protects one, of course, from such inadvertencies; nevertheless it does happen that the insufficient consideration of the counter-transference puts the patient into a condition that cannot be altered and which he uses as a motive for breaking off the treatment. One must just accept the fact that every new psycho-analytic technical rule costs the doctor a patient.

If the psycho-analyst has learnt painfully to appreciate the counter-transference symptoms and achieved the control of everything in his actions and speech, and also in his feelings, that might give occasion for any complications, he is threatened with the danger of falling into the other extreme and of becoming too abrupt and repellent towards the patient; this would retard the appearance of the transference, the pre-condition of every successful psycho-analysis, or make it altogether impossible. This second phase could be characterized as the phase of resistance against the counter-transference. Too great an anxiety in this respect is not the right attitude for the doctor, and it is only after overcoming this stage that one perhaps reaches the third, namely, that of the control of the counter-transference.

Only when this has been achieved, when one is therefore certain that the guard set for the purpose signals immediately whenever one's feelings towards the patient tend to overstep the right limits in either a positive or a negative sense, only then can the doctor 'let himself go' during the treatment as psycho-analysis requires of him.

Analytic therapy, therefore, makes claims on the doctor that seem directly self-contradictory. On the one hand, it requires of him the free play of association and phantasy, the full indulgence of *his own unconscious*; we know from Freud that only in this way is it possible to grasp intuitively the expressions of the *patient's unconscious* that are concealed in the manifest material of the manner of speech and behaviour. On the other hand, the doctor must subject the material submitted by himself and the patient to a logical scrutiny, and in his dealings and communications may only let himself be guided exclusively by the result of this mental effort. In time one learns to interrupt the letting oneself go on certain signals from the preconscious, and to put the critical attitude in its place. This constant oscillation between the free play of phantasy and critical scrutiny presupposes a freedom and uninhibited motility of psychic excitation on the doctor's part, however, that can hardly be demanded in any other sphere.

XV

TECHNICAL DIFFICULTIES IN THE ANALYSIS OF A CASE OF HYSTERIA[1]

(Including Observations on Larval Forms of Onanism and 'Onanistic Equivalents')

A PATIENT who was endeavouring with great intelligence and much zeal to carry out the directions for psycho-analytic treatment, and who left nothing to be desired in

[1] *Zeitschrift*, 1919, Bd. V. 34.

the way of theoretical insight, nevertheless, after a certain degree of improvement, probably due to the first transference, made no progress for a long time.

As the proceedings made absolutely no headway, I decided on extreme measures and fixed a date up to which I would continue to treat her, in the expectation that by this means I should provide her with an adequate incentive to effort. Even this, however, proved only of temporary assistance; she soon relapsed into her former inactivity, which she concealed behind her transference love. The hours went by in passionate declarations of love and entreaties on her side, and in fruitless endeavours on mine to get her to understand the transference nature of her feelings, and to trace her affects to their real but unconscious object. On the completion of the period set I discharged her uncured. She herself was quite content with her improvement.

Many months later she returned in a quite desolate condition; her earlier troubles were returning with all the old violence. I yielded to her request and again undertook the treatment. After a short time, as soon as the degree of improvement previously attained was once more established, she began the old game again. This time extraneous circumstances interrupted the treatment, which again remained incomplete.

A fresh exacerbation and the disappearance of the extraneous difficulties brought her to me for the third time. This time, too, we made no progress for a long time.

In the course of her inexhaustibly repeated love phantasies, which were always concerned with the doctor, she often made the remark, as though by the way, that this gave her feelings ' down there '. That is, she had erotic genital sensations. But only after all this time did an accidental glance at the manner in which she lay on the sofa convince me that she kept her legs crossed during the whole hour. This led us —not for the first time—to the subject of onanism, an act performed by girls and women for preference by pressing the thighs together. As on former occasions, she denied most emphatically ever having carried out such practices.

I must confess—and this is characteristic of the slowness with which an incipient new point of view irrupts into consciousness—that even then it was a long time before I hit on the idea of forbidding the patient to adopt this position. I explained to her that in so doing she was carrying out a larval form of onanism that discharged unnoticed the unconscious impulses and allowed only useless fragments to reach the material of her ideas.

I can describe the effect of this measure as nothing less than staggering. The patient, to whom the customary genital discharge was forbidden, was tormented during the interviews by an almost insupportable bodily and psychic restlessness; she could no longer lie at peace, but had constantly to change her position. Her phantasies resembled the deliria of fever, in which there cropped up long forgotten memory fragments that gradually grouped themselves round certain events in her childhood and permitted the discovery of most important traumatic causes for her illness.

The consequent impetus towards improvement certainly brought about distinct progress, but the patient—although she conscientiously carried out the above rule—seemed to reconcile herself to this form of abstinence and settled down to this stage of knowledge. In other words, she again ceased to exert herself, and took refuge in the sanctuary of the transference love.

Having had my wits sharpened by these previous experiences, however, I could now rout out the hiding-places in which she concealed her auto-erotic satisfaction. It appeared that she did, indeed, carry out the prescribed behaviour *during the hours of analysis*, but constantly transgressed it during the rest of the day. We learned that she knew how to *eroticise* most of her housewifely and maternal activities by pressing her legs together inconspicuously and unconsciously to herself; naturally she lost herself at the same time in unconscious phantasies which thus protected her from becoming aware of her activities. When the restraint was extended to include the whole day there was another but not even yet definitive improvement.

The Latin phrase, *naturam expellas furca, tamen ista recurrat*, seemed to be justified in this case.

I noticed frequently in the course of the analysis certain 'symptomatic acts', such as playful squeezing and handling of the most varied parts of the body. After the complete interdiction without any exception of the larval onanism, these symptomatic acts became *masturbation equivalents*. By this I understand apparently harmless stimulations of indifferent parts of the body which are, however, qualitatively and quantitatively substitutes for genital erogenicity. In this case the shutting off of the libido from any other path of discharge was so complete that from time to time it was increased to an actual orgasm at other indifferent parts of the body that are not by nature prominent erotogenic zones.

It was only the impression caused by this experience that enabled the patient to credit my assertion that she was wasting her whole sexuality in those little 'naughtinesses', and to consent for the sake of the treatment to forgo also these gratifications that she had practised since childhood. The annoyance she thus caused herself was great, but well worth while. All abnormal channels of discharge being closed to it, her sexuality found of itself, without any assistance, the way back to its normally indicated genital zone, from which it had been repressed at a certain time in development, as though exiled from its home to foreign countries.

This repatriation was hindered a little by the opposition of a temporary return of an obsessional neurosis experienced in childhood; this, however, was easily translated and easily understood by the patient.

The last stage was the appearance at unseasonable times of a *need to urinate*; the gratification of this was equally interdicted. One day she surprised me with the information that she had experienced so violent a stimulation of the genitals that she could not forbear rubbing the vaginal mucous membrane forcibly in order to get some relief. Though she could not immediately accept my explanation that this confirmed my assertion that she had passed through an infantile period of active masturbation, nevertheless she soon adduced ideas and dreams that did convince her. This masturbatory relapse, however, did not last long. Parallel with the reconstruction of her infantile defence reaction, she achieved, after all these worries, the capacity of obtaining satisfaction in normal sexual intercourse, which—although her husband was unusually potent and had begotten many children by her—had hitherto been denied her. At the same time many of the as yet unsolved hysterical symptoms found their explanation in the now manifest genital phantasies and memories.

From this extremely complicated analysis I have endeavoured to select only what was of technical interest, and to describe the manner in which I came upon the definition of a new rule in analysis. This runs as follows: during treatment one must also think of the possibility of larval onanism and onanistic equivalents, and, where indications of these are observed, abolish them. These apparently harmless activities can easily become hiding-places for the libido which has been driven away from its unconscious excitations by the analysis, and in extreme cases may replace an individual's whole sexual activity. Should the patient notice that these possibilities of satisfaction escape the analyst, he attaches all his pathogenic phantasies to them, short-circuits them constantly by motor discharge, and thus saves himself the irksome and unpleasant task of bringing them to consciousness.

This technical rule has since stood me in good stead in several cases. Long-standing resistances against the continuation of the treatment have been brought to an end by its means.

Observant readers of psycho-analytic literature will perhaps detect a contradiction here between this technical measure and the opinion of many psycho-analysts about onanism.[1]

The patients, too, with whom I had to employ this technique did not omit to object—'you stated', said they, 'that onanism is not dangerous, and now you forbid it me'.

[1] 'Über Onanie'. A discussion in the Vienna Psycho-analytic Society. [Translated in *Contributions to Psycho-Analysis*, chap. vi.]

The solution of this contradiction is not difficult. We do not need to alter anything in our opinion of the relative harmlessness, for instance, of the onanism of necessity, and yet maintain the demand for this kind of abstinence. We are here not concerned with a generalization about self-gratification, but with a provisory measure for the purposes and the duration of the psycho-analytic treatment. Besides, a treatment that has been successfully concluded enables many patients to give up this infantile or juvenile form of satisfaction.

Not all, however. Cases do even occur in which the patients during treatment, yield—for the first time in their lives as they say—to the need for masturbatory gratification and date the beginning of the favourable change in their libidinal attitude from this 'courageous deed'.

This last, however, can only hold for manifest onanism with a conscious erotic phantasy, not for the numerous forms of 'larval' onanism and its equivalents. These are to be regarded as pathological from the first, and in any case require to be cleared up by analysis. This is only to be obtained at the price of at least a temporary resignation of the activity itself, by which means its excitement is directed along purely psychic paths and finally into consciousness. Once the patient has learnt to tolerate the consciousness of his onanist phantasies he may be allowed to deal with it himself again. In most instances he will only make use of it in case of necessity.

I take this opportunity of saying something further about larval and vicarious onanist activities. There are many otherwise not neurotic people, especially many neurasthenics, who are, so to say, almost life-long onanists unconsciously. If they are men they keep their hands in their trouser pockets all day, and it is noticeable, from the movements of their hands and fingers, that in doing this they pull, squeeze, or rub the penis. They have 'nothing bad' in their thoughts at the time; on the contrary, they are perhaps sunk in profound mathematical, philosophical, or business speculations.

In my opinion, however, this 'profundity' must not

be taken too seriously. These problems certainly arrest their whole attention, but the real depths of the soul life—the unconscious ones—are meanwhile occupied with pure erotic phantasies and procure satisfaction by a short (as it were somnambulistic) path.

Others substitute for the burrowing in the trouser pockets a clonic quiver of the calf muscles, often very annoying to their companions, while women, whose manner of dress as well as sense of decorum forbids such noticeable movements, press their legs together or cross them. They like to create such unconscious 'secondary gain of pleasure', particularly while occupied with absorbing needlework.

Apart from the psychic consequences, this unconscious onanism cannot be held to be quite innocuous. Although or, indeed, because it never issues in full orgasm, but always only in frustrated excitement, it can play a part in the development of an anxiety neurosis. I know cases, however, where this continual excitement is accompanied by very frequent even if minimal orgasms (in men by prostatorrhœa also), and ultimately makes these people neurasthenic and diminishes their potency. Normal potency is only possessed by those who preserve and store up the libidinal impulses for a considerable latent period, and who can discharge them powerfully along genital channels on the occurrence of suitable sexual aims and objects. Constant squandering of small quantities of libido destroys this capacity. (This does not hold in the same degree for conscious, intentional, periodic masturbation.)

A second consideration, which seems to contradict the views previously stated, is the conception of *symptomatic acts*. We learnt from Freud that these manifestations of the psychopathology of everyday life are of use in the treatment as indications of phantasies which are repressed and therefore significant, but otherwise entirely innocuous. Now we see that they too can be intensively charged with libido displaced from other situations, and become onanism equivalents and no longer harmless. Transition stages are here discoverable between symptomatic acts and certain forms of *tic convulsif*, of which as yet we possess no psycho-analytic explanation.[1] My expectation is that on analysis many of these tics will blossom forth as stereotyped onanistic equivalents. The remarkable association of *tics* with *coprolalia* (for instance on the suppression of motor manifestations) would then be nothing else but the irruption of the erotic phantasies (mostly anal-sadistic) symbolized by the tics into the preconscious, with a spasmodic excitation of the corresponding word memory traces. Coprolalia would then owe its origin to a mechanism similar to the technique employed above which allows certain impulses, hitherto led off in onanistic equivalents, to break through into consciousness.

But after this digression into hygiene and nosology, let us return to the much more interesting technical and psychological considerations raised by the case recounted in the introduction.

I was compelled in this case to give up the passive part that the psycho-analyst is accustomed to play in the treatment, which is confined to the hearing and interpretation of the patient's ideas, and had by active interference in the patient's psychic activities to help over dead points in the work of the analysis.

We owe the prototype of this 'active technique' to Freud himself. In the analysis of anxiety hysterias on the occurrence of a similar stagnation—he had recourse to the method of directing the patients to seek just those critical situations which usually caused them an attack of anxiety; not with the idea of 'accustoming' them to these situations, but in order to free the wrongly anchored affects from their connections. We expect from this measure that the unsatisfied valencies of these free floating affects will above all attract to themselves their qualitatively adequate and historically correlated ideas. Here too we find, as in our case, the ligature of customary, unconscious paths of discharge of excitation and the enforcement of the preconscious cathexis and the conscious hyper-cathexis of the repressed material.

Since our knowledge of transference and of 'active technique' we are able to say that besides observation and

[1] [See Chap. XII. in this volume.—Ed.]

logical deduction (interpretation) psycho-analysis has also at command the method of experiment. Just as in experiments on animals the blood pressure in distant parts can be raised by the ligature of large arterial vessels, so in suitable cases we can and must shut off psychic excitement from unconscious paths of discharge, in order by this 'rise of pressure' of energy to overcome the resistance of the censorship and of the 'resting excitation' by higher psychic systems.

In psycho-analysis as distinguished from suggestion no influence is exercised over the new direction of the current, and we gladly let ourselves be surprised by the unexpected turns taken by the analysis.

This kind of 'experimental psychology' is adapted as is nothing else to convince us of the correctness of Freud's psycho-analytic doctrine of the neuroses and of the validity of the psychology constructed upon it and upon the interpretation of dreams. At the same time we learn the peculiar value of Freud's assumption of the *psychic 'instances'*[1] and become accustomed to deal with *psychic quantities* just as with other energy masses.

An example like the one described here shows anew that in hysteria it is not common 'psychic energies' but libidinal or, more exactly, genital impulses that are at work, and that the formation of symptoms ceases when one succeeds in re-directing the abnormally employed libido to the genitals.

[1] [The term 'instance', in German '*Instanz*', was originally a legal term, cf. 'court of first instance', and is used in psycho-analysis, as in law, in the sense of one of a hierarchy of functions or authorities.—J. R.]

XVI

THE FURTHER DEVELOPMENT OF AN ACTIVE THERAPY IN PSYCHO-ANALYSIS[1]

(An address delivered at the Sixth International Congress of Psycho-Analysis at The Hague on the 10th September 1920)

I

THE fundamentals of psycho-analytic technique have undergone little essential alteration since the introduction of Freud's 'fundamental rule' (free association). That my proposals do not aim at this either, I would emphasize at the beginning; on the contrary, their intention was and is to enable the patient, by means of certain artifices, to comply more successfully with the rule of free association and thereby to assist or hasten the exploring of the unconscious material. Besides, these artifices are only required in certain exceptional cases; for most patients the treatment can be carried out without any special 'activity' on the part of either doctor or patient, and even in those cases in which one has to proceed more actively the interference should be restricted as much as possible. As soon as the stagnation of the analysis, the only justification for and the only motive of the modification, is overcome, the expert will immediately resume the passively receptive attitude most favourable for the efficient co-operation of the doctor's unconscious.

Like almost every innovation, 'activity' on closer inspection is found to be an old acquaintance. Not only has it played an important part already in the early history of psycho-analysis; it has in a certain sense never ceased to exist. We are dealing here, therefore, with the formulation of a conception and of a technical expression for something which, even if unexpressed, has always *de facto* been in use.

[1] *Zeitschrift*, 1921, Bd. VII. 233

Nevertheless I consider such a definition and terminological fixation as not unimportant from a scientific point of view; only by this means does one become conscious in the true sense of the word of one's own actions, and only by its becoming conscious is the methodical, critical, and selective practice of a method of procedure rendered possible.[1]

The period of the Breuer-Freud *cathartic* procedure represented a phase of marked activity on the part of the doctor as well as on that of the patient. The doctor made the greatest efforts to revive the memories relating to the symptoms and made use of every assistance that the procedures of waking or hypnotic suggestion put at his disposal. The patient, too, made every endeavour to follow the directions of his guide, and had therefore to engage in marked psychic activities, had often indeed to exercise all his intellectual faculties.

Psycho-analysis, as we employ it to-day, is a procedure whose most prominent characteristic is *passivity*. We ask the patient to allow himself to be guided uncritically by his 'ideas'; he has nothing to do but to impart these ideas without reserve—of course after overcoming the inner resistances that struggle against this. The doctor should not fix his attention rigidly on any particular intention (for instance on the desire to cure or to understand), but should also yield himself passively to the play of his phantasy with the patient's ideas. Of course, if he is to influence the patient's further ideas, he cannot continue this phantasying indefinitely; as I have explained elsewhere,[2] as soon as he has been able to crystallize certain really valid opinions, he must direct his attention to them and on mature reflection must decide upon an *interpretation*. Communicating such an interpretation is, however, in itself an active interference with the patient's psychic activity; it turns the thoughts in a given direction and facilitates the appearance of ideas that otherwise would have been prevented by the resistance from

[1] The significance of bestowing names in scientific matters deserves a psychological research of its own.

[2] 'On the Technique of Psycho-Analysis'. See p. 177.

becoming conscious. The patient must comport himself passively during this 'midwifery of thought'.

More recent knowledge of the decisive significance which the distribution of the libido has for the formation of neurotic symptoms helped Freud to another method of procedure.[1] He distinguishes two phases in the therapy; in the first all the libido is forced from the symptoms into the transference; in the second the struggle with the libido that has been transferred to the doctor is dealt with, and the attempt is made to free it from its new object. This setting free of the libido is rendered possible by the alteration of the ego under the influence of education by the doctor. Of course, by the forcing of the libido into the transference an active encouragement of this tendency on the doctor's part is not meant; the transference occurs spontaneously; the doctor needs only the skill not to disturb this process.

The education of the ego, on the other hand, is distinctly an active interference of which the doctor is capable because of the authority which has been heightened by the transference. Freud does not evade calling this kind of influence 'suggestion', but indicates the essential characteristics that distinguish this from non-psycho-analytic suggestion.[2]

This influencing of the patient is certainly an active thing, the patient behaving passively towards this endeavour on the part of the doctor.

In what has been said so far, the passive and active conduct respectively referred exclusively to the patient's *psychic attitude*. Analysis demands no *activities* from the patient except punctual appearance at the hours of treatment; except for this no influence is exercised on the

[1] Freud, *Vorlesungen zur Einführung in die Psychoanalyse* (III. Teil. Allg. Neurosenlehre, S. 534 u. ff.) [Translated, *Introductory Lectures on Psycho-Analysis*.]

[2] Earlier suggestion generally consisted in persuading the patient of a conscious untruth. ('There is nothing the matter with you'—which is certainly not true, as the patient is suffering from the neurosis.) Psycho-analytic suggestion employs the transference to make one's own conviction of the unconscious motives of the illness accessible to the patient; the psycho-analyst himself must have a care that the belief so accepted is no 'blind belief' but the patient's own conviction, based on memory and actual experience ('repetition'). This also distinguishes psycho-analysis from the persuasion and explanation treatment of Dubois.

general mode of life: indeed it is expressly emphasized that the patient must deal with important decisions himself or they must be deferred till the power of making decisions is attained. The first exception to this rule occurred in the analysis of certain cases of *anxiety hysteria*; it happened that the patients, in spite of close compliance with the 'fundamental rule' and in spite of a deep insight into their unconscious complexes, could not get beyond 'dead points' in the analysis until they were compelled to venture out from the retreat of their phobia, and to expose themselves experimentally to the situation they had avoided because of its painfulness. As was to be expected, this brought with it an acute exacerbation of the anxiety, but, in exposing themselves to this affect, they at the same time overcame the resistance to hitherto repressed material that now became accessible to analysis in the form of ideas and reminiscences.[1]

I really meant that the description of 'active technique' should be applied to this proceeding, which does not so much represent an active interference on the part of the doctor as on the part of the patient upon whom are imposed certain tasks besides the keeping of the fundamental rule. In the cases of phobia the task consisted in the carrying out of painful activities.

I soon had the opportunity to apportion to a patient tasks that consisted in her *renunciation* of certain hitherto unnoticed *pleasurable activities* (onanistic stimulation of the genitals, stereotypies, and tic-like twitchings or stimulation of other parts of the body), and in the control of the impulse to such activities. The result was that new memories became accessible and the progress of the analysis was visibly accelerated.

The inference from this and similar experiences has been drawn *by Professor Freud in his Address to the Congress at Budapest.*[2] He was even able to generalize the theory

[1] Compare 'Technical Difficulties in the Analysis of a Case of Hysteria', pp. 189-198 of this book. A verbal statement of Freud's gave me the indication for this proceeding.

[2] 'Turnings in the Ways of Psycho-Analytic Therapy'. Freud's *Collected Papers*, vol. ii. 392.

obtained from these observations, and to lay down the rule that, in general, the treatment must be carried out in a condition of *abstinence*; the same renunciation that led to the symptom formation must be preserved throughout the whole treatment as the motive for the desire to get well; it is even useful to deny just *that* satisfaction which the patient most intensely desires.

In what I have just said I believe I have mentioned everything essential that has so far been published about activity in psycho-analytic technique, and everything in the generally recognized methods that can be designated as 'activity'.

II

I should now like to give excerpts from some analyses calculated to substantiate what has been said, and to deepen to some extent our insight into the play of forces at work in 'active technique'. The case of a young Croatian woman, a musician, who suffered from a host of phobias and obsessional states, occurs to me at once. I shall mention only a few of her endless symptoms. She suffered torments of stage fright; if she was asked to play in front of others at the music school, she became scarlet in the face; finger exercises, which when she was alone she readily performed automatically without any effort, seemed to her prodigiously difficult; she made mistakes on every occasion and had the obsessive idea that she *must* disgrace herself, which she accordingly did pretty thoroughly in spite of her unusual talent. In the street she believed herself constantly observed because of her too voluminous breasts, and did not know how to hold or conduct herself in order to conceal this (imagined) bodily deformity. Now she would fold her arms across her chest, now compress the breasts tightly against the thorax; but, as is customary with obsessional patients, each precaution was followed by the doubt whether she were not by these very means attracting attention to herself. Her behaviour in the street was now excessively shy, now provocative;

she was unhappy if in spite of her marked beauty no attention was paid her, but was no less disconcerted when actually spoken to by someone who misunderstood (or, rather, correctly interpreted) her behaviour. She was afraid that she had an offensive breath and went constantly to the dentist and the laryngologist, who naturally could discover nothing the matter. She came after an analysis of many months' duration to me (as the colleague concerned had been obliged to break off the treatment), and was already well initiated into her unconscious complexes; on continuing her treatment, however, I had to endorse the observation of my colleague that the progress of the cure had no relation to the depth of her theoretic insight and to the memories already laid bare. Things went on with me in the same way for weeks. At one interview a street song occurred to her that her elder sister (who tyrannized over her in every way) was in the habit of singing. After hesitating for a long time she repeated the very ambiguous text of the song and was silent for a long time; I extracted from her that she had thought of the *melody* of the song. I did not delay in asking her to sing the song. It took nearly two hours, however, before she could bring herself to perform the song as she really intended it. She was so embarrassed that she broke off repeatedly in the middle of a verse, and to begin with she sang in a low uncertain voice until, encouraged by my persuasions, she began to sing louder, when her voice developed more and more and proved to be an unusually beautiful soprano. This did not overcome the resistance; after some difficulty she confessed that her sister was in the habit of accompanying the song with expressive and indeed quite unambiguous *gestures*, and she made some clumsy arm movements to illustrate her sister's behaviour. Finally I asked her to get up and repeat the song *exactly* as she had seen her sister do it. After endless spiritless partial attempts she showed herself to be a perfect *chanteuse*, with all the coquetry of facial play and movement that she had seen in her sister. From now on she seemed to take pleasure in these productions and began to fritter away the hours of analysis with such things. When I noticed this, I told her we knew now that she enjoyed displaying her various talents and that behind her modesty lay hidden a considerable desire to please; it was no longer a matter of dancing but of getting on with the work. It was astonishing how favourably this little interlude affected the work. Presently memories of her early childhood, of which she had never spoken, occurred to her, memories of the time when the birth of a little brother had had a really unholy effect on her psychic development and had made of her an anxious, shy, and abnormally good child. She remembered the time when she was still 'a little devil', the darling of all her family and friends, when she displayed all her talents before people and generally showed an unrestrained pleasure in muscular movement.

I followed up this active measure and constrained the patient to carry out activities of which she had the greatest fear. She conducted in front of me (while at the same time she imitated the sounds of an orchestra) a long phrase from a symphony; the analysis of this notion led to the discovery of the penis jealousy by which she had been tormented since the birth of her brother. She played to me the difficult piano piece that she had to play at the examination; it was shown soon afterwards in the analysis that her fear of disgracing herself when playing the piano referred back to onanistic phantasies and onanistic disgrace (forbidden 'finger exercises'). She did not dare to go to the swimming-baths on account of her idea that her breasts were disproportionately large; only after she had overcome the resistance on my insisting was she able to convince herself during analysis of her latent desire to exhibit. Now that the approach to her most hidden tendencies was opened up, she acknowledged that during the analytic hour she occupied herself a great deal with her sphincter ani; sometimes she would play with the idea of passing flatus, sometimes contract the sphincter rhythmically, and so on.

As with every technical rule, the patient then tried to reduce activity to absurdity by exaggerating the tasks allotted her. I let her be for a time and then bade her give up these games, and after a not too prolonged labour we came upon the anal-erotic explanation of her anxiety that her mouth smelt offensively; soon after the reproduction of the associated infantile memories, while maintaining the prohibition against anal play, this showed marked improvement.

We owed the most marked impulse towards betterment to the patient's *unconscious onanism* which was rendered manifest by the help of 'activity'. Sitting at the piano she experienced, on every more vehement or passionate movement, a voluptuous sensation of the genital parts stimulated by the movement. She had to acknowledge these sensations to herself after she had been bidden to behave, as she saw many artists do, very passionately at the piano; but so soon as she began to take pleasure in this play she had on my advice to give it up. As a result we were then able to take cognisance of reminiscences and reconstructions of infantile genital play, the chief source perhaps of her exaggerated sense of shame.

It is time now to consider what exactly we were doing by these interferences, and to attempt a formulation of the play of psychic forces to which we owed the undeniable progress of the analysis. In this case our activity may be divided into two phases. In the first, the patient, who guarded herself from certain activities by a phobia, had to be commanded to carry out those activities, contrary to inclination; after the hitherto repressed tendencies had become pleasurable, she had in the second place to deny herself, that is, certain activities were *forbidden*. The commands had the result of rendering *fully conscious* inclinations hitherto repressed, or only manifested as unrecognizable rudiments, and ultimately rendering them *conscious as desires*, as ideas agreeable to herself. Then when the satisfaction of the now pleasurable activity was denied her, the psychic impulse once roused found the way to long repressed material, to infantile reminiscences, or they had to be interpreted as repetitions of something infantile, and the peculiarities and conditions of the childish procedures had to be reconstructed by the analyst with the help of the other analytic material (dreams, fancies, etc.). It was easy for the patient to accept such reconstruction as she could deny neither to herself nor to the doctor that she had recently actually *experienced* these activities and their accompanying affects. Thus the 'active therapy', hitherto regarded as a single entity, breaks up into the systematic issuing and carrying out of *commands* and of *prohibitions*, Freud's 'attitude of renunciation' being constantly maintained. I have already had occasion in a number of cases to make use of this measure, and not only (as in the case described) by the activation and control of sexual and erotic tendencies, but also of highly sublimated activities. Following certain hints, I constrained a patient who—apart from naïve attempts during adolescence—never wrote poetry, to put her poetical notions on paper. In this way she managed not only to unfold an unusual degree of poetic talent, but also the whole content of her—till then—latent longing for masculine productivity in general, which was connected with her predominantly clitoric eroticism and her sexual anæsthesia for men.

In the period of interdiction, however, during which literary work was forbidden her, it became evident that in her case we were dealing rather with a misuse than a use of a talent. Her whole 'masculinity complex' proved to be a secondary affair, the result of a genital trauma suffered in childhood that had turned her character—till then thoroughly feminine and yielding—in the direction of auto-eroticism and homosexuality by rendering heterosexuality disagreeable to her. The discoveries made during analysis enabled the patient to estimate her real penchant correctly; she is aware now that she usually seizes her pen when she fears that she cannot function fully as a woman. This analytic experience has assisted not a little in the return of the normal feminine capacity for gratification.

When the patient is 'active' from the beginning without being so commanded, when he masturbates, carries out obsessive and symptomatic acts and 'transitory symptoms' then naturally the first, 'the command period', falls out of itself, and the patient's task narrows itself to discontinuing such activities meantime for the purpose of furthering the analysis. (Of course, these little symptoms are often only rudiments of the latent tendencies, and the patient has first to be encouraged to develop them fully.) Among symptoms that have appeared and have been forbidden in the course of treatment I would mention the need of urination immediately before or after the analytic session, a feeling of sickness during the session, unseemly wriggling, plucking at and stroking the face, the hands, or other parts of the body, the playing with the sphincter already referred to, the pressing together of the thighs and so on. For instance, I noticed with one patient that, as soon as the contents of the association began to be uncomfortable or painful for him, instead of continuing the work he manifested affects, screamed, wriggled, and generally behaved in an unseemly fashion. Of course, it was the resistance against the analytic material already disturbed that caused this; he wanted literally to 'shake off' the painful thoughts.[1]

In seeming contradiction to the fundamental rule of analysis I had in a few cases to decide to encourage or discourage patients directly towards or against the production of *thoughts* and phantasies. I have in this way induced patients to carry out this plan who threatened to deceive me, for instance, to feign dreams. But where I became aware of the 'misuse of the freedom of association'[2] by means of misleading, futile, and side-tracking ideas or phantasies, I did not hesitate to show the patient that by this he was only trying to escape the more difficult task, and to bid him resume the interrupted train of thought. These were just cases in which the patients wished to avoid what touched them closely but painfully, by means of the so-called 'talking past' (Ganser)—one might rather say *thinking past*. This directing of the course of association, this hindering and furtherance of thought and phantasy, is certainly also an activity in the sense of the word employed here.

[1] The tics and so-called stereotypies require special consideration, which I have attempted in another paper. [*Internl. J. of Psycho-Analysis*, vol. ii. p. 19. Given also in Chap. XII. of this book.]

[2] 'On the Technique of Psycho-Analysis', pp. 177-183.

III

Little of general applicability can be said about the *indications* for activity; here, if anywhere, one must proceed on individual lines. The main thing about this technical auxiliary is, and remains, the utmost economy of its employment; it is only a makeshift, a pedagogic supplement, to the real analysis whose place it must never pretend to take. On another occasion I have compared such measures to obstetric forceps that also should only be used in extreme need and whose unnecessary employment is rightly condemned by medical art. Beginners, or analysts of no great experience, do better generally to refrain from it as long as possible, not only because they may easily mislead the patient by it (or are misled by them), but also because they easily lose in this way their only opportunity of obtaining the criteria and proofs of the dynamics of the neuroses, which are only to be gathered from the behaviour of the patient who is under no external control and subjected solely to the 'fundamental rule'.

I instance only a few of the many *contra-indications*. Such technical artifices are bad at the beginning of an analysis. Habituation to the fundamental rule affords the patient quite sufficient occupation, and at the beginning, too, the doctor must conduct himself with all possible reserve and passivity in order not to disturb the patient's spontaneous attempts at transference. Later during the actual course of the treatment, according to the nature of the case, activity may more or less frequently be of use or even unavoidable. Of course, the analyst must know that such an experiment is a two-edged sword; he must also have certain indications of the *powers of endurance of the transference* before he determines on it. Activity always works, as we have been, 'against the grain', that is against the pleasure principle. If the transference is weak, that is if the treatment has not yet become an obsession (Freud) for the patient, he easily makes use of the new and irksome task to free himself entirely from the doctor and to escape from the treatment. This is the explanation of the failure of 'wild psycho-analysts' who usually proceed too actively and masterfully and thus frighten away their clients. The conditions are different towards the end of an analysis. The doctor now need feel no anxiety lest his patient should run away; usually he has rather to combat the patient's attempt to carry on the treatment indefinitely, that is, to cling to the treatment instead of to reality. 'The end-game'[1] of the analysis is seldom successful without active interferences or tasks respectively that the patient must perform beyond the exact adherence to the fundamental rule. As such I would mention: the setting of a term to the conclusion of the treatment, the constraining to an already formed decision which has been postponed owing to resistance, the performance now and then of some particular sacrifice prescribed by the doctor, of a charitable or other alms. Sometimes after an at first compulsory and unwilling performance on the part of the patient, one is presented (as for example in Freud's case of 'Infantile Neurosis'[2]) with his final explanations and reminiscences as a parting gift, and not infrequently at the same time with an often small but symbolically significant present that is really donated by the patient in these cases and not 'solved' as at other times during the analysis.

Indeed there is no kind of neurosis in which activity might not be employed. I have already said of obsessive acts and anxiety-hysteria phobias, that one seldom manages without this technique. It is rarely necessary in true conversion hysteria, but I remember a case that I once treated in a similar fashion many years ago, without knowing that I was employing an active therapy. I will report the case briefly.

A man of bucolic appearance visited my consulting room at the worker's polyclinic, complaining of attacks of loss of consciousness. I considered his attacks to be hysterical and took him to my house to examine him more closely. He told me a long-winded family history of trouble

[1] [The author uses a term employed in chess.—TRANS.]

[2] [*Gesammelte Schriften*, Bd. VIII. *Collected Papers*, vol. iii.]

with his father, a well-doing farmer, who would have nothing to do with him on account of his unsuitable marriage, so that he 'had to work as a canal cleaner, while . . .' At these words he became pale, swayed and would have fallen, had I not caught him. He seemed to have lost consciousness and muttered incomprehensible stuff. I did not let myself be misled, however, shook him quite severely, repeated the sentence he had begun, and demanded forcibly that he should finish his sentence. He then said in a feeble voice that he had to work as a canal cleaner while his younger brother saw to the tillage; he would see him walking behind the plough with its span of six beautiful oxen and then going home after work was done and having his meals with his father, etc. He was going to faint a second time, too, when he spoke of the dissension between his wife and his mother; I forced him, however, to tell this to an end also. In a word, this man had the knack of hysterical fainting which he did whenever he wanted to escape from the unhappy reality into the beautiful world of phantasy, or from too painful trains of thought. The 'actively' compelled, conscious thinking out of the hysterical phantasies to their completion affected the patient like a miraculous cure; he could not get over his astonishment that I could cure him thus 'without medicine'. Sokolnicka[1] recently reported an hysterical attack, in a child suffering from an obsessional neurosis, which was similarly influenced by activity. She also suggested the very valuable idea that one should try to get at the symptoms that are in the service of the secondary 'gain of illness' by pedagogic means.

I take this opportunity to mention Simmel's analyses of traumatic war hysterias[2] in which the duration of treatment was appreciably shortened by active interference, and the experiences Hollós communicated to me orally in Budapest of the active treatment of catatonics. The *neuroses of children* and *mental illnesses* in general should offer a fruitful field for the employment of pedagogic and other

[1] 'Analyse einer infantilen Zwangsneurose', *Zeitschrift*, Bd. VI. S. 228.

[2] [Translated in 'Psycho-Analysis and the War Neuroses', Intnl. Psy.-An. Library, vol. ii.]

activity, but it must not be forgotten that such activity can only be described as a psycho-analytic one when it is used, not as an end in itself, but as an aid to the exploration of the depths.

IV

I myself have repeatedly been in the position of repudiating unmotivated, and in my opinion superfluous, or, indeed, quite misleading proposals for the modification of psycho-analytic technique. If I now advance some new proposals myself, then I must either withdraw my previously declared conservative views, or must show that these proposals are reconcilable with my earlier utterances. I am also prepared that my opponents of those days will not let slip the opportunity to tax me with inconsistency. I recall my criticisms of the technical proposals of Bjerre, Jung, and Adler.

Bjerre suggested that one should not be content in analysis with the discovery of the pathogenic sources, but should also undertake the patient's spiritual and ethical guidance. Jung wanted the psycho-therapeutics to lead the patient's attention away from the past—and to direct it towards the actual duties of life; Adler said that one had to concern oneself not with the analysis of the libido, but of the 'nervous character'. My present proposals show some analogy with these modifications, but the differences are far too striking to escape objective judgement.

The instructions that I propose to give the patient—and only, as stated, in certain exceptional cases—are not in the least concerned with the practical or spiritual conduct of life in general; they relate only to certain particular dealings, they are not *a priori* directed to morality, but only against the pleasure principle; they hinder the erotic tendencies (the non-moral) only in so far as it is hoped they will thereby remove an obstacle to practicable analysis.

It may just as well happen, however, that one tolerates, or even encourages, an erotic tendency that the patient has guarded against. An examination of character is never put in the foreground of our technique, for it does not play here the striking part it does for Adler; instead it is only touched on when certain abnormal traits comparable to the psychoses disturb the normal course of the analysis.

It might be objected that the 'active technique' is a return to the banal suggestion or cathartic—abreaction therapy. The answer to that would be that we certainly do not employ suggestion in the old sense, as we only prescribe certain lines of behaviour and do not foretell the result of the activity, do not, indeed, even know it ourselves. In requiring what is inhibited, and inhibiting what is uninhibited, we hope for a fresh distribution of the patient's psychic, primarily of his libidinal, energy that will further the laying bare of repressed material. What, however, this material will be we tell the patient all the less as we gladly let it take us ourselves by surprise. Finally, we neither promise ourselves nor the patient an immediate 'betterment'. On the contrary, the provoking of an opposition by activity disturbs to no small degree the comfortable but torpid quiet of a stagnating analysis. A suggestion, however, that only promises something so unpleasant differs not a little from the hitherto health-assuring medical suggestions and can hardly be any longer designated by the same name. Not less marked are the differences between 'activity' and the cathartic therapy. It was the task of catharsis to evoke reminiscences and to achieve the abreaction of inhibited affects by the awakening of memories. Active technique rouses certain activities in the patient, inhibitions, psychic discrepancies, or a discharge of affect, and expects *secondarily* the accessibility of the unconscious or of the memory material. In any event the activity roused in the patient is only means to the end; while the discharge of affect in catharsis was regarded as an end in itself. Where then the task of catharsis ends, the real work of the 'active' analyst only begins.

While, however, laying stress on the difference (to some extent the direct contradiction) between the methods and modifications just described, on the one hand, and active technique on the other, I do not deny that the uncritical employment of my proposals may easily lead to a distortion of analysis after the fashion of Jung, Adler, or Bjerre. One reason the more to employ these technical helps with the greatest care and only after a complete mastery of correct psycho-analysis.

In conclusion I should like to mention some conceptions by means of which I attempted to explain to myself the theory of the efficacy of active technique. Activity, in the sense described, chiefly effects an increase of the resistance, since it stimulates the ego sensibility. This causes an exacerbation of the symptoms due to the increased severity of the inner conflict. Active interference, therefore, recalls the stimulating treatments that are employed in medicine for certain torpid or chronic processes—a mucous catarrh that has become chronic proves refractory to any treatment—the acute exacerbation, however, brought about by artificial stimulation leads not only to the discovery of latent sources of disease, but also rouses the resisting powers of the organism that may be indispensable for the process of cure.

Quite another kind of theoretical consideration throws light upon the efficacy of active technique from the standpoint of psychic economy. When the patient gives up pleasurable activities or masters painful ones, there arise in him new states of psychic tension, most often increases of tension that disturb the peace of remote or deeply repressed psychic domains hitherto spared by the analysis, so that the derivatives from this—in the form of ideas that can be interpreted—find their way into consciousness.

The necessary shortening of the duration of treatment for external reasons, the numbers to be dealt with in the army and the polyclinics, etc., would suggest activity on a larger scale rather than the normal individual psycho-analysis. At any rate I can here draw attention from my own experience to two dangers. The one is that the patient as a result of such interferences is cured *too quickly* and therefore not completely.[1] For instance, I rapidly succeeded in encouraging an obsessional neurotic and phobic patient to seek out with

[1] Compare 'Discontinuierliche Analysen': [' Discontinuous Analyses ', page 233 of this book].

enjoyment all the situations that formerly she had anxiously avoided; from a timid creature who had always to be accompanied by her mother she became an unusually gay, independent lady who let herself be surrounded by a whole host of admirers. But it never came to the second, the renunciatory part of the active technique with her at all; I discharged her in the certain expectation that she would have to undergo the reverse of the active technique in a second analysis as soon as external difficulties had once more heightened the merely superficially resolved inner conflict to the pitch of symptom formation. The other danger is this: that as a result of stimulation of the resistances the treatment that was to have been shortened by the activity is much protracted, contrary to expectation.

Amongst the special indications for more active analysis I again mention cases of onanism, whose larval and often chameleon-like interchanging forms have consequently to be developed and inhibited, and this often occasions true onanistic activities for the first time. The unconcealed forms of onanism should be observed for a time till they have, so to say, developed themselves fully; one will probably never get hold of the unconscious (Oedipus) nucleus of the self-gratification phantasies without previous interdiction of the satisfaction itself.

In the treatment of impotence, too, the patient's attempts —mostly fruitless—are observed for a time without interference. In every case, however, these endeavours at self-cure must be forbidden at least for a period, and attempts at coitus dissuaded, until as a result of analysis the real libido with its unambiguous characteristics becomes apparent; cases certainly do occur in which one can carry out the treatment to a conclusion without any such influencing of the sexual capacity. It also happens that for the purpose of deepening the analysis sexual intercourse must temporarily be forbidden even subsequent upon the attainment of sexual capability. I have had to make a pretty extensive use of activity in the cases that might be called 'character analyses'. In a certain sense every analysis has to reckon with the patient's character when they are being gradually prepared to accept painful pieces of insight. There are cases, however, in which it is not so much neurotic symptoms but rather abnormal qualities of character that predominate. Qualities of character are distinguished from neurotic symptoms primarily in that with them, as in the psychoses, the 'insight into the illness' is lacking; they are as it were private psychoses endured, nay acknowledged, by the narcissistic ego, at any rate abnormalities of the ego whose modification is chiefly resisted by the ego itself. As we know from Freud, the patient's narcissism can limit the influence of analysis, especially as character is apt to form a wall of defence against the approach to infantile memories. If it is impossible, in Freud's phrase, to remove the patient into 'the seething heat of the transference love' in which even the most reserved qualities of character melt, then a last attempt may be made by the opposite method, and traits of character that are often only suggested may be stimulated by setting the patient unpleasant tasks, that is by activity, which will cause the former to be fully developed and reduced *ad absurdum.* That *this kind* of stimulation may easily lead to the breaking off of the analysis hardly needs to be mentioned, but if the dependence of the patient withstands this test then the effort of technique may be rewarded by the progress of the analysis.

In the cases so far dealt with the doctor's activity has consisted in his prescribing certain rules of conduct for the patients; that is he gets them to assist actively in the treatment by their behaviour. The question here principally concerned is whether the doctor is in the position to further the treatment *by his own behaviour in relation to the patient.* By compelling the patient to activity we are really showing him the path to self-education, which will facilitate the enduring of the material still repressed. The question now arises whether we may also employ the other pedagogical means of assistance, of which praise and blame are to be considered the most important.

Freud said once that in children analytic after-education is not to be separated from the actual lessons of pedagogy. Neurotics, however, have all—especially during analysis—

something childlike about them, and one has in fact sometimes to cool down a too impetuous transference by something of reserve, or to make some advances to the shy and by these means to establish the 'optimum temperature' of the relations between doctor and patient. The doctor must never, however, rouse expectations in the patient that he can or should not fulfil; he must answer for the sincerity of every statement till the end of the treatment. But within the limits of complete sincerity there is room for tactical measures as regards the patient. Once this 'optimum' is reached, one will naturally not occupy oneself further with this relationship but, as soon as possible, turn to the consideration of the main task of the analysis, the exploring of the unconscious and of the infantile material.

The efficacy of activity becomes partly understandable perhaps from the 'social' aspect of analytic therapy. How much more profoundly confession operates than self-acknowledgement, or being analysed than self-analysis, is a matter of general knowledge. The Hungarian sociologist Kolnai has just lately adequately acknowledged this effect. We aim, however, at a heightening of this effect when by our commands we constrain one or other patient not only to own deeply concealed impulses to himself, but to *enact them before the doctor*, and, by setting him the task of *consciously controlling* these impulses we have probably subjected the whole process to a revision that was despatched at some other time in a purposeless fashion by means of *repression*. It is certainly no accident that just infantile *naughtinesses* are so often developed during analysis and must then be given up.

The fact that the expressions of emotion or motor actions forced from the patients evoke secondarily memories from the unconscious rests partly on the reciprocity of affect and idea emphasized by Freud in *Traumdeutung*. The awakening of a memory can—as in catharsis—bring an emotional reaction with it, but an activity exacted from the patient, or an emotion set at freedom, can equally well expose the repressed ideas associated with such processes. Of course the doctor must have some notion about *which* affects or actions need reproducing. It is also possible that certain early infantile unconscious pathogenic psychic contents, which never were conscious (or preconscious) but which date from the period of 'unco-ordinated gestures or magical behaviour',[1] can not be simply remembered at all, but can only be reproduced by a re-living in the sense of Freud's repetition. In this, active technique only plays the part of *agent provocateur*; its commands and prohibitions assist in obtaining of repetitions that must then be interpreted or reconstructed respectively into memories. 'It is a triumph for the therapy', says Freud, 'when one succeeds in releasing by means of the memory what the patient would fain discharge in action.' Active technique desires nothing more and nothing less than to lay bare latent tendencies to repetition and by this means to assist the therapy to these triumphs a little oftener than hitherto.

XVII

CONTRA-INDICATIONS TO THE 'ACTIVE' PSYCHO-ANALYTICAL TECHNIQUE[2]

(*A paper read at the Ninth International Psycho-Analytical Congress at Bad Homburg, September* 1925)

The so-called 'active' technique which I attempted to present at the Hague Congress of our Association[3] in its main outlines, and to illustrate in later papers with examples,[4] met with a quite critical response from one group

[1] Compare 'Stages in the Development of a Sense of Reality', translated as chap. viii. of *Contributions to Psycho-Analysis*.

[2] Translated by John Rickman.

[3] (In 1920) 'Weiterer Ausbau der "aktiven Technik" in der Psychoanalyse', *Zeitschrift*, Bd. VII. 1921 (English translation, 'Further developments of the "active" technique'. See p. 198 of this book).

[4] 'Über forcierte Phantasien', *Zeitschrift*, X. 1924. (See p. 68) and 'Zur Psychoanalyse von Sexualgewohnheiten' ('Psycho-analysis of Sexual Habits'. See p. 261.)

of my colleagues, the response from another being friendly. One group of critics thought that psycho-analysis must take up arms against my innovations, asserting that in so far as they were acceptable they were not new but in so far as they transgressed the old established limits they were dangerous and therefore to be rejected. As you see, the arguments are the same as those which provided motives for burning the Alexandrian library.

I found that the extravagant praise of a few young persons troubled me more than these critics, for the former were ready to see in this 'activity' the dawn of a kind of psycho-analytical freedom. This they obviously understood to be no less than that it was no longer necessary to travel the hard road of the ever more complicated analytical theories—a courageous 'active' slash could loosen the most difficult therapeutic knot at a stroke. Now because I can look back over the experience of a number of years I believe the most useful purpose will be served if I renounce an all but sterile discussion with speculative opponents, and not troubling much about the unwelcome enthusiasm of particular adherents, put myself in the witness-box to indicate the weak points in the 'active technique'.

The first and perhaps most crucial objection that has appeared against my formulations is a theoretical one. Fundamentally it rests on a sin of omission. Obviously in order not to be done out of the pleasure of my discovery by difficult and therefore tedious psychological problems, I omitted in my expositions up to the present time to come to close grips with the relation between the increase of tension evoked by the technical device on the one hand and transference and resistance on the other.[1] I wish therefore so far as possible to repeat, and this time in unmistakable fashion, that 'activity' unquestionably stimulates the resistance of the patient in so far as it seeks to increase the psychical tension by painful frustrations, injunctions, and prohibitions, and so gain new material. That is to say, the ego of the patient runs counter to the analyst. This applies particularly to the old habits and character traits of

[1] I did so by allusion, however, in the paper at the Hague.

the patient, and I regard one of the duties of the active technique to be the inhibition and analytic dissection of these conditions. This statement is not only of theoretical importance; the important practical consequence follows that by omitting to observe it the success of the treatment may be endangered. Above all things, from this relation of the ego to frustration it follows that the analysis ought never to begin with active measures. On the contrary, for a long time the ego must be treated with forbearance or at least treated with circumspection, for otherwise no working positive transference will occur. Activity as a measure of frustration acts therefore as a disturbing or destroying agent of the transference; as such it is well-nigh inevitable at the end of treatment, and if applied in untimely fashion certainly disturbs the relation between physician and analysand. If handled with unrelenting force it drives the patient from the analyst as certainly as do the inconsiderate explanations of the 'wild analysts', which at once put the patient at enmity with his sexual expositions. This is not the same as saying that the activity is *only* to be applied as a means of eliminating the transference by disjunction, for it can do good service in the course of treatment if the transference-love is sufficiently tenacious; in every case a great deal of experience and practice is needed to estimate how much of it can be enjoined on the patient. It follows, once more, that the beginner should take care before he wanders from the tedious but instructive paths of the classical method to begin his career with the active technique. And there, to be sure, lies a great danger, which I have hinted at above several times. I have an impression that the analyst who is sure in his *knowledge* and is ready to take a chance on this method may make a part of the 'future prospects of psycho-analytic therapy'[1] which Freud hopes to see realized. In the hands of those who know less of the subject a reversion to the pre-analytic suggestive and enforcing method may very easily result from active technique.

I am not without justification in asserting that in the practice of the active measures there is besides the general

[1] See Freud's *Collected Papers*, vol. ii.

a special analytical qualification of competence required, though I do not think that this difficulty is insuperable. The so-called tuitional analysis gives a preference to activity (because it has sufficient opportunity and is indeed chiefly a character, that is, an Ego-analysis), so our younger men understand activity better and value it more correctly, but on the other hand they run the risk of over-valuing it.

Sincerity, however, bids me confess that in matters of activity even experience does not guard one completely from mistakes, and I must therefore tell you of the disappointments I have experienced. In particular cases I made an obvious mistake in estimating the time or the importance of the provocative measures, with the result that I was only able to keep the patient by making full acknowledgement of my mistake and after apparent loss of regard letting him disport his triumph over me. As a matter of fact this experience to some extent prejudiced the analysis, and I cannot help asking myself whether it was unconditionally necessary and should not have been avoided. I also saw at the end of this case that the demand of a greater activity from the patient is a *pium desiderium* so long as we are unable to give any clear indications for it. Provisionally I can only formulate these negatively and say that one should not employ activity if we cannot assert with a good conscience that all available methods of the not-active (the more passive) technique have been brought into use, the genetic details of the symptoms have been sufficiently 'worked through', and that only the throb of experience was lacking in order to convince the patient. It will indeed be a long time before we shall be in the position positively to formulate the indications for activity for every kind of neurosis separately.

Another series of difficulties arose from my putting forward certain injunctions and prohibitions far too strongly till I finally became convinced that these expressions themselves indicated a danger; they induce the physician forcibly to thrust his will upon the patient in an all too true repetition of the parent-child situation, or to permit the sadistic bearing of a schoolmaster. At length I gave up altogether either ordering or forbidding my patients to do things, but now rather attempt to gain their intellectual understanding of the projected measure and only then to put it into execution. In addition I no longer bind myself so firmly in arranging these procedures that I cannot retract them sooner or later if the difficulties are insuperable on the side of the patient. Our 'active' mandates must therefore not be too rigid, but, as one of the colleagues whom I analysed put it,—be of an elastic compliancy. If one does otherwise one formally induces the patient to misuse this technical device. The patient, particularly if he be an obsessional neurotic, will not fail to take the chance of making the injunctions given by the physician the subject of endless ruminations and idling away the time in over-conscientiousness in order among other things to anger the analyst. Only when they see that the physician does not regard the strict execution of the injunction as a *conditio sine qua non* does the patient not feel himself threatened with an unyielding compulsion, and then he complies with the intentions of the analyst; when it is a matter of analysing an obsessional neurotic to the satisfactory state where he regains the capacity to express his feelings and carry out acts without compulsion and ambivalence, the application in the analysis of a compulsion from without is the most unsuitable thing imaginable.

But the most important correction which I must make as a result of the experience of the last few years to the suggested 'active' measures concerns the setting of a limit to the analysis as a device for accelerating the ending of treatment. You know that this suggestion came from my friend Rank, and that I took it over from him without reserve as a result of a few surprising successes and recommended its general application in a book written jointly with him.[1] Recent experience compels me very fundamentally to restrict this generalization. The theory on which this technical aid was built up was the idea that in every analysis after working through the resistances and the pathogenic

[1] 'Entwicklungsziele der Psychoanalyse', by S. Ferenczi and Otto Rank (*Neue Arbeiten zur ärztl. Psa.* Heft 1, 1924). (To be published shortly in translation in the Mental and Nervous Disease Monograph Series.)

past sufficiently a stage is reached in which practically nothing else remains to be done but to detach the patient from the treatment and the analyst. In general that is correct, but what is exaggerated according to my present opinion is the second assertion which we put forward, namely, that this detachment always follows the shock of dismissal. The dismissal works brilliantly in particular cases; in others it misfires lamentably. It shows that even the experienced analyst can be misled in his impatience prematurely to regard the patient as ready for notice. But the beginner who lacks certainty in the judgement of the condition of readiness will sail far too easily into unseasonable vigour. I recall a particular case of severe agoraphobia in which after a year's analytic work I felt justified in speeding up the patient with 'active' aid, that is to say, to force the pace. This succeeded and in a quite remarkable manner advanced the analysis which had for a long time been stagnant. Encouraged by this and believing that the analytic material supported me, I thought the time had come to give him notice and set the fixed limit at six weeks at which I was going to end the treatment whatever happened. After overcoming a negative phase everything seemed to go well; then in the last week of treatment an unexpected relapse occurred in the symptoms which I hoped to overcome by a rigid adherence to the notice. But I was counting my chickens before they were hatched, acting, that is, without a correct judgement of the possible strangle-hold of the symptoms still existing—and so the fixed day for departure came without the patient being able to finish his treatment. There was nothing for me to do but to confess that my calculation was false, and it took me some time to dispel the bad impression of this incident under repeated hints of my ignorance. I learnt from this case not only that one must be extraordinarily cautious and only leave the beaten track on rare occasions, but also that one may only take on a mandate for this as for other 'activities' in agreement with the patient and with the possibility of retiring.

In the meantime Rank's views supported by his experience with giving notice to quit have turned into a theoretical extension of the theory of the neuroses. He found in the trauma of birth the biological basis of the neuroses generally and thought that in the process of cure this trauma must, under favourable conditions, be made to repeat itself and then be eliminated. In so far as this theory has coloured his technique in some measure it far exceeds what I wish to comprehend under the term 'activity'. As I have already explained elsewhere, the active technique if it is going to work at all and give satisfaction ought to bring about in the patient the psychical conditions under which repressed material comes forward more easily. I value the anxiety birth phantasies (which had no attention paid them before Rank pointed them out) so highly that I cannot simply regard them as a hiding-place for many painful birth and castration anxieties. As far as I can see, 'activity' has in no way to accommodate itself to this particular theory.

It is, of course, out of the question for one to set a limit to a patient who himself wants to force the analyst to do so, just as it is usually dangerous to give the patient even an approximate notion of the duration of the treatment. This is not only inadmissible because one estimate can be knocked to pieces by conditions which are ever deceptive (it is quite impossible for us to know in advance what difficulties we shall have to cope with in individual cases), but also because we put a dangerous weapon at the service of the patient's resistance by doing so. If the patient knows that he has only to persevere for a given time in order to be able to withdraw from the more painful features of the analysis and remain ill, this chance will certainly not be left unused, while the suspension of an analysis that is, so to speak, endless, will convince a patient sooner or later that our patience is greater than his, and this will finally induce him to give up his remaining resistances.

I shall take this opportunity to point out what appears to be a particularly crass misunderstanding regarding 'activity' which has become widespread. Freud, and I too, have always used the word 'active' only in the sense that the patient has to carry out tasks occasionally which are different from the mere narration of ideas; it was never intended that the activity of the physician should go beyond that of interpretation and the occasional setting of tasks. The analyst is, therefore, first and last inactive and independent, and may only occasionally encourage the patient to do particular actions. This clearly illustrates the difference between the 'active' analyst and the suggestionist. The second and even more important difference is that in suggestion the giving and fulfilling of tasks is everything, while in analysis it is only an aid to the attainment of new material, the *interpretation* of which is always the chief duty of analysis. So all the tendencious insinuations about a 'separatist movement' which my 'active measures' were expected to lead to can be left to settle themselves. On the other hand I must add if the assertion should be made that 'activity' (so far as it is correctly applied) implies absolutely nothing new, that this rather overshoots the mark. He who says this is, so to say, being more papal than the pope; Freud still finds in the strong emphasis of the factor of repetition and in occasional attempts to provoke this repetition a shade of difference.

I am now in a position to tell you something of the way in which patients reduce to absurdity the freedom of action allowed them. As a rule they begin with the question whether it is really allowed for them to scream out loud or get up from the *chaise longue* in order to look at the analyst's face, or to enter and leave the consulting-room, and so forth. . . . One takes such threats without being shocked, because these deeds are not only harmless but may lead to the discovery of repressed infantile impulses. Occasionally the patients attempt to express the early infantile desire to exhibit or attempt, naturally without result, to provoke the disapproval of the physician by craving to perform manifest onanism or incontinence. In cases that are not psychotic one may be sure that they could not carry out any act that could be dangerous for the physician or themselves.[1] In general the limits of the admissibility of the active technique allow the patient all possible modes of expression so long as

[1] The applicability of the method of 'draining away' is to be stressed occasionally even with psychotics.

the rôle of the physician does not exceed that of a friendly observer and adviser. The wish of the patient to receive signs of positive counter-transference must remain unfulfilled; it is not the task of the analysis to bring happiness to the patient by tender and friendly treatment (he must be referred to the real world after the analysis to get these claims satisfied), but to repeat under favourable conditions the reactions of the patient to frustration, as it happened in childhood, and to correct the disturbance in development which can be reconstructed historically.

With the assertion that activity is always a matter for the patient, I shall in no way be minimizing the importance of those discoveries which Rank and I have published in our joint work on the courageous interpretation of analytic material in terms of the psycho-analytic situation; on the contrary, I can only repeat here that for me and my analysis it is an advance that I take Rank's suggestion regarding the relation of patient to analyst as the cardinal point of the analytic material and regard *every* dream, *every* gesture, *every* parapraxis, *every* aggravation or improvement in the condition of the patient as above all an expression of transference and resistance. Alexander's admonition which he directed against us that transference and resistance at all times are the basis of analysis was unnecessary—every beginner in analysis knows that already—but, when he is unable to mark the difference between the methods proposed by us and the much more timid methods previously in general use, it is either because for all his gifts his susceptibility to shades of difference is not his strongest point, or because in his modesty he has felt it superfluous to tell us that he was already acquainted with the suggestions we put forward. To be sure I must add that on an unprejudiced examination the credit of priority belongs to Groddeck, who when the condition of one of his patients is aggravated always comes forward with the stereotyped question: 'What have you against me, what have I done to you?' He asserted that in the solving of this question the aggravation of the symptoms could always be removed, and that also with the help of such analytic devices he was able to understand more deeply the previous history of the case. I must add that the degree of value placed on the analytic situation is only indirectly concerned with activity, and that its increased consideration in no way implies activity in my meaning of the term.

* * * * *

In order not to weary you further with these methodological details and, therefore, for you to get the false impression that there only exist contra-indications for the active technique, I wish—so far as the time allotted to me permits—to tell you some of the things which I am pleased to regard as the further developments of 'activity'. In my last paper I spoke a good deal about muscle, particularly sphincter, tension, which I applied in several cases as a means of inducing an increase of tension. I have since then learnt that it is sometimes useful to advise *relaxation exercises*, and that with this kind of relaxation one can overcome the psychical inhibitions and resistances to association. I need hardly assure you that this advice is only put to the service of analysis, and only concerns the bodily self-control and relaxation exercises of the yogi in that we hope to learn from it something of the psychology of these adepts.

I long ago called attention to the importance of *obscene words* for analysis.[1] In a first attempt at an analytic approach to tic convulsif[2] I was able, among other things, to give a partial explanation of coprolalia. The opportunity which 'activity' gave me of making a deeper study of the emotional verbal expressions of the patient led me to the assertion that not only every case of tic was a disguised expression of obscene words, behaviour and coprophilic insults, but it is also a sadistic assault, and that the tendency to this is present in latent form in all cases of stammering and in nearly all cases of obsessional neurosis, and that with the help of 'activity' it can be brought to the surface from the condition of suppression. It was proved that quite a number of im-

[1] 'On Obscene Words', *Ztbt. f. P. A.*, 1911. (Translated in *Contributions to Psycho-Analysis*.)

[2] 'Psychoanalytische Betrachtungen über den Tic.' (A translation is included in this volume, p. 142.)

potent and frigid persons were not cured till one had evoked the infantile prohibition regarding the saying of obscene words, and indeed during the sexual act itself. The positive corollary of this kind of inhibition is the obsessive utterance of obscene words as a condition of orgasm which one could speak of as a new kind of perversion were it not so extraordinarily widespread.

That experiences of this kind not only advance technical ability but theoretical knowledge will hardly be disputed by anybody. To just these small advances in knowledge I owe the certainty that 'activity' as a method of work perhaps deserves some attention. I shall demonstrate this by a few examples.

A relative disturbance of potency proved in certain patients to be determined in part by an unusual over-sensitiveness of the mucous membrane of the glans penis. They took care, though for the most part unconsciously, in exposing the glans and in freeing it from the protecting covering of the foreskin; the softest direct contact with anything rough signified castration and was accompanied by correspondingly exaggerated feelings of pain and anxiety. When they masturbated they never did so directly on the glans but plucked at the foreskin, only rubbing the folds of this mucous membrane on one another and on the glans. One of these attempted in childhood to fill the cavity of the prepuce with water in order to evoke sexual enjoyment; another who like the rest had the greatest anxiety about sexual intercourse on account of the friction which is unavoidable in the act was fixated in his phantasies, among others, upon a servant girl, who, manifestly bearing his great sensitiveness in mind, had helped him as a youth to come to orgasm by simply *breathing* on his erect member. In such cases I hastened the analysis, as I believe, by advising the patient to keep the foreskin rolled back behind the corona glandis for a few days and to stop the rubbing and friction. The consequent advance in the analysis enabled me to have a deeper insight, as I believe, into the erotic importance of the prepuce generally; indeed, it led me to suppose a special foreskin erotism in childhood whose development appeared to accompany the phallic stage proper and could turn into a point of regression for neurotic symptoms. All this seemed to support my theory of the vaginal character of the prepuce.[1] I was also able to comprehend more clearly Freud's postulate concerning the displacement of clitoris-erotism in women on to the vagina. The vagina is a gigantic foreskin which takes over the erotogenic rôle of the hidden clitoris; analogous to this I call to mind the erotic game of boys who have coitus with one another in the foreskin. I communicated this to Roheim[2] in the hope that with his knowledge of these matters he would be able to throw more light on the psychological significance of certain puberty-rites, particularly circumcision. It seems to me extraordinarily probable that circumcision has at one and the same time a double aspect; on the one hand it is, as Freud has shown us, a means of inspiring terror, a symbol of castration by the father; on the other hand, it seems to be a kind of 'active therapy' among the primitives which has for its aim the hardening of the penis and the preparation for sexual activity by overcoming the castration-anxiety and the over-sensitiveness of the glans. If that were true it would follow naturally that the character of circumcized and uncircumcized men and people would develop differently, which may help a little to explain the Jewish question and anti-Semitism. Unfortunately, I must tell you the remark of a young colleague who came to know of these researches; he said, 'Now I know what active technique is, one lets the patient pull his foreskin back'.

In conclusion, a few words on the effect of the factor of experience resulting through 'activity' on the *conviction* of the patient. Brooding maniacs and other incurable doubters, who intellectually are able to grasp the most varied degree of probability concerning the analytic explanations but never reach the important degree of certainty

[1] See my *Versuch einer Genitaltheorie.* (A translation is appearing in the Mental and Nervous Diseases Monograph Series.)

[2] [Roheim gives me these references, 'Die Völkerpsychologie und die Psychologie der Völker', *Imago*, 1926, and a paper on 'The Scapegoat' read at the Bad Homburg Congress, to be published in book form under the title of *Animism, Magic and the Divine King.*—ED.]

needed for cure, attain this conviction with the help of the active technique; the analytic situation is used to bring about love for a person (namely, the analyst) without restraint, that is without ambivalence. This is not only practically but in a large measure also theoretically important. It shows us that along the path of intelligence, which is a function of the ego, really nothing in the way of 'conviction' can occur. The last and logically irrefutable word of the pure intellectuality of the ego on the relationship to other objects is a solipsism, which cannot equate the reality of other living beings and the whole outside world of personal experience, and speaks of them as more or less living phantoms or projections. When Freud ascribed to the unconscious the same psychical nature which one traces as a quality of one's own conscious ego, he made a step that was only probable in logic but never demonstrable in the direction of positivism. I do not hesitate to compare this identification with those which we recognize as the prerequisite of libidinal transference. They lead ultimately to a kind of personification or animistic conception of the entire world around us. All this is 'transcendent' viewed from the logical-intellectual standpoint. We ought to replace this mystic sounding word by the expression 'transference' or 'love', and courageously assert that the knowledge of a part, perhaps the most important part, of reality is not intellectual but only to be obtained *experientially* as conviction. (In order not to leave the opponents of experience and of science long in their triumph, I hasten to add that the experience of the importance of the emotions is in the end still itself an experience, so that in spite of all we need not be anxious about the fate of science.) I personally feel myself to be turned completely to the Freudian positivism, and prefer to see in you who sit there before me and hear my words not ideas in my ego but real beings with whom I can identify myself. I cannot put that on a logical basis for you. If, for all that, I am also convinced of it, I owe it only to an emotional factor—if you like to transference.

All this is apparently only loosely if at all connected

with active technique, but the tendency to repetition increased by activity was for me the path not only to practical but also theoretical progress in psycho-analysis. After I had pointed out to you the reverse side of activity and its contra-indications, I felt myself compelled to tell you something of its merits too. For the rest I expose myself, as my friend Eitingon said, to the danger of comparing myself with Balaam, who came to curse the Jews—and he blessed them.

XVIII

THINKING AND MUSCLE INNERVATION[1]

THERE are people who whenever they want to think something out tend to interrupt the particular movement in which they happen to be engaged (for instance walking) and to continue it only after completion of the intellectual act. Others again are incapable of carrying out an in any way complicated thought process while at rest, but must manifest active muscular movements throughout its duration (getting up from their chair, walking about, etc.). Those of the first category often prove to be strongly inhibited people in whom every independent effort of thought calls for the conquest of inner (intellectual and affective) resistances. The individuals belonging to the second group (who are usually described as of the 'motor type') are on the contrary people with a too rapid flow of ideas and a very active phantasy. The fact that the inhibited individual seems to employ the energy saved by the suspension of muscular innervation for overcoming resistances during the act of thinking, while the 'motor type', according to all appearances, must squander muscular energy if he wishes to moderate the otherwise all too 'easy overflowing of in-

[1] *Zeitschrift*, 1919, Bd. V. 103.

tensities' (Freud), that is, to restrain his phantasy and think logically, speaks for the inner connection between the act of thinking and motility. The degree of 'effort' necessary for thought does not always—as indicated—depend on the difficulty of comprehending the task to be mastered, but is—as analysis shows—very often affectively conditioned. Unpleasurably toned thought processes require, *ceteris paribus*, greater effort; inhibited thought often proves on analysis to be conditioned by the censorship, that is, to be neurotic. In mild cyclothymics one sees conditions of inhibited and exaggerated phantasy run parallel with variations in liveliness of movement. These motor symptoms of thought inhibition or of excitement occur in 'normals' also at times.[1]

Of course on a closer examination one finds that the appearance in these cases of muscular energy being transformed quite simply into 'psychic energy' is deceptive. One is dealing with complicated processes, with the splitting of *attention*, with *concentration*. The inhibited individual has to turn his attention wholly upon his organ of thought, and cannot, therefore, at the same time carry out a co-ordinated movement (also requiring attention). The rapid thinker, on the other hand, must to some extent distract his attention from his thought processes in order in some degree to retard their overwhelming rush.

During reflection, therefore, the inhibited thinker only suspends co-ordinated movements, but not the consumption of muscle innervation; on closer examination, indeed, one finds that during reflection the tonus of the (resting) musculature is always increased.[2] In the 'motor type' one is dealing not merely with an increased muscle tone (output of innervation) but with the interpolation of resistances to the attention.

Nor should one consider that the incapacity for syn-

[1] A patient who waggles her feet almost continuously (a tic-like habit of hers) always betrayed to me during analysis the moment that anything occurred to her by suddenly stopping the movement, so that I could always admonish her when she consciously withheld an idea from me. She waggled her feet ceaselessly during the association pauses that often lasted for minutes.

[2] The increase of muscle tonus during thinking is physiologically proven.

chronous thought and action is a characteristically neurotic phenomenon. There are numerous cases in which the neurotic masks a circumscribed, complex - conditioned thought prohibition just by exaggerated nimbleness and liveliness in the unprohibited psychic regions.

Psycho-analysis could assist a great deal in clearing up these complicated relations between psychic activity and muscle innervation. I refer to Freud's plausible explanation of *dream hallucinations*, according to which these owe their existence to a retrograde excitation of the perceptual system (regression) which is one result of the sleep embargo (paresis) at the motor end of the psychic apparatus. The second important contribution made by psycho-analysis to the knowledge of the relations between intellectual effort and muscle innervation is Freud's explanation of laughter at a witty or comic impression; according to his explanation, which sounds very plausible, such laughter is the *motor* discharge of a *psychic* tension that has become superfluous. Finally, Breuer and Freud's view of the *conversion* of psychic into motor excitement in hysteria may be referred to, and also Freud's explanation according to which the individual suffering from *obsessive ideas* is really substituting thought for action.

The regular parallelism of motor innervations with the psychic acts of thinking and attention, their mutual conditioning and frequently demonstrable quantitative reciprocity, speak at any rate for an essential similarity in these processes. Freud, therefore, is probably right when he considers thought to be an ' experimenting with the displacement of smaller excitation masses ', and also locates the function of *attention*, which periodically ' searches ' the external world and ' goes out to meet ' the sense impressions, at the motor end of the psychic apparatus.

XIX

DISCONTINUOUS ANALYSES[1]

FREUD has already pointed out that therapeutic success is often a hindrance to the thoroughness of the analysis; I was able to substantiate this in a number of cases. It may easily happen, if the irksome symptoms of the neurosis disappear during analytic treatment, that the still manifest indications of illness seem less troublesome to the patient than the continuation of the work of the analysis, which is often so hard and so full of renunciations. Should, however, the treatment really become *peior morbo*, the patient hastens (mostly also compelled by material considerations) to break it off and directs his interest to real life which he already finds satisfying. Such half-cured people in any case are usually still attached to their doctor by the bonds of transference; one learns that they talk somewhat exaggeratedly about the treatment and the person of the doctor, and they give indications, too, from time to time of their continued existence by picture postcards or other little attentions, in contradistinction to those patients who broke off the treatment in the midst of the resistance and wrap themselves in obstinate silence. The really cured, whose transference was dissolved, have no need to bother themselves particularly about their doctor, and do not do so.

Now it sometimes happens that the 'half-cured' fall ill again and want to continue the treatment. It then appears that internal or external factors were the exciting causes of the relapse which, as it were, activated the unconscious material not worked over at the analysis and jostled it out of repression. It may also be expected with certainty that on repeating the analysis things will come under discussion that either played no, or only a very small, part on the first occasion.

It has struck me very much how wonderfully quickly the

[1] *Zeitschrift*, 1914, Bd. II. S. 515.

old contact between doctor and patient can be reestablished. A patient, for instance, who had kept well for four years after an (unfinished) analysis, remembered on resuming the treatment every particular of the first time; it was still more remarkable how in the memory of the doctor (who in the meanwhile had in no way concerned himself with the patient but had worked intensively with so many others) the most insignificant details referring to the patient recurred spontaneously: the whole history of his childhood, the names of all his relatives, the dreams and thoughts, as well as their interpretations at that time, even to the colour of hair of people who had been spoken of. In two hours one was quite on the old lines, as though it had only been a matter of a rather prolonged week-end and not a separation of four years. The scientific result from the easily cured cases was mostly very small; the relapse allows a deeper insight into connections that at the time are only superficially recognized.

Freud's technical principle that even during treatment one must not spare the patient the shocks of reality is compulsorily disregarded in individual cases, as, for instance, when treatment must be carried out at a distance from relatives (the most important reagents for the neuroses). In such cases it may happen that the patient who had considered himself cured falls ill again with neurotic symptoms immediately upon, or shortly after, his return home, and returns with what speed he may to the doctor (by whom in any case he had been prepared for this eventuality). Contact with reality in these cases, too, forces to the surface psychic material thus far concealed.

A third indication for ' discontinuous analysis ' may be due entirely to external conditions. Patients who are very busy or live at a distance, or such as have usually only a restricted amount of time and money at their disposal for the purposes of treatment, come every year only for one or two months at a time. One cannot say that the time between the individual working periods passes without leaving a trace on these patients; a certain subsequent assimilation, a working out of what has been learnt during the treatment, is sometimes undeniable. This slight benefit, however, disappears against the great drawback that in this way the otherwise already wearisome treatment is dragged out interminably. Continuous analysis is therefore to be preferred to discontinuous analysis in every case.

In analyses that last more than a year, the treatment is also interrupted by the doctor's holiday time. For patients who really want to continue the treatment, *this* interruption does not mean a real discontinuity, so that the first session after the holiday actually does form the continuation of the analytic conversation that was interrupted by the separation.

XX

ON INFLUENCING OF THE PATIENT IN PSYCHO-ANALYSIS[1]

AT the penultimate International Congress of Psycho-Analysis in Munich, where so many differences of opinion till then latent came to light, Dr. Bjerre (of Stockholm), amongst others, delivered an address in which, not unlike the Zürich secessionists, he proposed to combine purely psycho-analytic therapy with a medical and ethical education of the patient. As at that time Bjerre explicitly opposed certain statements of mine contradictory to this and to his views, I saw myself compelled to defend the former, and to explain anew that psycho-analytic therapy must exhaust itself in the methodical clearing up and overcoming of the patient's inner resistances, and can achieve actual results without further active interference. On this occasion I uttered a special warning that psycho-analytic treatment should not be confounded with so-called suggestion (cure by transference).

Now there are two contradictory utterances to be found concerning this question, in an earlier number of our

[1] *Zeitschrift*, 1919, Bd. V. 140.

periodical.[1] Jones, in his lucid and severe criticism of Janet's conception of psycho-analysis, says amongst other things, 'A psycho-analyst should never advise a patient, least of all to sexual intercourse'.[2] At the beginning of a communication by Sadger, on the other hand, the behaviour of a patient is described after he, 'in consequence of my (the author's) advice, had performed coitus for the first time'.

I believe that the importance of the problem of whether the analyst may offer the patient advice justifies the opening up of the question afresh.

After what I said about it in Munich, it looks as if I must in this matter agree unconditionally with Jones and must reject Sadger's proceeding. That I do not do so, but consider Jones' statement to be an exaggeration, therefore requires justification.

In many cases of anxiety hysteria and of hysterical impotence, I found that the analysis went smoothly up to a certain point. The patients had full insight but the therapeutic result was always delayed; the ideas even began to repeat themselves with a certain monotony, as though the patient had nothing more to say, as though their unconscious were exhausted. This, of course—had it been true—would have contradicted the psycho-analytic theory of the unconscious origins of the neuroses.

In this predicament some verbal advice of Prof. Freud's came to my assistance. He explained to me that after a certain time one must call upon anxiety hysterics to give up their phobically strengthened inhibitions and to attempt to do just what they are most afraid of. The physician can justify such advice to himself, as to the patient, in this way, that each such attempt brings to the surface untouched

[1] *Zeitschrift*, Bd. IV. 39 and 48. ['Professor Janet über Psychoanalyse: eine Erwiderung.' Published also in the *Journal of Abnormal Psychology*, February 1915, vol. ix. p. 400, and reprinted in his *Papers on Psycho-Analysis* in the *second* edition (chap. xx. p. 373).]

[2] [The actual words in the paper quoted are '. . . it is no part of this [psycho-analytic] treatment to give advice of any kind to the patient, let alone advice of such a responsible and equivocal nature as the one he [Janet] suggests' (*i.e.* advising the patient to practise regular and normal coitus). This is by no means the same as the extreme statement here criticized.—ED.]

psycho-analytic material that without this shaking up could only have been obtained much later or not at all.

I followed my teacher's instructions, and can report excellently of their success. The treatment of many patients proceeded really by leaps owing to the improvement brought about by the 'shaking up'.

The opponents of psycho-analysis will object that this is nothing but treatment by suggestion or habit in another dress. I, however, reply to them 'si duo faciunt idem, non est idem'.

First of all, we never promise the patient that he will be cured by the attempt; on the contrary, we prepare him for the eventual worsening of his subjective condition immediately after the attempt. We only say to him—and that justifiably—that *in ultima analysi* the attempt will prove helpful in the treatment.

Secondly, we renounce thereby all the otherwise usual means of forcible or coaxing suggestion, and leave it to the patient whether he will decide to make this attempt. He must already have achieved a fairly good degree of psycho-analytic insight into the treatment if he carries out our request.

Finally, I do not in any way deny that in these trials an element of transference—of the same means therefore by which alone the hypnotist works—also comes into play. While, however, with the latter the transference to the doctor is supposed to act directly as a means of cure, in the Freudian psycho-analysis it only serves to weaken the resistances of the unconscious. At any rate, before the end of the treatment the physician lets the patient see even these cards, and discharges him fully independent.

In *this* sense I think that Sadger was right when he required of his patients a long avoided activity, and that Jones exaggerated when he said that the psycho-analyst never gives advice.[1]

I believe that this conception is not incompatible with the purity of psycho-analytic therapy that he defended against Bjerre.

[1] [This he never said.—Ed.]

XXI

ATTENTION DURING THE NARRATION OF DREAMS[1]

THE psycho-analyst, as is well known, should not listen with strained attention when the patient talks, but by 'suspended attention' allow scope to his own unconscious. I should like to make an exception to this rule, in regard to the narration of the patient's dreams, for here every detail, every shade of expression, the sequence of the content, must in the interpretation be put into words. One should also endeavour to observe accurately the wording of the dreams. Complicated dreams I often have narrated to me again, in cases of necessity even a third time.

XXII

RESTLESSNESS TOWARDS THE END OF THE HOUR OF ANALYSIS[2]

MANY patients become restless when the end of the analytic session is approaching; they interrupt their associations with the question 'Is it not four o'clock yet?' or with the statement 'I believe the hour is already up', etc. The analysis of this behaviour shows that these patients have been unpleasantly disturbed on previous occasions by my sudden uncompromising intimation that the session was at an end. The patient settled himself cosily with the doctor as though he could always remain thus confiding and secure with his spiritual guide. Being suddenly shaken up out of

[1] *Zeitschrift*, 1923, IX. 68. [Translated by Olive Edmonds.]
[2] *Zeitschrift*, 1915, Bd. III. S. 294. [Translated by John Rickman.]

this dream affects him strongly and may even involve certain transient symptoms, causing, for instance, hysterical giddiness.[1] The restless questions towards the end of the hour of analysis are a kind of defence formation against the unpleasant sensation experienced on these occasions.

The exaggerated modesty of the pretentious person forms the pendant to this behaviour from everyday life. He 'wishes to be a burden to no one', that is, he flies from every occasion on which his self-love might be hurt by the discovery that he could be a burden to anyone. The mechanism of this proceeding recalls that of the hysterical phobias; these also are defence formations against unpleasurable situations.

XXIII

SENSATIONS OF GIDDINESS AT THE END OF THE PSYCHO-ANALYTIC SESSION[2]

(*A Contribution to the Explanation of Bodily Symptoms of Psychological Origin*)

MANY patients have a sensation of giddiness on rising from the recumbent position at the end of the psycho-analytic session. The explanation—in itself rational—that this is the result of the sudden change of posture (cerebral anæmia) proves on analysis to be a successful rationalization; in reality the sensation on change of posture is only the means of expression of certain feelings and thoughts still under censorship. During the session the patient gave himself up wholly to free association and to its preliminary stipulation, transference to the doctor, and lives in the phantasy that he will always enjoy such well-being. Suddenly this (unconscious) phantasy is destroyed by the doctor's warning that the session is ended; he suddenly becomes conscious of the

[1] Compare my note on 'Sensations of Giddiness at the End of the Analytical Session'.

[2] *Zeitschrift*, II., 1914, p. 272.

actual facts; he is not 'at home' here, but a patient like any other; it is the paid doctor and not the helpful father that stands before him. This sudden alteration of the psychic setting, *the disillusionment* (when one feels as '*though fallen from the clouds*') may call up the same subjective feeling as is experienced in sudden and unexpected change of posture when one is unable to adapt oneself suitably by compensating movements and by means of the sense organs —that is to say, to preserve one's 'equilibrium'—which is the essence of giddiness. Naturally at the moment of this disillusionment that part of the *belief in the analysis* that did not as yet rest on honest conviction but only on a filial trust disappears very easily, and the patient is again suddenly more inclined to regard the analytic explanations as a 'swindle',[1] which word association may also facilitate the appearance of the symptom. The problem, however, is not solved but merely displaced by this discovery, for the question at once arises of why does one call the *deceiver* a *swindler*, that is, take him for a person who knows how to rouse feelings of giddiness in others? Probably just because he is able to waken *illusions* that at the moment of *disillusionment* will call up the feeling of giddiness (in the manner just described).

The end of the psycho-analytic session, moreover, brings with it necessarily also another kind of psychic 'swaying'. The complete freedom of association enjoyed during the session must suddenly be dammed up before leaving, and all the logical, ethical, and æsthetical barriers demanded by social life be re-erected. This complete change-over of the thought processes, their sudden subordination to the reality principle, was once expressed thus, in the motoring terminology that he affected, by a boy suffering from an obsessional neurosis and who felt marked giddiness after the session; he said he had to *brake* his thoughts from fifty to twenty-five miles an hour on getting up. This throwing on of the brakes, however, when the need for it is sudden

[1] [German '*Schwindel*'—*giddiness* as well as '*swindle*'. The interplay here of meaning and sound is untranslatable, but essential to the significance of the note.—Tr.]

can fail at the first go off; the 'engine' runs for a time in the new position, too, at the old 'velocity' till the compensating arrangement succeeds in mastering the situation, when the sensation of giddiness ceases. Naturally the most difficult thing is to resume the conventional attitude in regard to sexual matters immediately after an analytic session. The patient who a moment before was unreservedly revealing his most intimate secrets now confronts the doctor as a 'stranger' before whom he thinks he should be, and actually is, ashamed, like someone discovering that his clothes are not properly 'buttoned up'. In the case of a peculiarly sensitive patient the subsequent shame often lasted for a whole hour after the psycho-analytic session; she felt as though she were going about quite naked.

The minor symptom described here is of no particular pathological importance, causes the doctor no technical difficulties, and disappears for the most part when the patient gets accustomed to the sudden change-over of the psychic setting. I only described it because it forms an example of the manner in which psychic states of excitement overflow into the bodily sphere, which may help to the understanding of *hysterical conversion*. With a feeling of giddiness after the end of the analytic session, probably the feeling of the psychic change-over can only transform itself into the *sensation* of giddiness because both processes deal with an analogous disturbance of equilibrium. It is possible that the explanation of every psychogenic bodily symptom, and every manifestation of hysterical conversion, requires the assumption that between the particular psychic and physical process there must be present identity of the more delicate mechanism as a *tertium comparationis*.

XXIV

A TRANSITORY SYMPTOM. THE POSITION DURING TREATMENT[1]

In two cases men patients betrayed passive homosexual phantasies by shifting suddenly during the hour of analysis from the dorsal and lateral decubitus respectively on to their faces.

XXV

THE COMPULSION TO SYMMETRICAL TOUCHING[2]

A great number of nervous, but also many otherwise quite normal, people suffer from a superstitious compulsion; if they touch one part of the body by accident or purposely they are compelled to touch also the symmetrically corresponding part in exactly the same way. For instance, if they have reached up to the right ear with the right hand, they must immediately catch hold of the left ear with the left hand in a perfectly identical fashion. Should they omit to do this they feel restless, as is usually the case when an obsessional manifestation is checked.

[1] *Zeitschrift*, 1913, Bd. I. 378.
[2] *Zeitschrift*, 1916–17, Bd. IV. S. 266.

I only had the opportunity of analysing one such case, a girl, who, besides other neurotic symptoms, suffered also from this peculiarity (of which as a symptom, however, she was not subjectively aware). Direct interrogation of the origin of this symptom brought, as usual, no explanation. The first associating idea led to childish scenes. The very severe nurse, of whom she was much afraid, was very strict that the children when washing themselves should always wash both ears and both hands properly and not content themselves with the cleansing of one half of the body. On this information one would have been inclined to consider the symmetrical 'compulsion to touch' simply as a sort of 'post-hypnotic command automatism' that might have been maintained so many years after the admonition was received.

As always, this simple explanation had to be sacrificed in the further course of the analysis for a more complicated one. The same nurse who otherwise laid such stress on the thorough washing and rubbing of the body excepted one single part, the genitals, which the child was forbidden to wash or touch except in the most exiguous way possible. And yet this is just the part of the body the rubbing and washing of which was no unpleasant duty but rather a source of pleasure.

I formed the supposition that the compulsion to the exaggerated washing or touching of symmetrical parts of the body generally indicates a defiance in the guise of dutifulness and obedience. The compulsion to touch symmetrical parts of the body is the over-compensation for the doubt whether it were not better to touch a certain part of the body situated in the median plane.

The patient's sister, who was much of the same age and otherwise free of any neurosis, nevertheless shared with her this symptom of 'symmetrical compulsion to touch'.

XXVI

THE PSYCHIC CONSEQUENCES OF A 'CASTRATION' IN CHILDHOOD[1]

In the paper entitled 'The Little Chanticleer',[2] who in his earliest childhood suffered a quite negligible injury to the penis which then definitely influenced the whole of his impulsive life and mental development, I had to point out the great significance of the constitutional factor in the fear of castration, for which the actual experience only acted as a determining accident.

Chance brought me a patient about three years ago who could be considered as a counterpart to 'The Little Chanticleer'. He actually did undergo 'castration' when not quite three years old. Of course it was not castration in a medical sense, but another operation on the penis. The patient remembered exactly how it came about. He had trouble in passing urine (certainly due to a phimosis), whereupon it occurred to his father, a very headstrong country squire, in spite of his being a good Christian, to ask—instead of the district doctor—the advice of the village Jewish butcher, who suggested the only method of cure to be recommended from a medical point of view, namely, circumcision. The father immediately agreed; the butcher brought his long, sharp knife and carried out the removal of the foreskin on the desperately struggling boy, who, naturally, had to be forcibly held.

The incident concerned Mr. L., a Croatian agricultural functionary, who applied to me for treatment for impotence. He had remained celibate and, with the exception of the lowest types of prostitutes (even with them his potency was not very certain), had not yet had any serious relations with women. He lacked the necessary courage for this. It soon appeared that this lack of self-confidence completely

[1] *Zeitschrift*, 1916–17, Bd. IV. S. 263.
[2] [Translated in *Contributions to Psycho-Analysis*.]

dominated not only his sexual life but also the rest of his existence, and was to blame for the fact that in spite of his rather unusual intelligence he had not gone far either in social or material respects.

As the patient's position does not allow of protracted leave he only comes to me at fairly long intervals and always only for a few (1-3) weeks at a time, which, of course, considerably diminishes not only the therapeutic, but also the psycho-analytic, value of the case. Nevertheless in the course of time sufficient characteristic material has cropped up during the analysis to justify its communication.

At the first session (as we shall call the groups of analytical hours) it was unusually difficult to get the patient to talk. This powerful resistance, which could hardly be overcome, was occasioned by the fact that the patient had real sins to confess. He had the propensity of correcting his luck at cards, not only when a favourable opportunity presented itself accidentally, but also by deliberate preparation by the necessary manipulations of the playing cards. However, after such trickeries, which often led him into great danger, he felt dissatisfied, squandered the money in drink, and then reproached himself horribly. The bad name that the knowledge of his dishonest play would have given him, but which he had as yet escaped, he acquired for himself in another way; he frequently gets drunk and becomes violent and fraternizes in his intoxication with a low set (musicians, waiters, etc.) of whose acquaintance he is fearfully ashamed when he is sober. A revision of his sins backwards into his early childhood revealed only a few insignificant thefts; the most notable of these was the theft of a purse from his sleeping father's trouser pocket. This father was a crazy person who brought up his boys with a horse-whip, was often drunk, and died of alcoholic epilepsy. At this point in the tale came the account of the very rough operation already described.

After the patient had to some extent unburdened his soul by these confessions, the other side of his emotional life could display itself, and he appeared as a sensitive, kindly creature, desirous of being loved, with a gift for poetry and science. If he had to acknowledge one of his sins, however, or to recite one of his poems, he fought against it every time in a peculiar manner; his voice became forced, he cursed unrestrainedly, he contorted himself almost like an hysteric in opisthotonus, all his muscles were contracted to the utmost, his face flushed, the veins swelled till after the critical communication had been made the patient suddenly became calm and could wipe the sweat of anxiety from his brow.

He then told me that in such attacks he felt a powerful retraction of the penis and had the obsessive impulse to seize hold of the genitals of the man to whom he was speaking.

I was able to explain to him before parting that he had always lived in the discouraging consciousness of his mutilation, and that it was this that made him cowardly and was the basis for the compulsion to create certain advantages for himself by cunning and deceit. Moreover, the theft from his father's trouser pocket was also the symbolic equivalent of the despoliation he himself had suffered. The retraction of his penis reminded him of his inferiority on every occasion when he had to answer for anything; the impulse to seize a strange penis was due to a wish to rid himself of the torment of this idea, so that in phantasy he did possess fully efficient genitals.

At a later session he confessed, with the difficulties just described, the peculiarities of the myth-like phantasies that were apt to occur to him when he was quite alone. He felt himself soaring towards the sun with open eyes like an eagle. He flew up to the sun and fearlessly bit a piece out of its rim with his powerful beak, so that its brilliance waned as at an eclipse. By this sun-symbol phantasy the patient betrays to the initiated his insatiable thirst for vengeance against his father (the sun), on whom he would make good by a mutilation the sexual weakness which he attributes to him. The semblance of an eagle is a wish-formation to conceal the consciousness of the disturbances of erection. We can take the patient's complaint that his potency was injured most of all by a course of sun baths as a very apt confirmation of this interpretation of the sun as father. As an associative link between sun and father there was the father's shining, threatening eye, before which, in contrast to the daring of the phantasy, he had as a child always had to drop his eyes.[1]

His curious behaviour on communicating unpleasant ideas, or such as in his opinion were displeasing to the doctor, was very soon explained. The forced voice, the cursing, the flinging himself about was all nothing but the unconscious re-enacting the castration and his conduct during that act of violence. During less dangerous confidences he only felt the retraction of the penis as a suggestion of castration. The early psychic shock had (as I have also found it in many adult war neurotics) occasioned a permanent psychic and nervous association between the injured part of the body and his affective life, so that his feelings could have been described as a scale of retraction and castration sensations. All subsequent emotions at once roused the still painful scar in his soul and the corresponding part of his physical organism.

The impulse to seize in his fear a strange genital that was superior to his allowed of several explanations. It originated at first in the wish, already indicated, to possess a larger penis; the patient used this clutch also as a security against a repetition of the castration, as though he always held the penis of his supposed opponent in his hand as a pledge. (I had to explain his unusually protracted onanism similarly. He did not trust himself to let his penis out of his hand and to entrust it to a strange—perhaps dangerous—female. From the general importance of the castration complex one can assume that this motive plays a part for many onanists.)

Finally, I also discovered passive homosexual phantasies behind this compulsion; being castrated he regarded

[1] It is possible that the paternal eye generally acts as a *tertium comparationis* in the formation of the sun-symbol. Compare for this the well-known 'Eye of God' that is surrounded by sun-rays. I know an accomplished hypnotist who believes he owes his powers of suggestion to his piercing eyes. He defied his strict father as a child, and for a long time endeavoured to outstare the most dazzling sunshine.

himself as a woman and wished at any rate to participate in feminine enjoyment.

The disturbance of sexual development—probably just between the narcissistic and genital stages—must also afford the explanation for his unusual narcissism and the anal-erotic archaisms which he cherishes to this day. His ideas concerning these were often extraordinarily primitive. I will only mention that he preferred to defæcate into a stream near the house, and liked to follow up for a considerable time the farther adventures of these erstwhile parts of his ego, from which he parted only unwillingly. He has a peculiar *flair* for the anal-erotic origin of avarice; when, for instance, he found that his sister had prepared much too shabby a meal in his honour it occurred to him 'my sister got these doughnuts out of her arse'.

Having been robbed of his most valuable possession (supposedly), he dreaded every monetary outlay; he imagined himself cheated at every turn, 'curtailed'; hence, too, his tendency to *overreach* others. He was aware of a marked idiosyncrasy towards his tailor and barber.

The beginning of his neurosis is not well elucidated. As a young man he suffered for several years from the fear of becoming epileptic. An identification with his alcoholic epileptic father can safely be assumed from this, but the undoubtedly polyvalent meaning of this symptom has not been sufficiently analysed.

This case might take a terminal place in Freud's 'ætiological series'. It is probable that a child who was not in the least predisposed could be rendered neurotic by such a trauma.

As director of the neurological division of a military hospital I had the opportunity of interrogating Bosnian Mohammedans who had been circumcised in childhood. I learnt that there the operation is performed on children in their second year and entails no nervous consequences, and particularly no impotence. With the Jews the ritual circumcision is performed on the eighth day of the child's life; here, too, symptoms such as my patient's do not occur. It is therefore possible that this interference has a subsequent morbid effect only at the critical narcissistic age.

In this and similar cases one must—as does Freud also—recognize the immense significance of the 'masculine protest' for the symptom formation. This patient's most passionate driving desire is in fact to be a man; certainly not for the sake of 'superiority', but in order that he, like his father, may be able to love a woman and found a family. It is, moreover, no marvel that after this severe injury to his narcissism he should produce not only libidinal but also egoistic phantasies, phantasies of a self-love wounded by the circumcision.

XXVII

ON FALLING ASLEEP DURING ANALYSIS [1]

Patients sometimes complain of sleepiness during analysis (at the height of resistance), and even threaten that they will go to sleep. In this way they express their dissatisfaction with the aimless, senseless, and wearisome treatment. The doctor explains the significance of their threat, upon which they mostly cheer up again in proof that the right nail has been hit on the head. One of my patients, however, was not content with the threat, but really fell asleep once or twice. I quietly let him be and waited, knowing (if only from consideration of the expense of the time slept away) that he could not sleep peacefully for long—knowing, too, that this time he intended to reduce *ad absurdum* my method of letting him talk and of keeping silence myself. I kept silent, therefore, and the patient slept quietly enough for about five minutes; then, however, he started up and continued the work. He repeated this three or four times. On the last occasion of this kind he had a dream the interpretation of which justified the assumption that the patient chose this

[1] *Zeitschrift*, 1914, Bd. II. S. 274.

peculiar form of resistance because by it he could also give expression to unconscious passive homo-erotic phantasies. (A phantasy of being overpowered during sleep.) The wish of many patients that one should hypnotize them is to be explained similarly.

XXVIII

SILENCE IS GOLDEN[1]

An obsessional neurotic patient—otherwise usually taciturn and hesitating in his associations—showed himself distinctly chatty at one interview. On having his attention drawn to this he acknowledged himself the unwontedness of his garrulity, excusing it, however, with his peculiar humour, as of course 'silence is golden'. In connection with this idea I pointed out to him the symbolic identity of gold and filth, and told him that he was evidently in the habit of hoarding his words, as well as gold and filth, and that that day he was only accidentally in a prodigal mood. I moreover explained that his use of the notion that 'silence is gold' rendered the psycho-analytic interpretation of the proverb possible. Silence is 'gold' only because taciturnity in and for itself means a saving (in use). On this remark the patient broke into uncontrollable laughter and told me that that very same day he had—by exception—had a very copious action of the bowels, while usually—even if fairly regularly—he passed only small quantities. (The actual occasion for the expansiveness and prodigality was the sudden removal of an external compulsion; it became possible for him to forgo a journey that he would only very unwillingly have undertaken.)

Another patient (an hysteric) suffers amongst other things from two symptoms that always appeared at the same time and with the same intensity: spasm of the vocal

[1] *Zeitschrift*, 1916–17, Bd. IV. 155.

cords and of the sphincter ani. If he is in an elevated mood his voice is loud and clear, his evacuation copious and 'satisfying'. When depressed (particularly on the occasion of some inadequacy) or on intercourse with seniors and superiors, loss of voice and tenesmus occur at the same time.

(The analysis of this patient showed, amongst other things, that he was one of those not uncommon people who retain their motion because they expect a 'strengthening' ('physically and psychically') from it, while they fear to be 'weakened' by its evacuation.—In my experience so far, this intimate association of 'strength' and 'retention' is to be traced to childish accidents in which the patient was 'too weak' to retain the motion. This tendency to retention radiates out into psychic territory and leads to the retention if possible of all emotions, all 'ebullitions of feeling'; an outburst of feeling that could no longer be restrained may be followed by as powerful a feeling of distress as was formerly an anal incontinence.)

That there are certain connections between anal erotism and speech I had already learnt from Prof. Freud, who told me of a stammerer all whose singularities of speech were to be traced to anal phantasies. Jones too has repeatedly indicated in his writings the displacement of libido from anal activities to phonation. Finally I too, in an earlier article ('Über obscöne Wörte'),[1] was able to indicate the connection between musical voice-culture and anal erotism.

The communication of these cases seemed to me worth while as they justify the assumption that voice and speech culture are associated with anal erotism, not merely accidentally and exceptionally, but according to definite laws. The proverb 'silence is golden' might stand as the confirmation of this assumption in folk psychology.

[1] [Translated in *Contributions to Pyscho-Analysis*, chap. ix.]

XXIX

TALKATIVENESS[1]

WITH several patients talkativeness proved to be a method of resistance. They discussed all conceivable immaterial matters superficially in order not to have to speak or reflect on a few important ones.

[1] *Zeitschrift*, III. 294. [Translated by John Rickman.]

XXX

THE SCIENTIFIC SIGNIFICANCE OF FREUD'S 'THREE ESSAYS ON THE THEORY OF SEXUALITY'[1]

THE 'Three Essays' show us Freud, the psycho-analyst, for the first time engaged in synthetic work. Here the author endeavours for the first time to bring together, to classify, to co-ordinate the immeasurable wealth of experience yielded by the dissection of so many thousand minds, in such a fashion that there may result from it the clearing up of a great psychological domain. That he should choose sexuality as the object of his first synthesis was due to the nature of the material for observation that he had at command. He analysed patients with psycho-neuroses and psychoses and always discovered some kind of disturbance of the sexual life to be a fundamental cause for these ailments. Further researches connected with psycho-analysis convinced him that sexuality plays a far greater and more complicated part in the psychic activity of normal and healthy people also than had hitherto been considered possible—so long as one could only assess the evident manifestations of sexuality and was unaware of the unconscious. It appeared, therefore, that sexuality, in spite of its immense literature, is, in comparison with its importance, a very neglected chapter of human knowledge, and one that certainly deserves to be submitted to a thorough examination from a new point of view.

It is probably less modesty than the insatiability of the

[1] *Zeitschrift*, III. 227, and chapter vi. of the author's *Populäre Vorträge über Psychoanalyse*. [Dr. Ferenczi contributed this paper to his Hungarian translation of the third edition of Prof. Freud's book.—TRANS.]

scientist striving ever onwards that makes Freud in his latest conclusions point out the incompleteness of this endeavour. The student, however, who, so to say, acquires the intellectual possession of the new discoveries and perspectives indicated in these treatises without labour and effort, does not see the incompleteness, but rather the advantages of the work, and would advise the author to follow the French proverb and say to himself: *En me jugeant, je me déplais; en me comparant je suis fier.* Whoever compares the richness of the material of these treatises, the astonishing newness of their points of view, with the manner in which sexuality is handled elsewhere will certainly not react with feelings of dissatisfaction but with admiring esteem on reading them. He will gratefully acknowledge that the libido theory, whose problems were not even propounded before Freud, has been firmly established and partly elucidated, even if not yet fully elaborated, by the efforts of one single individual.

This success, as well as the success of Freud's psychiatric researches, is not due only to the author's acuteness, but also to the subsequent employment of a method of research and the firm adherence to certain scientific points of view. The psycho-analytic method of research—*free* association, free in every sense of the word—brought to light a hitherto unknown and unconscious *deeper layer* of the psychic life. And the hitherto unexampled strictness and consistency with which psycho-analysis employs the principle of psychic determinism, and the conception of evolution, permitted the fruitful scientific development of this new material.

The progress that we owe to this method of work is astonishingly great. Before Freud, psychiatry was a collector's cabinet of extraordinary and meaningless clinical pictures of disease, and the science of sexuality consisted of the descriptive grouping of repulsive abnormalities. Psycho-analysis, always true to determinism and the evolutionary idea, did not shun the task of dissecting and rendering comprehensible this psychic content also, however repugnant to logic, ethics, and æsthetics. Its self-control was richly rewarded; in the nonsense of the mental patient it recognized the onto- and phylogenetic primitive forces of the human psyche, the humus nourishing all cultural and sublimating endeavour, and it succeeded—particularly in the 'Three Essays'—in proving that the only path to the understanding of normal sexual life leads from the sexual perversions.

I hope that what I still have to say about the significance of these 'Essays' will not one day seem exaggerated. I do not exaggerate when I attribute to them an importance in the history of science. '*My object was to find out how much light psycho-analytic research can throw on the biology of human sexuality*', explains the author in his preface to the book. This seemingly modest endeavour, carefully considered, signifies the overthrow of accepted doctrine; hitherto no one had thought of the possibility that a psychological, much less an 'introspective', method could help to explain a biological problem.

One must go very far back to estimate this endeavour at its proper significance. We must remember that primitive science was anthropocentric and mystic; man took his own psychic functions as the measure for all phenomena. It was a great advance when this cosmology (*Weltanschauung*), which corresponded to the geocentric Ptolemaic system in astronomy, was overthrown by 'natural philosophy' or one might say the Copernican conception, which took from man his leading importance and relegated him to the modest position of a mechanism among endless others. This view tacitly involved the assumption that not only the bodily, but also the psychic human functions, are manifestations of mechanisms. Tacitly, I say, because up to the present day natural science contented itself with this quite general assumption, without vouchsafing the slightest insight into the nature of psychic mechanism, and indeed denied this ignorance to itself by covering up this gap in knowledge with sham physiological and physical explanations.

The first ray of light illuminating the mechanisms of psychic life came from psycho-analysis. By means of this knowledge psychology could master also those layers of the psychic life that lie beyond immediate experience, and could venture to inquire into the laws of unconscious psychic activity. It was in these 'Essays' that the next step was taken; a part of instinctual life is brought nearer our understanding by the hypostatizing of certain mechanisms acting in the psyche. Who knows whether we shall not also see the last step, the evaluation of the knowledge of psychic mechanisms in the field of organic and inorganic occurrences in general?

In so far as Freud attempts to solve problems of biology as well as of sexual activity by means of psycho-analytic experience, he returns to a certain extent to the methods of ancient animistic science. There is a safeguard, however, against the psycho-analyst falling into the error of such naïve animism. Naïve animism transferred human psychic life *en bloc* without analysis on to natural objects. Psycho-analysis, however, dissected human psychic activity, pursued it to the limit where psychic and physical come in contact, down to the instincts, and thus freed psychology from anthropocentrism, and only then did it trust itself to evaluate this purified animism in terms of biology. To have been the first in the history of science to make this attempt is the achievement of Freud.

I must repeat that it is not empty speculation but the careful observation and examination of psychic peculiarities and sexual aberrations (hitherto quite neglected) which have led to these great perspectives. The author himself is content to indicate them by brief notices and passing remarks, and hastens to return to the facts, to the individual cases, in order not to lose touch with reality and to build a sure and wide foundation for the theory.

The student, however, whose vocation is embellished by these discoveries, could not deny himself the pleasure of contemplating these perspectives, and also of drawing the attention of those who otherwise perhaps had heedlessly passed by that landmark for science—Freud's 'Three Essays'.

XXXI

COMPOSITE FORMATIONS OF EROTIC AND CHARACTER TRAITS[1]

In a whole series of cases we can observe that certain character traits regress easily to their erotic pre-stage—whose sublimation-product they really are—and in this way composite formations of erotic and character traits are brought about.

1. A boy confessed to the juvenile court at Pozsony that he had removed paper money from a collection box by smearing long sticks with his excrement and withdrawing the adhering bank-notes by their aid.

It is certainly not an accident that the boy in considering ways and means to satisfy his craving for money hit on this idea. The anal character trait concerned in the collecting of money only needed to revive his own fundamental anal erotism (coprophilia). This is in a way a return of the repressed material in what represses it.

2. Sufferers from 'housewife-psychosis' [*Hausfrauen-psychose*] employ their insatiable passion for cleaning by preference on lavatories. A combination of cleanliness (anal character) and coprophilia (anal erotism).

3. In many cases I could confirm a marked avarice, concerned, however, only with quite special expenses; such as paying for the laundry or for toilet paper. Very many people who in other respects live well economize noticeably in changing their linen, and can only with difficulty decide on the purchase of fresh toilet paper for their households (avarice—anal character + filth—anal erotism).

4. In an earlier paper[2] I instanced the case in which a child who wanted to have beautiful shining 'golden' coins swallowed the copper coins and recovered them from his fæces, literally brilliantly cleaned. The chemical

[1] *Zeitschrift*, 1916–17, Bd. IV. 146.
[2] [See chap. xiii. of *Contributions to Psycho-Analysis*, p 278.]

juices of the alimentary canal dissolved the tarnish off the coins. (Combination of two character traits ; love of money and cleanliness, along with the original anal erotism.)

5. The pedantry of many anal characters is in nothing so strict as in regard to the punctuality of bowel evacuation.

6. Obstinacy is well known as a typical anal character trait. A very popular method for expressing obstinacy is the baring of the buttocks and the invitation to coprophilic activities. The original anal erotism comes to life in this method of expression.

7. The analysis of many neurotics and the observation of the doings of children show us that 'setting on fire', the delight in conflagrations, indeed, too, the tendency to incendiarism, is an urethral-erotic character trait. Many incendiarists were excessive bed-wetters and the ambition that developed out of this inferiority selects (for reasons still unknown) by preference the Herostratic type of renown. In a collection of criminal cases of incendiarism there were quite a number in which incendiaries set fire to their *beds*, as though to indicate the still active enuristic primitive source of their pyromanic character trait.

8. A gentleman who well remembers his infantile bladder weakness became later a passionate volunteer fireman, which, after what has been said above, does not greatly surprise us. But though the extinguishing of fire itself is already a composite formation of the Herostratic character with urethral erotism, the persistence of the urethral tendency showed itself even more plainly in this person's choice of vocation. He became a doctor and selected urology as his speciality, in which he can constantly be occupied with the bladder functions of—other people.

If indeed any further proof were needed, then this series of observations might serve as an argument against Jung's mistaken hypothesis, according to which the erotic impulses uncovered in the analysis are not to be taken as 'real' but only as 'symbolic'. The constant admixture of erotic tendencies in the apparently already 'clarified' character traits shows us as nothing else does how true to life those unconscious impulses still are, and how they take advantage of every opportunity to realize themselves in any—and, as we have seen, often very transparent—garb.

XXXII

PSYCHO-ANALYSIS OF SEXUAL HABITS[1]

Some recent papers of mine have dealt with the amplification of our therapeutic technique by means of certain 'active' procedures. These papers were on the whole couched in general terms; no details were given as to the manner in which this psycho-therapeutic expedient should be employed, with the result that too wide a field for misconception was left open. I feel myself therefore in duty bound to publish a more detailed account of my experiences in this matter. Needless to say, owing to the complexity and wide ramifications of the material, I am not yet in a position to give a systematic account of the subject. I trust, however, that by adducing certain characteristic examples from my practice I may be able to show how this so-called activity may be employed with success; further, in what light the results have to be regarded theoretically and how the method can be correlated with other analytic knowledge. I shall of course avail myself of such opportunities as arise to indicate the limits within which the active method can be employed and shall not neglect to point out occasions on which application of them, instead of producing the anticipated result, may give rise to fresh difficulties. In common with all other detailed investigations, the present attempt is bound to give an impression of one-sidedness. The mere fact that one is supporting a thesis in the face of every conceivable criticism is of itself calculated to give the impression that the new proposals are being advanced to the detriment of what has previously been regarded as correct

[1] *Zeitschrift*, 1925, XI. 6-39. [Trans. by Edw. Glover.]

procedure: it is an easy step from defence to special pleading. To avoid producing this assuredly false impression the author can only repeat that his so-called activity is in no way intended to displace previous analytic methods, but rather in certain contingencies and at certain points to amplify them. Any attempt to substitute for the previous technique a series of active measures and abreactions would only end in disappointment and stultification. The aim and end of psycho-analytic therapy now, as always, is to bring about a mobilization of the repressed in the pre-conscious system by means of reawakened memories and of reconstructions arrived at by necessity. Activity is nothing more than an expedient which, skilfully applied, will advance analytic work.

The idea of arranging the phenomena about to be described under the title of 'Psycho-Analysis of Sexual Habits' suggested itself when in the course of writing it became apparent that the scientific associations to a theme originally purely technical in nature grouped themselves naturally round the subject indicated in the title.

1. *The Analysis of Urethro-Anal Habits*

One of the principal indications concerning the general attitude to be maintained towards analysands is found in Freud's formulation that analysis shall be conducted in a state of mental privation. Up to the present this has been taken to mean solely that the wishes and demands put forward by the patient in the transference have to remain unsatisfied, more particularly his longing for affection and the tendency, so to speak, to settle himself for life with the analyst. I would add by way of supplement that various other privations also can be advantageously imposed on the patient; in illustration I shall now detail the most important amongst my observations.

In one of my earlier papers I took as an illustration of active methods during analysis the case of patients who during the sitting exhibited as a transitory symptom a strong desire to urinate; such patients were as far as possible to be prevented from gratifying the compulsion. My expectation was that the increased tension produced in this way would, as it extended to the mental sphere, make it more easy to bring up the material which tends to gain cover behind such symptoms. Later I had occasion to regulate the process of defæcation with certain patients, especially those who exhibited excessive anxiety to observe regular intervals. Here again my expectations went no further at first than the hope that analysis would be advanced by this disturbance of habit. The actual results, however, exceeded my expectations. Cases with a urinary compulsion proved to be persons who urinate altogether too frequently, that is to say, who suffer from a very mild form of pollakiuria, behind which is concealed unconscious anxiety about imperfect control of the urinary sphincters. This is at once a derivative form and residue of infantile difficulties in settling down to the excretory discipline in question. The same can be shown to apply to stool-pedants. By exaggerated promptitude and punctuality they compensate for the infantile anal-erotic tendency to hold back the stool as long as possible; but here, too, an unconscious anxiety was operative lest, if the stool were kept back too long, too much excretory material would accumulate, giving rise to severe pain on ultimate defæcation. I had frequently to regulate anal and urinary processes in one and the same patient, chiefly with impotent men and frigid women.

The first reaction to such disturbance of excretory habits was as a rule the following: a urethral prohibition would be met with protestations from the patient that he could if he liked hold his urine for a whole day, that he had an exaggerated potency in this respect, and so on. On my reply that he should merely attempt to retain his urine as long as possible, this would result on occasion in quite astounding performances, the urine being retained from eight to ten hours, on one occasion for twenty-eight hours. This, of course, applied only to the first attempt or only for a brief period. As a rule the instruction to continue the attempt was not successfully carried out; indeed in some instances it required only one or two attacks of exhaustion, which had been covered by this 'hyper-potency', to unmask a tendency to enuresis with which the patient had been quite unfamiliar and which threw light on important parts of his early infantile history. It seemed as if a persisting weakness of the internal sphincters of the bladder had been counterbalanced by over-strong innervation of the external auxiliary sphincters, a disability which came to light only when the latter system was exhausted.

Similarly with closet-pedants the instruction was given to wait until the desire came of its own accord. Here the resistance took the form (occasionally observed in urinary cases also) of hypochondriacal apprehension. The bowel might rupture; retention would give rise to hæmorrhoids; the retained excreta would injure the constitution or cause poisoning; some complained of headache, loss of appetite, and mental incapacity; they quoted cases where prolonged constipation had given rise to fæcal vomiting, and they could only with difficulty be restrained from having recourse to their habitual pills or enemata. Nevertheless, their apprehensions proved to be merely phobia-constructions barring the way to repressed anal erotism and anal anxiety. If one persisted in the regulation, undeterred by these gratuitous prognostications, one gained on many occasions a deep insight into the instinctual life concealed behind character-peculiarities. Here, too, one came across obstinate patients who would retain their stools for four, five, eight, and, in one well-authenticated case, for eleven days in order to reduce my injunctions to absurdity. In the long run, apparently when they saw that I was not to be moved from my course, such patients would produce, accompanied by severe pains similar to those of labour, an extremely hard scybalum followed by an enormous stool.

In these cases, too, a single experiment was usually though not invariably sufficient to overcome the patients' obstinacy: if one gave them a renewed exhortation to retain the stools for the longest possible period, it proved no longer an easy matter to do so; indeed, in some instances it was possible in this way to relieve conditions of constipation which had persisted for incredibly long periods. Here again it seemed that an exaggerated functioning of the external sphincters had concealed a weakness of function of the internal sphincters.[1]

Obviously I should never have paid such close attention to the details of these two functions if I had not made the remarkable, and to me at first astonishing, observation that by the methods described one can open up otherwise impassable avenues of communication, on the one hand between character-peculiarities and neurotic symptoms, and on the other between their instinctual sources and the details of infantile development. The so-called 'character analyses' would seem to call specially for reduction, by means of these active manœuvres, to anal, urethral, and oral-erotic interests in order to bring into play new and distinct fusions and applications of instinctual energy.

My experiments on the retention of excreta proved, moreover, profitable in an unexpected direction, by bringing confirmation of the 'amphimixis theory' of genital function as set forth in my *Versuch einer Genitaltheorie*.[2] In some instances my attention was drawn to the fact that a urethral prohibition affected anal function in a quite unmistakable way; it was as if the tendency to evacuation had undergone displacement backwards, so to say. Patients would exhibit increased frequency in evacuation, increase in flatulence, and would pass wind copiously. But displacements of a different type were also observed, *e.g.* a definite effect on the appetite, and most remarkable and most important of all, in the case of impotent patients erections occurred even where these had been for a long time conspicuous by their absence. It was impossible to avoid correlating these phenomena with certain views I had put forward in my *Genitaltheorie* concerning the origin of the genital function. The facts observed could be regarded as experimental con-

[1] Those who are familiar with my observations on the often quite astounding 'hysterical materialization phenomena' (see *Hysterie und Pathoneurosen* [translated here in Chapter VI., page 89]) will not reject as *a priori* absurd the view that the unconscious can obtain direct expression through the form and structure of the excreta, a possibility to which Groddeck had already made half-joking reference in his *Seelensucher*.

[2] 1923. [Translation to be published shortly.]

firmation of my conclusion that anal and urethral innervation-characteristics are to be observed in a state of amphimictic fusion in the evacuation and retention functions of the bladder and of the rectum; further, that these tendencies are secondarily displaced to the genital organ, where they control the act of emission in copulation and its inhibitions. Apart from the theoretical importance of these discoveries it seemed to me to be of practical significance that by means of these active procedures there was greater possibility of reconstructing the pregenital formations in cases of impotence. Moreover, I am entirely in agreement with the view expressed by W. Reich [1] that not only manifest cases of impotence but, so to speak, all cases of neurosis show some disturbance or other of genital function, and I was able to demonstrate the suitability of urethro-anal activity in widely differing forms of neurosis.

In reply to the obvious criticism that retention must have given rise to mechanical stimulation of the adjacent genitalia, I may state that the erections were observed not only when the bladder was full but after it was emptied. A much more convincing argument in favour of the correlation mentioned above was found in the mental attitude displayed by the analysands in question. Individuals behind whose 'hyper-potency' was concealed a latent infantile weakness became much more unassuming, whilst those who succeeded through the retention procedure in overcoming a certain anxiousness exhibited a remarkable increase of self-confidence in sexual matters. In addition, they gained courage to bring up deep associations and memories and to advance the transference situation in a manner which up to that point had been impossible. Apart from this I am not altogether convinced that even the so-called 'bladder erection' can be explained solely on mechanical grounds, without the conception of amphimictic displacement of innervation.

These observations afforded me an opportunity of studying in detail, during the analytic 're-education', the

[1] 'The Therapeutic Importance of Genital Libido', Salzburg Congress, 1924. [Translation in preparation.]

nature of pregenital education in children. I found that the ultimate cause of the tendencies to urethral evacuation and to anal retention is anxiety about pain in the case of emptying the bladder, anxiety over the tension caused by a full bladder and, in the case of emptying the bowel, anxiety about pain associated with the stretching and dragging of the anal sphincter. Hence evacuation implies pleasure for the bladder, 'pain' for the rectum.[1] The *erotic* exercise of these functions calls for a relatively great increase in tension. Emptying the bladder gives rise to actual pleasure only when the distension has exceeded a certain limit: in the same way the erotic pleasure-premium in bowel evacuation, to which Freud first called attention, occurs only when the tension or 'pain' experienced before evacuation is appreciable. In my opinion the main specific character of erotism consists in a pleasurable overcoming of self-constituted organic difficulties.[2] Now many neurotics show themselves over-anxious and deny themselves the pleasure of anal and urethral erotism through fear of the unavoidable pain associated therewith; it would appear that the courage to face pregenital erotism is an indispensable factor without which satisfactory genital erotism cannot be established. In analysis the fight over anal and urethral habit-weaning is repeated and, on this occasion, carried to a more successful conclusion, presupposing, of course, the resolution of certain capacities and habits which would indicate superficially that this phase of education had been successfully carried through.

Yet not only did these retention experiments uncover significant physiological phenomena; they also gave rise to associative material of some importance. The child's identification with its parents has in fact a pregenital preliminary stage; preceding the attempt to measure his genital capacity with that of the parents, the child endeavours to outrival them by means of anal and urethral exploits. Here, as is suggested in my *Genitaltheorie*, excreta are equated with children, and the excretory organs

[1] Cf. also D. Forsyth's observations on this point.

[2] *Versuch einer Genitaltheorie*, p. 11.

are made to play the as yet sexually undifferentiated rôle of progenitor.

Active interference, particularly with bowel function, might thus be described in the following terms: by means of it we increase certain tensions until the pain of retention outweighs the anxiety of evacuation; with urethral cases the process might be described rather as one of growing accustomed to something together with the development of tolerance for tensions of the bladder-wall. Beside these physiological factors the part played by the physician, by virtue of parental transference, must obviously not be overlooked. Medical orders and prohibitions repeat to some extent the authoritative commands of the significant personages of childhood, with of course one important difference: in childhood everything tends in the direction of weaning from pleasure-gain; in analysis we substitute for the original training, which has been over-successful, a re-education which affords suitable latitude to erotic play.[1]

Associated with the regulation of anal and urethral function in analysis there occurs as a rule a revision of certain 'character-traits' which, as Freud has shown, are merely substitution, fermentation and sublimation products of these organic instinctual dispositions. Analytic reactivation of anal erotism takes place at the cost of anal character-traits. Patients who up to this point have been over-anxious and avaricious become gradually more liberally disposed, and that not with excreta alone; the inflammable urethral type, who has never been able to tolerate tension even in the mind without immediate discharge, becomes more restrained. Speaking generally, the methods tend to convince patients that they are able to stand more 'pain',

[1] The expressions 'order' and 'prohibition' are rather misleading and do not give an accurate idea of the manner in which, I hold, the procedure should be applied. I would call them rather positive and negative suggestions, implying thereby that they are not so much the authoritative commands familiar in the education of children as experimental modes of behaviour which are adopted by the patient either in agreement with the physician or because he has confidence in their ultimate utility. Nothing is farther from the psycho-analyst's intention than to play the part of omnipotent dictator or to indulge sadistic severity. To do so would be to sink to the level of the one-time psychotherapy of force. It is very seldom necessary to make continuation of treatment contingent on acceptance of our suggestions.

indeed, that they can exploit this 'pain' to extract further pleasure-gain; from this there arises a certain feeling of freedom and self-assurance which is conspicuously absent in the neurotic. Only with the assistance of this self-confidence will sexual tendencies of the advanced genital type be mobilized or courage gained to reactivate the Oedipus complex and to overcome castration anxiety.

When analysis is completed it becomes apparent that neurotic bowel and bladder symptoms are, in part at least, merely repetitions of the old adaptation-struggle between the instinct to evacuate and the earliest social demands. It becomes more and more clear that, as with neuroses generally, the actual traumatic force operative here is the tendency to flight from the Oedipus complex, hence from genital function; manifest and latent expression in neurosis of anal, urethral, oral, and other erotisms is most often secondary in nature, *i.e.* they are regressive substitutions for the actual neurosogenic factors, particularly for castration anxiety.

The anal and urethral identification with the parents, already referred to, appears to build up in the child's mind a sort of physiological forerunner of the ego-ideal or super-ego. Not only in the sense that the child constantly compares his achievements in these directions with the capacities of his parents, but in that a severe sphincter-morality is set up which can only be contravened at the cost of bitter self-reproaches and punishment by conscience. It is by no means improbable that this, as yet semi-physiological, morality forms the essential groundwork of later purely mental morality, just as, in my opinion, the physiological act of smelling (before eating) is the prototype or forerunner of all higher intellectual capacities in which there is a postponement of instinctual gratifications (thought).

It is not impossible that up till now we have greatly under-estimated the biological and physiological significance of the sphincters. Their anatomical form and mode of function seem to be specially adapted to the stimulation, accumulation, and discharge of tensions: they operate after the manner of sluices erected at the portals of entry and exit in the body, and their oscillating degrees of innervation permit an unending variation in states of tension and discharge, in that they facilitate or obstruct the increase and decrease of body-content. These phenomena have previously been regarded in a purely utilitarian light, and the importance of sphincter-play in stimulating pleasure and 'pain', and particularly its erotic significance, have been entirely neglected. It is easy to demonstrate the displacement of innervation from one sphincter to another or to several others. For example, a state of anxiety is usually heralded by marked constriction of the anal orifice, accompanied as a rule by a tendency to empty the bladder. In hysteria this contraction can be displaced to other organs, *e.g.* globus hystericus, laryngeal spasm (hysterical aphonia), pyloric contraction and the formation of atypical sphincters at various points of election in the intestinal canal. The source of all these difficulties is shown in hysteria to be anxiety over the corresponding innervation of the genital sphincters, illustrated in the male by disturbance of potency and in the woman by menstrual troubles (uterine contractions). These sphincter observations suggest that the explanation of many neurotic symptoms lies in their relation to castration anxiety, birth anxiety (Rank), and to the, as yet, incompletely understood anxiety of parturition. As a means of estimating the strength of fluctuations in emotion, in particular of anxiety, one might suggest that experimental psychologists should adopt manometry of anal sphincter-tension, just as paying attention to the oral and glottic sphincters has added to our knowledge of the physiology and pathology of breathing, speaking, and singing, more particularly in respect to their emotional relationship (S. Pfeifer, Forsyth).[1]

Patients who carried these retention exercises beyond a certain point usually displayed great anxiety, sometimes accompanied by temporary incontinence and frequently associated with the reactivation of infantile experiences. The appearance of incontinence can be regarded as a kind of panic when all regard for 'sphincter-morality' is abandoned

[1] See also my remarks on stammering (*Genitaltheorie*, p. 12).

and retreat is made to the stage of infantile-autochthonous self-gratification.[1]

I have already referred to the overflow of increased tension fron anal-urogenital orifices to general psycho-physical tonicity. In one instance dreams occurring during a period of activity showed quite definitely that 'stretching' represented, so to speak, an erection of the whole body, by means of which the patient unconsciously gratified a phantasy of coitus with the mother, the body taking the place of his penis, which he could not erect properly.

In my opinion this identification of the whole body with the genital will prove to be of great significance in the pathology of neurosis as well as in that of organic disease. When I submitted the present observations to Professor Freud, he summed the matter up briefly in the comment that impotent persons who have not the courage for sexual intercourse perform coitus in (unconscious) phantasy with the body as a whole. Perhaps this is the origin of all 'intra-uterine' phantasies.

I might adduce here some other striking instances of the way in which analysis can be favourably influenced by modification of excretory habits. A patient with an almost intolerable anal pruritus, followed by an irresistible tendency to anal and rectal masturbation, showed no signs of symptomatic improvement in spite of a tedious investigation by means of associations. It was only after he had gone through a prolonged voluntary retention experiment and had eliminated the associated feelings of tension in the rectum as pleasure-organ that the tendency to displace erotism to the genitalia became manifest. Another patient who was only capable of having intercourse when his bladder was empty, and not complete intercourse at that, succeeded in producing stronger and more continued erections after some successful attempts at retention of urine; at the same time he made considerable progress towards analytic understanding of his condition. In very many cases, amongst them some male patients, retention of the stools

[1] Cf. the sudden abandonment of all sphincter-control in states of great anxiety, terror, in hanging, etc.

afforded interesting insight into the parturition-significance of the act of passing fæces. The patient who defæcated only by dint of force and with whom excretion was accompanied by spermatorrhea, the price, so to speak, being paid by the genital system, abandoned this symptom after forced retention with painful evacuation.

It is difficult to lay down exact indications when and in which cases the attempt can and must be made; at any rate there must be very good grounds for the assumption that a displacement backwards (or disintegration) of genital erotism to its biological preliminary stages is present, *i.e.* that the original fear of genital castration has been displaced to the more harmless anal and urethral excretory functions. The method described then serves the purpose of bringing about displacement to the genital organ.

That large amounts of libido can be unconsciously attached to bowel function is shown by the following case. A patient had curious attacks associated with a feeling of 'eternity', during which she had to lie still free from all excitation in an introverted state. This 'eternity' actually represented an indefinitely postponed evacuation of the bowels, and was only cleared up when the painful experience of forced retention induced the irresistible compulsion to bring the 'eternity' to an end. It was only after she had permitted herself this anal orgasm that it proved possible for her to approach the previously inaccessible genital orgasm. A patient with exceptionally strong castration-fear was accustomed to pass a single and complete stool: it was a phobia of his to prevent any breaking up of the mass by the sphincters. He exhibited in addition a quite remarkable capacity for which I could find no satisfactory anatomical explanation; he could produce without any external assistance, and as a rule during defæcation, a temporary constriction of the penis just about a centimetre behind the glans. Once his erotism was displaced back to the genital system the chronic impotence improved, and a permanent cure followed the elucidation of his Oedipus complex and the overcoming of his sexual anxiety concerning the parents. Here as in many other cases the moulded fæcal substance represented a child. One of my pupils, v. Kovács, of Budapest, was able to correlate a facial tic which had persisted from childhood with latent tendencies to masturbation and displacement to the bowels; she was able to bring about a cure by means of psycho-analysis together with the imposition of certain bowel exercises.

These observations tend to confirm the view that 'bioanalytic' dissection of genital function is not only of theoretical importance, but is calculated to add to our therapeutic resources.

By way of supplement it should be said that 'activity' can be applied to the functions of nutrition as well as to those of excretion: renunciation of certain pleasures in eating and drinking, both qualitative and quantitative, together with compulsory eating of foods or substances which have previously been avoided for reasons of idiosyncrasy, can uncover the instinctual background of oral character-traits.

II. *The Analysis of Certain Sexual Habits*

In his address delivered at the Budapest Congress,[1] Freud told us most emphatically that the rule regarding the state of privation in which analysis should be conducted was not to be taken to mean permanent sexual abstinence during analysis. In the present section, however, I should like to adduce some evidence showing the various advantages to be gained if one is not deterred from imposing even this privation. The most convincing theoretical argument in its favour I have taken from one of Freud's latest works,[2] in which he shows us that a permanent bond in groups is based on the 'aim-inhibited' sexual impulses alone and that gratification continually weakens this bond. In my opinion the same applies to the 'group of two' represented in the analytic situation between physician and patient. Freud himself stated some considerable time ago that habitual sexual gratification renders the child ineducable, in all

[1] 'Turnings in the Ways of Psycho-Analytic Therapy', 1918, *Collected Papers*, vol. ii.

[2] *Group Psychology and the Analysis of the Ego.*

probability because indulgence increases the child's narcissism, thus making it independent of external influence. The same is true of that kind of re-education which we seek to effect by means of psycho-analysis. Educational and analytic work must both alike repeat the latency period (which I have made bold to regard as a residue of primeval deprivations dating perhaps from the Glacial Epoch) and bring it to a new and successful conclusion. In this work the physician must take over the rôle of father or primal father,[1] whilst the patient must be in that state of susceptibility which involves regression to the group mind (Freud). Continued lowering of sexual tension by gratification during the analysis implies an absence of those conditions which promote the psychological situation necessary for transference. The analyst produces the same effect on the patient as the despot who loves no one but is loved by all; by countermanding the habitual modes of gratification he ensures an affective relationship with the analysand, by means of which repressed material is freed and the relationship itself is ultimately dissolved.[2]

The necessity to combine analysis with sexual abstinence was not simply the result of speculation but arose from disappointing experiences in cases where the countermand was not given or where the temptation to transgress it was too strong. A young married woman with acute melancholia had a secret love-affair but, owing to my apprehension of her committing suicide, I had never dared to suggest complete abstinence from sexual relations; she proved amenable to my influence only while her mental condition was intolerable, but shortly afterwards became refractory and returned to her lover without completing analysis. Another young woman consulted me on account of an unhappy love-affair with a doctor who practised certain sexual activities with her but did not return her tender regard. Transference was easily established but, as analysis presented no prospect of gratification, she abandoned it on

[1] It is obvious that the physician must also occasionally play the part of mother.

[2] This last factor, it is true, differentiates the mental situation of the analysand from that of adherence to a religious or other sect in which obedience is strengthened by means of privation (hunger, thirst, sexual asceticism, sleeplessness, etc.).

several occasions and returned to the less scrupulous colleague. Again and again she came back penitently to resume treatment, only to break away when resistance increased. On the last occasion she kept away for a prolonged period, and the next I heard of her was a newspaper report of her suicide. I lost a very interesting case of obsessional neurosis, in spite of normal transference and unimpeded progress, simply because I had not forbidden energetically enough an affair with a man who, characteristically, had the same surname as myself. I had a similar experience with another neurotic woman who was accustomed to indulge in 'infidelities' of this kind during the summer holidays.

From these observations two conclusions are irresistible: first, that there is little prospect of analytically freeing anyone from an unhappy infatuation so long as actual gratifications with the love-object are taking place; secondly, that it is as a rule unfavourable if patients can enjoy sexual pleasures during analysis. Obviously a state of sexual abstinence is more easily attained with unmarried than with married people; in the latter case it can often be induced by temporary separation from the marriage partner.

Nevertheless, it is precisely with married neurotics that regulation of marital sexual relations is imperative. Semi-potent or three-parts potent men often strive after sexual achievements far exceeding their desire,[1] and revenge themselves on their wives by bad temper, or else exhibit or exaggerate neurotic symptoms. Moreover, it is often true of the apparently hyper-potent that their sexual performances merely compensate for feelings of weakness, something after the manner I have already described in urethral types. A disposition of this sort is not calculated to promote transference, and moreover the real state of affairs is concealed; hence if the analysis is to be advanced the disposition must be overcome. Take, for example, the following case, which is quite typical: a patient who had been neurotic since early youth was before his marriage 'cured' of impotence by

[1] Cf. also Rank, 'Perversion and Neurosis', INTERNATIONAL JOURNAL OF PSYCHO-ANALYSIS, vol. iv.

some urological treatment or other. The cure was effected by an obsessional neurosis being brought about, and by dint of carrying out innumerable ceremonials he was able to perform coitus with a semi-erect penis; in fact he had two children. The first regulation imposed during analysis was one of complete separation, which quite obviously ameliorated his condition. Thereupon he was given a urinary retention course, since his ceremonials were mainly of a urethral type, *e.g.* micturition immediately preceding intromission. In the meantime analysis of the obsessive impulses and thoughts was of course continued, and shortly afterwards these symptoms were correlated with the enforced but unconsciously dreaded sexual activities. The compulsion acted in this case, as Freud says it invariably does, as a corrective to doubt, which latter was motivated by castration anxiety. At a later stage of treatment the patient had spontaneous erections, but was enjoined to continue renunciation of gratification both with his wife and with other women. This procedure represented, of course, merely an extension to the genital organ of retention exercises previously associated with the urinary apparatus. Here again the tension had to increase beyond the limits set by anxiety, when it produced not only increased pleasure in aggression, physiologically speaking, but stimulated the mental courage necessary to attack the unconscious phantasies. In this manner the analysis described, and many others, were successfully stimulated by a kind of 'sexual anagogy'.

The necessity for such anagogy is not confined to neurotics; many unhappy married relations can be improved by this means. Nothing is more prejudicial to marriage than a pretence of greater tenderness, and particularly of stronger erotism, than is actually present, to say nothing of the suppression of hate and other 'painful' feelings. An occasional angry outburst and temporary abstinence can work wonders in the subsequent reconciliation. The husband often adopts a wrong attitude in sexual affairs from the very first night; he feels constrained to exercise to a bride who is quite unaccustomed to these demonstrations a degree of masculine potency far beyond the necessities of the occasion. The result is that their erotic relations cool off even during the honeymoon: the husband becomes morose and his wife is overcome with perplexity at the course of events. This may develop into a permanent source of damage to married relations. The husband begins to feel his ' conjugal duties ' as a regular compulsion against which his libido rebels with correspondingly compulsive polygamous inclinations. In such cases the abstinence-rule is of some service. By its very nature intercourse should not be a deliberate act, a matter of use and wont, but a sort of celebration during which dammed-up energies can spend themselves in an archaic fashion.[1] Moreover, psycho-analysis has taught us that owing to the equation of wife and mother, Oedipus anxiety is usually the source of disinclination for marital intercourse. Paradoxically enough, therefore, marital fidelity makes greater demands on potency than the most lurid polygamous existence. That so many love-marriages end unhappily is to be attributed to a diminution in tenderness resulting from overstressed gratification; both partners find their dreams shattered, whilst the husband even comes to regard himself as caught in the toils and doomed to lifelong sexual slavery.

As we know from the symptom-complexes of neurasthenia, genito-sexual overactivity can give rise to physical and mental disturbances, especially to states of depression. My experience of analytic treatment and cure of such symptoms has led to a deeper understanding of the pathology of this condition, which up to the present has been rather neglected by psycho-analysts. The ' inadequate discharge ', which Freud in his earlier works described as the cause of neurasthenia, proves on closer examination to be a protest of anxiety on the part of the corporeal and psychic ego against libidinal exhaustion; regarded from this point of view neurasthenia is seen to be founded on hypochondriacal ego-anxiety, in direct antithesis to the anxiety-neurosis, where anxiety is due to dammed-up object-libido. Even after normal copulation neurasthenics are plagued

[1] Cf. *Genitaltheorie*, p. 58.

with 'scruples of corporeal conscience' about masturbatory and other genital activities; they feel that orgasm has been brought about as one would forcibly pluck unripe fruit, that is to say, by gratification of as yet insufficient sexual tension at the cost of ego-function. This may account for the 'pulling off' symbol for masturbation. Of course, treatment of neurasthenia can only be purely palliative in nature, *e.g.* the abandonment of pathogenic types of gratification; nevertheless, it can be materially advanced by analytic discovery of the motivations behind masturbation-anxiety and its reduction in course of treatment.

W. Reich [1] is entirely in the right when he holds that it is by no means essential to prevent gratification of onanism which has previously been avoided from motives of anxiety. I should like to add that once the patient has learned to tolerate masturbation another stage remains to be gone through, viz. learning to endure still stronger sexual tensions even without masturbation, that is to say, toleration of complete abstinence. Only in this way can he overcome auto-erotism completely and find a path to normal sexual objects. In analytical terminology narcissistic libido-tension is required to reach a pitch where discharge is no longer a sacrifice but a relief and a source of pleasure.

An important fact disclosed by the study of neurasthenia, as indeed of nearly every neurosis or psycho-neurosis, is that nocturnal emissions are masturbatory acts exiled to dream life on account of their incompatibility with consciousness, and that they are often encouraged by the adoption of certain postures. Explanation of the unconscious desire for such gratification is accepted by the patient, after a more or less prolonged resistance, through sheer weight of evidence, and responsibility for this form of self-gratification is assumed, with the result that it is either greatly reduced or abandoned altogether. Emission dreams are without exception disguised incest-dreams, which fact of itself explains why they cannot be experienced as waking masturbation phantasies. Hence we are entitled to regard it as an advance when masturbation takes the place of the

[1] *Loc. cit.*

more pathogenic nocturnal emission; the former should then be allowed free play before complete abstinence is imposed.

Anxiety-neurosis, too, which we find at the root of every anxiety-hysteria and of most conversion-hysteria, can also be treated either by palliative measures or in a radical fashion; it likewise depends on two factors, on the one hand the amount of dammed-up libido, and on the other the sensitiveness to such libido-accumulations. As with onanistic over-expenditure of libido, abstinence is accompanied with anxiety ideas and sensations. The neurasthenic regards his semen as the most priceless sap, the loss of which will bring in its train all manner of grievous conditions and diseases, whilst the anxiety-neurotic is afraid that his dammed-up libido will poison him or cause him to have a stroke. The radical treatment in this case is the adoption, even in increased degree, indeed, of the abstinence-rule in spite of anxiety, together with continued analytic investigation and mastering of the anxiety itself and of its mental derivatives.

Abnormalities of ejaculation (ejaculatio praecox in the case of neurasthenia, and in anxiety-neurosis ejaculatio retardata) are certainly to be regarded as disturbances of the seminal vesicles and their sphincters in the urethral or anal sense. Hence they may require to be dealt with by a combination of genital and pregenital abstinence-rules. A Mohammedan conversant with Indian erotic customs informed me that, in common with his fellow-countrymen, he could perform coitus without ejaculation *ad infinitum* provided that during the act the woman exercised pressure with the fingers on his perineum, in this way relieving him of the necessity of controlling the ejaculatory sphincters.

As has already been pointed out, these various abstinence-rules, in addition to displacing repressed innervations to other parts of the body, bring about mental reactions by means of which much unconscious material is uncovered. We have already considered the anxiety-reaction: no less striking, however, are the frequent manifestations of rage and of desires for revenge directed naturally in the first instance against the analyst but easily traceable to infantile sources. And it is precisely this freedom of reaction which distinguishes the orders and prohibitions of analytic re-education from those which were experienced in childhood and later on gave rise to neuroses. But we shall return to this matter of aggression in somewhat greater detail below. Abstinences, especially the abandonment of sexual 'excesses', bring about a quite undeniable increase in mental capacity, suggesting that the libido saved thereby increases not only the muscular tone but the tone of the thinking apparatus, a view which incidentally was expressed by Schopenhauer. With neurosis, however, there can be no increased pleasure or increased capacity without analysis; increase of tone merely helps to bring repressed material to the surface, and only when this has been thoroughly sifted does increase in capacity occur. We know, since Freud's work, that, in the absence of analytic solution, neither abstinence nor gratification can resolve neurotic conflicts.[1]

III. *On Unconscious Phantasies of Sexual Lust-Murder*

Application of urethral, anal, and genital regulation during analysis of patients exhibiting genito-sexual excess has resulted in uncovering, with quite striking regularity, strong tendencies towards aggression, chiefly in the form of lust-murder. These are often expressed in sadistic phantasies of strangling, stabbing, or otherwise violently overpowering a woman, and sometimes are merely alluded to by jocular or playful illustrative references. To judge from the associations, this wish to murder the woman, which as a rule is only unconscious, is highly over-determined. First and foremost it is an act of revenge for the intention ascribed to the woman of robbing the man of his semen: secondly, it is an expression of castration anxiety, the threat from the father on account of sexual intercourse. This component of the murder-impulse is really transferred from the man (father) to the woman (mother). On the other hand, adopting Rank's use of the term, the anxiety in such cases can be interpreted as anxiety in regard to the mother's

[1] *Introductory Lectures on Psycho-Analysis*, p. 361.

vagina (vagina dentata = birth anxiety). It is not yet clear whether, and if so to what extent, the latter anxiety is to be regarded as an actual traumatic factor, as a repetition of the trauma of birth, or whether it is merely an expression of castration anxiety or parturition anxiety; possibly both factors are present in varying degree in individual cases.

At any rate, after a communication by S. Pfeifer at the Budapest Psycho-Analytic Society to the effect that a necrophilic dream was due to anxiety in regard to coitus, I was able to state this general principle, viz. that the sadistic impulses of neurotics are frequently based on coitus anxiety. Many neurotics unconsciously regard coitus as an activity which, either directly or subsequently, is calculated to injure life or limb, and in particular to damage the genital organ, *i.e.* an act in which are combined gratification and severe anxiety. Murder then at any rate partly subserves the purpose of avoiding anxiety by rendering the love-object incapable of inflicting injury; gratification can then be enjoyed undisturbed by castration anxiety. In these phantasies of aggression the woman is attacked in the first instance with external weapons (knife, dagger, or, in the case of throttling, with parts of the body which are not usually protected, *i.e.* the hand), following on which coitus is performed, that is to say, the penis is employed as weapon against a now harmless object. The close fusion of aggressive and libidinal impulses which exists in normal coitus here seems to be as it were 'defused' into two distinct actions. In the normal coitus of individuals who are not neurotic, the inner tension seeking for discharge finally overcomes anxiety, although, as suggested in my ontogenetic and phylogenetic 'catastrophe'-theory of coitus,[1] some traces of anxiety may still persist.

By imposing abstinence we compel the neurotic to endure powerful tensions which finally overcome anxiety about coitus. In one instance I was able to observe with special clearness in the dream-life of the patient a gradual development from phantasies of lust-murder to those of

[1] Cf. *Genitaltheorie*, chaps. v. and vi.

coitus. Following dreams in which the woman (mother) was killed came others depicting violent struggles with a man (doctor, father) and ending in emission. Still later there appeared active homosexual dreams, *i.e.* castration of men, and only when the man had been overcome and the principal danger thus averted did manifest dreams of coitus with women occur.[1]

It remains now to correlate these observations with my somewhat slender experience of manifest masochistic perversions. I have it on the authority of an extremely intelligent young man who suffered from this perversion that each masochist finds pleasure only in a special degree of humiliation and bodily suffering to which the partner in each case is specially enjoined to conform. The degree varies individually but, should the margin be overstepped, their desire cools and they abandon the passionate relationship as far as that particular object is concerned. It seems that the masochist's need for punishment, or, more broadly speaking, his need for suffering, the deeper sources of which have been brought to light in Freud's latest work on this subject,[2] subserves in addition, one might say, practical ends. These are somewhat akin to the purpose of my own experiments, which are intended to increase the capacity for tolerating pain beyond the anxiety-barrier in order to stimulate the courage necessary for coitus. Since their orgasm takes place during the infliction of pain, masochists never attain this position, and are either incapable of ordinary coitus or at most can perform coitus only when there has been some preceding painful experience. The parts of the body surrendered for algolagnia are almost invariably extra-genital, as it were a displacement of pain and anxiety to other parts of the body, in order to preserve genital gratification unhampered by castration anxiety. A masochist whose pleasurable phantasies were concerned with being beaten on the buttocks exemplified this state of affairs very well. As a child she had substituted anal erotism for genital

[1] Further research into this question would not only help to explain criminal lust-murders, but also ordinary murderous impulses.

[2] 'The Economic Problem of Masochism', *Collected Papers*, vol. ii.

masturbation, but then took pleasure in having blows administered on the buttocks immediately after defæcation. I fancy I should have made more progress with this case had I employed anal retention-exercises with a view to re-establishing genital erotism and so inducing tolerance for castration, birth, and parturition phantasies.

From this point of view it can be seen that sadistic murder-pleasure and masochistic enjoyment of suffering have a common motivation in mental and physical sensitiveness to pain involving the genital region, and in the resultant anxiety about normal sexual activity. Future investigation will show how far unconscious identification of the whole ego with the genital plays a part in this process.[1]

IV. *Habit and Symptom*

All the manifestations which we have so far classified as urethral, anal, and sexual habits can be defined as symptoms behind which analysis is able to disclose repressed desires and feelings. We shall now describe another, although very incomplete, series of 'symptom habits' which are not directly connected with the genital organ.

Special mention must be made of patients' movements during analysis to which we have already alluded. Many patients exhibit an exaggerated rigidity of all the limbs; when greeting the analyst or saying good-bye this may develop into almost catatonic rigidity without necessarily suggesting a condition of schizophrenia. As analysis progresses release of mental tensions may be accompanied by relief of muscular tensions, but sometimes this does not happen and we are compelled to draw the patient's attention to the habit and so to some extent to 'mobilize' it. As a rule this results in review of material previously hidden or repressed, in particular of affectionate or hostile tendencies which were inhibited owing to tension, and in addition of difficulties relating to sexual discharge and erection. The patient's handshake may afterwards become freer and his posture more mobile, whilst the mental attitudes may show

[1] Cf. *Genitaltheorie*, p. 52.

a corresponding change.[1] Some considerable time ago my attention was directed to certain 'transitory' symptoms[2] beside these constant symptoms just described; even the sudden cessation of a habitual rhythmic movement can be interpreted in analysis as signifying a suppressed thought, and as such can be explained to the patient.[3]

An unfamiliar gesture occurring during analysis may prove to be a sign of repressed emotion. Most significant, however, are the so-called 'naughty' or 'bad habits', nail-biting, nose-boring, scratching, fingering the moustache, etc. I have elsewhere[4] indicated the possibility that such habits are masturbation-equivalents. At any rate it is worth while paying them some attention and, when opportunity arises, suggesting to the patient that they should be abandoned. This should be done not so much by way of breaking a habit as in the expectation that increasing tension will force unconscious material to the surface, where it can be turned to analytic advantage. The most persistent of all 'transitory' formations, tic convulsif, can neither be understood nor improved without some such procedure.

A specially typical case was that of a man suffering from a severe narcissistic neurosis who was obsessed with the (imaginary) idea that his nose was misshapen and who made constant grimacing contortions of the facial muscles, which were particularly violent during times of emotional excitement. He had in addition innumerable mannerisms of posture and movement which on occasion were elaborated into obsessive ceremonials. Analysis of this condition was materially advanced by a strict prohibition during the hour of the very slightest tic-like movements: later on the prohibition was extended to movements occurring in extra-analytical periods, which, I need hardly say, involved some quite strenuous work for both patient and analyst. Never-

[1] Cf. 'On the Technique of Psycho-Analysis' (1919), pp. 177-189.

[2] Cf. Ferenczi, 'Transitory Symptom-Formations during Analysis' (1912), *Contributions to Psycho-Analysis*.

[3] There seems to be a certain relation between the capacity in general for relaxation of the musculature and for free association. Sometimes I require patients to relax particularly. Cf. 'Thinking and Muscle Innervation', pp. 230-233.

[4] 'Technical Difficulties in the Analysis of a Case of Hysteria', p. 189. 'Psycho-Analytical Observations on Tic', p. 142.

theless, by giving this tension conscious psychic discharge in place of reflex and, so to speak, symbolic discharge, we were able to discover the aim and motivation of each individual movement. The grimaces represented an unconscious, cosmetic manipulation of the nasal muscles, the earlier ideal form of the nose being thus reproduced through the movements of contraction and dilatation; this tendency was concealed by the horrifying effect of the facial distortion. The other mannerisms were also part of a system of beauty-culture.[1] Further associations brought memories of childhood from which it appeared that all these postures and movements had once been consciously and deliberately practised and cultivated, although later on the patient had little appreciation of their meaning and interpretation.

This observation is by no means an isolated one; indeed, to judge from my experience of hysterical and other neurotic physical symptoms, one might go so far as to suggest that none of these symptoms occurs without having had infantile forerunners of the nature of 'habits'. It is not for nothing that nurses make efforts to counteract so-called childish tricks, as when they threaten children who pull faces that they will be 'struck like that'. In most instances, certainly, they are not struck like it, but, where neurosogenic conflicts are present, suppressed infantile habits provide the repressed with symptom-forming material. When some hysterical symptoms strike us as being 'exaggerations' (*e.g.* isolated contractions of otherwise symmetrically contracting muscles of the eye or larynx, of the platysma, movement of the galea, modification of the involuntary processes of circulation, respiration, or of intestinal peristalsis) we must remember that the childish organism has other sources of excitation in auto-erotic or organo-erotic play which are not available in the adult. 'Education' consists not merely in learning to acquire capacities, but to no small degree in unlearning 'supernormal' capacities. Forgotten (or repressed) capacities can, however, return in the form of neurotic

[1] Incidentally, this example is one of many that go to confirm my contention that tics stand in a very close relation to narcissistic neuroses. Here, as so often, the narcissism was secondary, a displacement of the dreaded genital erotism back on to the whole body, indeed on to the whole psycho-physical ego.

symptoms.[1] For that matter, all obsessive ceremonials have one of their roots at least in childish games and activities. The curious idea which so many neurotics ventilate at the end of treatment, viz. that the illness which had tormented and incapacitated them so much was after all only 'a pretence', is quite sound in the sense that they have produced in adult life symptoms which during childhood they aimed at and sought after in play.

Moreover, psycho-analysis can be regarded as a long-drawn-out fight against thought-habits. Free association, for example, makes constant demands on both physician and patient if the latter is to be prevented from slipping back into directed thought. Should one, however, observe that rational associations of a painful character are being avoided with the help of free associations the patient must be induced to face the former.[2] On the other hand, some patients take up the whole hour with a monotonous series of hypochondriacal and querulous ideas which are a substitute for free association. Having allowed them a certain amount of latitude, I sometimes make the suggestion that instead of repeating the boring sequence over again, the patient should make a prearranged gesture to indicate that he is busy with the familiar train of thought. In this way he is unable to gain relief, with the result that the underlying material is more rapidly brought to light. In a similar way by prohibiting elliptical associations (obtuse loquacity) we can bring patients to complete a painful train of thought, not, of course, without considerable resistance on their part.

v. *The Metapsychology of Habits in General*

Hitherto our knowledge of the psychology of habit could be summed up in the proverb 'Habit becomes second nature'. The theory that paths of excitational discharge are 'canalized' by repetition tells us no more; it merely

[1] One neurotic with digestive trouble remembered as a child passing flatus audibly seventy times running; another with a respiratory complaint used at the age of three or four to lean hard against the edge of the table until an expiration-convulsion ensued.

[2] 'On the Technique of Psycho-Analysis: Abuse of Free Association', p. 177.

expresses the same proverb in artificial, physiological terminology. Freud's theory of instincts enabled us for the first time to understand the psychic motivation of the tendency to repeat earlier experiences as if they were habits: his repetition-compulsion is a derivative of the life-instincts and death-instincts which seek to reduce all animate matter to a state of equilibrium. At all events, repetition is associated with an ' economy of mental expenditure ', compared with which seeking after new paths represents a fresh adaptation, *i.e.* something relatively less pleasurable. Freud's latest work (*Das Ich und das Es*, 1923)[1] first gave us some idea of the psychic topography of the processes involved in habit-formation and habit-resolution. The dynamic and economic aspects of these processes had already been dealt with in his earlier work. In my opinion his subdivision of the ego, which had previously been regarded as an entity, into real ego, super-ego, and *id*, enables us to indicate with more accuracy the region of the mental system involved in converting voluntary actions into automatisms (habit-forming), and on the other hand the part involved in giving automatisms a fresh orientation or in altering them (habit-breaking). The region where we may conceive habit-tendencies to be piled up is that great reservoir of instinct and libido, the *id*, whereas the ego is only stimulated when the necessity arises to deal with a new and disturbing stimulus, that is to say, when adaptation is essential. In this sense the ego operates like an ' emergency-apparatus ', to use Bleuler's phrase: each fresh adaptation demands expenditure of attention, *i.e.* involves work on the part of the conscious perceptual layer, whereas habits are deposited in the unconscious of the person concerned. Habit-formation implies that the *id* has become responsible for a previous ego-activity (adaptation), whereas to break a habit implies that the conscious ego has taken over from the *id* a previously automatic method of discharge, in order to apply it in a new direction.[2] It is clear that this conception brings

[1] [No. 12 of the International Psycho-Analytical Library.]

[2] The feeling of decision according to free will, that of *liberum arbitrium*, is attached only to acts accomplished by the ego and not to the instinctive or ' habitual ' reactions of the *id*.

instinct and habit into one and the same category, a view to some extent justified by the fact that instincts themselves always tend to re-establish previous states. They are in that sense also merely habits, whether they lead directly to the peace of death or arrive there by the roundabout route which follows the 'sweet habit of life'. Nevertheless, it is perhaps better not to equate habit and instinct entirely, but rather to regard habit as intermediate between voluntary action and actual instinct, reserving the term 'instinct' for those long-standing habits which are not acquired during the lifetime of the individual but are handed on by inheritance. Habits would then represent, so to speak, the cambium layer of instinct-formation where even now the transformation of voluntary into instinctive action takes place and can still be observed. The sources of voluntary actions are perceptual acts, stimuli which impinge on the perceptual surface of the individual, a layer which, in Freud's opinion, alone guards the approaches to motility. In habit-formation outer stimuli are, so to speak, introjected and work from within outwards, either spontaneously or on minimal stimuli from the outer world.

Now analysis as usually carried out is really a fight against habits and is directed towards substitution of real adaptations in place of those unsatisfactory habit-like methods of resolving conflict which we call symptoms: hence it provides an 'instrument wherewith the ego can continually possess itself of more of the *id*' (Freud).

Of course the third ego-component, the super-ego, has also an important part to play in processes of habit-formation and habit-breaking. It is certain that habits would not be so easily acquired or given up if there were no previous identification with the educating forces whose example is built up in the mind as a pattern of behaviour. We need not go over again the libidinal trends and psychological group-bonds which are concerned in the process. We can, however, regard this introjection of external educative influences as a model for the formation of a new habit and for the appearance of a fresh instinct. At this juncture the problem of instinct-formation becomes involved with such other problems as the formation of mnemic impressions in the mind or in organic substance generally. It is perhaps more advantageous to explain memory processes in terms of instinct than to mask our knowledge of instinct in such irreducible terms as ' mnems '.[1]

Psycho-analysis aims at bringing unconscious components of the *id* which operate automatically once more under the disposal of the ego. The latter, by virtue of its closer relationship to all the forces of reality, can then give these components a fresh orientation, one more in keeping with the requirements of the reality-principle. Communication between conscious and unconscious comes about, as Freud tells us, ' by the interposition of preconscious links '. Now of course that applies only to unconscious presentations; in the case of unconscious inner trends which ' behave like the repressed ', that is to say, do not get through to consciousness either as emotions or sensations, interpolation of preconscious links will not bring them into consciousness. For example, unconscious inner ' pain ' sensations ' can develop driving force without attracting the ego's attention to the compulsion. Only resistance to the compulsion, a blocking of discharge-reaction can bring this " Something Else " into consciousness in the form of " pain ".'[2] Now our ' activity ' in technique holds up discharge-reactions (abstinence, privation, countermand of pleasurable activities, insistence on unpleasurable activities), increases thereby the tension of inner need, and connects up with consciousness ' pain ' which has hitherto been unconscious; hence it is to be regarded as a necessary amplification of purely passive association technique. The latter starts from whichever psychic superficies is present and

[1] Here we reach the problem of organic inheritance. ' The experiences of the ego ', says Freud in *Das Ich und das Es*, p. 46, ' seem at first to be lost to posterity ; when they have been repeated often enough and with sufficient intensity, however, in the successive individuals of after-generations, they transform themselves, so to say, into experiences of the *id*, the impress of which is preserved by inheritance.' Consideration of the process of habit-forming in the course of an individual life shows us, in my opinion, rather more clearly the path taken by this process of incorporation ; the inheritance of an individually-acquired attribute may by parallel induction or some other method influence the germ-plasm and so the succeeding generations. Cf. also *Genitaltheorie*, p. 91.

[2] Freud, *Das Ich und das Es*, p. 23.

works back to the preconscious cathexes of unconscious material: it might be described as 'analysis from above', to distinguish it from the 'active' method which I should like to call 'analysis from below'. In this connection the fight against 'habits' and particularly against larval modes of libido-discharge, which being unconscious attract no attention, is one of the most important means of increasing inner tensions.

VI. *Some Technical Considerations*

A review of the foregoing material enables us to correlate our theoretical anticipations with the results of former quite free experimentation by 'active methods' and, where occasion demands, to supply missing details or correct inaccuracies.

Granted that our view of the twofold direction of analysis is accurate, the question immediately arises: What is the relation of one method to the other? When, for example, should we commence analysis from below and how long should it be continued? To these questions no precise answer can be returned. Hence analysis from above should be regarded, now as before, as the classical method, not only from the point of view of scientific comprehensibility, but in that it conforms to the necessity for precise technical formulations. Nevertheless, I think the case-material I have brought forward, in particular the descriptions of urethro-anal and genital regulation, at least show us how active technique can promote non-active procedure. Moreover, I believe that our brief theoretical discussion has helped us to understand the rationale of the method. For the sake of completeness in presentation I should like now to put forward some of the ideas which have forced themselves on me during application of the technique.

So long as the existing inner tensions suffice to bring out the material which is essential for analytic progress, there is no necessity to increase them artificially, and we can direct our whole attention to analytic dissection of the material spontaneously produced. The appropriate procedure has been described with some detail in Freud's papers on technique. When, however, at a certain stage of the analysis the patient makes himself at home, so to speak, further progress can only be attained by adopting a certain degree of activity which will lead once more to the unhampered production of spontaneous associations. Many analyses are greatly stimulated by this alternation of emotional and intellectual phases; one cannot help comparing the process to one of driving tunnel-shafts, with this difference, that in analysis the work is carried out now from one end and now from the other.

With regard to the golden rule of activity, namely, privation, it is not advisable to accede at once to suggestions coming from the patient. Apart from the fact that one of course always first asks for associations to the suggested procedure, it is a good plan to advise the patient to abstain from such a course for the time being or indeed to recommend doing the reverse of what he has proposed. At any rate one is more likely to discover its psychic motivations in this way than if one permits the patient to follow his accustomed line of least resistance. Some patients try to find occasion for conflict in analysis, using a technique which has proved successful in their everyday life, and it is striking to watch the effect of treating them in an indulgent manner. One brings about in this way a state of privation, since it is more difficult for them to discharge certain affects in the face of indulgent treatment. In contrast to this, certain sensitive types who have been accustomed to petting and who leave no stone unturned to gain expressions of affection from the analyst should be treated with a certain degree of strictness or at least in a somewhat detached objective way. Of course it is obviously only feasible to go against the grain in this way when the patient's analytical attachment is sufficiently strong.

Generally speaking, it is a good plan to hold a watching brief for some time after the commencement of analysis, contenting oneself with study of the patient's reactions to the changing circumstances of his accustomed *milieu*. Gradually one commences to interpret and to offer analytic explanations, and still later, should the progress of analytic work demand it, one may occasionally lay down certain rules of conduct. These are directed in the first instance towards the patient's relationships with his family, friends, colleagues, or superiors, then to the modification of personal habits and customs, particularly in regard to details of eating, sleeping, dressing, and undressing, etc., and to his ways of physical gratification. Where patients are passionately fond of reading or engage in artistic pleasures, it is sometimes necessary to put a temporary ban on such pursuits. In certain instances one must remove the patient from his accustomed *milieu* for a longer or shorter period, although it is generally more advisable to end the analysis under the same external circumstances which the patient will encounter when he comes to exercise whatever fresh capacity for adaptation he has gained through treatment. Similarly with patients who come to analysis from a distance, it may be necessary to advise a temporary sojourn in their native surroundings in order to test the reaction of their newly acquired mentality to the old environment.

The most difficult situation to handle technically is that of the transference, in which the decisive battle between physician and patient, or rather between health and disease, is played out. In such cases the analyst must preserve an attitude of unwearied patience in the face of aggressive impatience: here impassivity has the same effect as the most extreme 'activity'.[1] When, for example, the love-transference is of a specially stormy nature and the patient responds to the analyst's attitude of unruffled objectivity with icy reserve, it may require weeks, even months, of laborious 'working through' to demonstrate that, in spite of the analyst's lack of response, the patient's positive feelings still exist in the unconscious. Recognition of this fact indicates marked analytic progress; it also implies some modification in the character-development of the patient who at some time or other in childhood has stuck in a phase of hate and sulkiness; transference-experiences of this kind

[1] Cf. 'On the Technique of Psycho-Analysis' (1919), pp. 177-189.

lead more easily to the discovery and reconstruction of the associated infantile memories.[1]

Moreover, the privation rule can often help us to overcome a by no means trifling difficulty, viz. what attitude the analyst must observe when the patient gives expression to impulsive affection. So long as the patient is in a state of resistance, we must, as previously indicated, draw his attention to the presence of unconscious feelings of tenderness; actually these must be allowed a certain time and latitude in which to develop. But it is not possible simply to respond to the patient's desire for affectionate treatment or flattery, as is so often done in suggestion or hypnosis. In analysis, transference-love must be entirely one-sided, and as soon as the previously repressed emotions take the form of wishes, or even compulsions, privation must once more be imposed.

All that I have described as 'activity' refers only to the patient's actions and behaviour; he alone, therefore, is under certain circumstances active, not the analyst. Nevertheless, it cannot be denied that in exceptional cases the analyst must employ the familiar educational instruments of friendliness and severity. Curiously enough, this is less frequently needed in cases of real neurosis than in actual psychopathic or psychotic cases; it is also more frequently indicated with persons who are treated for character abnormalities than with those suffering from neurotic or psychotic symptoms. The same may be said of the analysis of 'healthy' subjects. Character-analyses may prove almost as difficult as the analyses of psychoses. This is due to the fact that character traits, which are accepted by the ego, resemble symptoms concerning which the patient has no insight; at any rate their treatment involves the patient's narcissism. Character traits are, so to speak, secret psychoses; hence the paradox that sound people are more difficult to 'cure' than those suffering, for example, from transference-neuroses. In one instance a psychopathic patient with strong narcissism and a tendency to catatonic rigidity and mutism was freed from

[1] Cf. Ferenczi-Rank, 'Wiederholung der unerwiderten Oedipusliebe in der analytischen Situation', *Entwicklungsziele der Psychoanalyse*, 1924. [Being transl.]

his tension when I allowed him to strike me. It is my belief that by so doing I forestalled some impulsive action, possibly a dangerous one. On another occasion I took the unavoidable and salutary course of permitting a psychopathic patient who suffered from exceedingly severe anxiety-attacks to display his undeveloped genitalia before me for medical examination.

Using the terminology of ego-analysis, we may also describe our treatment in the following way: on some occasions it is a process whereby, using associative channels or by means of increased tensions, repressed *id*-excitations are brought to consciousness in the face of ego-resistances; at other times it is a process whereby over-strong *id*-impulses (often those excitations which are the first to be expressed) are prevented from obtaining discharge by the mobilization of more powerful ego-forces. The aim of analysis is the development of a personality with powerful instinctual trends but at the same time with great capacity for controlling them. We might say that a successfully educated or analysed individual is one who does not repress his desires but at the same time does not become their slave.

As to the forms of neurosis in which increase of tension or habit-frustration is indicated, it is difficult to lay down a general rule. In hysteria we encounter quite open and spontaneous expression of emotional and physical signs of stimulation, hence there is no necessity for artificial stimulation; even so, we can by suitable means hasten the displacement of this stimulation back to the genital organ. The obsessional neurotic, as is his wont, endeavours to shift the entire analysis on to an intellectual plane and tries to subvert the association method for purposes of obsessive brooding. Practically no obsessional case can be cured until his conflict has been displaced to the emotional level (usually by dint of activity), *i.e.* until the case has been temporarily metamorphosed into hysteria. In one instance a border-line case of schizophrenia, with visual hallucinations, was treated by extremely active analysis and exhibited the following modification of the clinical picture: a doubting mania, which had been in evidence prior to the psychosis, now took the place of the paraphrenic symptoms. Later on a series of conversion-symptoms appeared, followed by signs of anxiety-hysteria (typical phobias). For the first time at this stage analytic investigation of the libidinal basis of his illness became possible. I formed the impression that his disease gradually retreated before the analytic reconstruction, rallying, however, at each fixation-point in order to oppose treatment with fortified resistances. These and many other similar observations have convinced me that ' analysis from below ' is not merely an analytic accessory but advances our theoretical understanding. On many occasions it lays bare the structure of neurosis and gives us some idea of that phenomenon which I would characterize as ' oscillation in regard to the election of neurosis '.

VII. *The Process of Weaning from Psycho-Analysis*

Freud has taught us that in course of treatment analysis itself becomes a habit, indeed a symptomatic state or variety of neurosis which must itself be treated in due course. Up to the present, however, he has not communicated very much concerning the exact nature of this treatment. One gathers that this form of ' illness ' heals very slowly indeed when left to itself. If external reality does not press quite exceptionally hard, the patient has no inducement to bring to an end the analytic situation, which is in many ways pleasurable to him. In spite of the fact that treatment consists of a long-drawn-out series of abstinences and privations, injunctions and prohibitions, nevertheless it offers the patient through the transference-situation a new edition of his happy childhood. Indeed it does more: the new edition is more attractive than the old one. Analysis enters into the emotional and mental life of the patient in a more delicate, friendly, and above all in a more understanding way than was ever possible during the original upbringing. This may have been the reason why Freud, in a case which he has described to us in detail, set a time-limit by which the analysis should terminate.[1] The reaction to this very

[1] ' The History of an Infantile Neurosis ', *Collected Papers*, vol. iii.

active procedure was one of extreme violence and itself contributed much towards the solution of the patient's highly complicated infantile history. In Rank's opinion, which I have myself corroborated,[1] this ' period of weaning ' is one of the most important and significant throughout the analysis. I would repeat here that the advantages to be gained by this manœuvre if it is applied at the appropriate moment are very great. In order to distinguish between this kind of weaning and the methods I had previously adopted, I must have recourse to the simile used by Freud which he took from chess. Formerly I waited until the patient gave up and retired from the game as hopeless; move and counter-move went on until some external experience or other made it easier for the patient to face external reality. Setting a time-limit to analysis is to be regarded on the other hand as a final challenge, a sort of checkmate which the patient has to face when all other avenues of retreat are closed except that of becoming well.

Now this is all very specious, but before this procedure can be generally applied an answer must be found for a number of very difficult questions which immediately arise. Are there unequivocal signs that a patient is ready for weaning, and if so what are these signs? What is to be done should a mistake have been made and the patients, instead of recovering when notice is given, take advantage of some unobserved position and relapse? Can one in fact give notice to all cases without exception?

Even the first of these questions cannot be answered satisfactorily. One can only say that obviously the physician must first of all have complete insight into the structure of the disease and must have reduced the symptoms to a comprehensible unity. But the patient, too, must have worked through the various connections intellectually and must have arrived at the stage where transference-resistances alone prevent conviction. We may regard it as a delicate hint, so to speak, of returning health when, as mentioned above, the patient becomes positive that he has never been ill at all, that the whole condition was entirely ' put on ', etc. If

[1] Ferenczi-Rank, *Developmental Aims of Psycho-Analysis.* [Being translated.]

we take him at his word and suggest in a quite friendly manner that he will need only a few more weeks' analysis, he will of course take fright and pretend that he was only joking. He will also, so far as that is possible, have a slight symptomatic relapse. If we are not misled by such tactics and stick to the stipulated term of notice, our attempt to bring about analytical separation will in many instances, though not invariably, be crowned with success.

As we have already said, the technique of giving notice is not free from possibilities of error, and the consequences of any blunder may be distinctly unpleasant. Above all, one tends to forfeit the patient's confidence and to spoil his reaction to any subsequent imposition of a time-limit. In such circumstances our only course is to acknowledge the blunder, the more so that analysts are under no necessity to preserve a reputation for medical infallibility. When the end of analysis is determined by external circumstances, we are spared the necessity (and with it the associated difficulties) of giving notice. But wherever possible we should not be guided by the external conditions; nor should we allow them to determine the end of analysis, since the patient often uses reality for purposes of resistance. Under no circumstances should we agree to a termination of treatment which is dictated to us by the patient; on the contrary, we should counter his impetuosity by patiently carrying analysis to its conclusion. Dictation of this sort will become more frequent and will more often figure as resistance when the existence of a 'time-limit rule' becomes more widely known.[1]

In some cases it is necessary to drop a timely hint of a possible termination of analysis before actually giving notice; even this may give rise to massive reactions, thereby abating the vigour of later reaction when definite notice is given. We might describe this method as one of double proclamation (the period suggested is usually some weeks, in certain instances two to three months).

When I review my experience with this termination-

[1] This form of resistance is inevitable in training-analyses, where the analysand usually has knowledge of all the technical expedients before he begins his own analysis.

technique, which I have practised since the autumn of 1922, I can only reaffirm my opinion that for many cases it constitutes an effective means of hastening separation from the analyst. I must, however, abandon the view I held, in common with Rank, that the method is universally applicable. On several occasions I have found myself compelled to recommence treatment of patients who have been discharged apparently cured, in order to clear up certain unresolved material. Naturally I took care in such circumstances not to repeat the notice, but waited until the impossibility of obtaining real gratification through the analytic situation, together with the attraction of external reality, overcame a transference-relation the value of which was gradually depreciating.

Towards the end, occasionally even in the middle of treatment, dreams and transitory symptoms appear which prove on analysis to be birth-phantasies in Rank's sense of the term.[1] I had the impression that, as Rank has emphasized, analysis is advanced technically by re-experience of the birth-situation in transference, but I could not get accurate confirmation of this impression. Nevertheless, we are indebted to Rank for calling our attention to birth-phantasies: in common with intra-uterine phantasies, they certainly deserve consideration. It is not yet clear whether they are, as Rank suggests, only reminiscences of the birth-trauma or whether, as I am inclined to think, they represent a regression in phantasy from the Oedipus-conflict to the birth-experience; the latter having been already overcome is, relatively speaking, the less painful of the two.

Finally we must take to heart Freud's admonition concerning the end of treatment, viz. that it is no part of an analyst's ambition to force his own ideals on the patient. When it becomes apparent that the latter's ego can subordinate his desires (the *id*) to the requirements of his super-ego and to the necessities of reality, it is time for him to be independent. His further education may be left to fate.

* * * * *

[1] Rank, *Das Trauma der Geburt*, 1924. [Translated.]

The author is aware that in the present communication the principle of increasing inner tension through privation has been advanced in a rather one-sided way. Practically no notice has been taken of the principle of indulgence, although there can be no doubt that this form of mental influence, which is so widely employed in general medicine, must also on occasion be used in analysis. In his opinion the most important form of indulgence consists in temporary or permanent freedom from certain privation-exercises.

XXXIII

POLLUTION WITHOUT DREAM ORGASM AND DREAM ORGASM WITHOUT POLLUTION[1]

Patients often tell one that they have had a pollution during sleep, although the accompanying dream content had no sensual character, nor indeed betrayed any sexual connection. Analysis often discovers the threads leading from the harmless conscious dream content to an unconscious sexual phantasy that explains the seminal loss. It certainly shows a marked capacity for repression, however, when the substitute for the real can be adhered to till the last moment of organic satisfaction. Much more frequent, of course, are the cases in which the dream—as usual—begins with disfigurations and veilings of the phantasy, but at the moment of orgasm allows the dreamer to become conscious of the sexual or genital occurrence without any concealment.

There is, however, a typical form of these pollution dreams unaccompanied by orgasm that I had the opportunity of studying almost daily in a young man over a prolonged period. He had a pollution every night, but never accompanied with a sensual dream content. They

[1] *Zeitschrift*, 1916–17, Bd. IV. 187.

were *occupation dreams* that ended with a loss of semen; this confirms Tausk's assumption, therefore, according to which a pathological press of occupation represents a disfigured sexual activity.

For instance, the young man dreamt of a complicated mechanical discovery (he wished to be an engineer), of a flying automobile that combined all the advantages of a flying machine and of an automobile. The work was arduous, there were all sorts of hindrances in his way, but when the machine was finished and set in motion—he wakened with a pollution. At other times he dreamt of a difficult mathematical task the solution of which coincided with an ejaculation, etc.

As I knew from Freud that pollutions are mostly the recurrence of nocturnal onanistic activities (or at least of onanistic phantasies), I made strict inquiries about a history of masturbation from this patient, and learnt that he had put up an exceptionally strong defensive battle against it. His mother was one of those people—apparently unconcerned but really very sensual—who do not wish to recognize their sons' maturity, in order to prolong their physical intimacy with them. To protect himself from his, in this case frankly incestuous, phantasies, the lad could do nothing except transpose his sexuality into some other language—as harmless as might be. This he did consciously on his part when he relapsed into onanism. He masturbated 'without phantasies'. Since waking masturbation had been altogether suppressed; however, it recurred at night as an occupation pollution.

It would seem, therefore, that the subject of pollution without orgasm is particularly closely associated with *onanism unaccompanied by sexual phantasies*, about which one is so often told. We must, however, accept such statements by adults with the utmost caution; only in quite young children at the stage of 'primary onanism' can we allow of the possibility of a purely local genital excitement without the involvement of the rest of the psyche. After a time too one is certain to learn from adults that, during masturbation, certain 'thoughts', even if no sensual phantasies, come to them. These thoughts are often peculiar. Mathematical or mechanical problems (as in the case of the above young man), continuous counting, even—in one case—the reciting of the Hebrew alphabet.

The analogy here with compulsive thoughts and compulsive acts will not escape the psycho-analyst. Onanism is a kind of compulsive act that is to be deprived of its real meaning by association with certain meaningless or, in the given situation, nonsensical thoughts.

A closer analysis of the patient who repeated the Hebrew alphabet while masturbating (and also, it turned out, sometimes accompanied his masturbating with Hebrew prayers) yielded the following: it was also a case of an unconscious incestuous masturbation phantasy, whose repudiated content was, as it were, exorcised by the recitation of the sacred prayers (or of their remnants—the Hebrew alphabet).

Another eleven-year-old boy, while masturbating, imagined religious scenes without any sensual content. In most cases he occupied himself at these times with the apparition of the Holy Maria, which was the more understandable as his mother was called Maria.

The associating link facilitating the displacement of the phantasy from a form of genital activity to one apparently so remote as that of prayer may be the *automatism* that is common to both.

The automatic reciting of prayers that may even be associated with rhythmically automatic bodily movements (the forward and backward bowings of many Jewish sects, the complicated rhythmical bodily movements of the 'dancing dervishes', rhythmical beating of the breast, etc.) is adapted, just in consequence of this automatism, to become the disfigured representation of another rhythmic automatism, the genital one. The same can be said of the automatic reciting of the alphabet and of automatic counting, whose wholly 'abstract' nature too, stripped of all sensual thought-content, is of value in the flight from conscious sexuality. (In this connection I refer to the work of Freud on 'Obsessive Acts and Religious Practices'.[1])

[1] [Translated in Freud's *Collected Papers*, vol. ii. chap. ii.]

Pollutions or waking onanism in which—as in the case described above—ejaculation follows the solution of a difficult task are symptoms in miniature of an *anxiety neurosis*. Freud showed us that a greater part of the affects experienced by mankind as anxiety, as also anxiety dreams, are of neurotic origin; the libido, incapable of becoming conscious (or repressed) turns back, in disposed persons, into the bodily and psychic symptoms of anxiety. We are therefore dealing with anxiety pollutions such as occur sometimes in boys even in the waking state. The generation of anxiety by libido is a reversible proceeding. Great anxiety can also cause libidinous stimulation. (Reference is often made to this source of libido in Freud's works, such are 'Three Essays on the Theory of Sexuality',[1] 'Interpretation of Dreams'.[2])

A third group of pollution dreams without orgasm, we can apparently explain only with the aid of *synæsthesia*. One is told of nocturnal pollutions with orgasm whose psychic accompaniments were simply beautiful landscapes that were perhaps seen through the window of a railway carriage, or merely bright colours, fireworks, etc. A woman supplied me with a characteristic example of this kind of dream; after a long series of beautifully harmonious colours she suddenly saw a Japanese landscape before her, and at the moment when a volcanic eruption with the most wonderful light and colour effects occurred the 'eruption'—the orgasm—took place also in the genital sphere. In these cases it is as though the whole gamut of possible genital sensations was transposed into the optic-æsthetic sphere. Similar stimulations of heterogenous sensory areas are known to us as 'synæsthesias'. (*Audition colorée*, *odorée*, etc.)

We know, however, from psycho-analysis that optical sensation in and for itself is not free from erotic admixtures, and that scoptophilia plays an important—in certain pathological cases the whole—part in sexual excitement. If one considers also that 'landscapes' in dreams mostly

[1] [Translated by A. A. Brill. Mental and Nervous Disease Monograph Series, No. 7.]

[2] [Translated by A. A. Brill.]

represent sexual geography (Freud), one can interpret dreams of this kind simply as scoptophilic dreams in which the sexual pictures have been replaced by optical symbols. Instead therefore of bringing in 'synæsthesia' to explain these occurrences, we should make use of such observations to explain the peculiar occurrences of synæsthesia.

Pollution dreams without a manifest sensual content are therefore, as you see from this series of examples, no rarity. Rank has even advanced a theory that every dream, those also, therefore, that are apparently not at all sensual, at a certain stage of its construction approximates to an orgastic wish-fulfilment. Much rarer are unconcealed coitus-dreams with complete orgasm without the corresponding physiological accompaniment, without pollution.

I had only once the opportunity of studying such a dream, and I will report it, therefore, in detail as the patient told it to me.

Dream: *A little child has soiled the bed; a big broad-shouldered man looks out of the window, looks deliberately away from the bed with the child in it as though he were ashamed because of the child.*

Second picture: *I am in bed with my sweetheart, have connection with her, and obtain full gratification; I think that I have done so twice, once in normal fashion and once per anum.* As an obscure confused accompaniment to this last dream fragment I have the feeling *as though a friend, for whom I entertain a great esteem, and with whom I have to carry out an associated business undertaking, were in the next room and sends his child with some message into the bedroom where the sexual acts take place. Naturally, I feel ashamed to show myself so, but the child is quite unembarrassed. The child's father, too, seems to know of the sexual proceedings.* I wakened without the trace of a pollution having occurred.

The previous history of the dream is as follows: the patient suffers amongst other things from obstinate constipation, and is in the habit of promoting the natural evacuations by fluid injections. The evening before the dream, it happened that the injection acted so rapidly that he had not time to reach the closet, but had to evacuate the bowels in his room. It affected him somewhat unpleasantly, for he had to call the chambermaid and, after explaining the occurrence, had to request her to remove the night-stool.

Knowing this, it is not difficult to explain the first dream. The little child that behaved in this unseemly way can, according to the events of the evening of the dream, be none other than the dreamer himself. The feeling of ashamedness, too, which the behaviour of the grown-up represents, is the dreamer's own personal feeling still active in his sleep. We are concerned, therefore, with a 'dissociation' of the individual that certainly subserves wish-fulfilling tendencies. In the dream it is not he (the grown-up) but the little child that has behaved in this way. On the other hand the latent dream thought would run—I am ashamed to have behaved myself like a little child.

Only the second dream fragment has reference to our theme: here we have to deal with a case of a coitus-dream without pollution. If we look more closely, however, we come to the conclusion that this dream fragment—as so often—expresses the same dream thought as the first, only by means of different material; one can say, too, with Rank, with material from another higher layer of psychic life. The repudiated anal evacuation of yesterday is here changed into a genital ejaculation—certainly a wish-fulfilling disfigurement—for one does not need to be ashamed of this evacuation; on the contrary, it is a sign that one is no longer a child, especially if one can perform the act twice running. Something of an anal character, however, has crept into this dream fragment from the latent thoughts, and that is probably why the act is performed once 'per anum'.

Haltingly and associated with entirely other material, the feeling of ashamedness and the child from the first dream fragment are repeated. Shame that he has not yet achieved any of the work planned in common with his business friend; another equally real embarrassment about his relations with a no longer young woman (although he could have married the child of his esteemed and fatherly friend); all these in themselves very unpleasant thoughts are, as it seems, wish-fulfilling displacements of the most repudiated of all impulses, of anal erotism. In this dream fragment the anal mishap is at least raised to genital object-love by means of the symbolic identity of all organic dejecta (fæces, semen, etc.).

What help does an analysis of this dream give towards an understanding of coitus-dreams without pollution?

In my opinion the following: this dream is not (or is very much less) concerned with the satisfying of the yearning for the beloved so much as with the concealing of the unpleasant, indeed sleep-disturbing, thought of the shameful proceeding of the previous evening. Even though the material for this disfigurement was taken from the genital sphere, it would not be imbued with that impulsive force that may even set the organic genital mechanism in action in ardent desire for a woman.

The interpretation of the second dream fragment has a well-known model. We all remember the dream interpreted by Freud in which a lady, who has already lost a nephew, dreams of the death of the now sole-surviving and much-loved nephew. She rightly rejected the wish-fulfilling character of the manifest dream till she remembered, in the course of the analysis, that at the death of the first nephew she had seen for the last time the man she loved; the death of the second signified no satisfaction in itself, but the wished-for opportunity for another satisfaction (a meeting with the man).

In our dream, too, the wish-fulfilment did not lie in the sexual intercourse itself, but in the situation that permitted the mishap of the previous evening to appear as though it had not occurred; the sexual intercourse was not an end in itself, but a means to attain that other wish.

In conclusion we could therefore say that, in this case of pollution without a sensual dream, the unconscious wish is strong enough to set the organic genital process in motion, but too weak to break down the too strict censorship between

Ucs[1] and *Pcs*.[1] In the orgastic dream without pollution, on the other hand, the unconscious sexual wish would be too weak in and for itself to cause a loss of semen; it only serves the purpose here of taking the place of a thought insupportable to the *Pcs*.[1] This time it finds the gates of the censorship wide open and—precisely therefore in spite of its feebleness—becomes fully conscious. Only the powerful unconscious wish has access to bodily processes, while preconscious wishes are only capable of releasing psychic processes.

It indicates no exception to this rule if such orgastic dreams were to occur without pollution in cases of real weakness of the genital executive. Here, too, we would have to consider the unconscious part of the libido as feeble, and the dream rather as a fulfilment of the desire for pleasure.

XXXIV

THE DREAM OF THE OCCLUSIVE PESSARY[2]

A PATIENT recounted the following dream: *I stuff an occlusive pessary into my urethra. I am alarmed as I do so lest it might slip into the bladder from which it could only be removed by shedding blood. I try, therefore, to hold it steady in the perineal region from outside and to force it back or to press it outwards along the urethra*. . . . Here it struck him that in a dream fragment preceding this dream *the pessary was stuffed into his rectum.* Supplement: *in the dream I was aware that the elastic thing would spread itself*

[1] [In English translations the letters *Ubw*, an abbreviation of the German word *Unbewusst*, are rendered *Ucs*, a contraction for the system designated by the name ' The Unconscious ' ; similarly the letters in German, *Vbw*, meaning ' The Preconscious ' system are transliterated by *Pcs*. To complete the list : the initial for Consciousness is *Cs* (German *Bw*), and for ' Perception-consciousness ' *Pcpt-Cs* (German *W-Bw*).—ED.]

[2] *Zeitschrift*, 1915, Bd. III. S. 29.

[sic] *in the bladder and then it would be impossible to get it out again.*

To the patient who is otherwise quite a masculine person, this dream in which he—like a woman—takes precautionary measures against impregnation seemed quite nonsensical, and he also was curious to learn whether this painful dream was a wish-fulfilment.

Asked for the actual conditioning of the dream he at once related: 'I had an assignation yesterday. Naturally it was the female partner and not I who took precautionary measures; she does actually protect herself from consequences by means of an occlusive pessary.'

'Then in the dream you identify yourself with the woman. How does that come about?'

'I know that I am quite free from feminine tendencies. As a child I liked stuffing small objects into the apertures of my head (nose, ears), from which they were often removed only with difficulty, usually occasioning some anxious excitement. The tape that hangs from the rubber pessary reminds me of tapeworms of which I was also afraid. It now occurs to me that I played yesterday with some dogs and thought to myself I might get echinococci from them.'

'Tapeworms and echinococci', I remarked, 'can certainly easily be related to the idea of pregnancy; as eggs, or in some other early stage of development, they obtain entrance into the body and grow to a considerable size there, just like a child in the mother's body.'

'It would agree with that—that in the dream I dreaded lest the elastic thing might expand in the bladder. The echinococcus, too, is a bladder, isn't it? And then again! In sexual intercourse another danger worries me a great deal, that of venereal infection. I protect myself by means of a fish bladder.'

'Infection in dreams very often represents pregnancy in symbolic fashion. In your dream you seem to have interchanged or at least combined the two dangers that might threaten a single man. Instead of protecting yourself with the fish bladder and the woman with the pessary, you infect yourself as it were with the bladder-shaped instrument, that is, you impregnate yourself.'

'As the tapeworm really can do. The worm segments are, if I remember rightly, hermaphroditic!'

'This idea further substantiates our assumption, but we do not yet know how you came to impregnate yourself. What occurs to you about the "bloody operation" of the dream?'

'The following instance occurs to me at once: a short time ago the woman already referred to underwent an operation in the perineal region; at the birth of her little son she suffered a perineal tear that was insufficiently repaired at the time, and as a result the vagina and uterus subsequently prolapsed, which interfered not a little with her (and naturally also my) sexual enjoyment. The operation consisted in a subsequent repair of the perineum.'

'Your ideas seem to converge from all directions on to the situation of childbirth. I draw your attention to the fact that the story you have told, even allowing for considerable omissions, has already been recounted in the manifest dream; think about the *holding steady*, of the foreign body *in the perineal region*, *from outside*, and about *forcing it back* or *pressing it out* in the dream. It is as though you were describing with technical accuracy the protection of the perineum during childbirth. Whence have you this obstetric knowledge?'

'I was last interested in this subject on the occasion of the mentioned operation. I was afraid too that at a possible subsequent birth the woman might be damaged as a consequence of the narrowed genital canal.'

'Then for you anxiety lest there be a child is associated with the anxiety lest there should be none.'

'Yes, that is really the only thing that seems to hinder me from marrying this woman, who otherwise—as you know—is in every way suited to me. I know also the two motives that caused these worries to bother me but yesterday. Another young lady, whom I wanted to marry years ago, was presented to me yesterday as a bride. I thought to myself: she will certainly have a child soon.'

'Probably at the time it was just that prospect that allured you, but youth and virginity may also have proved attractive, especially in contrast to the no longer intact sex organs of your present friend. I would remind you, moreover, of the strong castration complex repeatedly confirmed in your case. Even the normal female genitals sometimes repel people like you; the association with perineal tear, operation, abnormal width, etc., can, however, disturb the sexual enjoyment of quite normal people. But you still owe me a second dream motive!'

'The second motive is probably this: yesterday evening I spent a long time with my mother, with whom a little six-year-old grandchild, my nephew, was staying. I am very fond of the boy, he is curious and intelligent; I treat him affectionately and tell him everything he cares to ask about and that I can answer. I did the same yesterday and thought: I was not so well treated by my mother—you know how strict she was with me.'

'You wanted to show your mother seemingly how a child should be treated, that is, how you should have been treated. You identify yourself as governess with your mother. From that, however, there is only one step to the other, primitive, maternal function; to birth, as you experienced it in the dream. It is really your own rebirth at which you play the part of mother and child at the same time. In its clumsy way the dream perhaps expresses too the naïve wish: if I cannot obtain a child from the older woman, and may not get one from the younger—then I shall make the child myself! Moreover, here too is the connection with the infantile auto-erotic desires that we have discovered in you on another occasion; I do not mean only the boring into nose and ears that you mentioned, but also the secondary erotic gain in micturition and defæcation. Urine and fæces were your first—urethral and anal—children.'

'If I cannot completely accept this last interpretation, I must say in agreement with it that as a child I was for a long time uncertain about how children came into the world. The prudery that ruled in my family made the asking of such questions impossible. Lately, however, I gave my little nephew these ultimate explanations too.'

'Dreams are capable of achieving even more daring disfigurements; I venture therefore to add the following to the interpretation I have just given: that you, as most children, probably first considered the rectum, and only later the urethra, as the place of birth. The dream cannot express this except by stating that the expanding pessary had been previously in the rectum and only then been stuffed into the urethra. Now the expression "to spread oneself" is a striking one not usually employed of objects.'

'In association with "to spread oneself" the words *cock of the walk*, *intruder* occur to me. All these descriptions might, however, be directed against myself. The brothers of my beloved have looked at me askance for a long time, and I have to humble myself with them. I often seem a coward to myself; also I am afraid that sooner or later something unpleasant will happen to me.'

'The "passing" through a narrow place might certainly represent a picture of your complicated position, just as the softness and yieldingness of the material of which the pessary is made would compare not badly with the cowardice and the humbleness with which you reproach yourself. And as it depends entirely on your own decision whether the situation is altered you are really, as in the dream, doing yourself the injury about which you make complaint. In the dream formation, too, the channel of verbal association — *pessary - passing* — may have been available.'

'Just as you were speaking of narrowness and width a bit of yesterday's dream occurred to me. I remember clearly now that *the pessary was too wide for the rectum and threatened to fall out; for the urethra, however, it was too narrow.*'

'I take it as a confirmation of my interpretation from the unconscious that you are able to supply this detail, but I beg you to continue.'

'I think now of two boyhood friends, J. M. and G. L., both of whom I envied because of the size of their members. Also there recurs to me again what I told you a short time ago, that the size of his genital organ which I saw once when bathing with my father frightened me greatly as a child.'

'Here you are putting into words another layer of your psychic life that has already been partly analysed. Your ideas and the dream indicate that formerly at one time when you felt yourself attracted by no other woman than by your mother, the disproportion between the bodily dimensions of a child and an adult troubled you. I would remind you too of your sexual explorations as an older child, which you recounted to me yourself, when you undertook (*sub titulo* "playing doctor") an examination of the genitals of the little girls in the house. It seems to me, therefore, that the too marked narrowness where these were concerned satisfied you as little as the too great width you suspected in the adult woman. You seem to be still in this state of uncertainty and general dissatisfaction, as you cannot decide on your choice between younger and older nor feel fully satisfied with either. The long period of self-gratification that you went through in your youth might be the result of this failure in a choice of object. Therefore in the dream *you make yourself into the pessary child* after you had met, on one and the same day, as representatives of your mischanced courtships, both the woman with the too wide and the bride with the too narrow vagina. In our technology this is called a "regression" from object-love to self-gratification. Now I must, however, return to the fact that at the beginning of the hour you declared the dream to be "nonsense". You are right, it is certainly nonsensical if any one stuffs a foreign body unnecessarily into his rectum or urethra; it is not less so for a man to employ a feminine means of prevention or to want to arrange that he shall impregnate himself or perform obstetric services for himself. It is an ascertained rule of dream interpretation, however, that mockery and scorn are concealed behind such nonsense dreams.'

'My next ideas concern you, doctor, though I cannot just at once see the connection. I remember that yesterday you suggested to me that presently I should not require your services any longer, and that I could now manage quite well alone. This, however, really only caused me regret, as I did not yet feel myself so far recovered as to be able to do without your assistance.'

'Now I understand. You mock at me by showing by the unskilful introduction of the pessary how wrong it is to leave you alone and to consider you capable from now on of being your own doctor. You may be partly right; on the other hand, the repeatedly confirmed transference to me that makes breaking off the analysis difficult for you shows itself in your dislike of my remarks. This tendency lets you under-estimate your own capabilities and exaggerates my importance and assistance. The child that you were making for yourself would therefore also be your own self-analysis.'

'I have, as you know, repeatedly tried to analyse myself. I sat at my desk, wrote down my ideas, covered many sheets of paper with associations, without making anything of it. My thoughts flow into the immeasurable, I cannot collect them properly, I find no clue to the tangle. On the contrary I often marvel at the skill with which you can reduce to order what seems so disconnected.'

'The immeasurable growth of associations would correspond then to the "spreading itself" of the instrument over which you lose control. It is, however, no accident that you demonstrate your incapability just on the genitals and the procreation of children; you are aware that we have often confirmed how despondent you were as a child, dispirited by the imposing size of your father and especially by his wealth of children. For a long time you believed you could achieve nothing to the purpose without his support; you did not think you would ever be able to get the length of founding a family. A few of your earlier dreams, too, on analysis, contained clear allusions to a certain degree of femininity in your attitude towards your father. Since then, however, I have taken the place of father for you. You like the part of patient and dread to be thrown back on yourself and to undertake the entire responsibility for your further destiny. I do not ask you to accept all these interpretations; subsequent ideas may perhaps make this possible for you. This much you will be able to grant me already, however, that this dream has succeeded in transforming all the unpleasant thoughts that might have been able to disturb your last night's sleep into that far less alarming phantasy of urethral and anal activity, which, however, is at the same time the fulfilment of your most ardent wish. That the dream succeeded in representing the wish-fulfilment, the child, out of the same material, that of the rubber pessary, which could easily have aroused in you most unpleasant thoughts of a lifelong childlessness does your capacity for dreaming the greatest credit.'

XXXV

WASHING-COMPULSION AND MASTURBATION [1]

I HAVE a very intelligent patient with a mixture of hysteria and obsessional neurosis. The strongest of her compulsive thoughts is that she must be crazy; she also has washing-compulsion. She was for a long time a fervid onanist, also after marriage. She always practised onanism with scruples of conscience because (as a child) her mother had threatened her that she would be (as a result of masturbation) mentally imbecile. Her present neurotic illness coincided with her abandonment of onanism. A few dream analyses convinced me that the compulsive thoughts of being deranged took the place of a mixture of perverse phantasies. *To become deranged = to commit mad, foolish, imbecile acts, naturally of a sexual nature.*[2] She produced a mass of prostitution phantasies; the unconscious sexual

[1] *Zeitschrift*, 1923, IX. 70. [Translated by Olive Edmonds.]

[2] *The hypochondriacal obsessional idea of being deranged* I have found in many cases to be a cloak for 'deranged sexual wishes'.

phantasies were concerned with her parents, which in part she replaced by her children. She loved her little son and called him 'little father' (in Hungarian not an extraordinary thing to do); the daughter she treated severely, and called her 'little mother'. But the point worthy of notice in the case is that she varied the washing till at length she provided herself thereby with genital gratification. *At last she masturbated with the nozzle of the irrigator and rubbed her vulva with a stiff brush.* Thereby was her conscience quieted; she only washed herself and did not practise onanism. Professor Freud's presumption, that compulsions which ought to be precautionary measures against onanism are really roundabout ways to onanism again, finds in this case an irrefutable confirmation.

XXXVI

PARÆSTHESIAS OF THE GENITAL REGIONS IN IMPOTENCE[1]

Psycho-sexually impotent patients are wont to complain that they 'do not feel' their penis; others mention marked feelings of coldness in the genital region, while others again speak of the sensation of the penis shrinking up; all these illusions are intensified at the moment of attempted coitus. During the course of the analyses the patients then often say spontaneously that they can 'feel' the penis better, that the cold feeling is decreasing, that the penis (unerected) 'has more consistence', is 'more turgid', etc. For technical reasons it is not advisable to undertake a physical examination on the strength of such complaints; in a few cases, however, I could not evade this, but was unable to confirm the occurrence of any particular 'coldness' nor of any anæsthesia nor analgesia, but there

[1] *Zeitschrift*, 1913, Bd. I. S. 379.

certainly was a shrunken-together appearance of the penis. Analytically the unconscious source for these sensations was ascertained to be an infantile castration fear which, as I have detailed elsewhere,[1] is also the origin for that feeling of retraction that many patients get at the root of the penis and in the perineum, especially when afraid of the analyst (father). One of these patients once wakened at night with the sensation that he had 'no feeling' of his penis at all; he experienced great anxiety and had to convince himself by touch that he really had a penis. The explanation was as follows: as a child he was threatened with castration for onanistic manipulation of his genitals; whence the 'dread of touching' the genitals. The anxious clutching at the penis proved to be a compromise between the wish to masturbate and the dread to be so sorely punished for it. ('The return of the repressed.') Those here described and similar paræsthesias often show quite well by their variations the improvements and aggravations in the patient's condition. Besides unconscious (onanistic) incest phantasies,[2] castration threats are the most frequent causes of psychic impotence; most often it is both (fear of castration on account of the incestuous wish).

XXXVII

SHUDDERING AT SCRATCHING ON GLASS, ETC.[3]

THE meaning of this very widespread idiosyncrasy was brought to light in the analysis of neurotics. A patient, whose blood ran cold at the sight of potatoes being peeled,

[1] Ferenczi, 'Transitory Symptom-Constructions during the Analysis'. [Chap. vii. in *Contributions to Psycho-Analysis.*]

[2] Ferenczi, 'The Analytic Interpretation and Treatment of Psychosexual Impotence'. [Chap. i. in *Contributions to Psycho-Analysis.*]

[3] *Zeitschrift*, 1923, IX. 68. [Translated by Olive Edmonds.]

brought me the first hint of the significance: he unconsciously identified these vegetables with something human, so that for him the peeling of the potatoes meant a flaying or tearing off of the skin, as much active (sadistic) as passive (masochistic) in the sense of talion punishment. Supported by this experience, I must trace back the above-mentioned peculiarity to childhood impressions, during an early period of life in which an alive and human conception of the inanimate is customary. The shrill tone of scratching on glass seems to the child to be a cry of pain from ill usage, and linen utters—in his opinion—a scream of pain when it is torn in pieces. The touching of stuff with a rough surface, the stroking of silk, are also often accompanied by 'shudders', apparently because such stuffs, when stroked the wrong way by the hand, make a 'disagreeable' noise. Though roughness of surface is enough in itself to call forth a sympathetic roughness and soreness of one's own skin, the striking of polished or yielding objects on the nerves of the skin themselves seems to have a soothing effect. The inclination to cultivate such idiosyncrasies is derived in most cases from an unconscious castration-phantasy. It is not impossible that such and similar motives are of significance in the æsthetic production of different stuffs and materials.

XXXVIII

INFANTILE IDEAS ABOUT THE FEMALE GENITAL ORGANS [1]

A PATIENT suffering from impotence as the result of masked castration threats, and who had been severely intimidated as a child, dreams that he buys his English language-mistress a necktie, but that it really was a coiled-up eel. The analysis showed that he wants to buy her a

[1] *Zeitschrift*, 1913, Bd. I. S. 381.

penis (fish-tie), as he has a horror of creatures without a penis (a castrate, a woman). To approach a woman without anxiety he has to imagine the vagina as a coiled-up penis.

Another patient recounted the conscious memory of the infantile view that women had a short but thick penis with a very wide urethra whose lumen was large enough to allow of penetration by the man's penis. The idea that there can be creatures without a penis is very painful from its association with the castration complex (Freud), so that boys have to excogitate all sorts of theories about the female genitals which all agree in this, that in spite of appearances to the contrary women have a penis.

XXXIX

PTYALISM IN AN ORAL-EROTIC[1]

An elderly medical man told me that whenever he has to sound a woman with a stethoscope, and for this purpose puts his head near to her breast, he experiences an unusual flow of saliva; as a rule his saliva secretion does not exceed the normal. I have no doubt of the infantile (oral-erotic) source of this peculiarity. (Compare also the case with ' mouth pollutions ' mentioned by Abraham in *Zeitschrift für Psychoanalyse*, IV. p. 71.)

XL

EMBARRASSED HANDS[2]

This is a symptom of very frequent occurrence among young people, but also quite frequent in adults—that they do not know what to do with their hands. An inexplicable

[1] *Zeitschrift*, 1923, IX. 67. [Translated by Olive Edmonds.]
[2] *Zeitschrift*, 1914, II. 378. [Translated by John Rickman.]

feeling compels those thus troubled to occupy their hands somehow, but they never find the suitable employment. For this reason they imagine they are watched by those present, and making all sorts of unusually awkward attempts to occupy their hands they become ashamed of their clumsiness, and this only increases their embarrassment further and leads to all sorts of symptomatic actions—upsetting things, overturning glasses, etc. Their attention at any rate is too much concentrated on the position and movement of the hands at the moment, and this conscious watchfulness disturbs the usual 'ease', that is, the automatism of deportment and of manual movement. Many people get themselves out of this difficulty by hiding their hands under the table or in their pockets; others clench their fists or hold their hands and arms in some awkward position.

In such cases according to my experience one is mostly dealing with *insufficiently repressed tendencies to onanism* (occasionally with imperfectly guarded tendencies to some other 'naughtiness' such as nail-biting, nose-picking, scratching, etc.). The suppression of the onanistic tendency has here only got so far that the aim of the movement to be carried out (masturbation) is no longer conscious, but the impulse to some movement still forces its way through. The compulsion to occupy the hands is only the displaced expression of this tendency, and at the same time the attempt to rationalize it. The peculiar phantasy of being watched is to be explained by the repressed desire for exhibitionism that primarily had reference to the genitals and was then displaced to the few remaining exposed parts of the body (face and hands).

The consideration of tendencies that were repressed during the latent period and try to emerge at puberty, but are rejected or misunderstood by consciousness, might perhaps lead us to a closer understanding of other 'curious' and 'funny' peculiarities of the period of puberty.

XLI

RUBBING THE EYES AS A SUBSTITUTE FOR ONANISM[1]

A PATIENT, an obsessional neurotic, in whose illness a suppressed tendency to onanism plays a great part, reacts to sexual excitement with a severe itching of the eyelids, which he tries to mitigate by rubbing. I draw attention to the symbolic identity of eyes and genitals.

XLII

AN 'ANAL HOLLOW-PENIS' IN WOMAN[2]

A MALE patient as a child had the following notion about the female genital; that there was a tube hanging down behind, which served as well the function of dejection as of receiving the penis, whereby he also satisfied the wish that women should have a penis.

XLIII

MICTURITION AS A SEDATIVE[3]

WHEN a small child is frightened its mother places it on the chamber and tells it to urinate. The child then quietens visibly and stops crying. Undoubtedly the child is here offered a libido reward similar to that given him at other times in the form of sweets or other eatables. That micturition should discharge the affect of fright so sucessfully may be due to the fact that it provides for the child a *sudden* relief (pleasure) adequate to the suddenness of the fright.

[1] *Zeitschrift*, II. 379.
[2] *Zeitschrift*, 1923, IX. 70. [Translated by Olive Edmonds.]
[3] *Zeitschrift*, 1915, Bd. III. S. 295. [Translated by John Rickman.]

XLIV

DREAD OF CIGAR AND CIGARETTE SMOKING[1]

THIS usually only takes the place of some other (erotic) enjoyment that the patient considers 'dangerous'. Smoking and sexual intercourse are both things that grown-ups only permit themselves, but withhold from their children by means of threats and intimidations. I would here recall my explanation of anti-alcoholism (*Jahrbuch f. Psychoanalyse*, 1911, Bd. III. S. 853, 'Alcohol und Neurosen').

XLV

OBSESSIONAL ETYMOLOGIZING[2]

THIS occurred in a patient by the inquiry into the origin of words being substituted for the question of the derivation of children. This identification would form the pathological pendant to Sperber's[3] theory of the sexual origin of speech.

XLVI

CORNELIA, THE MOTHER OF THE GRACCHI[4]

CORNELIA was for many years the wife of Tiberius Sempronius, to whom she bore twelve children. She reared two sons, Tiberius and Caius, and a daughter, Sempronia (who married Scipio Africanus, junior). After the death of her husband she refused the hand of the Egyptian King Ptolemy, in order to devote herself entirely to her children. Once, when asked about her jewels, she replied, pointing

[1] *Zeitschrift*, 1914, II. 383.

[2] *Zeitschrift*, 1913, I. 378. [Translated by John Rickman.]

[3] *Imago*, 1914, I. Jahrgang.

[4] *Zeitschrift*, 1919, Bd. V. 117.

to her children, 'These are my treasures, my jewels'. She bore the tragic fate of her two sons steadfastly, in profound retirement. Cornelia was one of the noblest Roman women, and was also honoured for her great culture; the beauty of diction of her letters was much admired. The Roman people perpetuated the memory of the 'Mother of the Gracchi' in a bronze statue.[1]

Thus much we learn about this noble Roman lady from Plutarch; our information about her person, however, is wholly at second hand, the two fragments of letters preserved in the writings of Cornelius Nepos not being considered genuine by connoisseurs.

It may certainly be considered an audacity if I venture, after more than two thousand years, to offer a new suggestion towards the understanding of Cornelia's character. It may be guessed, however, from its publication in this paper, that I do not owe the suggestion to fresh discoveries, but to psycho-analytic experience and reflection.

There exist to-day women of the noble Cornelia's type, women who, themselves retiring, modest, often somewhat austere, parade their children really as other women do their jewels; it also happens that such women develop a psycho-neurosis, and then the psychiatrist has the opportunity of analysing this trait of character too. He gains thereby a deeper insight into the peculiarity of the prototype Cornelia, and learns to understand better the universal interest that is taken in the anecdote recounted about her.

I have at my disposal the minimal number of cases necessary for a generalization, namely, two. I have actually completely analysed two such women, and in doing so have established remarkable conformities between their inner and outer destinies.

The first, a woman married for many years, for a long time began almost every analytic session with praises of her eldest and youngest children, or with complaints about one of the middle ones, 'whose behaviour leaves much to be desired'. But the intellectual gifts of these children, too, very often gave her occasion for affectionate tales about

[1] From the article 'Cornelia' in the Hungarian 'Pallas' dictionary.

them. Her appearance and her behaviour were worthy of a Cornelia. Unapproachable, she withdrew from the glances of such men as dared look upon her beauty with desire, and in this she showed not merely reserve but distinct repulsion. She lived only for her duty as wife and mother. Unfortunately this beautiful harmony was troubled for her by an hysterical neurosis which showed itself partly in irksome bodily manifestations and occasional alterations of mood, and partly—as the analysis soon discovered—in that her capacity of attaining sexual satisfaction, so to say, wore out. In the course of the analysis the manner in which she reacted to her youngest child gradually assumed peculiar forms. To her alarm she noticed that in fondling the child she experienced marked erotic paroxysms, even definite genital sensations, sensations that she did not experience during conjugal relations. There then appeared in the guise of a transference to the doctor traits quite unexpected to herself; behind the somewhat prudish and distant attitude there gradually showed a quite marked, one might say, quite normal, womanly desire to please that knew how to employ every means suited to direct attention to her charms. Then from her dreams it was easy to guess, with the help of a well-recognized symbolism, that *for her the child really represented the sexual.* It did not call for much perspicacity to go a step further and to guess that her tendency to *show her children to others was a substitute for the normal desire for exhibitionism.* It thus also appeared that this component impulse was very prominent with her constitutionally as well as in consequence of some experiences, and that its repression played a considerable part in the motivation of her neurosis. This impulse underwent a particularly severe repression when in her early youth she had to suffer a little operation in the genital area. From that time onwards she felt herself of no importance compared with other girls, transferred her interest to intellectual things, began—like Cornelia—to write beautiful letters, even little poems, and for the rest, developed the somewhat prudish character already described.

Her relations to finery help us to understand the comparison employed by the noble Cornelia. She was very modest in what concerned clothing and jewels. Every recurrence of the memory of her painful genital experiences in childhood, however, was signalized by the loss of some article of finery, so that she has gradually lost almost the whole of her jewelry.

In proportion as she achieved the capacity for sexual enjoyment and the consciousness of her exhibitionism her exaggerated desire to demonstrate her children's advantages diminished, along with which her relations with the children became more natural and affectionate. She was also no longer ashamed to acknowledge to herself her pleasure in women's gear of all kinds and showed a distinct modification in her exaggerated estimation of the intellectual in mankind.

The erotic sensations on touching her youngest child that had finally so alarmed the patient had their explanation in the deepest layers of her personality and in the memory of the earliest period of her development. This voluptuousness was a reproduction of feelings she had freely enjoyed before the powerful suppression of her infantile self-satisfaction, which, however, transformed itself into anxiety and—on its unexpected irruption into consciousness—had to give rise to fear.

In the face of such experiences who would maunder on about the 'as if' nature, the unreality of symbols? For this woman, children and jewels were certainly symbols, second in reality and validity to no other psychic content.

The other patient of whom I wish to speak betrayed her relation to jewelry and children much more strikingly. She became a diamond cutter, liked to bring her child with her in person in order to show it to me, and had—in the strongest contrast to her particularly decent, as she herself phrased it, 'governess' clothing—typical nakedness dreams.

After these observations I feel myself justified in considering the case of the famous Cornelia, in spite of its antiquity, just as I would that of a living woman of to-day, and in assuming that her beautiful character traits were the sublimation products of the same 'perverse' tendencies to exhibitionism as we were able to prove lay behind the same qualities in our patients.

In the series, genitals—child—jewels, the last is certainly the least literal, the weakest symbol. It was therefore very much to the point that Cornelia should draw her fellow-women citizens' attention to the unnatural character of their worship of this symbol, and should direct them by her own example to more natural love-objects. We, however, may permit ourselves the fiction of a much earlier primitive Cornelia who went farther and, when she noticed that her female companions went too far in their adoration of the symbol 'child', pointed to her genitals as though to say: *Here are my treasures, my jewels, and also the primitive source of the cult that you practise with your children.*

One does not need, however, to turn to primitive times for such an example. The next best female neurotic or exhibitionist can demonstrate *ad oculos* such a regression to the real meaning of this symbolism.

In an essay entitled 'The Analysis of Comparisons'[1] I declared that comparisons thrown out carelessly in the course of conversation often contain far-reaching conceptions derived from the unconscious. Cornelia's comparison should be added to the examples there set forth.

[1] [See Chap. LXXVII. of this book.]

FROM THE NURSERY

Short Papers

XLVII

THE 'GRANDFATHER COMPLEX'[1]

The preceding papers by Abraham and Jones[2] give an almost exhaustive account of the significance that their relationships to the grandparents often assume for the whole life of the grandchildren. In this connection I should like to mention briefly a few observations that I had collected on this subject.

I found that the grandfather plays a twofold part in the phantasy of the child. On the one hand he is really the imposing old man who commands even the otherwise all-powerful father, and whose authority, therefore, it—the child—would like to appropriate and play off in his resistance to the father (Abraham, Jones). On the other hand, however, he is also the helpless, feeble old man, very near death, who can in no wise measure himself (especially not in matters of sex) against the powerful father, and he therefore becomes an object of disparagement for the child. It is very often precisely in the person of the grandfather that the grandchild for the first time approaches the problem of death, of the final 'being away' of someone belonging to him, and the child can then displace his inimical phantasies, which are, however, repressed owing to ambi-

[1] *Zeitschrift*, 1913, Bd. I. S. 228.

[2] *Zeitschrift*, 1913, Bd. I. S. 219, 'Die Bedeutung der Grossvater für das Schicksal des Einselnen'. Ernest Jones [chap. xxxviii. in his *Papers on Psycho-Analysis*]. *Zeitschrift*, 1913, Bd. I. S. 225, 'Einige Bemerkungen über die Rolle der Grosseltern in der Psychologie der Neurosen'. Karl Abraham [Kap. xiv. in *Klinische Beiträge zur Psychoanalyse*. Translation in preparation by the Institute of Psycho-Analysis].

valency, about the death of his father on to the grandfather. 'If the father of my father can die, then my father will die some day, too (and I shall get possession of his privileges),' is the trend of phantasy that generally hides behind the cover-memories and phantasies concerning the death of the grandfather. By the death of the grandfather, moreover, the grandmother becomes single; many a child (in order to spare the father's life but still to possess the mother entirely) seizes the expedient of letting the grandfather die in phantasy, gives the grandmother to the father and keeps the mother for himself. 'I sleep with my mama, you should sleep with your mama,'[1] thinks the child and feels himself just and magnanimous.

Whether the *imago of the 'feeble grandfather' or of the 'powerful grandfather'* (in the latter case with tendencies to identification) becomes a fixation for the child, depends essentially on the part that the grandfather really plays in the family. Where the grandfather is the master in the house, actually the Patriarch, there the child in his phantasy goes beyond the powerless father and hopes to inherit the whole of the grandfather's power directly; in a case of this kind that I was able to examine analytically the child could never submit, after the death of the powerful grandfather, to the father who had come to power; he treated him simply as an usurper who had robbed him of his rightful possession.

The *imago of the 'feeble grandfather'* is particularly clearly impressed on the children in families in which (as often happens) the grandparents are badly treated.

[1] Remarks of this kind by little children have been communicated to me from trustworthy sources. There is a beautiful example of this kind in the 'Analyse der Phobie eines fünfjährigen Knaben' [*Gesammelte Schriften*, Bd. VIII. Translated in *Collected Papers*, vol. iii.], published by Freud (*Jahrbuch f. Psa.* I. Bd., 1909, S. 74), where little Hans appoints himself the husband of his Mother and therefore his own Father, while he relegates his Father to the latter's own Mother, therefore to the little one's Grandmother, whereupon Freud remarks, 'Everything turns out all right. The little Oedipus has found a happier solution than that permitted by fate. He grants to his Father, instead of removing him, the same happiness that he demands for himself; he appoints him to be the Grandfather and marries him to his own Mother.'

XLVIII

FLATUS AS AN ADULT PREROGATIVE[1]

It sometimes occurs that analysands have to resist the inclination to pass a clearly audible and also noticeable amount of flatus in the course of the hour; this usually happens when they are being refractory with the doctor. This symptom, however, is intended not only to insult the doctor but to intimate that the patient intends to allow himself things that his father forbade him, but permitted himself. The licence referred to here represents all the prerogatives which parents arrogate to themselves but strictly deny to their children, and which the patient now wishes to appropriate for himself.

XLIX

CHILDISH IDEAS OF DIGESTION[2]

Three-year-old boy: 'Uncle Doctor, what have you got in your stomach that makes you so fat?'

The family physician's joking reply: 'Ka-ka!'[3]

The boy: 'Do you eat so much Ka-ka?'

(The little one thinks of the belly as a hollow space in which what has been eaten is contained unchanged like the children in the fairy-tales or myths who are swallowed by Kronos, the wolf or the whale, etc., or are reborn by being vomited up. The small investigator's remark indicates that he has not as yet discovered the causal chain between eating and defæcation, and that he considers the latter as a function for itself. We know, of course, how difficult it is for humans to ascertain such associations. The third striking point about this childish remark is the matter-of-factness with which it takes the consumption of fæces for granted.)

[1] *Zeitschrift*, 1913, Bd. I. S. 380. [2] *Zeitschrift*, 1913, Bd. I. S. 381.

[3] ['Ka-ka' = German nursery word for fæces.—Trans.]

L

DISGUST FOR BREAKFAST[1]

MANY children often suffer from an unconquerable disgust for breakfast. They had rather go to school with empty stomachs, and if compelled to eat they vomit. I do not know if children's specialists have a physiological explanation for this symptom. I found a psychological interpretation for it that revealed itself during psycho-analysis.

In this patient's case the idiosyncrasy persisted into adult life, and had to be interpreted as a displacement of an unconscious disgust for the maternal hand. He was already, as a young child, aware of the sexual relations of his parents; he repressed this knowledge, however, as it was irreconcilable with his feelings of tenderness and his respect. But when his mother came from her bedroom in the morning and prepared the breakfast with the same hands that may have played a part in those repudiated activities, even perhaps let the child kiss her hand to begin with, then the suppressed feeling appeared as disgust for the breakfast, without the child becoming conscious of the true origin of his idiosyncrasy.

It would be the task of children's specialists to inquire whether this interpretation was valid for other or perhaps for all such cases. The way to a therapy would thus also be indicated.

On another occasion I pointed out that the peculiar association of a feeling of disgust with the movements expressive of spitting and vomiting indicates that in the unconscious there exists a coprophilic tendency to the swallowing of what is 'disgusting', that spitting and vomiting, therefore, are really to be taken as reaction formations against coprophagia. This conception holds, of course, also for the 'disgust for breakfast'.

[1] *Zeitschrift*, 1919, Bd. V. 117.

LI

THE CAUSE OF RESERVE IN A CHILD[1]

THE young mother of two children is inconsolable because the elder child (aged four) is so remarkably reserved; she endeavours by every means to get the child to be frank, and to gain her confidence, but all in vain. Even when her much-loved English nurse has to be sent away the child displays no emotion towards her mother. The mother begs her to be frank, she may tell her mamma everything that is bothering her. 'May I really tell everything?' asks the little one. 'Of course, just ask,' answers the mother. 'Well then, tell me where do children come from!' (a striking confirmation of Freud's assumption that the evasiveness of parents towards inquisitive children can become the source of permanent affective and intellectual disturbance).

LII

TWO TYPICAL FÆCAL AND ANAL SYMPTOMS[2]

IN two women whose obsessional fears were connected[3] with childlessness and in whose unconscious the regression from genital and parental to anal erotism proceeded as in an obsessional neurotic patient of Freud's,[4] *vermin* and *eggs* play a quite peculiar part. Both (it is almost incredible how minutely neuroses often repeat themselves) suffered from childhood from the dread that they had lice in their hair. Extraordinary to relate, they occasionally *actually* do discover, to their great alarm, representatives of these vermin on their heads, which, however, is no wonder as they display an incomprehensible carelessness regarding the toilet of the hair—apparently in contradiction to their phobia of parasites. In reality both of them unconsciously

[1] *Zeitschrift*, 1913, Bd. I. S. 382. [2] *Zeitschrift*, 1915, Bd. III. 292.

[3] The one woman certainly had a child, but this far from satisfied her unconscious.

[4] Freud, 'The Predisposition to Obsessional Nemosis', *Coll. Papers*, ii. 122.

endeavour to acquire such parasites as these offer them the most favourable opportunity of satisfying symbolically their deeply hidden wishes; the repressed longing for many, very many children (that actually develop as parasites of the mother),[1] as well as the sadism and anal erotism to which they had to regress after their sexual disillusionment (killing of the vermin, wallowing in dirt). To make the analogy of the two cases still more remarkable, they produced another fæcal and anal symbol that had hitherto been unknown to me as such, namely, an overweening interest in hens' eggs. One of the patients, when at last she began to interest herself in her house, often told me what an inexplicable pleasure it afforded her to rummage about in a basket of fresh eggs, to arrange and count them; were she not ashamed, she would occupy herself in this way for hours. The other (a country woman) is almost incapable of work; the only place where she could be employed is the fowl-yard; there she is able to stuff geese for hours, and to watch the hens lay eggs; on these occasions she assists delivery by inserting her finger into the cloaca of the animal and fetching out the egg. The symbolic identity of the egg with fæces and child is even more transparent than that of vermin. One should not, however, forget the money value of eggs; we know, of course, that everywhere the price of eggs provides a standard of the cheapness or costliness of the means of living, and that eggs, particularly in the country, serve for money, as a standard of value. It seems that under some conditions of life the ontogenetic transformation of anal erotism comes to a standstill in certain anal character traits. At any rate this fondness for eggs approximates much more closely to primitive coprophilia than does the more abstract love of money.[2]

Finally it may be pointed out that, incidentally, both fæcal and anal symbols (as was to be expected) also allowed their phallic meaning to be recognized.

[1] Compare my short paper, 'Vermin as a Symbol of Pregnancy'. [See Chap. LXVIII. in this volume.]

[2] Compare my paper, 'The Ontogenesis of the Interest in Money'. [Translated in *Contributions to Psycho-Analysis*, chap. xiii., 1916.]

LIII

NAKEDNESS AS A MEANS FOR INSPIRING TERROR[1]

THE accidental coincidence of two observations, of a dream and of a childish memory (in two different patients), forces me to the assumption that in the nursery and in the unconscious *nakedness* may be used as a means of inspiring terror. [Literally: ' of frightening off.']

1. A patient whose *grande hystérie* revived again after the unexpected loss of her adored elder boy, and who in her distaste for life was constantly preoccupied with suicidal ideas, dreamt one day amongst other things that she is standing in front of her younger boy hesitating whether she should undress and wash herself naked in front of the little fellow. ' If I do this ', she thought, ' the child will have an imperishable memory that might harm him or even prove his complete undoing.' After some hesitation, however, she does it all the same; she undresses in front of the child and washes her naked body with a sponge.

The thought indicated by inverted commas springs from waking life and refers to the intention of suicide; she knows, partly from her psychological studies, that her suicide might have a devastating effect upon the psychic life of the remaining child, who would thus be left a motherless orphan. On the other hand she has—especially since the death of the eldest—often quite conscious hostile feelings against the remaining child; indeed she had a phantasy in which the tragic fate of the elder was transferred to the younger.

This actually existing hesitation between suicidal intention and sense of duty, between love and hate towards the child favoured by fortune, becomes, however, in the dream, extraordinary to say, the hesitation between exhibitionism and its opposite. The patient provided the appropriate material for this from her own experience.

[1] *Zeitschrift*, 1919, Bd. V. 303.

She loved the elder boy so much that she never allowed him to be bathed and washed by anyone except herself. Naturally the boy returned this love; indeed his attachment sometimes assumed markedly erotic forms, so that his mother was once compelled to ask the advice of a doctor about this. At that time too she already knew a good deal about psycho-analysis but did not trust herself to bring the case before a psycho-analyst. She was afraid of the questions that might have arisen. (We can add that unconsciously she more probably feared perhaps the renunciation that the analyst would have had to lay upon her tenderness for her son.)

How does it come about, however, that the patient reverses the situation so that she washes herself with a sponge in front of the second child, instead of washing the first born, as really happened? We may represent the process of this reversal to ourselves in the following way: she was about to transfer her love to the living child and wished to wash him as she had hitherto the older one. (The washing of the younger child was not so exclusively the mother's prerogative.) This is connected with the idea of continued existence! But she cannot put it through as yet. To handle the younger as tenderly as previously she did the beloved dead seems to her a desecration. The decision once made, however, is carried out in the dream, only in place of the younger child she takes herself for the object of her admiration and tenderness and grants the little one only the part of onlooker—and with an outspoken evil intent into the bargain. There is no doubt that here the mother identifies her own person with that of the beloved dead. Did she not say countless times during the little fellow's life, 'he is just the same as me', or 'I and he are one'?

This exaggerated mother-love, however, gave her occasion to re-excite her very marked infantile narcissism —transferred to the child. She fled to this transferred narcissism because the expected satisfaction was denied her by her sexual object choice. Now she was also robbed of her child, and the narcissism had to manifest itself in the more primitive fashion. That it found expression just in the form of exhibitionism, is explained—as I suppose—by analogous infantile experiences.

The part played by *exhibitionism as a means of punishment and of instilling fear* remained unexplained in this case.

2. Another patient on the very same day submitted something very similar. He related the following childhood's *memory* that had made a very strong impression on him; his mother told him as a little child that her brother had been a 'mother's boy'; he had always run after his mother, would not go to sleep without her, etc. She had only been able to break him off this by on one occasion *undressing herself naked* before the child in order to *frighten* him away from her. This step—so ran the moral of the tale—had the desired effect. This method of inspiring fear seems to have been efficacious even in the second generation, namely, upon my patient. Even to-day he can only speak in terms of the deepest indignation of the treatment that befell his uncle, and I suppose that his mother also told him this tale with educational intent.

After these two observations one has still to ask oneself whether nakedness is really capable of inspiring fear in general, or of frightening a child. And this question can be answered in the affirmative.

We know from Freud that *repressed* libido transforms itself into anxiety. What we have so far learnt of the anxiety conditions of children is in this respect very similar; one is always dealing with too great accesses of libido against which the ego is on guard; the libido repressed by the ego transforms itself into fear and the fear then seeks out secondary suitable objects (mostly animals) to which it can attach itself. The sensitiveness of the ego against accesses of libido is explained by the time relations established by Freud between the ego development and the development of the libido. The as yet inexperienced ego of the child is frightened at the unexpected quantities of libido and at the libidinal possibilities with which it does not yet know what (or what more) to do.

It is possible that the popular consciousness has a presentiment of these relations, so that one is not dealing here with an idea peculiar to individuals.[1] Researches might discover a more frequent occurrence of educational and fear-instilling measures which dealt with *intimidating the ego by inadequate kinds and quantities of libido respectively.*

LIV

THE PSYCHO-ANALYSIS OF WIT AND THE COMICAL[2]

The interest of medical men in wit and the comical is not new. In classical times doctors whose teachings were held in esteem for a thousand years quite seriously recommended that patients should be stimulated to laughter in order that their diaphragms be shaken and their digestion promoted. In the present lecture, however, I shall not initiate my hearers into the means and methods of such an art of entertainment. On the contrary, it is my clear intention to destroy the effect that wit and the comical have upon the naïve listener. I take on the part of a typical character in *Borsszem Janko*,[3] that of the successful caricature, Professor Tomb, who instead of letting poetical works in their original form influence his students takes them to pieces and murders their beauties by his philological and æsthetic analysis. From this programme you can already foresee that to-day it is not the helpful physician anxious to cure who speaks in me, but the psychologist. I desire to make you acquainted with a book of Professor Freud's on wit.[4]

Like every caricature, that of Professor Tomb too has a core of seriousness. What this tedious philologist does in all simplicity, namely, making what is beautiful dull by

[1] In popular superstition, too, nakedness (as well as the baring particularly of individual parts of the body: the genitals and the buttocks) plays a great part as a means of magic and of inspiring fear.

[2] A lecture delivered at 'The Free School of Social Sciences' in Budapest. Published in *Populäre Vorträge über Psychoanalyse*, chap. vii.

[3] A humorous Hungarian weekly paper.

[4] Professor Freud, *Der Witz und seine Beziehung zum Unbewussten*, II. Auflage, Wien, 1921. [Translation by A. A. Brill, 1917. New York, Moffatt, Yard & Co.; London, Broadway House.]

his analysis and thereby producing a comic effect upon everyone, Professor Freud does quite deliberately and uses it to obtain astonishing psychological information. Previous to Freud many people had concerned themselves with the problem of wit, many indeed made valuable contributions to a psychology of the pleasure in wit, but they always illuminated only one or other side of the problem when they thought to have solved the whole question. Freud's work, on the contrary, embraces the whole complex and all the profundities of the questions involved, so that we can point to the great master of mental science and mental treatment as being also the pathfinder in the domain of æsthetics.

The very method by which he set out to analyse wit was an ingenious idea that, on the basis above mentioned, we might call 'the method of the tedious philologist'. Freud reflected that if we want to discover what it is in wit that evokes good humour and stimulates laughter, then we must first of all ascertain whether it is in the content or in the form, in the thought itself or in the manner of its expression—or indeed in both together—that the hitherto indefinable 'something' lies which drives the hearer with such irresistible force to innervate his muscles of laughter. Freud next asked himself the question whether even the best of jokes can be 'spoilt', that is, can be put in such a form, in spite of the complete and faithful reproduction of its content, that it no longer has an exhilarating action. If this is the case, then, undoubtedly, it is not the content but merely the form—or, as Freud says, the technique—that gives the joke its character. In this way Freud reached the astonishing conclusion that by this procedure, which he called the 'reduction of wit', almost every joke can be robbed of its exhilarating qualities; in other words there is no joke so excellent that cannot be spoilt by sufficiently thorough professional knowledge.

Let us see how Freud demonstrates this on a well-known play upon words. In one of Heine's *Reisebilder*, in the 'Bädern von Lucca,' the poet speaks of, amongst others, the Lottery-collector and Corn-curer Hirsch-Hyacinth of Hamburg, who boasts to the poet of his relations with the wealthy Baron Rothschild and finally says: 'and, as true as a God-help-me, doctor, I sat beside Salomon Rothschild and he treated me just like an equal—quite famillionaire'. Had Hirsch-Hyacinth related it thus: 'Rothschild treated me just like an equal, quite familiar, although he is a millionaire', the witty effect would have been wanting. This effect was therefore only attained by the condensation, the portmanteau word formation. To visualize this write the words under one another like two numbers that are to be added up and do the addition by letting the syllables that occur in both words figure only once in the result. The following is the resulting sum:

```
famil i   a r
  millionaire
-------------
famillionaire
```

What has really happened here? Nothing more than that by means of a superficial acoustic association the joke succeeded in condensing two widely dissimilar conceptions, that of the family and that of wealth, into one word, that is, conjured up both the ideas in one word. Now what is Freud's explanation of the laughter-provoking effect of such a condensation on its hearers? The laughter, as he shows by numerous examples, springs from the fact that the intellectual effort that we would normally have had to exert to associate the idea of the family with that of the millionaire, and which—by following the speaker—we have already set in motion, has as a result of the condensation suddenly become superfluous, so that the nervous tension that was already stored up for thinking purposes and which we have thus economized is abreacted involuntarily as a motor innervation of the muscles of laughter, is discharged in laughter.

To distinguish a 'good' from a 'bad' joke let us take also an example of the latter.

In a story for children that has accidentally come into my hands I read something like this: 'There is a strange country where all sorts of curious animals live, cana-rhinoceroses fly in the air, popinjizards sun themselves on the cliffs, an elephantast strolls about in the garden and the cook makes a camel pudding for the children'. Now these also are word condensations that link together widely separated conceptions, but there is no deeper meaning concealed behind the superficial association as there is behind the word 'famillionaire'; hence such word plays provoke in adults at most a smile, but there is lacking here the easement of laughter which is the effect of wit.

The most important thing, nevertheless, is the fact that even such a condensation of two words associated purely acoustically, and having no sense connection with one another, can have an exhilarating effect. This is the indubitable proof that the exhilarating effect of plays upon words springs only from the fact that for a moment we are saved the serious effort of intellectual work and 'play', as children are in the habit of doing, 'meaninglessly' with the words. Against those jokes, however, whose inner meaning is not caught, the logical censorship is rapidly mobilized, so that the witty effect is soon displaced by disgruntled criticism. This censorship only sanctions hearty laughter if the joker succeeds in concealing something 'subtle' behind the superficial acoustic condensation. It is this greater subtlety, therefore, which circumvents the otherwise most careful guardian of logical thought-processes, and, while he is still gnawing the intellectual bone flung to him, the child that survives in our unconscious has long since taken advantage of the situation and made heartily merry over his success in getting the best of logic—that tedious and irksome controller of the emotions.

Those of you who have already heard something about psycho-analytic dream interpretation will quite certainly be struck by the far-reaching resemblance between the dream work and that of the joker. In the dream as in the joke what is related to consciousness, that is, the manifest dream content, the joke as told, only becomes comprehensible and explicable when the meaning concealed behind it is plumbed. In the dream as in the joke the motive for the dream work as for that of the joke has its roots in the infantile; accordingly in our nocturnal phantasies, as also in the making or enjoyment of a joke, it is not strict logical order that rules but the so-called 'primary process' which is characterized by a childishly superficial association. According to the experience of our analyses this superficiality is much greater in the dream than in joke-making, which, of course, occurs in the waking state; nevertheless, even in dreams concatenation and conglomeration of words do sometimes occur that would also be possible in word jokes.

In a dream of my own, for instance, amongst other things there occurred the word 'hippolitaine', which sounds like a quite meaningless aggregation of syllables; on analysis, however, this turned out to be the condensation of the words Hippolyte Taine, hippopotamus and métropolitaine, and thus fulfilled all the rules of the technique of condensation word play.

It was, moreover, his work on dream interpretation that led Freud to tackle the problem of wit. It is instructive to hear how he came to do this.

When Freud's *Interpretation of Dreams* and the method of free superficial association therein employed was published it was to the author's no small astonishment received with merely a pitying smile by the whole corporate body of scientific men. There were also, however, some rough spirits who openly laughed at and flouted Freud about it. In this they behaved exactly like neurotics the contents of whose dreams we interpret and who defend themselves against the unpleasant truths contained in the interpretation by laughing.

Had one of us laid before the pundits of our profession the knowledge we had gathered during years of industrious effort and been met with such a reception on such flimsy grounds, we should certainly every one of us have angrily rebuked those who made light-heartedly merry over our life's work, mercilessly exposed their superficiality and ignorance, and, in a word, have rated them soundly. Not so Freud. He saw in the general laughter a psychic manifestation worthy of scientific investigation; he therefore set himself undeterred to work to plumb the psychology of laughter and wit, and did not rest till he discovered why the uninitiated must laugh away most of his own dreams and all dream interpretation. Probably for the reason—this was the result of his investigations—because dream and wit draw from one and the same psychic spring, from the unconscious strata of repressed infantile desires, and work with the same psychic technical means and mechanism. To use a joking condensation I might therefore say that when he was made fun of, only then did Freud write the book he could throw at the heads of those who mocked him.

I cannot here take up the different varieties of puns in detail. Whosoever reads Freud's book—and I can recommend it to everyone who wishes to be thoroughly informed on these questions and to enjoy the beauty of form of an exemplarily constructed scientific work — will convince himself that all the kinds of wit included under plays upon words, that is, all those forms 'employing similar material twice over', those 'erected upon a double meaning', and puns dealing with 'concealed insinuations', obey the same fundamental rules as the condensation jokes we have just examined more in detail. In each of them it is the childish play with the words that is the real source of pleasure, while the sense hiding behind the meaningless word concatenations and repetitions serve partly to befool the censorship, partly to heighten artificially the effect of the joke by the momentarily evoked but in the next instant manifestly superfluous thought-tension which, economized in this way, is discharged in laughter. [A paragraph is omitted here. It deals with puns and turns of meaning in the German language which cannot be translated directly into English.—Transl.]

Here is an example of a purely intellectual joke. 'Adolf and Moritz have a quarrel and part in anger. When Moritz reaches home later on he sees that Adolf has written the word 'scoundrel' on his door. Thereupon he hastens to Adolf's door and—leaves his card.'

Wherein lies the entertainment in this joke? Why do we consider it excellent and witty? It is senseless to reply to a brutal insult by an act of civility, by leaving one's card. The natural answer would probably have been for Moritz to write 'you are the scoundrel' on Adolf's door. But this would not be a joke but a stupid tit-for-tat. The incomprehensible and out-of-place politeness becomes a joke by Moritz deliberately misunderstanding the insult inscribed upon his door and behaving as though with the word 'scoundrel' Adolf had left his visiting card. In this way he succeeded in cloaking his retort as an act of politeness, that is, in representing his real intention by its opposite. The insult 'you are the scoundrel' is here by the employment of certain methods in the technique of wit transformed into a successful joke. Wherein lies the essence of this technique? Therein, that the witty person succeeds in smuggling something absurd, an error, something of childishly illogical judgement and deduction in general, into the reasonable thought-processes of a serious adult.

But even when we have robbed the joke of all its technicalities, just as if we had peeped behind its side-screens, we notice that even in this diminished form it can still excite laughter, a sign that it has not yet been sufficiently 'spoilt', that there is still something pleasurable behind it. This something, however, is no longer a joke; it is not the amalgamation of a piece of nonsense with something sensible, but the comedy of the situation. We find it comical and have to laugh that Adolf is placed in a helpless situation by the polite leaving of cards; he is, indeed, deprived of every possibility of carrying on the quarrel, although he understands only too well the uncommonly insulting intention concealed by the civility. When, as well as all this, we consider that this whole long explanation is really the analysis of one single action, the leaving of cards, we cannot doubt that the joke is at the same time a masterpiece of condensation. It takes, as we see, many artifices to get the adult human intellect which is addressed to the realities of life and inclined to seriousness to lay aside for a moment its inhibiting function and let us go back into the playful, crazy, laughing times of childhood.

The best intellectual jokes are those displacement

jokes, the intentional misunderstanding of a question, the unexpected gliding off along unnoticed side-lines. In exactly the same way the dream work is wont to displace the psychic stress from something essential upon something that is a side issue. Other methods of the intellectual joke are: representation by an opposite or by a quite slight insinuation, out-trumping, the crushing rejoinder by means of a sophism, etc.; all act exhilaratingly because they temporarily mislead our judgement, and in this way we economize a certain amount of inhibiting effort that we had already automatically set going from habit and can now laugh off.

What Freud says sounds paradoxical but is nevertheless true: namely, that in hearing a joke we really never quite know what it is we are laughing at; indeed, the drawing off of attention from the technique of the actual effect of the joke is one of the most important tools of the skilled joker.

If, however, we analyse jokes in this way we learn that there are jokes that are not particularly distinguished either by their intellectual content nor in respect of their technique, and that yet are very effective. When we consider these jokes more closely it turns out that they are without exception tendentious jokes, mostly aggressive, obscene, cynical, or sceptical in nature.

We are more amused, therefore, at jokes of an aggressive and sexual tendency than they would deserve from their intellectual content and witty technique. Freud knew from other sources that in all of us the hidden, strongly emotional, but usually deeply repressed, tendencies, of which our conscious thoughts perhaps would only take cognizance with a feeling of disgust or of shame, gladly seize the opportunity of affording them cathexis with their original affect, that is, with pleasure. This is what happens on the occasion of a joke, due to the smuggling in of a childish pun or an error, when the strictness of the psychic censorship slackens for a moment. In the tendentious joke the technique of wit only plays the part of attractive bait (fore-pleasure); the greater gratification comes secondarily from the temporary suspension of the moral inhibition.

Thus a sexual or an aggressive joke, even though ever so 'feeble', can put a whole company in good humour.

The lower the cultural level of a company, by so much the coarser, the less adorned, must the sexual insinuation be to achieve its pleasurable effect. But even in the best society there is a predilection for retailing jokes that are not to be distinguished in essence from the brutal jests of the populace except that their obscenity is concealed by subtle insinuation and the censorship is deceived by their intellectual and moral veneer.

After the demonstration of this unexpectedly novel and unexpectedly simple explanation of the action of wit, Freud analysed wit as a social manifestation, and did so with the greatest acumen. The joker by profession, as every neurologist can confirm, is generally a nervous creature with an unbalanced character who in his jokes really ventilates his insufficiently censored intellectual and moral imperfections, that is, his own infantilisms. He does not generally laugh at his own jokes, and rejoices only at the gaiety that he wakens in his hearers. The entertainment of his hearers is all the greater as they get the jokes so to say in a gift.

For the primitive form of sexually aggressive joke that is common amongst the lower classes of the populace, two persons do not suffice; it takes at least three, a woman as object of the aggression and two men of whom one plays the part of the assailant and the other that of onlooker. So far as sexual aggression is concerned one would think that the third person as onlooker must have a disturbing effect. In reality, however, the latter is a accessory whom the assailant disarms and corrupts by the bribe of listening to a sexual duologue, the substitute for a sexual action, and of looking on in company at the woman's reaction of modesty.

In better circles the woman no longer takes part personally in such conversation, but amongst themselves the men maintain the old tradition. If a company divides up according to sexes then presently someone amongst the men will crack the latest sexual joke, and thereby gives the opening for an endless series of ambiguous wit. The people who like to make or hear jokes of this sadistic or sexual tendency are in other respects very often morally strict individuals who have no idea how much their behaviour betrays to the initiated of the deepest springs of their natures, of which they themselves are unconscious.

The joke has a certain importance not only in such small circles but also in larger assemblies. Every speaker, every demagogue, gladly spices his address with jokes; he does not thereby want merely to provide æsthetic enjoyment, but seems also to imagine that the public, if bribed with a good joke, will accept a weak argument more easily. On the other hand, there is no personality so awe-inspiring—no scientific, political, or æsthetic endeavour so estimable—that could not be disparaged by a successful joke. For the crowd enjoyment surpasses everything; to-day, as a thousand years ago, it demands only *panem et circenses*.

The most effective are the tendentious jokes that, for a moment, switch off the moral inhibitions active in us all. Insinuations often, however, release much laughter, where an external hindrance such as consideration for someone present renders it necessary to clothe the aggression in the form of a joke. I quote the following 'Serenissimo joke' from Freud: 'His Serene Highness is making a journey through his states and notices in the crowd a man who strikingly resembles his own noble person; he beckons him to approach in order to ask, "Did your mother ever serve at any time in the Residency?" "No, your Highness," is the reply, "but my father did."'

This innocent seeming reply is the most terrible retort upon the aspersion which his Serene Highness cast upon the honour of the soldier's mother; but the joke, owing indeed to its harmless appearance, also saves the soldier from the consequences of his *lèse-majesté*. The audience, in any case, are hugely amused, for every 'underling' is delighted to hear an authority properly 'told off' without it being possible for anyone to be punished for it.

Apart from intellectual content, technical skill, and tendentiousness, actuality also heightens the witty effect. For instance, a joke about a girl who was compared with

Dreyfus 'because the army does not believe in her innocence' was certainly much more telling at the time of the Dreyfus trial than to-day when '*l'affaire*' no longer occupies public attention. The pleasurable effect of actuality is, according to Freud, to be explained exactly as is the enjoyment of repetition in the kind of word and intellectual jokes already mentioned.

If in what follows I concern myself comparatively much more briefly with another kind of exhilarating mental experience, with the psychology of the comic, I am only faithfully following Freud's book, which concerns itself much less fully with this department of æsthetic psychology and really deals exhaustively only with the distinctions between wit and the comic. While the tendentious joke requires three people—the joker, the derided, and the listener—the comic is content with two: with one person who is comical, and a second who perceives what is comic in him and enjoys it.

A witticism is 'made'; subsequent upon any impression there follows for a moment a 'thought vacuum' in consciousness during which the association of ideas dives into the unconscious to reappear again after a thorough elaboration, condensation, and displacement, 'enriched' with errors and superficial associations, as a completed joke. The psychological workshop of the joke is therefore situated in the stratum of unconscious psychic functioning. This submersion is not necessary for the achievement of comic effect; the scene of its origin is to be laid in the preconscious system, which is not inaccessible to consciousness even if it is not exactly at the focussing point of its attention.

A characteristic example of the comic is the naïveté at which we smile in children and in simple or inexperienced people. For instance, the question little Maurice asks his mother is naïve: 'Mama, is papa so poor that he has no bed-clothes?' 'Why?' asks his mother. 'Because the neighbour said that he shared a coverlet with a lady.' If one knows for certain that the child is not deliberately cloaking dissembled knowledge in a witty guise, one is really laughing at the child's stupidity and ignorance, or, more correctly, one compares one's own knowledge with the ignorance of the child, with whom one had momentarily identified oneself in thought. In so doing the difference of intellectual tension between the normal and the infantile intellectual attitude is discharged in laughter. In an old Hungarian jest there is a village notary who is in the theatre for the first time in his life, where Othello is being played. In his naïveté he takes the scene being enacted for real, and hurls himself upon the stage to rescue Desdemona from the murderous hands of Othello. The theatre-habituated public can laugh heartily at this, as its compares its knowledge with the ignorance of the provincial and abreacts the great difference between them. To a similar comparison is to be traced the sense of the comical that lies in the abnormal size or diminutiveness of persons or of parts of the body, in automatic movement as well as in automatic thinking, in absent-mindedness, etc. In these cases by means of 'empathy' one compares one's own attributes with those of the comic person and there results from this comparison a difference of psychic expenditure for which at the moment there is no other outlet and that is therefore capable of discharge and becomes a source of pleasure. A similar comparison is also made in comicalities of situation, but not between oneself and another person but between two different sorts of situations in the case of a third person. It is, for instance, comic if someone in the midst of a conceited or high-falutin' discourse is suddenly overcome by an urgent bodily need. It is also comic if someone is deceived in their expectations. 'How well', our preconscious thinks to itself, 'that we are not so stupid, so impulsive, so childish as he who definitely assumed without sufficient evidence that his hopes would be fulfilled.' In the 'exposure'-comedy aggressive tendencies play a considerable part.

Somewhere between wit and intentional comicality comes irony; it is really the easiest way of extracting a smile from anyone. Nothing more is necessary than always to say the opposite of what one thinks and of what one's mimicry, gestures, and speech intonations quite clearly mean to express. The ironical person never says 'you do not look well', but always 'you *do* look well!' He does not say 'I do not think you will pass the examination', but 'you will pass your examination nicely if you do not work', etc.

A much more refined way of making people laugh is that of humour. To explain humour Freud started from the fact that we cannot always laugh at a joke or at something comical. If we are harassed with cares or sad, if the subject of the jest is one too near our hearts, then we cannot laugh at all, or only bitterly, at even the best of jokes or the most comical of situations. Not so the man of humour. He rises above his own troubles, his anger, or his feelings, economizes in so doing his affective expenditure and employs this energy in laughter while the ordinary person abandons himself to his sad emotions.

The highest achievement of humour is probably the so-called 'gallows humour'; whoever is capable of this will not be so overcome even by the proximity of certain death as to be unable to laugh or smile at his own situation. In 'rising above things', however, in disparaging everything that stands in our way, we fall into the same 'megalomania' and grandiose boastfulness which as children we considered made our littleness and feebleness more supportable.

Thus Freud finally traces wit, as well as the comical and humour, to infantilism.

The joker plays with words and wants to make stupidity and unmannerliness acceptable; the comic person behaves exactly like a clumsy, ignorant child; and the humourist, too, takes the grandiose phantasies of children as his example.

Expressed more scientifically, the source of pleasure in the joke is economy of inhibition, in comicality it is economy in thought, and in humour economy of feeling. All three, however, have one aim, to transport us back again for an instant to that 'Paradise Lost', to the simplicity of childhood.

My present lecture, however, was only intended to waken fore-pleasure; you can obtain the real pleasure for yourselves by the perusal of Freud's book.

LV

INTERCHANGE OF AFFECT IN DREAMS[1]

An elderly gentleman was wakened at night by his wife, who was alarmed because he laughed so loudly and unrestrainedly in his sleep. He explained later that he had had the following dream: 'I was lying in my bed; an acquaintance came in; I wanted to turn up the light, but could not do it. I tried again and again—in vain. Thereupon my wife got up out of bed to help me, but she could not manage it either; but because she was embarrassed before the gentleman at being in her *négligé* she finally gave it up and went back to bed again; all this was so comical that I had to laugh exceedingly at it. My wife said, "Why do you laugh, why do you laugh?" but I only went on laughing,—till I wakened.' The following day he was very depressed and had a headache—'From laughing so much that I was exhausted', he thought.

Considered analytically the dream seems less cheerful. The 'acquaintance' who entered is, in the latent dream thoughts, the figure of death evoked on the previous day as the 'great unknown'. The old gentleman, who suffers from arterio-sclerosis, had on the previous day had occasion to think of dying. The unrestrained laughter takes the place of weeping and sobbing at the idea that he must die. It is the light of life that he can no longer turn up. This sad thought may have become associated with recently intended but unsuccessful attempts at cohabitation, in which not even the help of his wife in her *négligé* was of any avail; he was aware that he was already upon the downward path. The dream work was able to transform the sad idea of impotence and death into a comic scene, and the sobbing into laughter.

Similar 'interchanges of affect' and reversals of the gestures of expression are also to be seen in the neuroses and in the 'evanescent symptom formations' in analysis as well as in dreams.

[1] *Zeitschrift*, 1916–17, Bd. IV. S. 112.

LVI

DREAMS OF THE UNSUSPECTING[1]

We know how difficult it often is to interpret the dream of a patient undergoing psycho-analytic treatment. He is as though 'warned' and avoids producing dreams that are easily translatable and which finally he could interpret for himself. It is otherwise with the great mass of people who have no inkling of psycho-analysis. These people tell one another—at table or in any other general conversation—their, so to speak, primordial dreams, unmitigated by any psycho-analytic culture, and have no foreboding that in so doing they are betraying their most intimate and secret desires, even often concealed from themselves, to the sophisticated listener. I once spent several weeks at a Spa and was able to collect a little series of such easily interpreted dreams at meal-times.

'Just imagine what I dreamt last night,' said a lady, who was staying in the pension with her daughter, to a neighbour. 'I dreamt I was robbed of my daughter last night;—while we were walking in the forest some men came towards us and dragged my daughter from me by force. It was dreadful!' I did not share this opinion of the dream and thought to myself the lady would have liked to be rid of her already more than marriageable daughter. Confirmation was not long awanting. The very next day the lady complained how much nicer the previous season had been; there had been a whole crowd of young people then, now her daughter had no suitable companions, there were none but elderly men. The following day she announced that they intended leaving shortly, as they also did.

A colleague staying there said to me one morning: 'I dreamt about you last night. You were struggling in a canal with an *apache* who wanted to force you under the water. I ran for the police to fetch you help.'

'What have I done to you that you should be so angry with me?' I could not keep from asking.

[1] *Zeitschrift*, 1916–17, Bd. IV. S. 208.

'Why, nothing at all; I dreamt so vividly because I had severe colic all night.'

'That may have its share in the formation of the dream,' I replied; 'the *canal* in which I was to have been drowned may be an allusion to the alimentary canal, which, therefore, in the dream was to do me, not you, harm. I repeat, you must be annoyed with me about something!'

'You don't mean that I wanted to drown you because you had to refuse me that little favour yesterday? You will never make me believe that!' This, however, interpreted the dream for me as a revenge phantasy.

'What does it mean when one puts one's shoes on and off all night in a dream?' a remarkably pretty and young war-widow asks me at table. 'For heaven's sake don't ask me so loud!' was my only reply, and I succeeded in turning the conversation to other matters. The dreamer, however, was not so easily put off. She continued the dream next night, and now wanted to know the interpretation of the following dream: 'Last night I dreamt that I had married an elderly gentleman; my mother forced me to do it. Afterwards I had a whole crowd of shoes of all colours that I put on and off—black, brown, and yellow shoes!' Evidently the possession of this host of shoes gave her pleasure, for even in the telling of them she laughed gaily.

'Whom did the old gentleman, your husband in the dream, resemble?'

'Oddly enough it was the husband of a young friend of mine who actually did marry an elderly man. I consider such marriages unseemly; they are deliberately calculated to cause adultery.' I did not need to inquire further in order to understand the interpretation of the many coloured shoes; I merely thought to myself—elderly bachelors should beware of this lady.

Meantime the rumour that I was interested in dreams seems to have spread through the house, for one day the nurse of a patient staying there comes and recounts the following horrible dream: 'I saw a sack in a room; in it was the body of my dead sister; the sack itself was on a wooden vessel in which dirty water, perhaps from the decaying of the body, was gathering, but it had not at all an offensive odour. I kept on forgetting, oddly enough, that my sister was dead, and started to sing, and then kept on hitting myself on the mouth as a punishment. When I opened the sack I saw that my sister was not dead but only very pale. *Beside her lay the corpse of a little child.* There was an ugly eruption on my sister's face.'

To understand the dream one must know that the dreamer is a well-built person of thirty-eight to thirty-nine years of age, who, in spite of being apparently in every way well suited for motherhood, remained single and chose the calling of sick nurse. I had to interpret the peculiar coffin birth phantasy, the doubt whether the sister was alive or dead, as the identification of the dead sister with a living person. Her peculiar ambivalent behaviour towards the dead sister indicated that this living person might be the dreamer herself; she rejoices over the death—then she punishes herself for this joy. Perhaps she may at some time have envied her sister, who, I learnt, was married, and would have liked to have put herself in her place so that she, too, could have children. The question, then, that I put to the dreamer was the following: 'Did you not, after your sister's death, have the idea that your brother-in-law, as so often happens, would marry you?' 'No,' she replied; '*my brother-in-law did certainly ask me to marry him, but I turned down his proposal because I did not want to take the charge of my sister's four children upon myself.*'

I did not undertake to clear up the individual points in this dream by analysis; I understood already, however, from the telling, that the dreamer may secretly have repented of the decisiveness with which she had rejected her brother-in-law. Whether, as well, actual experiences had not a share in the dream formation—I am thinking, for instance, of an abortion—I leave undecided. If here, however, we must neglect the question: phantasy or reality—and we are justified in this in problems of the unconscious—nevertheless, from the mere telling of a dream, we have become aware of important forces in the psychic life of the dreamer.

LVII

TO WHOM DOES ONE RELATE ONE'S DREAMS?[1]

We analysts know that one feels impelled to relate one's dreams to the very person to whom the content relates. Lessing seems to have had an inkling of this, for he writes the following epigram:

> Alba mihi semper narrat sua somnia mane,
> Alba sibi dormit; somniat alba mihi.
>
> (Lessing, *Sinngedichte*, II Buch).

LVIII

THE DREAM OF THE 'CLEVER BABY'[2]

Not too seldom patients narrate to one dreams in which the newly born, quite young children, or babies in the cradle, appear, who are able to talk or write fluently, treat one to deep sayings, carry on intelligent conversations, deliver harangues, give learned explanations, and so on. I imagine that behind such dream-contents something typical is hidden. The superficial layer of dream-interpretation in many cases points to an ironical view of psycho-analysis, which, as is well known, attributes far more psychical value and permanent effect to the experiences of early childhood than people in general care to admit. The ironic exaggeration of the intelligence of children, therefore, expresses a doubt as to analytical communications on this subject. But as similar appearances in fairy tales, myths, and traditional religious history very often occur, and in the painter's art are also effectively represented

[1] *Zentralblatt für Psychoanalyse*, 1912, Bd. III. S. 258. [Translated by John Rickman.]

[2] *Zeitschrift*, 1923, IX. 70. [Translated by Olive Edmonds.]

(see the Debate of the young Mary with the Scribes), I believe that here the irony serves only as a medium for deeper and graver memories of their own childhood. Therefore the wish to become learned and to excel over ' the great ' in wisdom and knowledge is only a reversal of the contrary situation of the child. One part of the dreams of this content observed by me is illustrated by the pithy observation of the ne'er-do-well, when he said, ' If I had only understood how to make better use of the position of the baby.' Lastly, we should not forget that the young child is familiar with much knowledge, as a matter of fact, that later becomes buried by the force of repression.[1]

LIX

A STRIKING PICTURE OF THE ' UNCONSCIOUS '[2]

In O. Liebmann's *Gedanken und Tatsachen* (2. Aufl., Strassburg, 1899) we find the following observation: ' There are dramas which would be quite unintelligible except for what goes on behind the scenes. The human mind is such a drama. What is enacted on the stage in the full light of consciousness are only detached fragments and scraps of the personal mental life. That would be inconceivable and indeed impossible without taking into account what occurs in the wings, which are unconscious processes.' (Quoted from M. Offner, *Das Gedächtnis.*)

[1] I do not believe that this communication has in any way exhausted the interpretation of this type of dream, and intends only to turn the attention of the psycho-analyst to it. (A recent observation of the same kind showed me that such dreams illustrate the *actual* knowledge of the child on sexuality.)

[2] *Zentralblatt für Psychoanalyse*, 1912, Bd. III, 52. [Translated by John Rickman.]

LX

POMPADOUR PHANTASIES[1]

One could give this name to that type of hetæral phantasy in which even the most chaste women indulge—in day dreams. The exaltation of the partner to kingly rank makes thoughts and wishes possible which would otherwise be rejected as immoral.

[1] *Zeitschrift*, III. 294.

SYMBOLISM

Short Papers

THE SYMBOLISM OF THE BRIDGE[1]

LXI

In establishing the symbolic relation of an object or an action to an unconscious phantasy we must first have recourse to conjectures, which necessarily undergo considerable modifications and often complete transformation with wider experience. Indications flooding in on one, as they often do, from the most diverse spheres of knowledge offer important confirmation; so that all branches of individual and group psychology can take their share in the establishment of a special symbolic relation. Dream-interpretation and analysis of neuroses, however, remain, as before, the most trustworthy foundation of every kind of symbolism, because in them we can observe *in anima vili* the motivation, and further the whole genesis, of mental structures of this kind. A feeling of certainty about a symbolic relation can in my opinion be attained only in psycho-analysis. Symbolic interpretations in other fields of knowledge (mythology, fairy-tales, folk-lore, etc.) always bear the impress of being superficial, two-dimensional: they tend to produce a lurking feeling of incertitude, an idea that the meaning might just as well have been something else, and indeed in these fields there is always a tendency to go on imposing new interpretations on the same content. The absence of a third dimension may well be what distinguishes the unsubstantial allegory from the symbol—a thing of flesh and blood.

Bridges often play a striking part in dreams. In the interpretation of the dreams of neurotics one is frequently confronted with the question of the typical meaning of the bridge, particularly when no historical fact apropos of the

[1] *Zeitschrift*, 1921, VII. 211. [Translated by C. M. Baines.]

dream-bridge occurs to the patient. It may have been due to some coincidence in the material furnished by my practice that I should be able to replace the bridge in a whole series of cases by sexual symbols as follows: the bridge is the male organ, and in particular the powerful organ of the father, which unites two landscapes (the two parents in the giant shapes in which they appear to the infant view). This bridge spans a wide and perilous stream, from which all life takes its origin, into which man longs all his life to return, and to which the adult does periodically return, though only by proxy—through a portion of himself. That the approach to this stream in dream-life is not direct but by means of some kind of supporting plank or stay is intelligible in the light of the special characteristic of the dreamers: they were without exception suffering from sexual impotence, and they made use of this genital weakness to protect themselves against the dangerous proximity of women. This symbolic interpretation of the bridge-dream proved true in numerous cases; I also found confirmation of my assumption in a popular folk-tale and in a French artist's drawing of an obscene topic: in both an enormous male organ figured, which was extended over a wide river, and in the fairy story it was strong enough to carry a heavy team of horses with their load.

My view concerning this symbol received final verification, and at the same time took on the deeper significance that belonged to it but had been previously lacking, from the communications of a patient who suffered from bridge-anxiety and from *ejaculatio retardata*. Besides a variety of experiences which were calculated to arouse and to heighten in the patient the apprehension of castration or death (he was the son of a tailor), the analysis disclosed the following terrifying episode from his ninth year; his mother, a midwife (!), who idolized him, would not be parted from him even on the night of agony in which she gave birth to a girl-child, so that the little boy, if he could not see the whole process of the birth from his bed, was at least obliged to hear everything, and from the remarks of the people tending the mother was able to gather details about the appearing of the infant and then its withdrawal for a time once more into the mother's body. The boy could not have escaped the apprehension which irresistibly seizes the witness of a scene of birth; he imagined himself in the position of the child, which was going through that first and greatest anxiety, the prototype of every later anxiety, which for hours together was being drawn to and fro between the mother's womb and the outer world. This to and fro, this isthmus between life and what is not yet (or no longer) life, thus gave the special form of bridge-anxiety to the patient's anxiety-hysteria. The opposite shore of the Danube signified for him the future life which, as is usual, was modelled upon prenatal life.[1] Never in his life had he gone over a bridge on foot, only in vehicles driven very fast and in the company of a strong personality dominating his own. When, after adequate development of the transference, I induced him for the first time to drive across the bridge with me once more after a long interval, he clung to me like a vice, all his muscles were stiffened to tautness, and his breath was held. On the return journey he behaved in the same way, but only as far as the middle of the bridge; when the bank this side, which for him meant life, became visible, he loosed his grip, became cheerful, noisy, and talkative. The anxiety had vanished.

We are thus enabled to understand the patient's apprehension in the proximity of female genitals, and his incapacity for complete surrender to a woman, who always meant for him, though unconsciously, deep water with the menace of danger, water in which he must drown if some one stronger does not ' hold him above the water '.

In my opinion, the two meanings ' bridge = uniting member between the parents ' and ' bridge = link between life and not-life (death) ' supplement each other in the most effectual manner: the father's organ is actually the bridge which expedited the unborn (the not yet born) into life.

[1] Cf. Rank's detailed discussion of the Lohengrin-legend with confirmations from folk-psychology.

This latter additional interpretation alone gives to the simile that deeper sense without which there can be no true symbol.

It is natural to interpret the use of the bridge symbol as it occurs in cases of neurotic bridge-anxiety as representing purely mental ' connections ', ' linking ', ' associating ' (Freud's ' word-bridge ')—in a word, as a mental or logical relation, that is, to take it as an ' autosymbolic ', ' functional ' phenomenon in Silberer's sense. But just as in the given instance solid material ideas about the events at a confinement form the basis for these phenomena, my own view is that there is no functional phenomenon without a material parallel, that is, one relating to ideas of objects. Of course, in the case of narcissistic stressing of the ' ego-memory systems ',[1] association with object-memories may fall into the background, and the *appearance* of a pure autosymbolism may be produced. On the other hand, it is possible that no ' material ' mental phenomenon exists which is not blended with some memory-trace, even though only a faint one, of the self-perception accompanying it. Finally, it may be recalled in this connection that in the last analysis nearly every symbol, perhaps indeed every one, has also a physiological basis, *i.e.* expresses in some way or other the whole body or an organ of the body or its function.[2]

There are contained, I think, in what has been so far intimated, the main outlines along which a topographical description of the formation of symbols might be constructed; and since the dynamics of the repression active in it has been already described on a former occasion,[3] there still remains to be supplied (in order to gain ' metapsychological ' insight, in Freud's sense, into the essential nature of symbols) a knowledge of the distribution of the psycho-physical quantities concerned in this interplay of

[1] See my article on Tic. (*The International Journal of Psycho-Analysis*, vol. ii. p. 1, Chap. XII. of this book.)

[2] Cf. the observations relative to this in the article ' The Phenomenon of Hysterical Materialization ', Chap. VI. of this book.

[3] See ' The Ontogenesis of Symbols '. Ferenczi, *Contributions to Psycho-Analysis*, 1916, chap. x.

forces, and more exact data as to its ontogenesis and phylogenesis.[1]

The psychic material brought to the surface in the 'bridge-anxiety' appears also in the patient in a symptom of conversion hysteria. A sudden shock, the sight of blood or of some bodily defect, may bring about faintness. The occurrence which was the forerunner of these attacks was supplied by his mother's story that he came half-dead into the world after a difficult birth and that respiration was brought about with great trouble. This recollection was the original trauma, to which the later one, his presence at his mother's labour, could attach itself.

It need scarcely be specially mentioned that bridges in dreams may also originate in historical dream-material and be without any symbolic significance.

LXII

BRIDGE SYMBOLISM AND THE DON JUAN LEGEND[2]

In the preceding paper on Bridge Symbolism I have tried to disclose the numerous layers of meaning which the bridge has attained in the unconscious. According to that interpretation the bridge is: (1) the male member which unites the parents during sexual intercourse, and to which the little child must cling if it is not to perish in the 'deep water' across which the bridge is thrown. (2) In so far as it is thanks to the male member that we have come into the world at all out of that water the bridge is an important vehicle between the 'Beyond' (the condition of the unborn, the womb) and the 'Here' (life). (3) Since man is not able to imagine death, the Beyond *after* life, except in the image of the past, consequently as a return to the womb,

[1] Cf. Ernest Jones's essay on 'The Theory of Symbolism', chap. vii. of *Papers on Psycho-Analysis*, 1918.

[2] *Zeitschrift*, 1922, VIII. 77. [Translated by John Rickman.]

to water, to Mother Earth, the bridge is also the symbol of the pathway to death. (4) Finally the bridge may be used as a formal representation of 'transitions', 'changes of condition' in general.

Now in the original version of the Don Juan legend the motives (1-3) mentioned are so closely related to a strikingly clear bridge symbol that I may claim this relationship as a confirmation of my interpretation.

According to the legend the famous lady-killer, Miguel Monara Vicentello de Leco (Don Juan), *lighted his cigar with the devil's cigar across the Guadalquivir.* Once he met his own funeral and wanted to be buried in the crypt of a chapel built by himself in order to be trodden on by the feet of men. Only after the 'burial' did he change and become a repentant sinner.

a. I wish to interpret the cigar lighted across the river as a variation of the bridge symbol, in which (as so frequently happens with variations) much of the unconscious repressed material has returned. By its form and the fact that it burns the cigar reminds us of the male organ burning with desire. The gigantic gesture—kindling the cigar from one side of the river to the other—is eminently fitted to serve as a representation of the gigantic potency of a Don Juan whose organ we wished to portray in colossal erection.

b. His presence at his own burial may be explained by the idea that this phantasy of a double represents a personification of the chief part of Don Juan's bodily ego, namely, his sexual organ. In every sexual intercourse the sexual organ is actually 'buried' and of course in the same place as that of birth, and the rest of the 'ego' may look anxiously at this 'burial'. The psycho-analysis of numerous dreams and of neurotic claustrophobia explains the fear of being buried alive as the transformation into dread of the wish to return to the womb. Moreover, from the narcissistic point of view every sexual act, every sacrifice to woman, is a loss, a kind of castration in Stärcke's meaning,[1] to which the offended ego may react with fear of death.

[1] *The International Journal of Psycho-Analysis*, vol. ii. p. 179.

Scruples of conscience, phantasies of punishment, too, may contribute to the fact that a Don Juan feels himself nearer to hell, to annihilation, with every sexual act. If we explain, with Freud, the Don Juan type of love-life—the compulsion to sequence-formation, to the conquest of innumerable women (Leporello's list!)—as a series of substitutes for the one and only love which is denied even to the Don Juan himself (the Oedipus-phantasy) we understand better the phantasy of punishment mentioned above: it requites for the supreme ' mortal sin '.

Of course I do not pretend in these few lines to have revealed the hidden meaning of the Don Juan legend which still has many inexplicable traits (for example, I may hint at the probably homosexual signification of the lighting of one cigar by another); I only wished to give a confirmation of the phallic, life and death symbolism of the bridge by its appearance among the typical symbols of death, birth, and sexuality.

LXIII

SIGNIFICANT VARIANTS OF THE SHOE AS A VAGINA SYMBOL[1]

A PATIENT dreamt that ' he had to look for a rubber shoe (galoshes) on the dirty ground, while his brother and many others with their wives had long ago gone on ahead '. (The scene occurs on going home from an entertainment or something of the kind.) The patient is unmarried, his younger brother married a long time ago. The patient is attached to a married woman no longer young who has had to have the results of a perineal tear treated by operation. On the day before the dream there had been unsatisfactory sexual intercourse, where the patient did not ' get finished ' (as in the dream). The ' dirt ' was an allusion to the disgrace that he would suffer if the husband knew of the matter. For this reason probably, too, the normal shoe symbol was changed into muddy, and also very extensible galoshes.

[1] *Zeitschrift*, 1916–17, Bd. IV. 112.

LXIV

THE SYMBOLISM OF BED-LINEN[1]

(*a*) A YOUNG man has a pollution regularly every time that his bed-linen is changed. Interpretation: he wishes to soil what is clean (woman); at the same time he compels (unconsciously) the females belonging to the household, who attend to the bed, to concern themselves with his potency.

(*b*) A man suffers from relative impotence: he can only achieve coitus if previously, with his own hands, he rumples up the bed-linen, which must be quite smooth, or if his wife lies upon a sheet of smooth paper which he crumples up immediately before the act. The symptom proves to be over-determined; its elements are: 1. love for the (wrinkled) grandmother; 2. sadism (as in the first case); 3. memories of onanism with the help of the bed-clothes.[2]

LXV

THE KITE AS A SYMBOL OF ERECTION[3]

A PATIENT relates of his uncle who suffers from delusions of persecution that although the latter was already more than thirty years of age he always played with boys, would sometimes show them his member, and was particularly fond of, and skilled at, constructing gigantic paper kites with long tails. He would let the kites fly so high that they went out of sight, then he tied the string to a chair, and made a boy sit upon it, and was delighted when the pull of

[1] *Zeitschrift*, 1913, Bd. I. S. 378.

[2] For the identification of skin and bed-linen (both of course are washed !) and of wrinkles and the folds of bed-linen, compare the following joke from *Fliegenden Blätter*. 'What do you want, child, with the flat-iron ?' 'I want to make grandpapa's face smooth.'

[3] *Zeitschrift*, 1913, Bd. I. S. 379.

the kite upset him. The association of paranoia with homosexuality is also shown in this example. In connection with this I am reminded of the mentally afflicted Mr. Dick in Dickens' *David Copperfield*; he, too, always plays with boys, and flies kites on which he scribbles his phantasies about the death of King Charles the First. If this occurred in one of our patients we should have to regard him, even though he were just as good-natured as Mr. Dick, as an unconscious parri- (regi-) cide, but who, on the other hand, worshipped the insignia of the paternal dignity.

[For the symbolism of kite-flying see the story (No. 6) from Grosz-Frankfurt 'Kite-flying' related in the VIIth volume of Anthropophyteia. A little boy asks his papa why children only fly kites in the autumn. His papa explains: 'It can only be done when the fields are cut, because one must run long distances; but I, I let my kite fly all the year round.']

LXVI

ON THE SYMBOLISM OF THE HEAD OF MEDUSA[1]

In the analysis of dreams and fancies, I have come repeatedly upon the circumstance that the head of Medusa is the terrible symbol of the female genital region, the details of which are displaced 'from below upwards'. The many serpents which surround the head ought—in representation by the opposite—to signify the absence of a penis, and the phantom itself is the frightful impression made on the child by the penis-less (castrated) genital. The fearful and alarming starting eyes of the Medusa head have also the secondary meaning of erection.[1]

[1] *Zeitschrift*, 1923, IX. 69. [Translated by Olive Edmonds.]

LXVII

THE FAN AS A GENITAL SYMBOL[1]

A PATIENT dreamt *I saw a woman with a fan in place of genitals; she walked on this fan; her legs were cut off.* The patient's powerful castration complex is repelled by the feminine lack of a penis; he has, therefore, to imagine the vulva as a fan-shaped split penis, but nevertheless still a penis.[2] He preferred to sacrifice the woman's legs.

Compare with this the occasionally observed perversion that is only satisfied by lame or amputated women. I once read in the 'agony column' of a daily paper an advertisement by someone who wished to correspond with women who had had a leg amputated.

LXVIII

VERMIN AS A SYMBOL OF PREGNANCY[3]

IN several cases, behind the exaggerated fear of vermin and the affectively toned cover-memories concerned with the disgrace of the discovery of this kind of uncleanliness, lay the unconscious phantasy of being pregnant. What pregnancy and having vermin have in common—in addition to the disgrace—is the sheltering of little living things in and on the body. The same holds for intestinal worms—child = little worm.[4] Vermin in dreams are also to be interpreted in this sense.

[1] *Zeitschrift*, III. 294.

[2] The spreading of a fan appears to be employed in dreams as an indubitable penis (erection) symbol.—[Note by Editor of *Zeitschrift*.]

[3] *Zeitschrift*, II. 381.

[4] [The German word 'Würmchen' (little worm) is applied to children as an affectionate diminutive.—TRANS.]

LXIX

PECUNIA OLET[1]

I

A YOUNG merchant was under my care for a prolonged period on account of obsessional and anxiety conditions. I could not pursue the case to an end, for the improvement that set in was, as so often, used by the resistance as a motive for breaking off the treatment. As the analysis soon showed, the actual cause of his illness was his relationship to his wife. I had to explain to the patient on the strength of very clear indications that he was coming to grief over the conflict between his love of money (anal erotism) and the rest of his sexuality. He married a more than well-to-do woman with whom he was not in love, while his unconscious dreamt of disinterested devotion; amongst other things he often thought consciously about a quite penniless but most charming woman, by whose side he had perhaps found the happiness for which he longed. I had, of course, to make clear to the patient that this happiness, too, would not have been unclouded, since his other no less powerful passion, the love of money, would have been unsatisfied.

At one of our talks the patient gave me absolute confirmation, according to my views, of the preceding interpretation. He recalled that shortly after his engagement, during an intimate association with his bride, he was alarmed by an unpleasant odour from her mouth. He left her abruptly, hastened to a confidential friend, and wanted to break off the engagement at once. He was soothed, however, and as the bad smell did not occur again he gave up his intention—the marriage took place.

I had to explain this memory as follows: an evidently insignificant odour from the lady's mouth became associated with the patient's primitive anal erotism from which was

[1] *Zeitschrift*, 1916-17, Bd. IV. S. 327.

derived his love of money; he was nigh owning to himself that he was about to marry for money; he wished to escape from this possibility as anxiously as he did from his own badly repressed anal erotic impulses. This was, therefore, a case of *character regression*, the falling back of a character trait (love of money) on to its erotic pre-stage.[1] For a moment the unconscious phantasy succeeded in converting the bride's mouth into the anal orifice.

Anyone who has not had considerable psycho-analytical experience will find this explanation extraordinarily forced and certainly very disagreeable. He will ask, as I hear so often, 'Why *must* the so-called "anal erotism" play a part again here? Is the case not to be explained more simply by the quite comprehensible dislike of any cultured person for an unpleasant smell, which was present in the given case, without dragging in "character regression"?'

Instead of dealing with this question I shall briefly recount a second case.

II

I suggest to a lady who imagines herself passionately in love with her husband that various of her symptoms indicate that she married mainly from interested motives, and that because she considers anything of the kind irreconcilable with her character she exaggerates her passionate attachment to her husband. After a prolonged resistance, she had to own to herself and me that at the time of her engagement she had really preferred another young man to her future husband, further that she and her family had at that time been in great material want, and, finally, that her husband had been thought a wealthy heir.

As in the above case, I drew her attention to her anal erotism, whereupon the patient at once reacted with the following reminiscence.

[1] Compare 'Passagère Symptombildungen während der Analyse' and 'Mischgebilde von erotischen und Charakterzügen'. ['On Transient Symptom Formation during Analysis', chap. vii. of *Contributions to Psycho-Analysis* and 'Composite Formations of Erotic and Character Traits', Chap. XXXI. of this book.]

'When I saw for the first time after my engagement the young man with whom I was previously in love, the following incident occurred. He greeted me and kissed my hand; at the moment the thought flashed through my mind that I had shortly before been to the closet and had not yet had an opportunity of washing my hands. He will smell fæces on my fingers! My anxiety was so great that I had at once to carry my fingers to my nose and smell them, whereupon it seemed to me as though a girl friend of mine who was present smiled ironically.'

Naturally I interpreted this reminiscence as a confirmation of the assumption already indicated, and added that she was really alarmed that the young man might 'smell' from her that she was marrying from motives of interest. Behind this scene I had to suppose, moreover, the repetition of infantile fæcal games. The patient had dim memories of having carried on games of this kind in the closet with her brother.

I must leave it to the reader to explain the marked resemblance between the two cases as accidental, or to afford it a meaning, ultimately the meaning that psycho-analysis attributes to it. On this occasion, however, I must emphasize that psycho-analysis never founds its theses on speculation, but always on the piling up of such correspondences, therefore on facts. The reply to the question of whence these correspondences originate is another matter, and analysis will not leave it unanswered. But it must not be impatient to give explanations so long as it only commands facts. It is in any case unjustifiable to reject the testing of facts on grounds of logic.

The Latin proverb which, in an alternative wording, I chose for the title of this article appears in a new light after the above explanation. The sentence, money does *not* smell, is a euphemistic reversal. In the unconscious it is certainly: *pecunia olet*, that is money = filth.

LXX

AN ANAL-EROTIC PROVERB[1]

A PATIENT from Erdely (Siebenbuergen) told me that in his district they say of someone who has had an incredible piece of luck, *e.g.* success in a lottery, 'He is as lucky as though he had fed on filth as a child.'

LXXI

SPECTROPHOBIA[2]

THE hysterical phobia for mirrors and the dread of catching sight of one's own face in a mirror had in one case a 'functional' and a 'material' origin. The functional one was dread of *self-knowledge* ; the material, the flight from the *pleasure of looking and exhibitionism.* In the unconscious phantasies the parts of the face represented, as in so many instances, parts of the genitals.

LXXII

THE PSYCHIC EFFECT OF THE SUNBATH[3]

FOR a neurotic whom I analysed the soothing effect of the sunbath depended for the most part on his tremendous father-transference. For him the sun was a father symbol, which he gladly let shine upon him and warm him; it had in addition an exhibitionistic significance.

[1] *Zeitschrift*, III. 295. [2] *Zeitschrift*, III. 293. [3] *Zeitschrift*, II. 378.

APPLIED PSYCHO-ANALYSIS

LXXIII

THE PROBLEM OF ACCEPTANCE OF UNPLEASANT IDEAS—ADVANCES IN KNOWLEDGE OF THE SENSE OF REALITY[1]

Not long after I first made acquaintance with psycho-analysis I encountered the problem of the sense of reality, a mode of mental functioning which seemed to be in sharp contrast to the tendency towards flight from 'pain' and towards repression otherwise so universally demonstrable in mental life. By means of a kind of empathy into the infantile mind, I arrived at the following hypothesis. To a child kept immune from any pain the whole of existence must appear to be a unity—'monistic', so to speak. Discrimination between 'good' and 'bad' things, ego and environment, inner and outer world, would only come later; at this stage alien and hostile would therefore be identical.[2] In a subsequent work I attempted to reconstruct theoretically the principal stages in the development from the pleasure-principle to the reality-principle.[3] I assumed that before it has experienced its first disappointments a child believes itself to be unconditionally omnipotent, and further that it clings to this feeling of omnipotence even when the effectiveness of its power in the fulfilment of its wishes is bound up with the observance of certain conditions. It is only the growing

[1] *Zeitschrift*, 1926, XII. 241-252. [Translated by Cecil M. Baines.]

[2] The child will learn 'to distinguish from his ego the malicious things, forming an outer world, that do not obey his will', *i.e.* he will distinguish subjective contents of his mind (feelings) from those which reach him objectively (sensations). 'Introjection und Transference' (1909), *Contributions to Psycho-Analysis*.

[3] 'Stages in the Development of the Sense of Reality' (1913), *loc. cit.*

number and complexity of these conditions that compel it to surrender the feeling of omnipotence and to recognize reality generally. In describing this development, however, nothing could at that time be said of the inner processes that must accompany this remarkable and important transformation; our knowledge of the deeper foundations of the mind—especially of instinctual life—was still too undeveloped to allow of this. Since then Freud's penetrating researches into instinctual life and his discoveries in the analysis of the ego have brought us nearer to this goal; [1] but we were still unable satisfactorily to bridge the gap between instinctual life and intellectual life. It was plain that we still needed that supreme simplification into which Freud has been at last able to reduce the multiplicity of instinctual phenomena; I refer to his view concerning the instinctual polarity that lies at the basis of all life—his doctrine of the life-instinct (Eros) and the death-instinct or destruction-instinct.[2] Yet not until one of Freud's latest works appeared—'Die Verneinung',[3] under which modest title lies concealed the beginnings of a psychology of the thought-processes, founded on biology—have the hitherto scattered fragments of our knowledge been gathered together. As always, here once more Freud takes his stand on the sure ground of psycho-analytical experience, and is extremely cautious in generalization. Following in his footsteps, I shall attempt once more to deal with the problem of the sense of reality in the light of his discovery.

Freud has discovered the psychological act of a *negation of reality* to be a transition-phase between ignoring and accepting reality; the alien and therefore hostile outer world becomes capable of entering consciousness, in spite of 'pain', when it is supplied with the minus prefix of negation, *i.e.* when it is *denied*. In negativism, the tendency to abolish things, we see still at work the repressing forces which in the primary processes lead to a complete ignoring of whatever is 'painful'; negative hallucinatory ignoring

[1] *Group-Psychology and the Analysis of the Ego* (1921). *The Ego and the Id* (1923). [Translations in this Series.]

[2] *Beyond the Pleasure-Principle* (1920).

[3] *Imago*, 1925, 'Negation'. [Translated in *Intnl. Jnl. of P.-A.* vol. vi. p. 367.]

is no longer successful; the 'pain' is no longer ignored, but becomes the subject-matter of perception as a negation. The question naturally arises at once: what must take place in order that the final obstacle to acceptance may be also removed from the path, and the affirmation of an unpleasant idea (*i.e.* the complete disappearance of the tendency to repression) made possible?

The suspicion also arises immediately that this is a question that is not to be easily answered; but since Freud's discovery this, at least, is clear from the outset: the affirmation of an unpleasant idea is never a simple thing, but is always a twofold mental act. First an attempt is made to deny it as a fact; then a fresh effort has to be made to negate this negation, so that the positive, the recognition of evil, may really be assumed always to result from two negatives. To find anything comparable to this in the familiar realm of psycho-analysis we should have to draw an analogy between complete denial and the mental state of a child who still ignores everything unpleasant. In the same way I endeavoured some time ago to show that the fixation-point of the psychoses is to be found at this stage,[1] and I explained the uninhibited capacity for constant euphoria that is found in cases of megalomanic paralysis as a regression to this phase.[2] The stage of negation has an analogy, as Freud has shown, in the behaviour of a patient during treatment, and especially in a neurosis, which is similarly the result of a half-successful or unsuccessful repression and is actually always a negative—the negative of a perversion. The process by which recognition or affirmation of something unpleasant is finally reached goes on before our eyes as the result of our therapeutic efforts when we cure a neurosis, and, if we pay attention to the details of the curative process, we shall be able to form some idea of the process of acceptance as well.

We note, then, that at the height of the transference the patient unresistingly accepts even what is most painful;

[1] 'Stages in the Development of the Sense of Reality.'

[2] 'Psycho-Analysis and the Psychic Disorders of General Paralysis' (Ment. and Nerv. Dis. Monogr. Series).

clearly he finds in the feeling of pleasure accompanying the transference-love a consolation for the pain that this acceptance would otherwise have cost him. But if, at the close of the treatment, when the transference also has to be renounced, the patient were not successful in gradually finding for this renunciation, too, a substitute and consolation in reality, no matter how sublimated that substitute might be, there would undoubtedly follow a relapse into negation, *i.e.* into neurosis. In this connection we are involuntarily reminded of a very fruitful work by Victor Tausk, an analyst whose too early death we all deplore. In his 'Compensation as a Means of Discounting the Motive of Repression '[1] he adduced the weakening of the motives of repression by compensation as a condition of the cure. In a similar fashion we must suspect the presence of a compensation even in the very first appearance of an acceptance of something unpleasant; indeed in no other way can we conceive of its originating in the mind, for this moves always in the direction of least resistance, *i.e.* according to the pleasure-principle. As a matter of fact, we find as early as in Freud's *Traumdeutung* a passage which explains in a similar manner the transformation of a primary into a secondary process. He tells us there that a hungry baby tries at first to procure satisfaction by a kind of hallucination; and only when this fails does it make those manifestations of 'pain' that lead to a real satisfaction as their result. We see that here for the first time the mental mode of reaction seems to be conditioned by a quantitative factor. The recognition of the hostile environment is unpleasant, but at the moment non-recognition of it is still more painful; consequently the less painful becomes relatively pleasurable, and, as such, can be accepted. It is only when we take into consideration the fact of compensation and avoidance of a still greater 'pain', that we are able in any way to understand the possibility of an affirmation of 'pain' without being compelled to renounce the universal validity of the search for pleasure as the fundamental psychical trend. But by doing so we are clearly postulating the intervention

[1] *International Journal of Psycho-Analysis*, 1924.

of a new instrument into the mental mechanism—a sort of reckoning-machine, the installation of which confronts us again with fresh and possibly still more puzzling enigmas.

We shall return later to the problem of psychical mathematics; meanwhile let us consider the mental content of the materials in relation to which a baby accomplishes the acceptance of reality. When Freud tells us that a human being ceaselessly or at rhythmic intervals observes his environment by 'feeling after', 'handling' and 'tasting' little samples of it, he clearly takes a baby's procedure when it misses and feels after its mother's breast as the prototype of all subsequent thought-processes. A similar train of thought led me in my bio-analytical essay [1] to assume that smelling or sniffing the surrounding world shows a still greater likeness to the act of thinking, since it allows of finer and more minute samples being tested. Oral incorporation is carried out only when the result of the test is favourable. The intellectual difference between a child that puts everything indiscriminately into its mouth and one that only turns to things that smell pleasantly is therefore quite an important one.

Let us keep, however, to the example of the baby that wants to suck. Let us assume that up till now it has always been appeased in good time, and that this is its first experience of the 'pain' of hunger and thirst; what probably takes place in its mind? In its primal, narcissistic self-assurance it has hitherto only known itself; it has known nothing of the existence of objects outside itself, which, of course, include even the mother, and could therefore have no feelings towards them, either friendly or hostile. There apparently occurs—possibly in connection with the physiological destruction produced in the organic tissues by the absence of nutrition—an 'instinctual defusion' in the mental life as well, which finds expression first of all in unco-ordinated motor discharge and in crying—manifestations which we may quite well compare with expressions of rage in adults. When after long waiting and screaming

[1] *Versuch einer Genitaltheorie.* [Appearing in translation in the Mental and Nervous Disease Monograph Series.]

the mother's breast is regained, this no longer has the effect of an indifferent thing which is always there when it is wanted, so that its existence does not need to be recognized; it has become *an object of love and hate*, of hate because of its being temporarily unobtainable, and of love because after this loss it offers a still more intense satisfaction. In any case it certainly becomes at the same time, although no doubt very obscurely, the subject of a 'concrete idea'. This example illustrates, it seems to me, the following very important sentences in Freud's paper, 'Die Verneinung'. 'The first and most immediate aim of testing the reality of things is not to find in reality an object corresponding to the thing represented, but to find it *again*, to be convinced that it is still there,' and 'We recognize as a condition for the testing of reality that objects which formerly had brought satisfaction must have been lost.'[1] We are only tempted to add further that the ambivalence indicated above, *i.e.* instinctual defusion, is an absolutely necessary condition for the coming into existence of a concrete idea. Things that always love us, *i.e.* that constantly satisfy all our needs, we do not notice as such, we simply reckon them as part of our subjective ego; things which are and always have been hostile to us, we simply deny; but to those things which do not yield unconditionally to our desires, which we love because they bring us satisfaction, and hate because they do not submit to us in everything, we attach special mental marks, memory-traces with the quality of objectivity, and we are glad when we find them again in reality, *i.e.* when we are able to love them once more. And when we hate an object but cannot suppress it so completely as to be able to deny it permanently, our taking notice of its existence shows that we want really to love it, but are prevented from doing so only by the 'maliciousness of the object'. The savage is therefore only logical when after killing his enemy he shows him the greatest love and honour. He is simply demonstrating that what he likes best of all is to be left in peace; he wants to live in undisturbed harmony with his

[1] In my *Genitaltheorie* I trace back the feeling of gratification—the feeling of attaining *erotic reality*—to a similar recurrence of finding *again* and recognizing *again*.

environment, but is prevented from doing so by the existence of a 'disturbing object'. When this obstacle appears it leads to a defusion of his instincts, so that the aggressive, destructive component comes to the fore. After his revenge is satisfied the other—the love-component—seeks satisfaction. It seems as if the two classes of instincts neutralize each other when the ego is in a state of rest, like the positive and negative currents in an electrically inactive body, and as if, in just the same way, special external influences were needed to separate the two currents and thus render them once more capable of action. The emergence of ambivalence would thus be a kind of protective device, instituting the capacity for active resistance in general, which, like the mental phenomenon accompanying it, recognition of the objective world, signifies one of the means of obtaining mastery over it.

We perceive, however, that while ambivalence no doubt leads to acceptance of the existence of things, it does not carry us as far as objective contemplation; on the contrary, things become alternately the objects of passionate hate and equally passionate love. In order that 'objectivity' may be obtained it is necessary for the instincts that have been released to be inhibited, *i.e.* again mixed with one another, a fresh instinctual fusion thus taking place after recognition has been achieved. This is probably the mental process which guarantees the inhibition and postponement of action until the external reality has been identified with the 'thought-reality' (Freud); the capacity for objective judgement and action is thus essentially a capacity of the tendencies of loving and hating for neutralizing each other—a statement that certainly sounds very like a platitude. I think, however, that we can in all seriousness assume that the mutual binding of attracting and repelling forces is a process of mental energy at work in every compromise-formation and in every objective observation, and that the maxim *sine ira et sine studio* must be replaced by another, namely, that for the objective contemplation of things full scope must be given to an *equal amount* both of *ira* and of *studium*.

Clearly, then, there are stages in the development of the capacity for objectivity too. In my essay on the development of the sense of reality I described the gradual surrender of personal omnipotence, and its transference to other higher powers (nurses, parents, gods). I called this the period of omnipotence by means of magic gestures and words; as the last stage, that of insight derived from painful experience, I regarded the final and complete surrender of omnipotence—the scientific stage, so to speak, of our recognition of the world. In psycho-analytical phraseology, I called the first phase of all, in which the ego alone exists and includes in itself the whole world of experience, the period of introjection; the second phase, in which omnipotence is ascribed to external powers, the period of projection; the last stage of development might be thought of as the stage in which both mechanisms are employed in equal measure or in mutual compensation. This sequence corresponded roughly to the representation of human development broadly outlined in Freud's *Totem und Tabu* as a succession of magical, religious, and scientific stages. When, however, I attempted much later to bring some light to bear critically on the manner in which our present-day science works, I was compelled to assume that, if science is really to remain objective, it must work alternately as pure psychology and pure natural science,[1] and must verify both our inner and outer experience by analogies taken from both points of view; this implies an oscillation between projection and introjection. I called this the 'utraquism' of all true scientific work. In philosophy ultra-idealistic solipsism means a relapse into egocentric infantilism; the purely materialistic psychophobic standpoint signifies a regression to the exaggerations of the projection-phase; while Freud's maintenance of a dualism completely fulfils the utraquistic demand.

We are justified in hoping that Freud's discovery of negation as a transition-stage between denial and acceptance of what is unpleasant will help us to a better understanding of these developmental stages and their sequence, besides

[1] Introduction to my *Genitaltheorie*.

simplifying our view of them. The first painful step towards recognition of the external world is certainly the knowledge that some of the 'good things' do not belong to the ego, and must be distinguished from it as the 'outer world' (the mother's breast). Almost at the same time a human being has to learn that something unpleasant, that is, 'bad', can take place within him (in the ego itself, so to speak) which cannot be shaken off either by hallucination or in any other way (hunger, thirst). A further advance is made when he learns to endure absolute deprivation from without, *i.e.* when he recognizes that there are also things that must be relinquished for good and all; the process parallel to this is the recognition of repressed wishes while realization of them is at the same time renounced. Since, as we know now, a quota of Eros, *i.e.* of love, is necessary for this recognition, and since this addition is inconceivable without introjection, *i.e.* identification, we are forced to say that recognition of the surrounding world is actually a partial realization of the Christian imperative 'Love your enemies'. It is true that the opposition with which the psycho-analytic doctrine of instinct meets certainly proves that reconciliation with our inner foe is the most difficult task that humanity is called upon to accomplish.

When we attempt to bring our fresh knowledge into connection with the topographical system of Freudian metapsychology, we surmise that at the stage of absolute solipsism only *Pcpt-Cs*, *i.e.* the perceptual superficies of the mind, is functioning; the period of negation coincides with the formation of *Ucs* repressed strata; the conscious acceptance of the outer world requires further that hypercathexis of which we are made capable only by the institution of another psychical system—the preconscious (*Pcs*)—interposed between the *Ucs* and the *Cs*. In accordance with the fundamental law of biogenesis the racial history of the evolution of the mind is thus repeated in the psychical development of the individual; for the serial sequence here described is the same as that by which we must imagine the progressive evolution of psychical systems in organisms.

In organic development, too, we find prototypes of the progressive adaptation of living creatures to the reality of the external world. There are primitive organisms that seem to have remained at the narcissistic stage; they wait passively for the satisfaction of their needs, and if this is denied them permanently they simply perish. They are still much nearer to the point of emergence from the inorganic, and on that account their instinct of destruction has a shorter path to travel back, *i.e.* it is much stronger. At the next stage the organism is able to thrust off parts of itself that cause pain and in this way save its life (autotomy); I once called this sort of sequestration a physiological prototype of the process of repression. Not until after further development is the faculty for adaptation to reality created—an organic recognition of the environment, so to speak; very fine examples of this can be seen in the mode of life of organisms that are symbiotically united; but the fact is patent in every other act of adaptation. In connection with my 'bio-analytical' point of view, we can accordingly distinguish even in the organic between primary and secondary processes—processes, that is, which in the realm of the mind we regard as stages in intellectual development. That would mean, however, that in a certain degree and sense the organic also possesses a kind of reckoning-machine, which is concerned not simply with qualities of pleasure and 'pain', but also with quantities. To be sure, organic adaptation is characterized by a certain inflexibility, seen in the reflex processes which are undoubtedly purposive but immutable, while the capacity for adaptation shows a continual readiness to recognize new realities and the capacity to inhibit action until the act of thinking is completed. Groddeck is therefore right in regarding the organic *id* as intelligent; but he shows bias when he overlooks the difference in degree between the intelligence of the ego and that of the *id*.

In this connection we may instance the fact that in organic pathology too we have an opportunity of seeing the work of negation (autotomy) and adaptation in operation. I have already attempted to trace certain processes of organic healing (of wounds, etc.) to the flow of a current of libido (Eros) to the injured place.[1]

We must not disguise from ourselves that all these considerations still furnish no satisfactory explanation of the fact that, both in organic and in psychical adaptation to the real environment, portions of the hostile outer world are, with the assistance of Eros, reckoned as part of the ego, and, on the other hand, loved portions of the ego itself are given up. Possibly here we may have recourse to the more or less psychological explanation that even the actual renunciation of a pleasure and the recognition of something unpleasant are always only 'provisional', as it were; it is obedience under protest, so to speak, with the mental reservation of a *restitutio in integrum*. This may hold good in very many cases; there is evidence for it in the capacity for regression to modes of reaction that have long since been surmounted and are even archaic—a capacity that is preserved potentially and in special circumstances brought into operation. What looks like adaptation would thus be only an attitude of interminable waiting and hoping for the return of the 'good old times', differing fundamentally, therefore, only in degree from the behaviour of the rotiferæ which remain dried up for years waiting for moisture. We must not forget, however, that there is also such a thing as a real and irreparable loss of organs and portions of organs, and that in the psychical realm also complete renunciation without any compensation exists. Such optimistic explanations, therefore, really do not help us; we must have recourse to the Freudian doctrine of instinct, which shows that there are cases in which the destruction-instinct turns against the subject's own person; indeed, that the tendency to self-destruction, to death, is the more primary, and has been directed outwards only in the course of development. We may suppose that whenever adaptation is achieved a similar, as it were masochistic, alteration in the direction of aggression plays a part. Further, I have already pointed out above that the surrender of loved parts of the ego and the introjection of the non-ego are

[1] *Hysterie und Pathoneurosen.*

parallel processes; and that we are able to love (recognize) objects only by a sacrifice of our narcissism, which is after all but a fresh illustration of the well-known psycho-analytical fact that all object-love takes place at the expense of narcissism.

The remarkable thing about this self-destruction is that here (in adaptation, in the recognition of the surrounding world, in the forming of objective judgements) destruction does in actual fact become the 'cause of being'.[1] A partial destruction of the ego is tolerated, but only for the purpose of constructing out of what remains an ego capable of still greater resistance. This is similar to the phenomena noted in the ingenious attempts of Jacques Loeb to stimulate unfertilized eggs to development by the action of chemicals, *i.e.* without fertilization: the chemicals disorganize the outer layers of the egg, but out of the detritus a protective bladder (sheath) is formed, which puts a stop to further injury. In the same way the Eros liberated by instinctual defusion converts destruction into growth, into a further development of the parts that have been protected. I admit that it is very hazardous to apply organic analogies immediately to the psychical: let it serve for my excuse that I am doing it deliberately, and only with regard to so-called 'ultimate problems', where, as I have explained elsewhere, analytical judgements take us no further, and where we have to search for analogies in other fields in order to form a synthetic judgement. Psycho-analysis, like every psychology, in its attempts to dig to the depths must strike somewhere on the rock of the organic. I have no hesitation in regarding even memory-traces as scars, so to speak, of traumatic impressions, *i.e.* as products of the destructive instinct, which, however, the unresting Eros nevertheless understands how to employ for its own ends, *i.e.* for the preservation of life. Out of these it shapes a new psychical system, which enables the ego to orientate itself more correctly in its environment, and to form sounder judgements. In fact it is only the destructive

[1] Cf. S. Spielrein, 'Die Destruction als Ursache des Werdens', *Jahrbuch für Psychoanalyse*, Bd. iv. 1912.

instinct that 'wills evil', while it is Eros that 'creates good' out of it.

I have spoken once or twice about a reckoning-machine, the existence of which I assumed as an auxiliary organ of the sense of reality. This idea really belongs to another connection, which to my mind explains the scientific, mathematical, and logical sense, but I should like to make a reference, although briefly, to it here. I can make a very useful beginning with the double meaning of the word 'reckon'. When the tendency to set aside the surrounding world by means of repression or denial is given up, we begin to *reckon* with it, *i.e.* to recognize it as a fact. A further advance in the art of reckoning is, in my opinion, the development of the power to choose between two objects that occasion either more or less unpleasantness, or to choose between two modes of action that can result in either more or less unpleasantness. The whole process of thinking would then be such a work of reckoning—to a large extent unconscious, and interposed between the sensory apparatus and motility. In this process, as in modern reckoning-machines, it is practically the result alone that comes into conscious view, while the memory-traces with which the actual work has been performed remain concealed, *i.e.* unconscious. We can dimly surmise that even the simplest act of thinking rests on an indefinite number of unconscious reckoning-operations, in which presumably every kind of arithmetical simplification (algebra, differential calculus) is employed; and that thinking in speech-symbols represents the ultimate integration of this complicated reckoning-faculty. I believe, too, in all seriousness that the sense for mathematics and logic depends upon the presence or absence of the capacity for perceiving this reckoning and thinking activity, though it is also performed unconsciously by those who do not seem to possess the mathematical or logical faculty in the slightest degree. The musical faculty might be ascribed to a similar introversion (self-perception of emotional stirrings, lyricism), as well as the scientific interest in psychology.

Whether and how far a given person forms 'correct'

judgements (*i.e.* has the ability to reckon the future beforehand) probably depends on the degree of development this reckoning-machine has reached. The primary elements with which these reckonings are performed are our memories, but these themselves represent a sum of sensory impressions, and therefore ultimately are reactions to various stimuli of different strength. Thus psychical mathematics would only be a continuation of 'organic mathematics'.

However this may be, the essential thing in the development of a sense of reality is, as Freud has shown, the interpolation of an inhibitory mechanism into the psychical apparatus; negation is only the last desperate effort of the pleasure-principle to check the advance to a knowledge of reality. The ultimate forming of a judgement, however, resulting from the work of reckoning here postulated, represents an inner discharge, a reorientation of our emotional attitude to things and to our ideas of them, the direction of this new orientation determining the path taken by action either immediately or some time afterwards. Recognition of the surrounding world, *i.e.* affirmation of the existence of something unpleasant, is, however, only possible after defence against objects which cause 'pain' and denial of them are given up, and their stimuli, incorporated into the ego, transformed into inner impulses. The power that effects this transformation is the Eros that is liberated through instinctual defusion.

LXXIV

THE PSYCHE AS AN INHIBITING ORGAN[1]

Some Remarks on Dr. F. Alexander's Essay on 'Metapsychological Considerations'

In the interesting work in which Alexander seeks to connect the Sexual (life) instincts and Ego (death) instincts,

[1] *Zeitschrift*, 1922, VIII. 203. [Translated by Olive Edmonds.]

as distinguished by Freud, with the most general biological and physical rules, he says, among other things, 'I would ask you now to test well my statement of the inhibiting function of the system "Conscious". That system "Conscious" was understood by Freud as something active, which governs motility. And he considers that in this system or at its boundaries a pre-eminently active function is performed by the censorship. *To understand the act of consciousness as an entirely passive perception of outward and inward occurrences lies far from psycho-analytical theory.*[1] . . . And yet if we sift the psycho-analytical material we find that all positively directed activity is derived from the remoter depths, that dynamically in the final analysis only the instincts are functioning. The only power, which belongs to the "Conscious", the higher system, is an inhibitive one: it may repress, it may restrain the development of impulses or their gratification, or it may direct them.'

This line of thought is a consistent deduction from a psycho-analytic consideration of mental occurrences, and agrees quite with my own convictions on the subject; a few errors, however, which it contains, ought not to remain unchallenged.

1. The conception of the act of consciousness as an entirely passive performance is not only not foreign to psycho-analytical theory, but has been accepted from the beginning as a universally known part of it. In *The Interpretation of Dreams*, where Freud attempted the topical localization of mental functions in 'psychic systems' for the first time, he speaks of the Conscious as a sense organ for (unconscious) psychical qualities, by which the passive perceptive nature of the conscious act is clearly indicated. But also the preconscious (which Alexander somewhat too schematically combines with consciousness, although the latter presupposes a more recent super-cathexis) is always understood by Freud as a system resulting from the selective activity of the censorship. It arises from the unconscious which is deeper and lies

[1] The italics are my own.

nearer to the instincts, through repression and a raising of the psychic level.

2. This conception is not only the personal view of Freud, but is shared by all psycho-analytical authors. I can here refer to one of my own works of the year 1915, which postulates the assertion of Alexander not only for the conscious but for the whole psyche. I will quote the passage referred to:[1]

'The mystical and inexplicable, which persists in every act of the will or concentration of attention, vanishes for the most part if we decide upon the following presumption: the primary fact, in acts of concentration of attention, is the *inhibition* of all acts with the exception of those intended. If all ways leading to the Conscious, with the exception of a single one, are blocked, the psychic energy flows spontaneously in the only direction left open, without any effort being necessary (which, moreover, would be inconceivable). If I wish to contemplate something attentively, I do this by cutting off all senses with the exception of the sense of sight from my consciousness. The intensified attention of the optic impulse comes into existence of itself, just as the raising of the level of a stream occurs spontaneously if the outlets become blocked. *Unequal inhibition is therefore the essence of every action;* the will is not like a locomotive which rushes along on rails, but it resembles more the pointsman, who closes all paths except one only to the undifferentiated energy—the real locomotive power—so that it must travel along the only one remaining open. I suspect that this is true of all kinds of action, even of physiological action, so that the innervation of a particular group of muscles is only a result of the *inhibition of all antagonists.*'

These theorems, which understand all psychical and even complicated physiological occurrences as repressions of primitive tendencies to the satisfaction of instincts (the real mainsprings of action), have probably remained hitherto undisputed, because they fit in well with psycho-analytical theory.

[1] 'Analysis of Comparisons', *Z.* III. Jahrg. p. 275. [See Chap. LXXVII.].

3. The opinion advanced by Alexander, according to which Freud assumes that 'in the system "Conscious" or at its boundaries a pre-eminently active function is performed by the censorship', is not correct. Also Freud understood by the activity of the censorship nothing else than the direction of the impulses, that is, the repression of the primitive forms of expression. The 'Capital' of every psychical undertaking is furnished according to Freud by the impulses, while the higher instances,[1] powerless in themselves, only see to the regulation of given instinct-forces.

4. From all this no one can doubt that Freud never understood the control of the motility by the preconscious in the sense that the preconscious possesses its own motor power, which can be discharged through the muscular system, but that the preconscious controls the *paths* to motility, so that, as in the above analogy of the pointsman, it grants or denies a motor outlet to impulses derived from deeper sources.

5. It goes without saying that these psycho-analytical conceptions will apply to all 'higher', 'social', mental actions of the preconscious, as well for intellectual as for moral and æsthetic ones. Freud has said quite emphatically that the 'urge towards perfection' of mankind is no other than an ever-repeated reaction against the primitive, amoral impulses which persist in the unconscious and are ever demanding satisfaction. Even if these tendencies attain an apparent secondary independence; their real source is still always the instinct-life, whereas the rôle of the higher systems is confined to their 'social' transformations, their attenuation, the regulation of the instinct-forces, and therefore their repression.

6. But these reflections by no means exclude a part of the tendency towards instinct gratification that splits off at a very early stage, perhaps at the very moment of the genesis of life, and derivatives of this may have acquired a relative autonomy, may have established themselves as a regeneration, reproductive life and perfection impulses, and so may have come ever to oppose themselves to the

[1] [See note on page 197.—J. R.]

egotistical quiescence and death instincts. One can therefore—in opposition to Alexander's conception—quite well accept Freud's idea of independently organized inherent life-impulses. If one only remains conscious that the sources of these impulses are always *ab ovo* exogenous, one will escape the danger of falling into mysticism, such as that of the 'creative evolution' of Bergson.

The commendable inclination of Alexander to hold fast to the monism of the universe should not and need not betray him into a premature denial of the twofold nature of the forces that is everywhere psycho-analytically and biologically traceable. For it is not only more enticing but also more correct and heuristically more promising to follow carefully the conflict of the warring forces before one attempts the philosophical unification of all psycho-physiological dynamics.

I must take this opportunity to point out that the expression 'monism' itself has not been defined unambiguously. There are certainly many among us who would like to suppose that ultimately everything physical, physiological, and also psychical can be reduced to one primary system of laws; these might well in a certain sense be called monistic. The acceptance of such laws for all departments of human experience is not, however, identical with that monism which believes that the explanation of these experiences must come from one single principle.

LXXV

CONCERNING THE PSYCHOGENESIS OF MECHANISM [1]

Critical Remarks on a Study by Ernst Mach

The psycho-analyst, who has learnt to meet the almost unanimous rejection of his science by mankind whose soul

[1] Published in *Imago*, 1919, Bd. V. S. 394, and in *Populäre Vorträge über Psychoanalyse*.

it has disquieted, with a certain fatalism, is, at long intervals of time, temporarily shaken out of this mood by certain experiences. While the savants who set the fashion are unremittingly occupied in destroying and burying our science for the *n*th time, there appears now in furthest India, now in Mexico, in Peru or Australia, a lonely thinker, a doctor or observer of humanity, and declares himself to be a follower of Freud. It is still more surprising when it turns out that a psycho-analyst has been at work silently in our very midst and suddenly publishes the psycho-analytical knowledge he has been accumulating for years. Most rarely of all, however, is one in the position to discover in the works of recognized leaders of present-day science traces of psycho-analytic influence, or a parallelism between their thought tendencies and those of the psycho-analysts.

In this state of affairs every one will find it pardonable and understandable that on reading the preface to Ernst Mach's work, *Kultur und Mechanik*,[1] I for a moment dropped the fatalistic attitude—which is, of course, only forced upon one and is hard to bear—and gave myself up to the optimistic idea that I could salute and esteem as of one mind with me one of the foremost thinkers and scientists at present living.[2]

My, as it soon proved, mistaken expectation will be echoed by every psycho-analyst who reads this preface—the contents of which I here in part repeat.

'In the introduction to the author's *Mechanic*, which appeared in 1883, the view is expressed'—it says at the beginning of the preface—'that the teachings of mechanism have been obtained by intellectual refinements from the treasures of handicraft experience.'

'The possibility now presented itself of going a step further, *as my son Ludwig, who from his earliest childhood was mechanistically inclined*, succeeded at my request, *by constantly repeated efforts of memory, in reproducing in essentials that early period of his development with many details*, which showed that the powerful *inextinguishable dynamic sensational experi-*

[1] Stuttgart, Verlag von W. Spemann, 1915.
[2] Ernst Mach has died since these lines were written.

ences of that time transport us suddenly *nearer the instinctive origins of all contrivances such as tools, weapons, and machines.*'

'Convinced that a further elucidation of such experiences might render possible *an incomparable increase in our knowledge of the primitive history of mechanism*, and, besides, might also lead to *the founding of a general genetic technology*, I have undertaken these studies as a modest step in this direction.'[1]

In these sentences the psycho-analyst rediscovers ideas that have long been familiar to him and working methods in which he is expert.

To derive the essential foundations of a highly organized psychic formation by means 'of constantly repeated memory efforts' from a primitive one, and to find its roots ultimately in infantile experience, is the essential thing in the psycho-analytic method and its most important result. Freud has not wearied for more than twenty years of testing this method, with similar results, on the most various psychic formations, on the neurotic symptoms of patients, the complicated psychic manifestations of the healthy, even also on certain human social and artistic creations. Some of Freud's students have indeed already published psychogenic theories and principles, derived from experience, that throw some light on Mach's special subject, the development of mechanism.

In Mach's introductory sentences, however, there are also subsumed other views as yet championed, or first expressly emphasized, almost solely by psycho-analysis. The words 'inextinguishable sensational experiences of early childhood' sound like the Freudian phrase about the indestructibility and timelessness of the infantile and the unconscious. The plan of inquiring for the primitive history of mechanism by methodical genealogical researches into the individual psychic life, instead of by excavations, merely repeats the psycho-analytic thesis, according to which not only the psychic tendencies and contents of their own childhood, but also those of their racial ancestors, can be

[1] The italics are the commentator's.

demonstrated in the unconscious of adults. Mach's idea of searching for the cultural history of mankind—on the basis of the fundamental law of biogenesis—in the psychology of the individual is a commonplace in psycho-analysis. I merely mention Freud's epoch-making book, *Totem und Taboo* (1913),[1] in which the nature of these, as yet unexplained, social institutions is brought nearer an understanding by means of individual psychic analyses reaching back into childhood.[2]

I must anticipate at once and say my hope that Mach had used or considered the achievements of psycho-analysis in his researches was not fulfilled. It is, however, nowhere said of what nature the 'constantly repeated memory efforts' which the author employed were, nor are we told the origin or the result of this psychological experiment, only the conclusions that could be drawn from it. But even these conclusions allow us to conclude in turn that it is simply a matter of repeated efforts to remember the past by a *conscious* direction of the attention to it. Whether and in how far *suggestion*, certainly not inoperative here because paternal, helped to overcome the resistances to memory—something in the sense of Freud's first attempts at analysis—we are not told. Free association, however, does not seem to have been employed in any way, that is to say, the only method that can get over all the affective resistances to which infantile amnesia is due and allows the past to be almost completely reproduced. Correspondingly, therefore, the affective determination of infantile (and archaic) mechanical discoveries is not sufficiently appreciated in this book of Mach's, and the advances in technique are described almost entirely from the rationalistic standpoint, as a progressive development of the intelligence.

[1] [Translation by A. A. Brill, published by Geo. Routledge, London.]

[2] See also the writings of Storfer, *Zur Sonderstellung des Vatermordes*, Sperber's work on the psychogenesis of language, Gieses's on that of work-tools, the writings of Abraham and Rank on the genesis of myths and poetry, and the as yet unpublished researches of Sachs on plough cultivation and its precipitate in the psychic life of mankind. I have myself attempted to explain ontogenetically the peculiar interest human beings have in money. *Internationale Zeitschrift für ärztliche Psychoanalyse*, 1914, Bd. II. S. 506 ff. [Chap. xiii. of *Contributions to Psycho-Analysis*.]

Mach's conception of the genesis of early childish and *primitive* discoveries is to be taken from the following sentences: 'Looking back (on childhood in primitive times), we see with amazement that our whole further life is only a continuation of our behaviour at that time; we endeavoured to overcome our environment, to understand it and thereby to attain our will.' . . . 'Suddenly it strikes us how uncounted generations, favoured somewhat at times by climate and soil, in an obscure need to live better, but generally under conditions whose hardship we can no longer even guess at, struggled for long centuries and created objects whose present ultimate forms we hold in our hands.' . . . 'If we *think* and *dream*, however, about these things of long vanished ages, then, like illusions, old memories of experiences and feelings waken in us, and, sinking back into our once childish world of sensation, we dimly apprehend and await the manifold developments and means of discovery of those contrivances of such immeasurable range.'

This perfectly correct programme, from our point of view, is also, however, only incompletely carried out by Mach. As he disdains to employ the method of psycho-analysis to complete the conscious dreams and thoughts and the infantile covering memories by laying bare their unconscious background in order to understand their distortions, his knowledge must remain superficial and—as the libidinal motives are mostly repressed and unconscious—almost all his efforts could only achieve rationalistic explanations of technical progress, or, to express it more correctly, could throw light only upon the rational side of the motivation.

Earthen bowls first originated perhaps 'as substitutes for the hollow of the hand in drinking', while perhaps 'the water collecting in hollow fragments of stone gave the incentive to the making of vessels, rough lumps of clay in which hollows are pressed by the hand'. But why 'the easily accessible fine plastic clay must always have been a very stimulating material' is not further examined into. Yet psycho-analysis supplies this missing part of the explanation by enabling this curious 'stimulation' to be traced back to quite distinct erotic components of the libido.[1]

Mach investigates just as little why, for instance, 'the plaiting and twisting of textile substances is a powerful instigation for the occupational impulse—a perpetual pleasure'. He contents himself with the assumption of a primary impulse for occupation, whose memory traces blaze up like lightning, and are made use of in times of need.

'The smoothing of existing cylindrical bodies like round twigs probably belonged to the games of the most primitive periods. We have practised it countless times as children and have rolled such a little rod backwards and forwards by hand in some channel without any axial displacement, whereupon any roughness on it drew a beautiful gutter . . . and so on.' (Primitive form of the *turning-lathe.*)

'. . . In earliest childhood our own playing fingers devised the *screw* for us. Something like a screw fell into our hands . . . turning it round in play we felt how it bored into the flat of the hand—a peculiarly mysterious feeling for us at that time, that constantly beguiled us into repeating it. . . .'

Mach explains in a similar fashion the origin of the *fire-stick* and *friction machines*, of *water raising* and *pumping apparatus*, etc. Always and everywhere he sees the action of an occupational impulse that, favoured by a happy accident, leads to a discovery. 'Discoveries are made where circumstances are most favourable and difficulties least.' According to Mach, therefore, discoveries can 'in the course of immense periods of time have crept into the lives of our ancestors quite without the connivance of peculiar personalities and individualities'.

The teaching of psycho-analysis is different. In a more programmatic work on the development of the sense of reality[2] I had to assume on the grounds of psycho-analytic experiences that in the development of art as well

[1] See Freud, *Charakter und Analerotik*, as well as the commentator's article already mentioned, 'Zur Ontogenes des Geldinteresses'. [See last footnote.]

[2] *Zeitschrift*, 1913, p. 124. [*Contributions to Psycho-Analysis*, chap. viii.]

as in that of the individual, therefore also in the development of human culture, *necessity* may have acted as a driving motive. I pointed out particularly the hardships of the ice ages, which may have occasioned an important developmental impulse. If, according to Mach's statement, 'the inventive faculty of the *Eskimo* is, according to unanimous evidence, inexhaustible', it is difficult to accept a peculiar favourableness of the climate and soil as accidental causes of inventiveness. It is much more plausible to postulate peculiarly adaptable individuals, personalities who, compelling the never-lacking 'accident' to their service, became discoverers.

In the adaptation to reality, however, psycho-analysis sees only one side of the problem illuminated. It teaches that discoveries almost always have a libidinal as well as an egoistic root in the psychic life. The child's enjoyment of movement and occupation in kneading, boring, drawing water, squirting, etc., flows from the erotism of organ activity, one sublimation form of which is represented by the 'symbolic' reproduction of these activities in the external world. Certain details—especially the nomenclature—of human work-tools still show traces of their partly libidinal origin.[1]

Mach, however, who is unaware of human analytic psychology, is quite remote from such views. He even calls the views of the Hegelian E. Kapp, 'who conceives of mechanical construction as an unconscious organ projection', jokes, that one must beware not to take seriously as 'nothing in science is elucidated by mysticism'. Spencer's idea, however, according to which mechanical contrivances are *organ prolongations*, is unexceptionable.

Our psycho-analytic conception contradicts none of these explanations; indeed, in my opinion, neither do they

[1] Mach's views on this subject, which do not consider the libidinal impulses at all, are just as incomplete as the opposite exaggeration of Jung, according to which tools represent only repressed erotic tendencies; for instance the fire drill is the suppressed genital activity. According to our view discoveries originate as said, from two sources, an egoistic and an erotic one. It must be granted, however, that very often a libidinal organ function is the prototype for the ultimate shaping of the tool.

contradict one another. There really are *primitive* machines that do not yet signify projections of organs but *introjections* of a part of the external world by means of which the sphere of influence of the ego is enlarged—thus the stick or the hammer.

The self-acting machine, on the other hand, is already almost a pure *organ projection*; a part of the external world is 'given a soul' by human will and works instead of our hands. The introjection and projection machines—as I should like to call them—do not therefore exclude one another; they only correspond to two developmental stages in the conquest of reality. Mach too, moreover, cannot quite get away from the striking analogy of certain machines with organs.[1]

I do not wish to belittle the great value and importance of Mach's work by these remarks; my object was only to indicate from what rich sources of knowledge our scientists shut themselves off by failing to take psycho-analysis into consideration. We psycho-analysts, too, desire nothing more ardently than the collaboration of psychology with the exact sciences demanded by Mach in this book, but we require that the exact sciences shall also employ our methods of psychological research in questions of psychogenesis, and shall not artificially isolate the psychological problems that interest them from the remaining psychic material. Mach himself considers it a mistake 'from among the abundance of impressions acting on the individual . . . to follow out just the mechanical ones, while in nature, in life, the most varied and instinctive and empirical perceptions have undoubtedly once on a time developed with and out of one another' (and therefore there are in this book examples not only of mechanical, but also of metallurgical, chemico-technological, even indeed of biological and toxicological discoveries).

In another part of the book he insists that the whole of mechanism is an idealization, an abstraction, incapable of exactly representing irreversible (thermodynamic) processes.

[1] Compare the instructive book, *The Machine in Caricature*, by Ing. H. Wettich (with 260 pictures), Berlin, 1916, Verlag der *Lustigen Blätter* (Dr. Eysler & Co.).

With the same impartiality, however, with which Mach marks out the boundaries of his special province, he could have acknowledged to himself that the consideration of the development of our mechanical capacities, apart from other psychic relations, 'necessarily loses in probability from neglect and oversight', as he would have expressed it, and must remain an idealization remote from reality.

We would take exception to only one other suggestion of Mach's. 'A strikingly important aid to an experimental ethnography', he says, 'would be the observation of children isolated and withdrawn from their environment from the very start, and left as much as possible to themselves. As experience shows that elementary learning is rapidly overtaken even by older individuals, this would in no case imply any disturbance in the life of the person concerned; on the contrary, it is to be expected from the decisive and directing influences exercised upon the whole of life by the character of the first period of development that such a proceeding would waken reciprocally important qualities in the individual, and thus new and far-reaching values be created.'

I believe I have at last found the decisive argument against the possibility of this scheme, which constantly recurs amongst poets and philosophers (due to its origin from a profound, particular, unconscious wish), of the education of such uncultured 'children of nature'. It is impossible to bring up a little primitive man, because we should have to transplant the new-born babe—if he is to be absolutely untouched by culture—immediately on birth into a primitive human family prior to the discovery of the first mechanical tools. Everyone will probably understand at once that this cannot be done. At the most one might let him be adopted by a Dravidian or South Sea Islander family; this, however, is quite superfluous, as, in any case, the Dravidian or South Sea Islanders have children of their own—the ethnologist only requires to journey thither in order to be able to observe them. The idea, however, of leaving a child to itself 'without a *milieu*' is nonsense; there never has been a human being, not even a primitive human being, without his corresponding *milieu*, achieved by means of the culture, however humble, already attained. The beginnings of culture are to be found already in our animal ancestors—Mach himself attributes mechanical talents to them on keys. The kind of experimental ethnology suggested will therefore never be able to be put in practice; I am not sure either whether a child that were left to itself—' without a *milieu* '—would not become an imbecile. Even talent requires stimulation from without. Jungle-book phantasies therefore are better left to the poets.

In spite of these criticisms, which are unessential, I have to declare, after reading this book, that Mach is a psycho-analyst, however emphatically the critical author of *Erkenntnis und Irrtum* may have guarded against it and have rejected psycho-analysis as ' mysticism '.

' It may well be that unconsciously sensation and understanding have their roots in our or our ancestors' memories ' . . . ' childhood and ancestral emotions give their profound appeal to works of art touched with archaic feeling.' These are phrases that might occur just as well in an article on psycho-analysis—that have certainly already so occurred; also only psycho-analysis can adduce exact proofs of the actuality of these assertions.

' Caught up by the stage of culture into which we are born, we hasten in a short tuition time (as in the fœtal condition) through tremendous periods of work and development. . . .' Were culture suddenly lost, then machines—starting with the simplest skills of natural man—would have to be built up again in the old series. Mach seems here to have grasped boldly the irrefragable causal chain that rules in psychic matters (perhaps in organic matters in general), and that was demonstrated first of all by Freud. He describes complicated mechanical (and other) culture as the highest human achievement, which, however, even to-day still springs from the simplest occupational impulses and is only to be regenerated from them.

Therefore Mach—hitherto entirely occupied with the intellectual work that finds its completion in the scientific literature of mechanism—now takes the simple worker, the child, the primitive man, for the object of his research; he has perceived that the knowledge of simple relationships is 'the necessary preliminary foundation and condition' for the understanding of the more complicated. In this, too, we would fain see a parallelism with the working of the psycho-analysts who would in general look for the explanation of the most complicated cultural achievements of the waking normal human being in childish things, or in the psychic life that in dream or illness has regressed to the stage of childhood.

I must not leave unremarked the freely *Animistic* spirit permeating the work of such a prominent authority in the world of *Physics*. He does not hesitate to acknowledge that a mechanism would have to be immovable of itself, for 'movement is only introduced into a mechanism by *force*'; Leibnitz, however, had the happy phrase: 'Force is something akin to the soul'.

When will the physicist, who finds the soul in the mechanism, and the psycho-analyst, who perceives mechanisms in the soul, join hands and work with united forces at a *Weltanschauung* free from one-sidedness and 'idealizations'?

LXXVI

SUPPLEMENT TO 'THE PSYCHOGENESIS OF MECHANISM'[1]

In a paper on the 'Psychogenesis of Mechanism' I criticized *Kultur und Mechanik*, the last publication of the late Viennese physicist and philosopher, Ernst Mach, from the psycho-analytic point of view. Amongst other things I mentioned that the little book gave the reader an impression as though the author had had Freud's discoveries in mind when he suggested discovering the infantile element in the sense for mechanism in his grown-up son, by means

[1] Published in *Imago*, 1920, Bd. VI. S. 384, and in *Populäre Vorträge über Psychoanalyse*.

of methodical memory efforts. From the fact that Freud is nowhere quoted by Mach, and from the one-sided intellectualistic bias of the article, I concluded, however, that Mach had perhaps hit upon this idea independently of Freud. Now, however, Dr. Pataki (engineer) has brought to my notice that in the *Prinzipien der Wärme-Lehre* (on pp. 443 and 444 of the second edition) there is a note which proves that Mach had already for a long time been familiar with the basic idea of psycho-analysis when he wrote his book about the psychological conditions of the development of the mechanistic sense, and if he makes no reference to it, then we are dealing with a case of *cryptamnesic rediscovery* of an idea.

It is characteristic that the place forgotten by Mach is just that concerned with the becoming unconscious and the continued activity of certain ideas. He speaks there 'of the remarkable fact that an idea, so to say, *continues to exist and act without its being in consciousness*.' . . . 'In this connection the excellent observations of W. Robert concerning dreams (Seippel, Hamburg, 1886) might be illuminating. Robert has observed that those series of associations that are disturbed and interrupted by day are elaborated by night as dreams.' . . . 'I have found Robert's observations confirmed in my own case on countless occasions and can also add *that one saves oneself unpleasant dreams if by day one thinks out thoroughly any unpleasant thoughts that may accidentally occur*, *or talks them over or writes them down fully*, *a proceeding which is also warmly to be recommended to all persons with a tendency to gloomy thoughts*. One can also observe phenomena in the waking state that are related to those mentioned by Robert. I am in the habit of washing if I have had a handshake from a damp, perspiring hand. Should I be prevented from doing this by some accident, I preserve a sense of discomfort, the cause for which I sometimes quite forget, but which I only lose when it strikes me that I had meant to wash my hands and when this has been carried out. It is quite probable, therefore, *that ideas once formed*, *even if they are no longer in consciousness*, *nevertheless maintain their existence*.

This seems peculiarly the case if these ideas, on entering consciousness, have been prevented from liberating their associated ideas, movements, etc. In these circumstances they seem to act as a sort of *charge . . . to a certain extent related to these are the phenomena which Breuer and Freud described recently in their book on hysteria.*'

That we are really dealing here with a cryptamnesic discovery is strengthened by the fact that the circumstance that beguiled Mach into this psychological side-issue was just a work which the author was writing on the conditions favouring or hindering *scientific discoveries* (*Korrektur wissenschaftlicher Ansichten durch zufallige Umstände*, S. 44). He speaks, amongst other things, of the importance of accident in *technical life* also; 'it can be illustrated by the discovery of the telescope, the steam engine, of lithography, daguerreotypes, etc. Analogous processes can finally be traced back to the beginnings of human culture. It is extremely probable that the most important cultural advances . . . were introduced neither according to plan nor intentionally but by accidental circumstances. . . .' *This train of thought is repeated in detail in Mach's last book* (Kultur und Mechanik), *which I reviewed; he then relates the results of the above-mentioned efforts of memory on the part of his technically gifted son, only that Breuer and Freud's work, quoted in the* Prinzipien, *and whose main interest, as is known, centred just on attempts at reviving long-forgotten memories, and which, therefore, must have served Mach as a prototype for his theory and method, remains unmentioned, the memory of it evidently overwhelmed by repression.*

The psycho-analyst may also venture to guess at the *motive* for such a repression from certain indications. Where he wants to illustrate the activity of unsatisfied, unconscious ideational complexes by an example drawn from his own experience, Mach betrays a part of his inhibition that signifies more, perhaps, than exaggerated cleanliness and pedantry.[1] Such hypersensitiveness to contact

[1] For the unconscious meaning of examples in general, see my essay 'On the Technique of Psycho-Analysis' [see Chap. XIV.], and 'The Analysis of Comparisons' [see Chap. LXXVII.].

with bodily moisture and the phobia against moistness of the hands, according to other analyses, springs ultimately from a defence against certain sexual ideas and memories. Such people, too, are wont to shy at *the intellectual* contact with sexual things.

Now Breuer and Freud's first communications were almost 'asexual'. Only subsequent experience compelled Freud to complete the theory of the neuroses by the sexual theory. It seems that these researches of Prof. Freud's (who was teaching at the same university) were not quite unknown to Mach, but were wholly antipathetic, and as such were rejected and forgotten by him. The displeasure connected with the sexual theory, however, took into repression with it the memories also of the still 'harmless' *Hysterie-Analysen* of Breuer and Freud. This is why they are not quoted in *Kultur und Mechanik*, although they are still mentioned in the *Prinzipien* as remote analogies, and therefore Mach had to rediscover (cryptamnesically) the idea inspired in him by Breuer and Freud of the methodical memory effects.

Now, too, we understand why Mach conceives of the psychogenesis of the mechanistic sense only as a progressive unfolding of intelligence, and that when he comes to speak of impulse he contents himself with the assumption of an 'occupational impulse' that, taking advantage of lucky accidents, leads to discoveries, while psycho-analytic consideration of the problem, from which he withdrew owing to unconscious motives, would have permitted the further dissection of that occupational impulse and the proof of the sexual elements in it.

LXXVII

THE ANALYSIS OF COMPARISONS[1]

Patients' Comparisons—Concentration and Repression—Functions of the Censor—Action and Inhibition—the Pleasure of Comparison.

MANY patients have the tendency to express their ideas and fancies by comparisons. Sometimes they are far-fetched analogies, little suited to express what the patient wants to make clear, but often the comparisons are really apt, clever, or witty. I find that these productions of the person analysed deserve particular attention and that they often give direct access to hidden psychic material. I should like to demonstrate this by a few examples, and for this purpose select the comparisons of a few patients who never tired of remarking on their impressions of the progress of the analysis. Here are comparisons of psycho-analysis.

'*The analysis is tedious*,' said one patient; '*it is like the irksome work of separating poppy from rice seeds.*'

The choice of this comparison was not accidental: the 'searching for seed' led straight to childish themes—infantile fixation—in the patient's life.

'*The work of analysis is like the shelling of pods*,' said another patient; '*one throws away the shells and keeps the beans.*' The analysis of this idea led deeper. The patient recalls that as a child he called the little bits of fæces that his sister passed 'beans'. A path was opened up from this memory that led to the patient's anal erotism.

'*I think the difference between hypnotism and analysis is this: hypnotism is like the beater that beats the dust farther into the clothes, but analysis is like the vacuum-cleaner, it sucks out the symptoms.*' This excellent comparison is on a level with Freud's well-known one in which hypnosis and analysis are likened to the technique of painting and sculpture as

[1] *Zeitschrift*, 1915, Bd. III. 270.

characterized by Leonardo da Vinci.[1] From the homosexual, masochistic point of view, the comparison with the beating as well as that with the sucking had a purely autobiographical significance which the analysis then laid bare.

'*Analysis is like treatment for the expulsion of worms,*' said one patient; '*one may get rid of ever so many segments, so long as the head remains one gets no benefit.*' I do not think that the tendency of psycho-analytic therapy has ever been more aptly characterized. The symptoms are really only separated 'segments' of a psychic organization that has its nucleus, 'its head', from which it derives its strength, in the unconscious; so long as the head is not brought to light, one must reckon on the reappearance of the—perhaps temporarily mitigated—symptoms. For the purpose of analysing the patient this simile was made use of to lay bare infantile anal experiences. It contained also the foreboding, later justified, that the treatment would be broken off prematurely, and that from considerations of expense. The patient would not let himself be deprived of the anal head of his neurosis worm.

'*During analysis I feel like a captured wild animal in its cage.*'

'*I feel like a dog tugging unavailingly at its chain.*'

'*The interpretations you put upon my ideas place me in the situation of a scorpion surrounded by flames; wherever I want to go I am scorched by the fire of your remarks—in the end I shall have to commit suicide.*'

These three similes are by a patient who had a peculiarly aggressive background to his manifest sensibility and gentleness, which I unavailingly tried to demonstrate to him. These, and many other, similes—he compared himself with wild, biting, and poisonous animals—I was compelled to interpret as substantiating my assumptions.

Sometimes one suspects something important behind an apparently haphazard choice of metaphor; when a patient characterized his psychic condition by the words, '*I feel as though there were a spot on my soul*'—this spot one could

[1] Freud, *Gesammelte Schriften,* Bd. VI. S. 15. [Translated—'On Psychotherapy'—in *Collected Papers,* vol. i. 253.]

not take metaphorically but in the original meaning of the word. The stain, of course, was not on his 'soul'.

'*A difficult birth*,' said one patient mockingly, as the analysis made no progress. He was unaware that the choice of this expression was determined by the difficult labour from which his own wife had suffered. On account of this difficult birth he could not hope for offspring, although meantime his first-born had died.

'*You seem to me like a farmer who knows his way about even the darkest places of the primordial forests of my soul*,' said another patient. His own juvenile Robinson Crusoe phantasies, of course, afforded the material for this rather forced comparison.

In analysing this last simile one must consider not only biographical but also co-operation of deeper symbolic determinants. When we consider that the comparison comes from a patient whose sexual inferiority was traced back to a narcissistic homosexual fixation, his outburst may be taken as a sign of transference to the doctor and the 'dark places of the primordial forests of his soul' as sexual symbolism.

Much clearer is the symbolism in the following comparisons of other patients:

'*Analysis is like the storm that stirs up the weeds from the bottom of the sea*' [sic!].

Taking this imagery in connection with what I already knew I had to regard it as derived from unconscious birth phantasies.

'*I cannot reconcile myself to this treatment in which the patient is left to himself and is not helped with his ideas. Analysis simply bores into the depths and trusts that what is concealed will shoot up of itself, like an artesian well; where, however, the internal pressure is so low as it is with me, one should be helped along with some pumping arrangement.*'

It suffices for the understanding of the sexual symbolism in this comparison to indicate that it concerns a patient with an unusually strong father fixation who transferred his feelings to the doctor.

A patient tells how at the feast after his sister's marriage he delivered the following health to his new brother-in-law: '*Your noble thoughts, when they have first passed through the retort of your spouse, will crystallize out again even more nobly*'. As this comparison was drawn on the occasion of a marriage, it must have been taken by all its hearers as an allusion to sexual and birth matters. Only the speaker himself was unaware of this implication.

'*If you succeed in penetrating to my unconscious thoughts, then you will seem to me like the hero who broke in the brazen gate of Constantinople with a blow of his club.*'

It will serve to explain the comparison that the patient's symptoms and dreams—although he will not hear of it—allow one to deduce a powerfully sadistic component in his sexual constitution.

This series of examples suffices to let one form an idea of the psychic conditions in the making of comparisons. When anyone concentrates his attention on searching for a comparison for anything, he is concerned only with the likeness, the resemblance, and is, on the other hand, quite *indifferent* to the material from which he takes his comparison. We notice then that in the circumstances this 'indifferent' material is almost always derived from the repressed unconscious. This makes it our duty to examine patients' similes carefully for their unconscious background. The analysis of comparisons proves to be, along with the analyses of dreams, mistakes, and symptomatic acts, a not unimportant weapon of analytic technique.

We were also able to establish that the material contained in the comparisons—like parts of the manifest dream content—proved sometimes to be memory traces from the patient's life history, therefore to be taken as real, and sometimes to be the symbolic expression of unconscious tendencies; of course both sources of comparison can participate in one and the same comparison.

The most important thing seems to me to be that the concentration of attention (of interest, perhaps also of a part of the libido) on the search for the comparison has a mitigating effect on the censorship similar to that we have come to know in the dream work; in the concentration on the hunt for a comparison, what has so far been repressed can —even if in disfigured or symbolic form—come into consciousness, just as it can in the concentration of interest on the wish to sleep. The sleeper, too, is only concerned with the maintenance of the sleeping state; everything else is at the time indifferent to him. Naturally of this 'indifferent' psychic material that part which, in consequence of the heavy pressure bearing upon it, has until now been more strongly under tension, that is, the repressed material, comes to the fore. The strength of the 'forward tendency' must correspond with that of the previous repression.

This reciprocal relationship of attention to the accessibility of the repressed material is well known to us from numerous other quarters. '*Free association*', the chief weapon of psycho-analytic technique, only becomes available by adherence to Freud's 'fundamental rule' that the patient must endeavour to react as indifferently as possible towards his ideas. Only when this prescription is followed does the material to be interpreted and co-ordinated appear from repression; if one endeavours by conscious attention to fathom a symptom or an idea, the censorship is only spurred on to increased wakefulness. Freud, moreover, has taught us that the psycho-analyst, too, achieves the correct interpretations not by logical efforts only, but rather by allowing his ideas free play, for which a certain indifference to the patient's ideas is necessary. An undue eagerness for information or for cure leads to nothing or into side-issues.

The indicated reciprocity is shown most markedly in the psychopathology of everyday life. The treacherous mistakes of the 'absent-minded professor' are the result of mental concentration on one subject and indifference to everything else. (Compare Archimedes: *noli turbare circulos meos*.)

People carry out their 'symptomatic actions' the more completely the more they are absorbed by something else. In the '*forgetting of one's own name*' the conscious search for it usually avails nothing; with cessation of the effort the forgotten word recurs of itself.

The symptomatology of hypnosis and suggestion also

becomes more comprehensible by consideration of the reciprocal relations of concentration and repression. We could maintain that hypnotic submission is to be traced back to blind obedience, but this again to the transference of the paternal fixation. There are only two kinds of hypnosis: father-hypnosis (that might also be called fear-hypnosis), and mother-hypnosis (in other words coaxing-hypnosis).[1] The concentration on the affects of fear and love render the individual hypnotized indifferent to everything else. The psychic state of the person cataleptic from fright would be expressed in the following phrases: 'I feel, do, and say everything that you wish, only do not be angry with me'. The love cataleptic might say, 'For love of you I see and do whatever you wish. Everything except your love is indifferent to me.'

Whatever the type of hypnosis concerned, however, the result of the cathartic method of Breuer and Freud demonstrates that here, in consequence of the fascination by the hypnotist and of the indifference towards everything else, psychic material, otherwise deeply repressed, easily becomes conscious.

Moreover, that concentration plays a great part in hypnotism is shown by the tricks of optical and acoustic concentration often helpfully employed in hypnotism.

In connection with this I must point to the practices of the so-called Crystal-gazers or Mirror-gazers (lecanoscopes, lecanomancers) who fix their attention firmly on an optical point, and prophesy. Siberer's researches[2] show that in these divinations it is really the individual's own unconscious that becomes articulate; we would add, in consequence of the mitigation of the censorship over repressed material which had become more indifferent due to concentration elsewhere.

The same thing can be observed in the too powerful excitation of an affect, for instance, in an outburst of hate

[1] Ferenczi, *Introjection und Übertragung*. (II. Psychoanalyse der Hypnose und Suggestion.) *Jahrbuch f. Psychoan.*, II. Bd. [Translated in *Contributions to Psycho-Analysis*, chap. ii., 1916.]

[2] H. Silberer, 'Lekanomantische Versuche'. *Zentralblatt für Psychoanalyse*, II. Jahrgang.

that is ventilated in curses. In a psychological study 'On Obscene Words'[1] I indicated that although—or perhaps just because—the person cursing is animated solely by the desire to inflict a great affront, careless of what it may be, on the object of his hate, in the wording of his curses he also expresses his own deepest repressed anal and Oedipus wishes, this time quite undisguised. (I refer to the obscene curses of the lower classes and to their milder forms amongst cultured people.)

Proof of this functional relationship between repression and degree of interest is also to be found in the pathology of the psyche. In the flight of thought of the maniac the most repressed material comes easily to the surface. We can take it that for him, in contradistinction to the inhibited melancholiac, it has become indifferent. In paraphrenia (dementia præcox) the essence of which is indifference to the external world and to all object relations, we see that the secrets so carefully guarded by the neurotic are simply babbled out. Paraphrenics are notably the best interpreters of symbols; they explain the significance of all sexual symbols to us without any trouble, after they have become meaningless for themselves.

From our psycho-analytic cases, moreover, we see that a certain 'indifference' is perhaps generally the condition on which the repressed can become conscious. Patients only attain to a conscious insight into a repressed impulse, when in the course of the treatment it has gradually become more indifferent to them, and their libido has been displaced on to other objects.

To return to a territory nearer to our starting-point, I refer to the psychic process of wit described by Freud, in which the attention is held by the wit-technique and this withdrawal of attention permits the most repressed tendencies to find expression. Finally I quote a verbal statement of the psycho-analyst Dr. Hanns Sachs, according to which the words in which poets clothe their ideas often indicate the deeper unconscious sources of those ideas.

[1] *Zentralblatt für Psychoanalyse,* Bd. I. S. 390 ff. [Translated in *Contributions to Psycho-Analysis,* chap. iv.]

Here too, one must consider, in analogy with the drawing of comparisons, that in the poets' case also concentration on the idea renders possible the irruption of repressed material in the haphazard words of the poem.

Pfister, moreover, found that wholly careless (therefore certainly indifferent) scribblings often contain astonishing communications from the unconscious psychic life.[1]

From the fact, then, that in all the cases of 'concentration' here cited, the severity of the censorship is relaxed in proportion to the demands otherwise made upon it, one is forced to conclude that there is employed in concentration a fund of energy otherwise functioning as the repressing censorship. (Whether we are dealing here with libidinal energy or interest, or both, must in the present state of psycho-analytic knowledge be left undecided.) This vicariousness of the two functions becomes more comprehensible when we reflect that really all kinds of concentration indicate a sort of censorship; the withholding from consciousness of all (inner or outer) impressions, with the exception of those that originate from the object of attention or that correspond with the psychic presentation on which one is concentrating. Everything that disturbs sleep is 'repressed' by the censorship of the sleeper, just as in the waking state thoughts are incapable of becoming conscious because of their immorality. The scholar concentrated on his subject becomes deaf and blind for everything else—that is, his censorship represses those impressions that have no reference to his object. We must suppose a similar—even if only evanescent—process of repression in all other cases of concentration also, and so, too, in the drawing of comparisons. After all this it is more comprehensible that the energy for such an evanescent repression (censorship) should be derived from the influence always active between the unconscious and consciousness and at its expense.

In any case, in the censorship we have to do with a system of limited functioning. If the demands on one of its functions be increased, then this can only be met at the

[1] Kryptolalie, Kryptographie und unbewusstes Vexierbild bei Normalen, *Jahrbuch f. Psa.*, Bd. V. S. 117.

expense of the other.[1] This corresponds exactly, therefore, with the point of view suggested by Freud, according to which there are active in the psychic system mobile quantities of an energy-excitation undifferentiated in itself.

As well as this purely 'economic' description of the process, however, one can also conceive the dynamics of the supposed displacement of energy during concentration. The mystical and inexplicable element that still clings to every act of will or attention disappears for the most part, if we reconcile ourselves to the following considerations: the primary thing in an act of attention is the *inhibition* of all other activities except the one intended. When all the roads that lead to consciousness are closed with the exception of one only, then the psychic energy-excitation flows spontaneously and without need for any individual 'effort' (which, moreover, would be inconceivable) in the one patent direction. If, therefore, I want to look at something attentively, I do it by shutting off all my senses except the sense of sight from consciousness; the heightened attention for optical stimuli occurs then of itself, just as the rising of the river level occurs of itself when the communicating canals are closed. *Unequal inhibition is therefore the essence of every action;* the will is not like the locomotive that dashes along on the rails: rather it resembles the pointsman who shuts off, in front of the, in itself, undifferentiated energy—the essential locomotive force—all the lines with the exception of one single one, so that it must run on the only lines remaining open. I imagine that this holds good for all kinds of 'activities', therefore also for physiological ones; that the innervation of a particular group of muscles therefore results *only* from the *inhibition of all antagonists.* Psychic concentration on the drawing of comparisons is therefore only possible by, and in consequence of, this inhibition of or indifference to interest in everything else, and amongst other things in what is

[1] This seems to hold good for the censoring authorities of the mass-mind (the State) also. I think that since, in consequence of the war, the censorship has become so exceptionally severe in political matters, that it has slackened in severity against erotic literature.

otherwise repressed, which then seizes the opportunity of finding expression.

I should have liked—for reasons of psycho-analytic observation—to have been able to communicate some new matter about the pleasure experienced in the drawing and hearing of apt comparisons. I found nothing, however, but the applicability of Freud's theory of wit to these æsthetic sources of pleasure also. In that the attention, and with it a part of the activity of the censorship, is concentrated on the establishing of similarities (already in itself somewhat pleasurable) between apparently disparate things; other, hitherto severely censored, complexes are freed from the oppression weighing upon them, and this saving of inhibition is the *essential* pleasure (' the end-pleasure ') that is to be attributed to the comparison. The pleasure of the resemblance (similarity) would therefore have to be considered as analogous to the *fore-pleasure* set free by the technique of wit. There is of course a continuous series from simple comparisons that set free no unconscious sources of pleasure up to the ' subtle ' and ' witty ' comparisons in which the principal pleasure is derived from the unconscious.

The pleasure, peculiar to comparisons, of rediscovering the same thing in quite different material is certainly to be classified with the saving of intellectual effort that is responsible for the fore-pleasure of wit technique. Possibly, however, behind this *pleasure in repetition* there is also a peculiar *pleasure in rediscovery.*

There are people who have the talent of discovering, in strange faces, even the slightest traces of resemblance to their friends. They seem to protect themselves by the feeling of familiarity roused by the resemblance against the unpleasant effect of quite new impressions (quite unknown physiognomies). We notice, too, with what pleasure we revisit a town that we already know, while it takes a certain time (thus here, too, some repetition) before the rawness of quite new travelling experiences is lost. I believe that the things that we have once ' psychically assimilated ', introjected, are even, as it were, ' ennobled ' by this and participate in our narcissistic libido. Finally, this may be the source of the enjoyment we feel when, in drawing a comparison, we rediscover the old familiar impression in a new one. The peculiarly odd impression that psycho-analysis makes on patients may perhaps be the reason why many of them, as the examples given at the beginning show, are at once compelled to mitigate this impression by a whole series of comparisons. The tendency to rediscover what is loved in all the things of the hostile outer world is also probably the primitive source of symbolism.

LXXVIII

ON SUPPOSED MISTAKES[1]

THERE is a peculiar kind of mistake in which one erroneously supposes that one has made a mistake. Such 'suppositious' mistakes are by no means infrequent. How often does it not happen to someone who wears glasses to hunt for them under the table, although they are perched on his nose; how often does one not think that one's pocket-book is lost, until, after an eager search, it is found where it should have been looked for at first; not to speak of the 'losing' and 'finding again' of the store-cupboard key by our housewives. At any rate this kind of mistake is typical enough to entitle one to examine it for a mechanism and dynamics of its own. The first case of this kind that I was able to unravel by analysis was a somewhat complicated, doubly mistaken performance.

A young lady, who is very interested in the theory of psycho-analysis (I owe to her the observations on 'Little Chanticleer'[2]), was in the habit of coming to see me now and then at lecture time. I had to cut one of her visits short with the intimation that I had a great deal to do.

[1] *Zeitschrift*, 1915, Bd. III. S. 338.
[2] [Chap. ix. of *Contributions to Psycho-Analysis*.]

The lady said good-bye and went away. She returned, however, in a few seconds and said she had left her umbrella in the room, which, however, certainly could not have been true as she had her umbrella in her hand. She remained for a few minutes longer and desired to ask me the direct question whether she were not suffering from an inflammation of the Parotid Gland (Hungarian, Fült*ömirigy*); she made a slip of the tongue, however, and said Fült*öürügy*, that is, Parotid *Pretext*. The German words 'Drüse' and 'Vorwand' (gland and pretext), which are so dissimilar, in Hungarian sound pretty much alike (mirigy and ürügy). The lady acknowledged, on my questioning her, that she would have liked to have stayed longer with me, so that her unconscious may have used the supposed forgetting of the umbrella as a *pretext* for prolonging the visit. Unfortunately I could not proceed further with the analysis, so that it had to remain unexplained why the intended forgetting was only supposed and did not actually happen. A hidden tendency (pretext) is equally characteristic of all mistakes.

I examined much more thoroughly the following case of supposed mistake. A young man was his brother-in-law's guest in the country. One evening a jolly company assembled, a gypsy orchestra was soon at hand, there was dancing, singing, and drinking in the open till late into the night. The young fellow was not accustomed to drinking, and soon became pathologically sensitive, especially when the gypsies started to play the doleful song 'The Corpse lies Coffined in the Court'. He wept bitterly, since it made him think of his not-very-long-buried father, of whose death the jolly tipplers thought as little as in the song the corpse in its coffin in the court is 'bewept by none, by none'. Our young man immediately withdrew from the boisterous company, and went for a solitary walk to a lake near by that was wrapped in night and fog. Following an—subsequently inexplicable—impulse (he was, as stated, himself somewhat 'befogged'), he suddenly took his pocket-book out of his pocket and threw it into the water, although the money it contained had only been given him to take care of and belonged to his mother. He could only give a short account of what he did later. He returned to his friends, drank some more, fell asleep, and was conveyed, sleeping, back to town in a carriage. He wakened late next morning in his bed. His first thought was—the pocket-book. He was in despair over what he had done, told no one about it, however, and sent for a carriage; he would go to the lake although he had not the least hope of finding the money again. At this moment the chambermaid appeared and handed him the pocket-book, which she had found under the pillow of the supposed loser's bed.

The complication of the intoxication renders this case unsuitable for any generalization about supposed mistakes. The psycho-analytic examination certainly showed that here —as so often—the alcohol did not itself create the symptom, but only assisted the eruption of an ever ready emotionally toned complex.[1] The pocket-book with the money entrusted to, and thrown away by him, was the symbolic representation of his mother, whom he—so strong was his father-fixation—in his unconscious really wished to drown. This behaviour might be translated into the language of the unconscious thus, 'If only mother had died instead and not father'.[2] The patient had to explain the incident to himself in this fashion: that when he was wandering about the lake in a befogged condition, he had only waved the pocket-book about over the water, then evidently, however, he put it into his pocket again, hid it carefully on undressing under the pillow, took, therefore, every precaution not to lose it, but forgot just these very measures and awakened with the certain memory of his misdeed. In psycho-analytic terms, the mistake was caused by an expression of his ambivalence. After he had killed his mother—in the unconscious phantasy —he went to bed with her and took good care of her. His

[1] Compare my little essay, 'Alcohol und Neurosen', *Jahrbuch für Psychoanalyse*, III. Bd., 2 Halfte, 1912.

[2] The fullness of the pocket-book was an illusion to the primitive sources of the patient's mother-hatred. His parents' marriage was unusually prolific, almost every year brought him a new brother or sister. At the same time the money pointed to an infantile anal-birth theory; the drowning to a converse of the saving from the water, etc.

exaggerated grief for his father was also to be interpreted as 'two-sided'; it played the part, too, of concealing his joy that he had at least inherited the paternal possessions (and the most valuable one, his mother). Of the ambivalent tendencies only the positive (tender) one was able to transform itself into fact, while the negative one could only perpetrate itself as a falsification of memory, in a much less dangerous form.

Another case that has a similar explanation, but the advantage that it was not complicated by any external influence (as the last was by alcoholic intoxication), is as follows.

It suddenly struck a doctor who had to give a patient some medicine that he has given his charge the wrong medicine and poisoned him. He administered antidotes. His indescribable anxiety only disappeared when a careful scrutiny proved the impossibility of the incident. Labouring under an over-strong 'hostile brother complex' he—in his phantasy—had here rid himself of a rival, while in reality he only took precautions for his safety; it was well that he did him no harm with these.

A similar thing once happened to me when I was wakened late at night to see a patient who was very ill. She had been to see me on the afternoon of the same day and had complained—amongst other trifling disorders—of a scratching feeling in her throat. An examination revealed nothing organic, but a 'touch of hysteria'. The patient's financial position forbade my suggesting so expensive a treatment as psycho-analysis; I contented myself therefore with the usual reassurements, and to help her throat trouble, gave her a box of *Formamint* pastilles that the makers had sent me as a sample; she was to take three or four daily.

On the way to the patient the painful thought occurred to me whether I may not have poisoned her with the pastilles. The preparation had hitherto been unknown to me; it had been sent to me just that day. I imagined it might be a *formalin compound*, perhaps a *form-amin* (sic), that is, a powerfully poisonous disinfectant. I found the patient suffering in some degree from stomach-ache, but otherwise looking so reassuring that I went home considerably relieved. Only on the way did it occur to me that formamint could only be a harmless preparation of menthol, which, of course, was verified next day. The whole poisoning phantasy proved, on analysis, to be the expression of my annoyance at the disturbance of my night's rest.

It would really seem as though behind this kind of mistake peculiarly dangerous aggressive tendencies lurked, whose road to motility must be carefully barricaded off, though they are still allowed to falsify inner perception.

Normally, as is well known, consciousness controls the approach to the motor end of the psychic apparatus. In these cases, however, it seems to be arranged, even in the unconscious, that the actions repudiated by consciousness shall in no circumstances come into being; consciousness could then occupy itself all the more securely with the—of course negatively toned—aggressive phantasies. This behaviour recalls the freedom of phantasy of the dreamer, for whom the sleeping state inhibits all action in general.[1]

There exists here a certain resemblance between the mistakes described and worry; here, as there, a just completed act is subsequently criticized, only the worrier becomes *uncertain* whether he has carried out the intended action *correctly*, while the 'supposedly mistaken' individual is erroneously *certain* that he has done so *incorrectly*. We are here concerned with delicate differences, which we cannot as yet conceive of metapsychologically, in the mechanism of testing reality. The analogy of these mistakes with obsessional neurotic symptoms strengthens us, moreover, in our assumption that the supposed mistakes—as the compulsion manifestations also—act as safety valves for ambivalent feelings.

The mechanism of this kind of mistake may also be described as the opposite of that of symptomatic acts. In the supposed mistake, consciousness supposes it has carried out an action (originating in the unconscious), whereas in

[1] My friend Dr. Barthodeiszky rightly drew my attention to the fact that 'supposed mistakes' occur oftenest in professional or other well-practised activities that are 'automatic', that is, unconscious yet to be depended on.

reality the motility was never properly censored. In the so-called symptomatic acts, on the other hand, the repressed tendency—unobserved by consciousness—succeeds in finding a motor discharge. Symptomatic act and mistake, however, have this in common, that in both there is a discrepancy between two functions of the unconscious, that of inner perception and the guarding of the approach to motility, while at other times both functions are wont to be equally competent or equally prejudiced.

The technique of the 'mistaken mistake' is also comparable with that of the 'dream within a dream'. Both protect themselves by a sort of reduplication against the too utterly repudiated manifestations of the unconscious. The mistaken mistake is, *eo ipso*, a correction, just as the dreaming in a dream robs a part of the dream content of its dream character. If one is aware that one is dreaming, one is no longer dreaming as at other times, when one takes what is dreamt as true, and if one forgets to carry out a mistake, then it simply does not occur.

The insinuation in the 'supposed mistake' is best shown by the following student joke: 'Excuse me for knocking up against you!' says a student in passing to a passer-by. 'You didn't knock up against me at all!' is the reply. 'I can soon remedy that,' retorts the student, and deals him a stiff dig in the ribs.

The joke, however, allows the unmasked tendency of the supposed mistake to be enacted at the end, while at other times one is only too happy to have recognized one's mistake and to have escaped an imaginary danger.

LXXIX

THE 'FORGETTING' OF A SYMPTOM AND ITS EXPLANATION IN A DREAM[1]

A PATIENT who has the habit of looking under her bed at night lest a robber be concealed there *forgot* one night to

[1] *Zeitschrift*, 1914, II. 384.

carry out this precautionary measure. That night she dreamt that she was followed by a young man and threatened with a knife. From the dream the associations led to infantile sexual experiences on the one hand, and on the other to a phantasy that occurred before falling asleep. This usually very prudish patient permitted herself to imagine sexual scenes between herself and a companion of her girlhood. One can assume that the intermission of the examination of the room served the purpose of allowing this phantasy—although disfigured by anxiety—to be further elaborated during the night—since the 'robber' had not been looked for, the thought of him could the more readily 'disturb' the patient's sleep.

LXXX

THE 'FAMILY ROMANCE' OF A LOWERED SOCIAL POSITION[1]

Some years ago I received a telegram from a fashionable winter resort, asking me to act as consultant in the case of a certain young countess. The summons came as rather a surprise. Psycho-analysis, especially in those days, had not aroused any great interest in aristocratic circles, and in any case, although I was on friendly terms with the physician calling me in, he could scarcely be regarded as an enthusiastic supporter of our science.

The history of the case which was communicated to me on arrival soon solved the mystery. The young lady had broken her leg tobogganing, and whilst in a state of unconsciousness following the accident had screamed out the most obscene oaths and generally used foul language and invective of a quite outrageous kind; since then there had been a few seizures of the same type, and the family

[1] Published in the *Zeitschrift*, 1922, Bd. VIII. S. 326, and in *The International Journal of Psycho-Analysis*, 1923, vol. iv. pp. 475-476.

physician, concluding that this might well be 'a case of hysteria of the Freudian type', called me in to see her.

On the days following my arrival, I was able to take a kind of rough psycho-analytic history of the case. The patient was an attractive girl of nineteen. Her rather tender-hearted father had pampered her; her mother, on the other hand, although attentive and affectionate, treated her a shade more strictly. She had already a strong transference to the doctor who about eight days before had put the limb in plaster; her attitude towards myself was much more reserved. Still, with the assistance of my colleague and of her parents, I was able to piece together the following details. The patient had always behaved in a curious fashion; whenever possible she escaped from the private quarters of the castle down to the servants' hall. Her special friend here was a nurse, whom since earliest childhood she had treated as a confidante. When the countess was sixteen this nurse left the castle and went to live on a distant part of the estate; nevertheless, till she was eighteen our patient continued to visit her crony there; indeed, often spent whole days at a time with her, helped her in her housework, scrubbed floors, fed the cattle, cleaned out stalls, etc., all in opposition to her parents' wishes. She detested the society of people of her own class; and only with the greatest difficulty could she be induced to pay calls or receive visitors, only indeed when these social activities were quite unavoidable. Aristocratic suitors, no matter how eligible, were sent brusquely about their business.

Some years before she had suffered from a neurosis which her mother described to me as follows: The patient became suddenly depressed and tearful but would confide to no one the cause of her grief. In the hope that social amusement would cheer her up, the mother took her to Vienna, but in spite of this the emotional condition remained unaltered. One night she came to her mother's bedroom in tears, crept into her bed, and made a clean breast of her trouble. She was weighed down by a terrible fear: she feared that she had been raped by some one whilst in a state of unconsciousness. The attack had probably been made on an occasion when, after accompanying her mother to the railway station, she had driven back to the castle in the family carriage, a journey lasting not more than five minutes. On the way back she felt ill and probably, she thought, lost consciousness: the coachman had taken advantage of her condition to assault her. She couldn't actually remember whether the latter had really done anything to her; she only knew that when she revived the coachman said something or other to her, exactly what she didn't know. Her mother tried to reassure her that her anxiety could have no basis in reality, pointing out that an attack of this kind could not possibly have been made on her by daylight in an open carriage on a busy high-road. Nevertheless, the girl's anxiety was not allayed until her mother had taken her to a number of eminent gynæcologists, all of whom were able to assure her after examination that she was *virgo intacta*.

During my two days' stay in the district I became convinced that the case was one of hysteria with traumatic exacerbation, that there was a definite relation between the coarse obscenity of the patient, her infatuation for the peasant-woman, and the defloration-phantasy, and that psycho-analysis alone could explain the condition. Without going further, I was able to hazard a guess, which was confirmed by witnesses of the accident, viz. that the accident was really deliberate, due perhaps to some tendency towards self-punishment. I learned subsequently that instead of psycho-therapeutic treatment, as I suggested, the patient underwent convalescent surgical treatment in a sanatorium, showed increasing interest in surgery, worked as a nurse during the war, and in spite of parental opposition married a young surgeon of Jewish extraction.

I had no opportunity of filling the gaps in this case-history by analytic observation, but there can be no doubt that the case exemplified a reverse of the neurotic Family-Romance: one of sinking in the social scale. The usual forms of the neurotic romance represent a phantasy of parental ennoblement: the parents are raised from modest or even poor surroundings to aristocratic and sometimes to royal station. The work of Rank on mythology has shown us that in the best-known hero-myths (Moses, Oedipus, Romulus and Remus, etc.) a similar story is to be found; all are of noble birth, are brought up by poor country folk (or even by animals), and in the end regain their rank. He holds the very plausible view that these rustic (or animal) foster-parents, on the one hand, and the aristocratic parents, on the other, constitute merely a *reduplication* of the parental imago in general.

Now whilst in myth these 'primitive' parents are generally treated as provisional figures which ultimately make way for parents of high rank, in this case the yearning was from an aristocratic to a primitive environment. Irrational as this longing may appear, it is by no means unique. A whole series of observations on young children has shown me that many children feel much more at home with the peasant class, with the house-servants and people of lowly origin, than in their own more cultivated *milieu*. Frequently this takes the form of a longing to lead a nomad gypsy life, or indeed to be turned into some creature or other. An untrammelled love-life (incestuous, of course, in addition) has an irresistible appeal for these children; to attain this freedom they are prepared to sacrifice rank and position. One might in this sense speak of helpful underlings and gypsies who abet the child's sexual needs, just as helpful animals are spoken of in fairy-tales.

As is well known, this tendency to return to nature is sometimes carried out in reality: innumerable stories are told, and repeated with alacrity, of affairs between countesses and coachmen or chauffeurs, or between princesses and gypsies. The great interest such tales arouse has its origin in tendencies common to all.

LXXXI

MENTAL DISTURBANCE AS A RESULT OF SOCIAL ADVANCEMENT[1]

I HAVE a series of observations on neurotics with whom social advancement of the family, at a time when the patients were young children, chiefly in the latency period, proved a most significant ætiological factor. Three of the cases were men suffering from sexual impotence; another was that of a woman with *tic convulsif*. Two of the impotent cases happened to be cousins, whose parents became wealthy and 'refined'—both at the same time, viz. when the children were seven to nine years old. All three impotence cases had gone through an infantile period of 'polymorphous perverse' sexuality of more than ordinary intensity and variety. There had in fact been nothing in the way of control or conventional restraint during this stage. At the age noted they came to live under refined conditions to which they were entirely unaccustomed, and to a large extent had to exchange a rustic environment for the social conditions of town and city life. They lost by this exchange their former composure and self-confidence; the more so that their previous lack of restraint necessitated a specially vigorous reaction-formation, if they were to conform even partly to the ego-ideal standards of the new and more refined *milieu*. It is in no way surprising that this wave of repression involved in a very marked degree their sexual aggressiveness and genital capacity.

In all these cases, but even more with the *tic* patient, I found a condition of narcissism widely exceeding normal limits: this was evidenced by excessive 'touchiness'. They took the slightest remissness in salutation as a personal injury; they all suffered from an 'invitation complex', and were capable of returning a personal slight with lifelong hatred. Naturally there was hidden behind this sensitive-

[1] Published in *Zeitschrift*, 1922, Bd. VIII. S. 328, and in *The International Journal of Psycho-Analysis*, 1923, vol. iv. pp. 477-478.

ness a feeling of their own social inferiority, but more particularly of the unconscious operation of 'perverse' sexual excitations. The *tic* patient and one of the cases of impotence had this additional factor in common, that their advancement during the latent period was not merely social but moral in nature: they were both legitimized during that period. A younger sister of the *ticqueuse* and the older and younger brothers of one of the impotent patients were not affected, perhaps because the change in surroundings was effected either before the close of the infantile sexuality period or when the stage of puberty had already commenced: in both cases the change could lead to no more harm. The latency period is of extraordinary importance as the time during which character-traits are formed and the ego-ideal built up. Disturbance of this process, due perhaps to alteration of the moral standards of life with unavoidable conflict between ego and sexual instincts, may lead much more often than we have hitherto supposed to the development of neurosis.

LXXXII

THE SONS OF THE 'TAILOR'[1]

In an extraordinarily high percentage of cases—in proportion to the number of patients—one finds among male neurotics those whose fathers have a calling that is in some sense 'imposing'. On another occasion I pointed out that the detachment of the Father-ideal from the person of the father—a necessary step for independence—is especially hard if the father himself is in a high position, to the occupant of which one would usually have liked to transfer one's filial feelings (princes, teachers, the intellectually great, etc.). This is, in my opinion, the explanation of the fact that the immediate descendants of important people

[1] *Zeitschrift*, 1923, IX. 67. [Translated by Olive Edmonds.]

and of men of genius so easily become 'degenerate'. But there are—as I must now add—callings which, though enjoying no such social esteem, leave impressions as strong as these, and which are often ineradicable, in the mental life of the child at least. These are the callings whose practice is associated with the handling of sharp instruments. First among them is the calling of the *tailor*, then those of the barber, the soldier, the butcher, perhaps also the doctor. Of the seven patients whom I am treating at the moment, for example, two are sons of tailors. Of course it is a question with both of them, as with all similar cases that I have observed, of a monstrous exaggeration of castration-fear, which brings about a crippling of potency.

LXXXIII

'*NONUM PREMATUR IN ANNUM*'[1]

It is a well-known fact that many artists and authors part unwillingly with their productions; others (for instance, Leonardo da Vinci) treat them badly and soon lose all interest in them. A special group is formed by those artists and authors who carry an idea—worked out mentally in minute detail—around with them for months at a time, without being able to decide upon realizing it. I learn from Prof. Freud, and can substantiate from my own experience, that obsessional neurotics have a peculiar tendency to put aside quite complete working projects.

I had occasion to examine psycho-analytically a young author who suffered from this hesitation, as well as from other neurotic manifestations, in a marked degree, and proved that this conduct was to be interpreted as a remote derivative from his abnormal narcissism. For this patient, hesitation over the working out and publishing of his ideas showed itself in the following peculiar fashion. So long as

[1] *Zeitschrift*, 1915, Bd. III. S. 229.

he had his subject ' at heart ' he guarded it like a secret; if he spoke of it he was troubled by the idea that it might be taken from him. Preferably he occupied himself with it on lonely walks or in his study. But even here he did not ' work out ' his subject for any length of time; at the most he would note down any new points in a few words that later he often did not himself understand. If now and then, nevertheless, he did publish something it occurred under the following conditions: he had to hit upon a new idea that he esteemed more highly than the one he had hitherto entertained; indeed he had to consider this new idea so important that—compelled by his artistic conscience—he finally set himself down to work it out. *Instead of this, however, he always fell back upon the notion of executing the old superseded idea, which he now worked out almost unhesitatingly*, while he continued to keep the new idea to himself. We had to relate his conduct to his narcissism. For the patient, everything that he produced was as sacred as a part of his very self, and only when his idea became relatively worthless for him could he bring himself to express it in words, that is, to separate himself from it; this, however, did take place when his narcissism became ' pregnant ' of another, new, more valuable idea. But even during the working up of the older idea he had from time to time to interrupt his efforts, if the importance and value of the older material came to the fore once again.

The analysis showed that his ideas really were the ' children of his soul ', which, however, he did not wish to part with, but to preserve within himself. These spiritual children corresponded in his unconscious to bodily ones that he wished to conceive in a genuinely feminine fashion. The patient's behaviour reminded me of those mothers who always love their youngest child the best. It is well known that it is not the severing of the umbilical cord but the gradual withdrawal of the libido that indicates the real freeing of the child from the mother. Corresponding to this passive trait in his character, the patient's anal erotism was very marked; the games he had played as a child with his fæces recalled the way he treated his intellectual creations. He passed his fæces also only after he had retained them a very long time and they had lost their value for him.

As we know from Freud that obsessional neurotics have a markedly anal-erotic sexual constitution, we may suppose that their tendency to hesitation is analogous with that of the case here described.

The motto of poetic art, '*nonum prematur in annum*', might also owe its origin to a similar psychic disposition on the part of its author. Not only does the suspicious number 9 speak for this, but also the double meaning of the verb *premere*.

At any rate observations of this kind show how incorrect it is to regard laziness, as do the Zürich people, as the final and ultimate cause of neurosis, only to be corrected by 'admonitions for the life-task'. Abnormal laziness—like that of my patient's—always has unconscious motives that are to be discovered by psycho-analysis.

LXXXIV

STAGE-FRIGHT AND NARCISSISTIC SELF-OBSERVATION[1]

AMONG persons who are embarrassed by 'stage-fright' when speaking in public or in musical or dramatic productions one finds that at such moments they have frequently fallen into a state of self-observation: they hear their own voices, note every movement of their limbs, etc., and this division of attention between the objective interest in the thing produced and the subjective in their own behaviour disturbs the normal, automatic, motor, phonetic or oratorical performance. It is a mistake to believe that such people become awkward as a result of their excessive modesty; on the contrary, their narcissism asks too much of their own

[1] *Zeitschrift*, 1923, IX. 69. [Translated by Olive Edmonds.]

performance. In addition to the negative-critical (anxious) observation of their own performance, there is also a positive-naïve, in which the actors are intoxicated by their own voices or other doings, and forget to bring about an accomplishment with these. The 'doubling of the personality' in speaking is often also a symptom of inner doubt about the sincerity of what is said.

LXXXV

HEBBEL'S EXPLANATION OF 'DÉJÀ VU'[1]

THE inexplicable feeling of familiarity conjured up by something that is met for the first time, as if it had been known already for a long time or previously experienced in exactly similar fashion, is explained by Freud as due to forgotten or repressed *day-dreams* that dealt with a similar situation. In connection with this I was in many cases able to trace back the 'déjà vu' to *nocturnal dreams* from the previous[2] or from a long-past night.[3] In the following poem by Hebbel—notable for other reasons as well—I find the latter explanation. (From the poems of the years 1857–1863 in Friedr. Hebbel's collected works, vol. ii. p. 12 ff., Leipzig, Max Hesses Verlag.)

Master and Man

'Away with that face! I can suffer it no longer! Where is the second huntsman?' Thus the Count spoke fiercely, and the old huntsman slinks troubled away; he, who is the best forester of them all.

Now the hunting horn sounds in the wood. For the first time he visits the castle amongst the dark pines; hitherto he has only seen it, now and then, from afar in the moonlight.

They ride away. What is it cowers yonder on the path

[1] *Zeitschrift*, 1915, Bd. III. S. 250.

[2] Freud, *Zur Psychopathologie des Alltagslebens*. [Translation, *The Psychopathology of Everyday Life*.]

[3] Ferenczi, *Zur Psychopathologie des déjà vu*. *Centralblatt*, Bd. II. 648.

beyond the elder? It is the old man who points to his grey head; but the youth curses and storms, 'Never come before me again!'

Why suddenly so fierce though usually so gentle? is asked on all sides. 'I have seen the man do ill before, though now I cannot recall the deed and know neither the place nor the hour.'

He hunts alone, chasing the black boar in the depth of the wood. The others are far behind and, wounding his foot on a stone, his horse falls.

The old man, sent by God, soon appears. He receives the fierce onslaught of the beast skilfully on his lance, and there it lies expiring.

Silently he turns to reach a hand to his lord, but springing up he says, 'Still there? Then is your end at hand!' and swings his spear.

But at last anger heats the loyal blood of the old man too; he draws his knife recklessly and hardly has he raised it than he has run the youth through.

Covered with blood and terrified to death he remains bending there. The dying man looks around for a moment and mutters, 'I saw it thus already in a dream'.

The psycho-analyst recognizes in the lineaments of the greybeard the marks of the helpful but terrible *father* who is armed with a life-saving (squandering), but also death-bringing, dangerous lance.

LXXXVI

POLYCRATISM [1]

By analogy with Schiller's poem 'The Ring of Polycrates' one could give this name to the superstition that dreads lest things should 'go too well' with one, because then a proportionately heavier punishment is to be expected from God. In an analysis it could be traced to a bad conscience due to personal phantasies that were reprehensible.

[1] *Zeitschrift*, 1915, III. 294.

MEDICAL JURISPRUDENCE AND RELIGION

LXXXVII

A LECTURE FOR JUDGES AND BARRISTERS[1]

EACH advance in psychology brings with it developments in every branch of mental science. If our knowledge of the human mind takes only one step forward we must revise every discipline whose objective is connected with the psychic life. Of what could one maintain this with more justification than of legal science and sociology? The aim of sociology is to instruct us in the laws that control the vital relationships of people combined into large groups; and the law moulds into the form of exact rules the principles to which man must adapt himself if he is to remain a member of society. This adaptation is above all a psychic process; therefore regarded from a higher, more general point of view, legal as well as social science are really only applied mental science, and as such must follow with attention every newly discovered fact, every new orientation of psychology. I should like to acquaint you with the important advances made during the last decennia in mental science. These advances are associated with the name of the Viennese neurologist and professor, Dr. Sigmund Freud, who subsumed his new method of psychic research, and the domain of knowledge discovered by its help, under the name of psycho-analysis.

If I were asked what was the greatest scientific merit of psycho-analysis and by what means could it inspire fresh activity into the dead waters of psychology, I would reply that it was the discovery of the laws and mechanisms of the unconscious mental life.

[1] Delivered in October 1913 to the 'State Association of Judges and Barristers' in Budapest. Published in *Populäre Vorträge über Psychoanalyse*, chap. viii.

What the philosophers who so much over-estimated the significance of the conscious mental life hitherto simply held to be impossible, what a few, indeed, dimly imagined but believed to be *eo ipso* inaccessible to exact knowledge—the mental life below the threshold of consciousness—it is precisely this that Freud's investigations made accessible to us. I cannot here reproduce in detail the evolution of this science, so recent yet so rich in experiences and in results. I only make brief mention of the fact that Freud from the study of mental diseases was in a position to lay bare the deeper strata of the human psyche. Just as experience with bodily illnesses brought enlightenment concerning certain hitherto quite unknown protective and adaptive arrangements in the organism, so the neuroses and psychoses proved to be caricatures of normal psychic functioning and let us perceive more strikingly, more acutely, the processes that play their part unnoticed in healthy people also. A satirical Englishman once said: 'If you want to study human nature, go to Bedlam' (the mad house). Our alienists, however, have so far allowed their unique opportunities for increasing human knowledge to escape them; they have devoted themselves exclusively to humanitarian efforts and scientifically have achieved little more than non-committal groupings of symptoms upon the basis of the most dissimilar principles. In particular they have utterly neglected psychological points of view in the study of mental diseases. The scalpel, the microscope, and experiment, however, proved completely unable to assist us in an understanding of these diseases. Breuer and Freud were the first to discover behind the grotesque incomprehensible manifestations of hysteria that magnificent protective arrangement, the mechanism of repression, which enables the mind to escape from tormenting ideas, from insight into the painful reality, by submerging such contents of consciousness into a deeper psychic stratum, into the unconscious whence it is only allowed to re-emerge in a distorted and, even for the patient himself, incomprehensible and therefore more supportable form, by way of psychic symptoms. To begin with, Freud searched for this repressed ideational material by recalling to hypnotized patients all the painful complexes from which they had taken refuge in illness. Later he gave up hypnotism and only made use of the so-called 'free association of ideas'; he got the patient to tell him unselectively everything that occurred to him without regard to the logical, ethical, or æsthetic value of the ideas. In this way there came to light, usually after the overcoming of powerful resistances, the ideas hitherto repressed or their clear or interpretable indications. The analysis of dreams, the scientific interpretation of dreams, gave us our first glimpse into the unconscious mental world of healthy people also. Then in turn came the little slips of everyday life, the psychological analysis of forgetting, of slips of the tongue, of the pen, of lesser and greater awkwardnesses, concerning which it was shown how incorrect it was always to put the responsibility for them upon accident, and how very much oftener they were determined by the wish of our unconscious. Thus with the psycho-analysis of wit and the comical, Freud made the first step towards a deeper understanding of æsthetic effect. The astonishing and remarkably uniform result of all these investigations was the demonstration that in the unconscious of the adult and in every way normal individual there also survives a collection of latent repressed primitive human or, more correctly, animal instincts at the same level at which they were condemned to silence in childhood by cultural adaptation. We learn also that these instincts are not inactive; they seek even yet for opportunity to break through the restraints of reason and morality and to make themselves felt. Even where such restraints are sufficiently powerful these instincts manifest themselves at least in the childish, absurd, or malicious guise of jokes, or they annoy our higher logical consciousness by parapraxes, and where all this does not suffice they live themselves out in the symptoms of mental disease. It thus turned out that the neuroses and psychoses in general originate from the conflict between the individual's sexual instincts and his life interests, and that the same thing holds good of the characteristic qualities of healthy people.

Whosoever desires to understand the real nature of

mental life must also abandon all romantic ideas about the 'innocence' of the child mind. The mind of the child is characterized by boundless and ruthless self-assertiveness, and by erotic tendencies which are usually dismissed with the euphemism 'bad habits'. They display violence and cruelty which may alternate with self-humiliation, playful preoccupation with excreta (which they also like smelling or tasting), enjoyment in the exhibition of their own and in the contemplation of another's nakedness. To these 'habits' is added in the earliest childhood, often as a suckling, the mechanical chafing of the genitals. The mental life of the child as concerns its ego instincts is therefore to be regarded as egoistic and anarchistic, but from the standpoint of the libido as perverse. We have no right to complain about this: it is rather we ourselves who deserve censorship for having forgotten our entire knowledge of the animal nature of mankind, of the recapitulation of the whole evolutionary journey by each individual, and who wish to idealize the child into a creature which from the first submits joyfully and spontaneously to higher social ends. In reality it is the concern of education to tame and mitigate the asocial instincts, to 'domesticate' children. We have two adjuvants towards this objective, repression and sublimation. The former endeavours by severity and fear to paralyse completely the primitive instincts, and to prevent their forcing their way into conscious thinking and willing. Sublimation, on the contrary, wishes to get the benefit of the valuable sources of energy active in these instincts by directing them to socially useful ends. Certain 'reaction formations' due to the conversion of instinctive impulses into their exact opposites are examples of sublimation in present-day education; for instance, the conversion of sexual tendencies into disgust and shame, the directing of primitive instincts into æsthetic activities, of transferring childish curiosity and the acquisitive instinct to scientific investigation. Reaction formations and the products of the conversion of primitive instinctive impulses can thus achieve a socially useful part. Of the two kinds of cultural adaptation repression is undoubtedly the more hurtful, as it increases the disposition to disease, and is at the same time uneconomical owing to its paralysing action on valuable mental energies; it is therefore to be avoided as much as possible in education, though its entire exclusion is in any case not feasible. A pedagogy informed by psycho-analysis will make use of sublimation wherever possible, will avoid all superfluous severity and force, endeavour to manage by the giving and withholding of affection and, in the older child, by rewards of a moral nature, and will in individually varying ways make instincts socially valuable. It is well that we should know that even the humane activities of many a distinguished surgeon are based upon a tendency to cruelty which has been guided along favourable lines, and which in childhood perhaps showed itself in the tormenting of animals; many seek in self-sacrificing altruism only the compensation for some never-to-be-gratified part of their personal happiness. The development of the kinds of instinctual gratifications is, nowadays, naturally only rarely so favourable as in the cases just mentioned. Much more frequently the cruel and passionate person becomes an unhappy member of society who is incapable of work. The pedagogue of the future, however, will not leave this development to chance, but on the basis of a knowledge of the instincts and the possibilities of their conversion will himself create the situations necessary for development, and thereby guide character formation into proper channels.

So important an increase in our knowledge of the individual mind could not leave the conception of the manifestations of the group-mind untouched. Freud and his students very soon took the products of the popular mind, above all the myths and fairy-tales, as objects for research, and made it clear that precisely in their very allegorical and symbolical manifestations repressed human instincts are demonstrable as they are in the symptoms of hysterics, and in the dreams of healthy people. The Oedipus myth, for instance, whose content is incestuous intercourse with the mother and parricide, and the pendant to which crops up in the mythical ideational cycle of every people, has only become comprehensible since we have learnt from psycho-analysis that these tendencies survive in people to-day, even if unconsciously, as atavistic vestiges of a primitive human condition. The study of the mind of present-day ' savages ' made it possible for psycho-analysis to reconstruct the first stage of cultural adaptation, and to demonstrate in detail the parallelism between this phase of human development and the development of the individual child mind. The most primitive religion is the totem cult, in which the superstitious worship of an animal reverenced as an ancestor alternates with its solemn sacrifice and dismemberment. This remarkable cult has been explicable since psycho-analysis has demonstrated many subtle traces of this ' totem religion ' in the relationship between children and their parents, for instance, in the ' shy respect ', in which ambivalent emotions of love and mutiny are mingled. Investigators of the science of comparative religion saw already, before Freud, the prototype of all religions in the totem cult. Freud put the finishing touches by making it clear that the consciousness of guilt and the longing for atonement, those essential ingredients of every religion, were atavistic vestiges of an appalling tragedy that had once upon a time taken place in the primal history of humanity. This was a revolution in which the ' horde of brothers ' conspired together and with brutal ferocity tore the father to pieces, who, as the strongest, had laid claim to all material and sexual property, in order that they might obtain possession of those goods. As we learn, however, the desired gratification remained denied to the brothers even after the removal of the tyrant. None of the brothers could lay claim to the paternal strength and to the chief possession, the mother, for himself alone, so that all the spilling of blood proved of no avail. The murderers, thereupon, were overcome with deep repentance for their bloody deed, they longed once more for the paternal authority holding equal sway over them all, constituted a patriarchy on a still severer basis, and developed the idea of a gigantic father and supernatural patriarch, the idea of God. The ceremony of the 'sacrifice', however, affords a concealed symbolic expression, even in present-day religions, to the ancient parricidal and anthropophagous tendencies.

Just as totemism was the first religion, so the 'taboos' were the first unwritten laws that are, moreover, still to-day the basis for sentence in Central Australia. The 'taboo' forbids certain things to be touched: the person of the king, female blood-relations, children and the dead, and the property of strangers. Every infringement of the 'taboo', according to the belief of these races, is followed of itself by the death punishment. The whole tribe keeps jealous guard that the 'taboo' prohibitions are observed. All are afraid that they must immediately die if they venture to look at the king; if, however, any one does so and nevertheless remains alive, then he himself becomes a dangerous 'taboo'. Many people had already attempted to explain how this most primitive form of feeling for the law could arise. The all too rationalistic explanation that it was the chiefs themselves who invented this system for their own use and advantage, and dressed it up in superstitious and mystical form for the benefit of the stupid populace, leaves the real psychological problem of taboo unexplained; why should the populace, in spite of its numerical superiority, deliver itself supinely to the magic of a single individual, to that of the chief or king? If, however, we follow Freud, and conceive loyalty also as a derivative of the belated repentance after that primal parricide (humanity's real original sin), we have a better prospect of discovering the primal source of 'respect for the law', of a sense of law.

There is a peculiar neurosis, called obsessional neurosis, which is characterized by a whole series of superstitious self-restrictions, the infringement of which involves the obsession of making all sorts of sacrifices. Obsessional neurotics are always afraid that they may have done some one an injury; in order that this may not occur they take anxious care not to touch any object that might come even into indirect contact with the person or thing concerned in the morbid fear. Were he compelled against his will to touch such an object, then only hour-long washing of his hands, or perhaps only a considerable sacrifice of money, or a self-inflicted pain could restore his peace of mind again. The psycho-analysis of such obsessional neurotics shows that in their unconscious these patients cherish feelings of hate and cruelty against precisely the people they so carefully guard, and that they fearfully avoid any occasion that might unleash the cruelty which consciously they loathe. The behaviour of savages and the analysis of neurotics, however, teach us also to understand the indignation that overwhelms the civilized person when he witnesses an infringement of the law. We must by degrees appreciate that the legal punishment is not only to be regarded as an arrangement suited for the protection of society, that it does not aim merely at correction of the sinner or deterrence from punishable action, but in part also it always gratifies our thirst for vengeance. This feeling of revenge itself, however, can be explained in no other way than that we are unconsciously indignant that the criminal dared to do something which we all unconsciously had the greatest inclination to do. We scorn and avoid the criminal chiefly because our unconscious for good reason is afraid of the infectiousness of the bad example. Naturally this explanation of the consciousness of guilt and the willing submission to punitive sanctions cannot but have an effect upon criminology and upon the kind of punishment for crime.

This leads almost of itself to the idea that a time must come when the psycho-analytic investigation and treatment of crime must be put in the place of the present customary automatic punitive measures. It is only in rare cases that a lasting improvement can be expected from a deprivation of liberty, just as the influence of suggestion upon a neurotic symptom can only be a passing one. Only the thorough investigation of the whole personality, the complete self-knowledge which psycho-analysis makes possible, can paralyse the environmental influences that have been effective from childhood and bring the hitherto unconscious and uncontrolled innate instincts under the guardianship of conscious reason. But even if the hope of curing the criminal prove deceitful it would be our duty to carry out these analytic investigations merely to obtain insight into the mental determinants of crime. Moreover, the experiences of analysis hitherto justify the assumption that, for instance, the damage caused by ' heedlessness ' or ' carelessness ' must in many cases be traced to an unconscious ' wish ', that often the tendency to theft and murder is only the expression of distorted forms of libidinal instincts, etc.

' *Principiis obsta, sero medicina paratur.*' This principle holds not only for medical science. Doctor and judge busy themselves with the Sisyphus task of curing and patching past and recurring evils; we could only begin to speak of a real advance if there were a social prophylaxis for these evils.

If in accordance with a common analogy we compare society to an organism, then we can also quite well divide this great organism into two groups, that of the libidinal and that of the egoistic instincts. The demand of the populace for bread and games exhausts to-day even as in ancient times the crowd's every requirement; at the most the idea of ' bread ' or ' pleasure ' may vary or become more complicated. If a community is to have stability, then the egotisms and the libidinal tendencies of the single individuals must be reciprocally adapted; that is, the individual must renounce the quite untrammelled gratification of his instincts. He does this in the hope that society will at least, in part, make good this sacrifice to him. One might describe the progress of social development in psycho-analytic terms as the gradual conquest of the pleasure principle by the reality principle. The constitutional state and its social-democratic ideal developed out of the individualism and oligarchy of primæval times and the tyranny and oligarchy of ancient times and of the Middle Ages.

Sociologists and politicians, however, are all inclined to forget that the renunciation of individuality, ' the state ', should not be an end in itself but only a means to the welfare of the individual, and that it is senseless to sacrifice to the community a greater share of personal happiness than is absolutely necessary. The exaggerated asceticism that distinguishes those states founded on religion precisely as it does the social-democratic ones is the crowd-psychology equivalent to that repression of affect whose harmful results for the health of the individual have been shown by psycho-analysis. Indeed we may put the question whether social diseases also are not to be traced to the repression of instincts. The analogies from the theory of the neuroses speak for the probability of this assumption. The religious fanaticism of whole peoples has already been brought into relation with obsessional neurosis. The paroxysms of revolutions and wars are like hysterical discharges of pent-up primitive instincts; one might call the psychic infection with the ideas of false prophets and philosophers which often spread like wildfire social insanity.

Between anarchy and communism, however, between unrestrained individual licence and social asceticism, there must be somewhere a reasonable individual-socialistic *juste milieu* that cares also for individual welfare as well as for the interests of society, that cultivates the sublimation instead of the repression of instincts, thereby preparing a quiet path for progress assured from revolutions and reactions.

I have always to come back to educational reforms when I consider the treatment of social troubles. At present even the wildest Socialist leader brings up his child to be a slave or a tyrant if, instead of allowing free play to that liberty he elsewhere clamours so loudly for, he plays the tyrannical father to his family, and thus accustoms his environment to the blind worship of authority. The *pater familias* should descend from the dangerously shaky throne of supposed impeccability and renounce as regards his children the almost divine omnipotence he has hitherto enjoyed, nor should he conceal from them either his weaknesses or his human impulses. Some part of authority might possibly be lost in this way, but only that part that sooner or later collapses of itself. A wise father, even after the loss of his dishonest advantage, keeps sufficient of their respect to allow him to bring up his children. The same thing holds good for the 'Fathers' of the great human communities.

If, then, in place of the dogmas inculcated by authority, which through modern education enslaves the power of independent judgement, insight into the natural instincts of our inner natures took over control, we should not need to disturb ourselves unduly about the social order. Always supposing, if such a new order came into being, that it did not merely take the interests of a few powerful people into consideration.

LXXXVIII

PSYCHO-ANALYSIS AND CRIMINOLOGY [1]

The 'International Psycho-Analytic Association' and its local branches have been endeavouring since 1908 to make the new method of research and investigation into mental science, which was, to begin with, only a form of medical treatment, accessible to all who wished to employ Freud's knowledge in the wide circle of theory and practice.

No one has as yet taken up the psycho-analytic revision of sociology; in this domain nothing has been done so far except a few essays of general interest. I consider it urgent that this task should be begun at the earliest opportunity by professionally equipped men.[2]

One must not wait, however, till the foundations of this new science (which is ancillary to sociology) have been comfortably laid and walls and roof erected over them. At the beginning such tasks should be placed upon the programme from which, in the meantime, practical results of importance may be expected. Such a task, in my opinion, would be the laying down of a psycho-analytical criminology.

Criminology has till now traced crime theoretically to temptation and to the influence of environment; in practice, however, it recommended for the prevention of crime eugenic, pedagogic, and economic reforms. This programme is essentially right and thoroughly exhausts all the

[1] From *A pszichoanalizis haladasa*, Budapest, 1920, S. 126 ff. (First published in *Az Uj Forradalom*, I., Budapest, 1919, then in German in *Populäre Vorträge über Psychoanalyse*, chap. ix.)

[2] Aurel Kolnai's book on *Psychoanalyse und Soziologie* has appeared since this. [Translation, *Psycho-Analysis and Sociology*. London: Geo. Allen & Unwin.—Ed.]

possibilities, but it was superficial in execution and flatly contradicted the 'determinism' constantly advocated by its representatives, in that it left entirely out of account amongst the driving forces of crime the most powerful determinants of all, namely, the tendencies of the unconscious mental life, their origin, and the prophylactic measures for guarding against them.

The conscious confessions of criminals and a statement of the circumstances of the crime, be it ever so complete, will never sufficiently explain why the individual in the given circumstances had to commit just that act. External circumstances very often do not motivate the deed at all, and the doer, did he wish to be frank, would mostly have to acknowledge that he really did not himself exactly know what impelled him to it; oftenest, however, he is not so frank, not even to himself, but subsequently looks for and finds explanations for his conduct, which was in many ways incomprehensible and psychically only imperfectly motivated; that is to say, he rationalizes something irrational.

As a doctor I have had occasion sometimes to explore psycho-analytically the psychic life of nervous patients who, besides other signs of disease such as hysterical or obsessional symptoms, showed the tendency or impulse to criminal acts. With some of them it was possible to trace the tendency to violence, theft, fraud, incendiarism, etc., to unconscious mental driving forces, and to weaken or even completely to annul these tendencies precisely by means of psycho-analytic treatment.

On the basis of such minor successes I was encouraged in my view that crime should be made the object of thorough psycho-analytic investigation, not merely as a by-product of the neuroses but also in and for itself. Psycho-analysis, therefore, should be at the service of criminological psychology and a criminological psycho-analysis should be set up.

In my opinion the execution of this programme should not meet with any insuperable difficulties.

To begin with, it will be necessary to collect a rich reserve of criminological psycho-analytic material.

It seems to me that professional psycho-analysts should

undertake the task of visiting confirmed criminals under legal sentence in the prisons and there analysing them properly.

A condemned person has no further reason for concealing anything of the thoughts and associations by means of which the unconscious motives for his actions and tendencies might be brought to light. Once the treatment has been begun, then the so-called 'transference', the emotional bond with the person of the analyst, will even render him desirous of and pleased with being dealt with in this way. The comparative investigation of similar offences will then render it possible to fill in the gaping lacunæ of criminological determinism with solid scientific material.

This would be the theoretical result to be expected from these researches. But practically, too, I think this work is not without prospects. Leaving out of account the fact that the road to pedagogic prophylaxis of crime is only to be found on the basis of a real psychology of the criminal, it is my conviction also that the psycho-analytic treatment of criminal natures, that is an analytic criminological therapy, is not impossible; in any case it has more prospect of success than the barbarous severity of prison warders or the pious admonitions of prison clergy.

This possibility of psycho-analytic treatment and re-education, respectively, of criminals opens up a wide perspective.

'Punishment' was hitherto largely motivated by the need for 'the maintenance of the outraged law'; others expected a prophylaxis of crime from its deterrent effect. In reality, however, we can easily discover in the present-day sentence and its fulfilment wholly libidinal elements that gratify the sadism of the punitive bodies. Psycho-analytic insight and the method of treatment based upon it would necessarily neutralize this extremely noxious factor of pleasure in punishing on the part of those bodies enforcing the sentence, as also on the part of public opinion in general, which in itself would contribute not a little to render possible the psychic 'rebirth' of criminals and their adaptation to the social order.

LXXXIX

BELIEF, DISBELIEF, AND CONVICTION[1]

Novel scientific conceptions are wont to be received with a measure of mistrust and disbelief that quite oversteps the limits of objectivity and betrays marked hostility. Many people entirely avoid any scrutiny of facts that contradict too abruptly the established order—especially from the methodological aspect—by declaring them to be *a priori* improbable; other people visibly endeavour to emphasize the unavoidable weaknesses and incompletenesses of a new point of view in order to drop the whole thing on this account, instead of weighing impartially its advantages and deficiencies, or even, indeed, of welcoming the novelty with a certain kindliness and letting criticism have its fling only subsequently.

Sharply opposed to this 'blind disbelief' is the blind belief with which other communications—perhaps much less probable in themselves—are accepted as soon as the personality of their sponsor or his method enjoys a considerable respect and authority with the scientific public.

These are emotional factors that are capable, too, of confusing scientific judgement.

In psycho-analysis, which gradually causes the persons analysed to alter radically their conception of many things, there is ample opportunity of observing this contradictory behaviour towards novel statements, of dissecting it into its elements, and of examining into the conditions for its existence.

Many patients, for instance many hysterics, start the treatment with an exaggerated ecstasy of belief; they accept all our explanations without distinction, and are never weary of singing the praises of the new method. These are the cases that may give the beginner wrong ideas of the rapidity and promptitude of the effects of psycho-analysis. It is only on deeper analysis during the course

[1] A paper read at the Congress of the International Psycho-Analytical Association in Munich, 1913.

of which, too, the resistances are put into words, that it is shown that these patients were not really convinced of the correctness of the psycho-analytic explanations, but had believed them blindly (dogmatically, as a matter of doctrine); they successfully repressed all their suspicions and objections only in order to keep secure the filial love they had transferred to the doctor.

Other patients—especially obsessional neurotics—immediately oppose the utmost intellectual resistance to anything that the doctor says.[1] Analysis traces this hostile attitude to the disillusionment about the truthfulness (the reality of the love) of those in authority, which results in so many people tending to repress their belief and to display only their disbelief. A peculiar kind of obsessional neurosis, doubting mania, is characterized by inhibition of the power of judgement: belief and disbelief come into play here simultaneously, or immediately after each other, with equal intensity, and prevent the formation either of a conviction or of a refusal of a statement, that is, of any judgement whatsoever.

The paranoiac, indeed, does not scrutinize the attempted explanation put before him at all, but sticks to the question, what motive, what interest can the doctor have for making that statement, what purpose is he pursuing thereby; and, as he can easily find or invent such motives he will go no deeper with the analysis.[2] There must, therefore, be at least a trace of a capacity for transference (belief), that is confidence, present in the person to whom one wishes to demonstrate something; at least the possibility that one may be right must not be excluded from the first.

Generally speaking, the disbelief that is based on insufficient grounds proceeds from two emotional sources: from the previous disillusionment with the capacity of

[1] 'In men patients the most important resistances to the treatment seem to proceed from the father complex and to resolve themselves into fear of the father and mutiny against and disbelief in the father!' Freud, 'The Future Prospects of Psycho-Analytical Therapy', *Zentralblatt für Psychoanalyse*, I. 1. [Translated in Freud's *Collected Papers*, vol. ii. chap. xxv.]

[2] Neurotics, too, occasionally behave in the same way; to this category also belong the 'scientific' objections to psycho-analysis, that the analyst only wants to make money, to attain power, to destroy the patient's morals, etc.

persons in authority to explain things and occurrences, or from the disillusionment with their benevolence as regards real enlightenment. The first form is a reaction to the original trust in parental omniscience and omnipotence which subsequent experience does not substantiate; the latter is the reaction formation to the originally assumed and actually experienced parental benevolence. Indeed, only the former kind of intellectual negativism in which authority in general has gone by the board deserves to be called 'disbelief', while the second form is better described by the word 'distrust'. In the first case all authorities are equally deprived of their divinity, in the second—although negatively—they continue to be reverenced; only belief in God is transformed into a kind of belief in the devil, into a belief in an omnipotence exclusively at the service of malevolent intentions. This is most clearly shown in patients suffering from delusions of persecution, who attribute to their persecutor, or, more correctly, to their negative conception of the father imago, superhuman powers and supernatural capabilities, as, for instance, control over everyone else, over all physical and occult forces (electricity, magnetism, telepathy, etc.), which all serve only the more surely to destroy him (the persecuted). Moreover, there is hardly an analysis during the course of which the patient does not temporarily, or for a more prolonged period, identify the doctor who takes the father's place with the devil himself; many a one sees in the doctor alternately his helpful, omniscient deity, whom one must blindly believe in in all things, and his equally omnipotent but demoniacally malevolent destroyer, whom one may not believe even in apparently obvious matters.

All these facts indicate, and our analyses daily confirm, that the abnormalities of belief, extreme ecstasies of belief, doubting mania, as well as disbelief in general and distrust, are symptoms of regression to or fixation at those infantile stages in the evolution of reality which I have called the magical and projection phases of the sense of reality.[1]

[1] See my essay, 'Stages in the Development of a Sense of Reality', *Internationale Zeitschrift für Psychoanalyse*, I. Jahrgang, S. 132 und S. 135. [Translated in *Contributions to Psycho-Analysis*, chap. viii.]

After the child, made wise by experience, begins to lose belief in his own omnipotence which brought him gratification of all his desires merely by vivid wishing, and later by gestures and word signals, it gradually dawns on him that there are 'higher, divine' powers (mother or nurse), whose favour he must possess if gratification is to follow on the heels of his magical gestures.[1] In racial history this stage corresponds to the religious phase of humanity.[2] Humanity has learnt to renounce the omnipotence of its own wishes but not the idea of omnipotence in general. The latter was simply transferred to other 'higher' beings (gods) who benevolently grant man everything so long as certain ceremonies pleasing to them are punctually performed (for instance, certain of the nurse's demands concerning cleanliness and other behaviour, or certain prayer formulæ that are pleasing to God). The tendency on the part of many people to blind belief in authority can be regarded as a fixation at this stage in the conception of reality.

The disillusion as regards one's own powers is, however, soon followed by that as regards the power and benevolence of these higher powers (parents, gods). It is recognized that the benevolence and power of these authorities does not go very far, that they themselves must obey other still higher powers (*i.e.* the parents must obey their superior the king), that these idolized figures often show themselves to be petty, egotistical creatures who consider their own well-being at the price of other people's; and finally, the illusion of the existence of a divine omnipotence and all-benevolence disappears altogether, to make way for an insight into a uniform and unfeeling order in the cosmic process.

The consequence of this last disillusionment is the projection—according to Freud the scientific—phase of the reality sense. But every standpoint achieved along this painful road of evolution can at the same time, owing to its overwhelming effect, create a vulnerable spot traumatically,

[1] *Op. cit.* 132.

[2] For this see Freud [*Totem and Taboo: Resemblances between the Psychic Lives of Savages and Neurotics.* 'Animism Magic and the Omnipotence of Thought'], *Imago*, ii. (*Gesammelte Schriften*, Bd. X.).

a 'fixation point' in the psychic life to which the libido is always inclined to regress, and to which it returns in certain manifestations of later life. I regard the various manifestations of blind belief, of doubting mania, of disbelief in general, and of distrust as forms of this 'return' of what has been (apparently) overcome.

As is well known, the child experiences his very first disillusionment, of his own omnipotence, that is, with the dawning of needs that can no longer be gratified by mere wishing, but only by 'modification of the external world'. This compels humanity to objectivate the external world in general, to perceive and recognize it as such; sense perception is, therefore, almost the sole warranty for the objectivity, the reality, of a psychic content. This is the 'primal projection', the separation of the psychic content into the 'ego' and the 'non-ego'.[1] Only such things are held as 'real' (that is, as also existing independently of our thought) that 'force' themselves independently of our will, often, indeed, in spite of it, upon our sense perceptions. 'Seeing is believing.'[2]

The child's first article of belief at the beginning of his knowledge of reality runs, therefore: everything is real, *i.e.* is effective external to myself, which, even when I do not wish it, forces itself upon me as a sense perception. 'Palpableness' and 'visibility', therefore, remain throughout life the basis of all 'proof'. Later experience teaches, of course, that sense perceptions, too, can deceive, and that only simultaneous and successive reciprocal control of sense impressions (already presupposed, of course, by the development of an *M* (memory) system alongside the original *P* (perceptual) system)[3] can create the 'immediate certainty of perception' which for brevity we call proof. In the course of the progressive development of the reality sense, logical

[1] Ferenczi, 'Introjection und Übertragung' (Introjection and Transference), *Jahrbuch*, I. S. 430. [Translated in *Contributions to Psycho-Analysis*.]

[2] 'The ground of all certainty is objective—in the sense, that is, of being something directly and immediately determined *for* the subject and not *by* it.' (The article on 'Belief' in the *Encyclopædia Britannica*, vol. 10, p. 597.)

[3] For this terminology consult the last section of Freud's *Traumdeutung*. [Translation by A. A. Brill.]

thought forms are evolved, that is, those kinds of intellectual activities relating ideas to one another by means of which one can always judge, reason, forecast events, and act purposively, ' correctly ' (that is, never contrary to experience). Undisputed proof, therefore, belongs to the laws of logical thought (and of mathematics) as well as to the evidence of the senses, but as the latter are really a precipitate of experience, Locke's view, according to which all proof depends upon intuition, remains in the end correct.

Amongst the ' objects ' of the external world that oppose the child's will and whose existence he must, therefore, recognize, other people play a quite peculiar and ever increasingly important part. With the other objects of the outer world the child gradually comes to terms; always and unalterably they put in his way the same hindrances, that is, their unalterable or self-consistently altering properties on which he can reckon, and by means of his knowledge of them more or less control. On the other hand, other living creatures, especially other people, are for the child incalculable, self-willed objects, that oppose not only passive but active resistance to his will, and perhaps just this apparent illimitableness may cause the child to transfer omnipotence phantasies to specially imposing fellow-creatures—to grown-ups. The other great difference between people and the other objects of the external world is that the other objects never lie; if one is mistaken about one or other attribute of an object in the end one always discovers that the mistake lay in oneself. The child at first treats words as objects (Freud)—that is, he believes them, he takes them not only as true but for fact. While, however, he gradually learns to correct his error in regard to other objects he is deprived of this possibility as regards the statements of his parents; not only because they impress him so much from the beginning with their real and their supposed omnipotence that he does not *dare* to doubt them, but also because he is often forbidden with threats of punishment and of deprivation of love to convince himself of the correctness of adult statements. Innate tendency and educational influences co-operate, therefore, to give the child a blind belief as regards the statements of impressive personalities. This belief is distinguished from conviction in that belief is an act of repression, conviction, on the contrary, an impartial passing of judgement.

A peculiarly complicating fact rendering adaptation still more difficult is that adults do not check the development of the child's judgement uniformly. They may, nay must, judge correctly about certain so-called 'harmless' things; manifestations of childish intelligence are even acclaimed with jubilation and rewarded with special demonstrations of affection so long as they do not concern sexual and religious questions or the authoritative position of the adults; on the last-mentioned matters, however, children are expected to adopt an attitude of blind belief—in opposition to all proof—and to suppress all doubts and any curiosity; one might, therefore, say that they have to surrender any independent effort of thought. As Freud has frequently pointed out,[1] every child does not achieve this partial surrender of its own judgement, but may react to it by a general inhibition of thought, one might almost say by a kind of affective feeble-mindedness. From those who remain permanently at this stage are recruited the people who succumb to the influence of every energetic personality, or who in submission to certain specially powerful suggestions, never venture beyond the narrow circle of these surroundings. Something of this disposition must be present in persons who are easily hypnotized, for hypnosis is nothing else than a temporary return to this phase of infantile self-surrender, credulity, and submission.[2] At any rate the analysis of such cases usually exposes mockery and scorn concealed behind the blind belief. The phrase *credo quia absurdum* is really the bitterest self-irony.

Children with a precociously developed reality sense only carry out to a certain extent the demand for the partial repression of their powers of judgement. This doubt, frequently displaced upon other ideas, returns very easily from

[1] See in particular, Freud, 'Eine Kindheitserinnerung des Leonardo da Vinci.' *Gesammelte Schriften*, Bd. IX. [Translated.]

[2] For this see my paper, 'Introjection and Transference', *Jahrbuch für Psychoanalyse*, I. [Translated in *Contributions to Psycho-Analysis*, chap. ii.]

repression. Lichtenberg's saying that 'disbelief in one thing is in most people based on blind belief in another' is borne out in these cases. They accept certain dogmas without criticism, but revenge themselves by an exaggerated distrust in regard to all other statements whatsoever.

It is in relation to his own subjective feelings that the child's credulity is most heavily taxed. The grown-ups demand that he shall consider things that for him are pleasant as 'naughty', and the renunciations that irk him as 'nice' and 'good'. The double significance of the words 'good' and 'bad' (that means good- and bad-tasting, and also well and badly behaved) contributes not a little to render the statements of third persons about one's own feelings debatable. It is here that we should look for at least one source of the peculiar distrust with which psychological statements are met, while so-called 'exact' mathematically formulated statements, or such as are based on technico-mechanical methods of proof, are often met with unwarranted confidence. This sticking fast at the doubting stage often involves a permanent weakening of the power of judgement, a psychic condition that is most clearly marked in obsessional neurosis.[1]

The obsessional neurotic is not to be influenced by hypnosis or suggestion; on the other hand, he is incapable of ever forming independent conclusions.[2]

[1] See Freud, 'Notes upon a Case of Obsessional Neurosis' (*Gesammelte Schriften*, Band VIII.). [Translated in vol. iii. of *Collected Papers*.]

[2] In this connection the striking fact may be emphasized that of the neuroses, hysteria, which succeeds completely in repressing out of the psychic into the physical sphere any doubt and emotion in general that is repugnant to consciousness, is apparently becoming rarer; we may couple with this the fact that more recent observations record a much diminished number of persons who can be hypnotized. On the other hand, the number of obsessional neurotics seems to be on the increase; indeed, it can be said that there are nowadays few so-called normal people without certain obsessional manifestations. One is tempted to trace the cause for this to the undeniable slackening of religiosity in society. Even those who esteem the social value of religiosity highly must, moreover, concede that the rigid religious dogmas instilled early into children can permanently damage the independence of their judgement. Schopenhauer pointed out the connection between the lack of adult freedom of thought and the religious education of children. He said, 'By relegating the mind in earliest childhood to the manipulation of priests we attempt not only to make the statement and the communication of the truth but even thought and discovery itself impossible' (*Parerga und Paralipomena*).

We can now better understand why present-day society has become partly incredulous and sceptical, partly dogmatically credulous as regards scientific statements also. The exaggerated and frequently unwarranted regard for technico-mathematical, graphic, and statistical methods of proof, and the marked scepticism especially for psychological matters, for instance, as regards psycho-analytic teachings, now become more comprehensible.

The old proverb is apparently being borne out; he who has once lied is not believed even when he tells the truth. The disillusionment that was experienced in connection with certain psychological (sexual and religious) matters as regards the love of truth on the part of parents and teachers has made people unduly sceptical in relation to psychological pronouncements; they therefore demand special assurances in order not to be deceived again.

This demand is only too well justified; it only becomes illogical when those who make the demand for 'proof' avoid the one possibility of obtaining it.

This one possibility—in psychic matters—is one's own experience.

The patient who submits to the irksomeness of analytic treatment, and who at first takes all our statements with bantering disbelief, can convince himself of the truth of these only by the renewal of old memories and, where these can no longer be obtained, 'by the painful way of transference' (transference upon something real, especially upon the doctor treating him). Indeed, he must almost forget that it was us who put him upon the right track, and must find the truth for himself. So far does this instinctive distrust of everything instructional and authoritative go, that an insight already acquired by the patient may be once more imperilled if he is reminded that he got it from us.

He is no less distrustful of every perceptible tendency in his doctor; whenever he notices an 'intention' in the latter he is out of humour, that is to say sceptical. Therefore, the doctor who has to deal with sceptics must adduce all explanations unemotionally and with uniform emphasis, and must never let them know what it is to which he attaches most importance, and also he must leave the discovery of the varying degrees of importance to the sceptic himself. Everyone who wishes to explain, to teach anyone anything, becomes a substitute for the father- and teacher-*imago*, and takes upon himself all the disbelief that these personalities formerly roused in the child. The widespread disinclination for so-called problem plays and novels in which the moralizing intention is too heavily underlined may similarly be traced to this source. The reader, however, accepts the same tendencies willingly, indeed gladly, if they are, as it were, concealed in a work of *belles-lettres* and must be discovered by the reader himself. It is well known, too, that nearly all the psycho-analytic teachings are accepted even by psychiatrists and joyfully acknowledged if they are tricked out as wit or demonstrated as the doom of one particular individual.

Hence it follows that in works of poetry psychological proof can only be obtained by means of exemplification (that is again by detailed experience), not, however, directly on the grounds of logical conclusions. In psychological matters the phrase quoted earlier stands as modified, thus: feeling is believing. Nothing that one ever learns from psychology in other ways ever attains the degree of certainty of what one has oneself experienced, and remains permanently at some stage of plausibility. Otherwise 'one hears the message '—but lacks belief.

These views about the circumstances in which one can achieve psychological convictions place us in the position of critically considering the psycho-therapeutic methods hitherto suggested, and of comparing their value. As the least serviceable of all, Dubois' ' persuasion ' and ' moralizing ' method is easily distinguished. So long as, in accordance with its programme, it really consists only of ' dialectic ' and ' demonstration ', endeavouring to bring the patients to see ' often by means of simple syllogisms ' that their symptoms are psychical—that they ' are nothing but the natural consequences of a disturbance of the emotions '—this therapy must remain ineffectual; in so far, however, as it is effectual it is so because of concealed or patent influences upon the patients' disposition, whereby, however, it ceases to be 'rational' (that is, to affect the reason only by logical means) and becomes a variant, and not even a skilful one, of suggestive (emotional) influence. The attempted moralizing and logical persuasion must, on the grounds mentioned above, immediately rouse the patients' whole resistance. They adopt a war footing towards the doctor, no longer concern themselves with whatever of truth may be contained in his statements, but look for (and find) only the weak places in his arguments; if in the end they cannot escape they may indeed declare themselves conquered, but they do not feel that the doctor is right but only that he carried his point. In the minds of those thus convinced looms last as first the doubt whether they have not succumbed merely to the doctor's dialectical skill, and merely been unable to expose his false conclusions.

The effectiveness of suggestive and hypnotic therapy consciously directed towards influencing the mind is beyond doubt. Several considerations, however, stand in the way of its general employment. One is the frequently emphasized lack of real suggestibility and capability for being hypnotized in most people. (I hold it to be unpermissible to announce as 'hypnotic' certain quite ineffectual proceedings during which the patient, in spite of mystic darkness and brow strokings, retains all his scepticism as regards the doctor's pronouncements. A great deal of self-deception lurks behind the expression 'waking suggestion'; one has only to discover the derision the patients who underwent such treatment heap upon the doctor they duped.) But this undoubtedly successful suggestive or hypnotic influence has also no prospect of inculcating in the patient permanently a feeling of conviction concerning the doctor's statements, and with so deep a belief as to give him the strength to maintain, even in spite of proof, the feeling of the absence of symptoms (that is, to maintain a negative hallucination). The sick person, as is well known, only achieves this 'self-denial' if and so long as the doctor represents parental authority for him and makes good this attribute by occasional recurring proofs of love or threats of punishment (that is, by sternness). ('Father' and 'mother' hypnosis.) A third more practical objection is whether it is justifiable deliberately to reduce a person once more to that childish stage of credulity which, as the symptoms attest, he would fain rise above. For this self-humiliation, if it is to be effective, is never confined to one quite particular complex, but affects the whole personality. However this may be, thus much is beyond a doubt, that the sick person can never by means of suggestion achieve for himself real 'convictions' adapted to serve him as a basis for a permanently symptom-free, that is, a more economical and more supportable, psychic existence.

While 'rational' (more correctly, rationalizing) and suggestive hypnotic psycho-therapies wish to influence patients intellectually or emotively without considering the conditions [1] necessary for the development of convictions and insight of sufficient import to modify the psychic attitude hitherto held, Freudian psycho-analysis demands full consideration of the intellectual as well as of the feeling life. It starts out from the fact that real convictions are only obtained from emotionally toned experiences, and that their formation is hindered by repressed emotions of hate and disbelief. By the help of free association it puts the patient in the position of reliving repressed memories and phantasies that were formerly wrongly disposed of, that is, repressed, and of critically reviewing by their help his own psychic life independently and uninfluenced. As, however, psycho-analysis allows the patient's affects (positive and negative) to be expressed in words in the form of the transference to the doctor (and here it must be stressed that this process is the patient's own doing and is hardly ever provoked by the doctor), it makes it possible for the patient really to experience dramatically complexes whose conscious traces are lost and no longer recoverable, and which therefore seemed to him utterly extraordinary, and to convince himself of their existence in a manner precluding all dubiety. Psycho-analysis evokes the patient's confidence quite simply; it forces nothing upon the patient, neither its authority, nor,

[1] (With which, moreover, their protagonists are unacquainted.)

by means of its authority, its teachings. On the contrary, it grants the person being analysed every kind and every degree of disbelief, of mockery and scorn of its methods and of their representative—the doctor—and wherever it observes hidden or repressed traces of this disbelief it brings it pitilessly to light. When the patient perceives that he may also be distrustful, that his thoughts and feelings are being in no way interfered with, he also begins to consider the possibility whether there might not be something worth while to be made of the doctor's statements.

The so-called Breuer-Freudian cathartic method of treatment to which individual doctors as, for instance, B. Frank and Bezzola have adhered, still bears too many traces of the historical evolution of psycho-analysis from hypnosis. In this method of treatment the doctor's authority—owing to the neglect of the transference—remains untouched, whereby the patients do not attain the full independence necessary to independent judgement.

Adler's psycho-therapy that would force all neurotic psychic life into the Procrustean bed of one single formula (inferiority and its compensation) may rouse interest and understanding in many neurotics by its characterological refinements, and in Adler's teaching they rediscover precisely their own (wrong) views about their condition and are delighted therewith. Therapeutically, however, nothing is achieved by this, as no attempt is made to assist the patient to new convictions that would essentially modify his pre-existing attitude.

A therapeutic modification such as that of Jung, which lays no special stress on the patient's re-living over again each individual traumatic infantile experience, and contents itself with a general indication of the archaic character of the symptoms or with a few examples that are to convince the patient of this, surrenders by this abbreviation of the treatment the advantage of including in the stable edifice of psychic determination by means of exact localization what is unknown to the patient. Generalized teaching and moralizing may carry the patient away for the moment; but this kind of insight, as it can only be forced upon one suggestively or dialectically, is beset with all the faults of the authoritative and so-called ' rational ' therapy discussed above; so this modification, too, deprives the patient of the possibility of achieving his own convictions, that is to say, of the one way in which in psychological matters proof can be obtained at all.

It is therefore only the Freudian method, psycho-analysis, which can procure the degree of inner certainty that deserves to be called ' conviction '.

XC

OBSESSIONAL NEUROSIS AND PIETY[1]

THE case of a patient, in whom a superstitious piety alternates with a state of compulsion, serves to illustrate Freud's theory that obsessional neurosis and religious practice are essentially identical (that is, are both taboo symptoms). So long as she is ' well ' (that is, free of obsessional symptoms), she conscientiously observes every religious ceremony; often, too, in secret, strange to say, those prescribed for religions other than her own, and sanctions every superstition of which she gets to know. On the instant that the dreaded obsessional symptoms appear, she becomes a sceptic and irreligious. Her rationalization for this is as follows: ' Since God (or Fate) has not protected me from the return of the illness in spite of my strict adherence to every precept, I abandon useless precautionary measures '. In reality, religion and superstition are superfluities for her, for reasons of which she is unconscious, as soon as she begins to cultivate her ' individual religion ' (the obsessional neurosis). When, however, she gets better, the socially recognized superstitious and religious exercises reappear, she becomes a believer once more. I have grounds for assuming that the obsessional periods correspond with powerful libidinal impulses.

[1] *Zeitschrift*, 1914, Bd. II. S. 272.

BIBLIOGRAPHY

1899–1926

SÁNDOR FERENCZI

[1] 1899. *Spiritismus.* Gyógyászat.

[2] *Uterus didelphys.* Gyógyászat. [Pregnancy in the isolated uterus.]

[3] 1900. *Öntudat, Fejlödés.* Gyógyászat. [Consciousness, Development.]

[4] *A morphium alkalmazása öreg embereknel.* Gyógyászat. [The use of morphia among aged persons.]

[5] *Bradycardia senilis.* Gyógyászat.

[6] *A menstruatio magyarázatának ujabb kiserlete.* Gyógyászat. [A new attempt at explaining menstruation.]

[7] *Két téves kórisme.* Gyógyászat. [Two mistakes in diagnosis.]

[8] 1901. *Apoplexiás roham sikeres gyógykezelése.* Gyógyászat. [Successful therapy in a case of apoplectic stroke.]

[9] *A térdtünet viselkedéséröl epileptikus rohamok alatt.* Orvosi Hetilap. [The behaviour of the knee-jerk in the epileptic attack.]

[10] *Coordinált és assimilált elmebetegségekröl.* A lecture in the Neurological Section of the Royal Society of Physicians in Budapest. [On co-ordinated and assimilated mental diseases.]

[11] *A jobboldali agyfélteke gócmegbetegeaése. Agytalyog.* Orvosı Hetilap. [Localized disease of the right hemisphere. Cerebral abscess.]

[12] *A szerelem a tudományban.* Gyógyászat. [Love in the sciences.]

[13] *Olvasmany és egészség.* Egészségügyi lapok. [Reading and health.]

[14] 1902. *Csigolyalob idegszövödményei.* Gyógyászat. [Neurological complications in a case of spinal caries.]

[15] *Tébolyodottságról.* Gyógyászat. [On Paranoia.]

[16] *Az agykéreg érzöterületéröl.* Orvosi Hetilap. [On the sensory Region of the Cortex Cerebri.]

[17] *Homosexualitas feminina.* Gyógyászat. [Female homosexuality.]

[18] 1903. *A kórházi segédorvosi intézményröl.* Gyógyászat. [On the organization of the work of Assistant Physicians in the Hospitals.]

[19] *Bromismus és arsenicismus.* Gyógyászat. [Bromism and Arsenicalism.]

[20] *Neuritissel szövödött tabes.* Gyógyászat. [Tabes dorsalis complicated by neuritis.]

[21] 1904. *A villamosság mint gyógyszer.* Gyógyászat. [Electricity as a factor in cure.]

[22] *Lázas betegséghez társult labyrinthbantalom.* Gyógyászat. [Pyrexia with affection of an occluded labyrinth.]

[23] *A hipnózis gyógyito értekéröl.* Gyógyászat. [On the therapeutic value of hypnotism.]

[24] 1905. *A neurastheniáról.* Gyógyászat. [On neurasthenia. A paper delivered at the Third National Congress of Hungarian Psychiatrists.]

[25] *A korai arteriosclerosisról.* Gyógyászat. [On arteriosclerosis in the young.]

[26] *Az arteriosclerosist kiséró ideges tünetekröl.* Gyógyászat. [On the nervous symptoms accompanying arteriosclerosis.]

[27] 1906. *Sexualis átmeneti fokozatokról.* Gyógyászat. [On the intermediate sex.]

[28] *Gyogyitás hypnotikus suggestióval.* Gyógyászat. [Treatment with hypnotic suggestion.]

[29] 1907. *Balesetbiztositási tapasztalátok.* Gyógyászat. [Experiences with death insurances.]

[30] 1908. * *A neurosisok Freud tanának megvilágitásában és a psychoanalysis.* Gyógyászat. [Actual- and psycho-neuroses in the light of Freud's investigations and psycho-analysis.]

[31] † *Analytische Deutung und Behandlung der psychosexuellen Impotenz des Mannes.* Psychiatrisch-neurologische Wochenschrift, x. 1908. [Analytical interpretation and treatment of psycho-sexual impotence in men.]

[32] * *Über Aktual- und Psychoneurosen im Sinne Freuds.* Wiener klin. Rundschau, 1908, Nr. 48-51. [On actual- and psychoneuroses in Freud's meaning of the terms.]

[33] *Amániás-depressiv elmezavar suggestiv világitásban.* Gyógyászat. [Manic-depressive disease in subjective elucidation.]

[34] *Über Psychoneurosen.* [On the psycho-neuroses—a lecture delivered before the Budapest Medical Society, 1908.]

[35] 1909. *Sorozatos elöadasok az ideg- es elmekortan köreböl.* Gyógyászat. [A course of lectures on nervous and mental diseases in the Budapest Medical Society.]

[36] † *Introjektion und Übertragung.* Y.i. 422-457. [Introjection and Transference.]

[37] 1910. † *Die psychologische Analyse der Träume.* [On the psychological analysis of dreams. Based on a lecture delivered in the Royal Society of Physicians, Budapest, October 1910.] Psychiatrisch-Neurologischen Wochenschrift, xii. Nr. 11-13. English translation, *Amer. Jnl. Psychology*, April, 1910.

[38] *Psychoanalyse und Pädagogik.* [Psycho-Analysis and Pedagogics. Abstract of a lecture at the First International Psycho-Analytical Congress, Salzburg.] C. i. 129.

[39] *Referat über die Notwendigkeit eines engeren Zusammenschlusses der Anhänger der Freudschen Lehre und Vorschläge zur Gründung einer ständigen internationalen Organisation.* [Abstract of a paper on the necessity of a closer relation of the followers of the Freudian theory and proposals for establishing a permanent international organization.] C. i. 131.

[40] 1911. *Alkohol und Neurosen.* [Alcohol and Neurosis. A reply to the Criticisms of Prof. E. Bleuler.] Y. iii. 853-857.

[41] † *Über obszöne Worte.* [On obscene words.] C. i. 390-399.

[42] *Reizung der analen erogenen Zone als auslösende Ursache der Paranoia.* [Stimulation of the anal erotogenic zone as precipitating factor in the outbreak of paranoia.] C. i. 557-559.

[43] * *Az élc és a komikum lélektana.* Gyógyászat. [The psychology of Wit and the Comical.]

[44] *Anatole France als Analytiker.* [Anatole France as Analyst.] C. i. 461-467.

[45] *A pszichoanalitikusok szervezkedése.* Gyógyászat. [On the Organization of the Analyst.]

[46] † *Über die Rolle der Homosexualität in der Pathogenese der Paranoia.* Gyógyászat, 1911. [On the part played by homosexuality in the pathogenesis of paranoia.] Y. iii. 101-119.

[47] 1912. *Über lenkbare Träume.* [On dreams that can be steered.] C. ii. 31-32.

[48] *Zur Begriffsbestimmung der Introjektion.* [On the definition of Introjection.] C. ii. 198-200.

[49] † *Über passagère Symptombildungen während der Analyse.* [On Transitory Symptom-constructions during the Analysis.] C. ii. 588-596.

[50] *Ein Fall von ' déjà vu '.* [A case of ' déjà vu '.] C. ii. 648.

[51] *Zur Genealogie des ' Feigenblattes '.* [On the genealogy of the ' fig-leaf '.] C. ii. 678.

[52] *Metaphysik = Metapsychologie.* [Metaphysics = Metapsychology.] C. ii. 678.

[53] 1912. * *Ein treffendes Bild des ' Unbewussten '.* [A striking picture of the ' Unconscious '.] C. iii. 52.

[54] *Deutung unbewusster Inzestphantasien aus einer Fehlleistung (von Brantôme).* [The interpretation of unconscious incest phantasies from a parapraxis (von Brantôme).] C. iii. 53.

[55] *Paracelsus an die Ärzte.* [Paracelsus on doctors.] C. ii. 678.

[56] *Goethe über den Realitätswert der Phantasie beim Dichter.* [Goethe on the reality-value of phantasy in the poet.] C. ii. 679.

[57] *Dr. S. Lindner.* C. ii. 162.

[58] † *Symbolische Darstellung des Lust- und Realitätsprinzips im Ödipus-Mythos.* [Symbolic representation of the Pleasure and Reality Principles in the Oedipus Myth.] I. i. 276-284.

[59] *Philosophie und Psychoanalyse.* [Philosophy and Psycho-Analysis.] I. i. 519-526.

[60] † *Über Onanie.* [On Onanism. A contribution to the symposium on Onanism held by the Vienna Psycho-Analytical Society. Published in the *Diskussionen der Vereinigung*, ii. 1912. Verlag Bergmann, Wiesbaden.]

[61] ¶ *The Psycho-Analysis of Suggestion and Hypnosis.* Transactions of the Psycho-Medical Society, London, 1912, iii. Part 4.

[62] 1913. * *Wem erzählt man seine Träume?* [To whom does one relate one's dreams?] C. iii. 258.

[63] *Zur Genese der jus primae noctis.* [On the genesis of the jus primae noctis.] C. iii. 258.

[64] *Liébault über die Rolle des Unbewussten.* [Liébault on the rôle of the unconscious in conditions of mental illness.] C. iii. 260.

[65] † *Entwicklungsstufen des Wirklichkeitssinnes.* [Stages in the development of the sense of reality.] Z. i. 124-138.

[66] * *Zum Thema: ' Grossvaterkomplex '.* [The grandfather Complex.] Z. i. 228-229.

[67] † *Ein kleiner Hahnemann.* [A little Chanticleer.] Z. i. 240-246.

[68] † *Zur Ontogenese der Symbole.* [On the ontogenesis of symbols.] Z. i. 436-438.

[69] † *Zur Augensymbolik.* [On Eye Symbolism.] Z. i. 161-164.

[70] *Aus der ' Psychologie ' von Hermann Lotze.* [From the ' Psychology ' of Hermann Lotze.] I. ii. 238-241.

[71] *Zähmung eines wilden Pferdes.* [Taming a wild horse.] C. iii. 83-86.

[72] * *Erfahrungen und Beispiele aus der analytischen Praxis.* [Experiences and Examples from Analytical Practice.] *Ein ' passagère ' Symptom. Position während der Kur.* [A transient symptom: the position during treatment.]

[73] 1913. * *Zwanghaftes Etymologisieren.* [Obsessional Etymologizing.]

[74] * *Symbolik der Bettwäsche.* [The symbolism of bed-linen.]

[75] * *Der Drachenflieger als Erektionssymbol.* [The kite as a symbol of erection.]

[76] * *Parästhesien der Genitalgegend bei Impotenz.* [Paræsthesias of the genital region in impotence.]

[77] * *Der Flatus, ein Vorrecht der Erwachsenen.* [Flatus as an adult prerogative.]

[78] * *Infantile Vorstellungen über das weibliche Genitalorgan.* [Infantile ideas about the female genital organs.]

[79] * *Kindliche Vorstellungen von der Verdauung.* [Childish ideas of digestion.]

[80] * *Ursache der Verschlossenheit bei einem Kinde.* [The cause of reserve in a child.] Z. i. 378-382.

[81] *Az idegkórtanban értékesithetö néhány megfigyelés a szemen.* Orvosi Hetilap. [Observations on the eye of use in neurology.]

[82] 1914. † *Einige klinische Beobachtungen bei der Paranoia und Paraphrenie.* [Some clinical observations on paranoia and paraphrenia.] Z. ii. 11-17.

[83] † *Zur Nosologie der männlichen Homosexualität (Homoërotik).* [On the nosology of male homosexuality (Homo-eroticism).] Z. ii. 131-142.

[84] † *Zur Ontogenie des Geldinteresses.* [On the ontogenesis of an interest in money.] Z. ii. 506-513.

[85] * *Reiben der Augen ein Onanieersatz.* [Rubbing the eyes as a substitute for onanism.] Z. ii. 379.

[86] * *Angst vor Zigarren und Zigarettenrauchen.* [Dread of cigar and cigarette smoking.] Z. ii. 383.

[87] * *Zwangsneurose und Frömmigkeit.* [Obsessional neurosis and piety.] Z. ii. 272.

[88] * *Schwindelempfindung nach Schluss der Analysenstunde.* [On the feeling of giddiness at the end of the analytical hour.] Z. ii. 272-274.

[89] * *Einschlafen des Patienten während der Analyse.* [Falling asleep during the analysis.] Z. ii. 274.

[90] * *Zur psychischen Wirkung des Sonnenbades.* [The psychic effect of the Sunbath.] Z. ii. 378.

[91] * *Diskontinuierliche Analysen.* [Discontinuous analysis.] Z. ii. 514.

[92] * *Das 'Vergessen' eines Symptoms und seine Aufklärung im Traume.* [The 'forgetting' of a symptom and its explanation in a dream.] Z. ii. 384.

[93] * *Ungeziefer als Symbol der Schwangerschaft.* [Vermin as a symbol of pregnancy.] Z. ii. 381.

[94] 1914. * *Über verschämte Hände.* [On embarrassed hands.] Z. ii. 378.

[95] *Allgemeine Neurosenlehre.* [General Neurology—a survey of the literature.] Y. vi. 317-328. (Gyógyászat, 1916.)

[96] 1915. * *Psychogene Anomalien der Stimmlage.* [Psychogenic anomalies of voice production.] Z. iii. 25-28.

[97] * *Analyse von Gleichnissen.* [The analysis of comparisons.] Z. iii. 270-278.

[98] * *Über vermeintliche Fehlhandlungen.* [On supposed mistakes.] Z. iii. 338-342.

[99] * *Der Traum von Okklusivpessar.* [The dream of the occlusive pessary.] Z. iii. 29-33.

[100] * *Die wissenschaftliche Bedeutung von Freud's ' Drei Abhandlungen zur Sexualtheorie '.* [The scientific significance of Freud's ' Three Contributions to the Theory of Sexuality '.] Z. iii. 227-229.

[101] * ' *Nonum prematur in annum.*' Z. iii. 229.

[102] *Die psychiatrische Schule von Bordeaux über die Psychoanalyse.* [The Bordeaux school of psychiatry on psychoanalysis.] Z. iii. 352-369.

[103] * *Erfahrungen und Beispiele aus der analytischen Praxis.* [Experiences and Examples from Analytical Practice.]
Zwei typische Kopro- und Pädosymbole. [Two typical fæcal and anal symbols.]

[104] * *Spektrophobie.* [Spectrophobia.]

[105] * *Geschwätzigkeit.* [Talkativeness.]

[106] * *Pompadour-phantasien.* [Pompadour-phantasies.]

[107] * *Der Fächer als Genitalsymbol.* [The fan as a genital symbol.]

[108] * *Polykratismus.* [Polycratism.]

[109] * *Unruhe gegen das Ende der Analysenstunde.* [Restlessness towards the end of the hour of analysis.]

[110] * *Urinieren als Beruhigungsmittel.* [Micturition as a sedative.]

[111] * *Ein analerotisches Sprichwort.* [An anal-erotic proverb.] Z. iii. 292-295.

[112] 1916. † *Contributions to Psycho-Analysis.* Authorized Translation by Ernest Jones. Richard Badger, Boston, pp. 288, price $3.00 net. [This appeared in a second edition under the title *Sex and Psycho-Analysis.*]

[113] 1916–17. * *Über zwei Typen der Kriegsneurose.* [Two types of war-neurosis.] Z. iv. 131-145.

[114] * *Mischgebilde von erotischen und Charakterzügen.* [Composite formations of erotic and character traits.] Z. iv. 146.

[115] 1916–17. * *Affektvertauschung im Traume.* [Interchange of affect in dreams.] Z. iv. 112.

[116] * *Sinnreiche Variante des Schuhsymbols der Vagina.* [Significant variation of the shoe as a vagina symbol.] Z. iv. 112.

[117] * *Schweigen ist Gold.* [Silence is golden.] Z. iv. 155.

[118] * *Pollution ohne orgastischen Traum und Orgasmus im Traume ohne Pollution.* [Pollution without dream orgasm and dream orgasm without pollution.] Z. iv. 187-192.

[119] * *Von Krankheits- oder Pathoneurosen.* [Disease- or Pathoneuroses.] Z. iv. 219-228.

[120] * *Träume der Ahnungslosen.* [Dreams of the unsuspecting.] Z. iv. 208.

[121] * *Die psychischen Folgen einer ' Kastration ' im Kindesalter.* [On the psychical consequences of ' castration ' in infancy.] Z. iv. 263-266.

[122] * *Symmetrischer Berührungszwang.* [The compulsion to symmetrical touching.] Z. iv. 266.

[123] * *Pecunia—olet.* Z. iv. 327.

[124] 1917. *Ostwald über die Psychoanalyse.* [Ostwald on psychoanalysis.] Z. iv. 169.

[125] 1918. *A ' friss levegö ' és a ' jó levegö ' üditö és gyógyitó hatdsa.* Gyógyászat. [The refreshing and curative effect of ' fresh air ' and ' good air '.]

[126] 1919. * *Technische Schwierigkeiten einer Hysterieanalyse.* [Technical difficulties in the analysis of a case of hysteria.] Z. v. 34-40.

[127] * *Zur psychoanalytischen Technik.* [On the technique of psycho-analysis.] Z. v. 181-192.

[128] * *Denken und Muskelinnervation.* [Thinking and muscle innervation.] Z. v. 102.

[129] * *Die Nacktheit als Schreckmittel.* [Nakedness as a means of inspiring terror.] Z. v. 303-305.

[130] * *Sonntagsneurosen.* [Sunday neuroses.] Z. v. 46-48.

[131] * *Ekel vor dem Frühstück.* [Disgust for breakfast.] Z. v. 117.

[132] * *Cornelia, die Mutter der Gracchen.* [Cornelia, the mother of the Gracchi.] Z. v. 117-120.

[133] * *Zur Frage der Beeinflussung des Patienten in der Psychoanalyse.* [On influencing the patient in analysis.] Z. v. 140-141.

[134] ¶ ‡ (with Karl Abraham, Ernst Simmel, Ernest Jones) *Zur Psychoanalyse der Kriegsneurosen.* (Int. Psa. Bibl. Nr. 1.) Psycho-Analysis and the War Neuroses. Introduction by Sigmund Freud. Int. Psa. Press (now incorporated under the Institute of Psycho-Analysis), London, 1921, pp. 59.

[135] 1919. * *Zur Psychogenese der Mechanik.* (Kritische Bemerkungen über eine Studie von Ernst Mach.) [On the psychogenesis of mechanism.] I. v. 394-401.

[136] * *Hysterie und Pathoneurosen.* [Hysteria and Pathoneuroses. See Nos. 5, 6, 9, 10, 15, 31, in Table of Contents.] Int. Psa. Bibl. Nr. 2. Int. Psa. Verlag, Wien. Hungarian, Verlag Manó Dick.

[137] 1920. * *Nachtrag zur 'Psychogenese der Mechanik'* [supplement to No. 135]. I. vi. 384-386.

[138] * *Weiterer Ausbau der aktiven Technik in der Psychoanalyse.* [Further developments of 'active' technique. Read at the Sixth International Psycho-Analytic Congress at the Hague, September 1920.] Z. vii. 233-251.

[139] 1921. * *Psychoanalytische Betrachtungen über den Tic.* Z. vii. 33-62. Psycho-Analytical Observations on Tic. J. ii. 1-30.

[140] *Tic-Diskussion.* (Reply to criticisms.) Z. vii. 395.

[141] * *Die Symbolik der Brücke.* Z. vii. 211-213. [The Symbolism of the Bridge.] J. iii. 163-168.

[142] *Allgemeine Neurosenlehre.* (Bericht ü. d. Fortschritte d. Psa.) [General Theory of the Neuroses Trans. in J. i. 1920, 294.]

[143] 1922. ‡ § (with S. Hollos) *Zur Psychoanalyse der paralytischen Geistesstörung.* Supplement No. 5 to *Zeitschrift.* Int. Psa. Verlag, Wien, 1922. Psycho-Analysis and the Psychic Disorder of General Paresis. Translated by Gertrude Barnes and G. Keil. R. xii. 88-107 and 205-233. Published by Nervous and Mental Disease Publishing Co., New York, 1925.

[144] * *Populäre Vorträge über Psychoanalyse.* [Popular Lectures on Psycho-Analysis (many of them are included in this volume).] Int. Psa. Bibl., Bd. xiii. Int. Psa. Verlag.

[145] * *Die Psyche ein Hemmungsorgan.* [The psyche as an inhibiting organ.] Z. viii. 203-205.

[146] ¶ *Freuds 'Massenpsychologie und Ich-Analyse'. Der individual-psychologische Fortschritt.* [Freud's *Group Psychology and the Analysis of the Ego.* The progress in the psychology of the individual.] Z. viii. 206-209.

[147] *A Psychoanalysis haladása.* [The advance of psychoanalysis.] Hungarian, Verlag Manó Dick.

[148] * *Soziale Gesichtspunkte bei Psychoanalysen.* Z. viii. 326-328. [Social Considerations in Some Analyses.] J. iv. 475-478. See Nos. 80 and 81 in Table of Contents.

[149] 1922. *Die Brückensymbolik und die Don Juan-Legende.* Z. viii. 77. [Symbolism of the Bridge and the Don Juan Legend. J. iii. 167-168.]

[150] *Versuch einer Genitaltheorie.* [Attempt at a Genital theory.] Published by Int. Psa. Verlag, Wien.

[151] *Lélekelemzés.* Hungarian, Verlag Manó Dick. [Psycho-analysis.]

[152] *Lelki problémák a pszichoanalizis megvilágitásában.* Hungarian, Verlag Manó Dick. [Psychical Problems in the light of Psycho-analysis.]

[153] *Ideges tünetek keletkezése és eltünése.* Hungarian, Verlag Manó Dick. [The coming and going of nervous symptoms.]

1923. *Erfahrungen und Beispiele aus der analytischen Praxis.* [Experiences and Examples from Analytical Practice.]

[154] * *Ptyalismus bei Oralerotik.* [Ptyalism in an oral erotic.]

[155] * *Die Söhne der ' Schneider '.* [The sons of the ' tailor '.]

[156] * *Die ' Materialisation ' beim Globus hystericus.* [' Materialization ' in Globus hystericus.]

[157] * *Aufmerken bei der Traumerzählung.* [Attention during the narration of dreams.]

[158] * *Das Grausen beim Kratzen an Glas usw.* [Shuddering at scratching on glass, etc.]

[159] * *Zur Symbolik des Medusenhauptes.* [The symbolism of the Medusa's head.]

[160] * *'Lampenfieber' und narzisstische Selbstbeobachtung.* [Stage-fright and narcissistic self-observation.]

[161] *Ein ' analer Hohlpenis ' bei der Frau.* [An ' anal hollow-penis ' in woman.]

[162] * *Der Traum vom ' gelehrten Säugling '.* [The dream of the ' clever baby '.]

[163] * *Waschzwang und Masturbation.* [Washing-compulsion and Masturbation.] Z. ix. 69-71.

[164] 1924. † § (with Otto Rank) *Entwicklungsziele der Psychoanalyse.* [The developmental aims of Psycho-Analysis.] Neue Arbeiten z. ärztl. Psychoanalyse Nr. 1, Int. Psa. Verlag, Wien, 1924.

[165] * *Über forcierte Phantasien.* [On forced phantasies.] Z. x. 6-16.

[166] 1925. * *Zur Psychoanalyse von Sexualgewohnheiten.* Z. xi. 6-39. Auch separat als Brochure erschienen. Int. Psa. Verlag, Wien. [Psycho-Analysis of Sexual Habits.] J. vi. 372-404.

[167] *Charcot.* Z. xi. 257-260.

[168] 1925. *Kontraindikationen der aktiven psychoanalytischen Technik.* [Contra-indications to the 'active' psycho-analytical technique. A lecture given at the Ninth International Psycho-Analytical Congress, Bad Homburg, September 1925.] Z. xii. 3-14.

[169] 1926. *Zum 70. Geburtstage Sigm. Freuds. Eine Begrüssung.* Z. xii. 235-240. [Freud's 70th birthday. A Greeting. J. vii. 297-302.]

[170] * *Das Problem der Unlustbejahung.* [The problem of the acceptance of Unpleasant Ideas: Advances in Knowledge of the sense of reality.] Z. xii. 241-252.

[171] A review of Rank's *Technik der Psychoanalyse*, Bd. I., *Die Analytische Situation*, is to appear in Z. xii. and in translation in J. viii. (*i.e.* in Jan. 1927).

[172] 1927. *Bausteine zur Psychoanalyse. Bd. I. Theorie. Bd. II. Praxis.* [These two volumes are a collection of the Author's papers in the German language, and are similar in scope to this book. They will be published by the Int. Psa. Verlag, Wien, in the spring of 1927.]

[173] [All the publications that have appeared in German have been collected and translated into Hungarian in five volumes entitled:

i. *Lélekelemzés* (Psycho-Analysis).

ii. *Lelki problémak a pszichoanalizis megvilágitásában* (Psychical Problems in the light of Psycho-Analysis).

iii. *Ideges tünetek keletkezése és eltünése* (the Origin and Disappearance of Nervous Symptoms).

iv. *A hisztéria és a pathoneurozisok* (Hysteria and Pathoneuroses).

v. *A Psychoanalysis haladása* (the Progress of Psycho-Analysis.)]

C = *Zentralblatt für Psychoanalyse.*

Y = *Jahrbuch für psychoanalytische Forschungen.*

Up to 1919, Vol. v.—Z = *Internationale Zeitschrift für ärztliche Psychoanalyse.*

From 1920, Vol. vi. and onwards,—Z = *Internationale Zeitschrift für Psychoanalyse.*

I = *Imago.* [A journal devoted to the application of psycho-analysis to the mental sciences.]

J = *International Journal of Psycho-Analysis.*

R = *The Psychoanalytical Review.*

The *Zentralblatt* and *Jahrbuch* no longer appear; the former is out of print. These and the *Zeitschrift* and the *Imago* are obtainable at the Internationaler

Psychoanaltyischer Verlag, Wien.' The *Journal* is published by the Institute of Psycho-Analysis, London. The *P.A. Review* is published at 3617 10th Street N.W., Washington, D.C.

* = Translation appears in this volume.

† = Translation appears in *Contributions to Psycho-Analysis*.

‡ = Written in collaboration.

§ = The translation has been or may be included in the Mental and Nervous Disease Monograph Series.

¶ = Translation into English published elsewhere.

LIST OF TRANSLATORS

[The numbers refer to the chapters in this book, not to the bibliography references.]

Jane Isabel Suttie: 1, 2, 3, 5, 6, 8, 9, 10, 11, 12, 13, 14, 15, 16, 18, 19, 20, 23, 24, 25, 26, 27, 28, 29, 30, 31, 33, 34, 36, 38, 41, 44, 46, 47, 48, 49, 50, 51, 52, 53, 54, 55, 56, 60, 63, 64, 65, 67, 68, 69, 70, 71, 72, 75, 76, 77, 78, 79, 80, 81, 83, 85, 86, 87, 88, 89, 90.

Cecil M. Baines: 61, 73.

Olive Edmonds: 7, 21, 35, 37, 39, 42, 58, 66, 74, 82, 84.

Edward Glover: 32.

John Rickman: 4, 17, 22, 40, 43, 45, 57, 59, 62.

ERRATA

Bibliography ref. [108a] *Hebbels Erklärung des 'déjà vu'*. [Hebbel's Explanation of 'déjà vu'.] [1915] Z. iii. 250.

[144] This contains Nos. 32, 34, 37, 43, 44, 58, 59, 71, 100, 115, 120, 132, 135, 137, and Nos. 3, 87, 88, 89 in Table of Contents.

ADDENDA
TO BIBLIOGRAPHY
(1899–1933)

[2*a*] 1899. *Hypospadiasis ritkább esete.* Orvosi Hetilap. [A rare case of hypospadiasis.]

[2*b*] *Pemphigus esete.* Orvosi Hetilap. [A case of pemphigus.]

[2*c*] *Strictura recti esete.* Orvosi Hetilap. [A case of strictura recti.]

[2*d*] *Furunculus gyógyítása.* Orvosi Hetilap. [Therapy of furunculosis.]

[7*a*] 1900. *Hyperdactylia esete.* Orvosi Hetilap. [A case of hyperdactylia.]

[17*a*] 1902. *Megfigyelések agyvérzések és gyógyításuk körül.* Gyógyászat. [Observations on cerebral hæmorrhages and their therapy.]

[20*a*] 1903. *Izomhüdésekkel szövödött tabes.* Orvosi Hetilap. [Tabes complicated by muscle paralysis.]

[20*b*] *Cretinismus két esete.* Orvosi Hetilap. [Two cases of cretinism.]

[20*c*] *Facialis bénulás infectiosus alapon.* Orvosi Hetilap. [Facial paralysis of infectious origin.]

[20*d*] *Paralysis et lues conjugalis.* Orvosi Hetilap. [General paralysis and lues in consorts.]

[20*e*] *Szoptatástól kiváltott thyreogen tetania.* Orvosi Hetilap. [Thyrogenic tetany caused by suckling.]

[20*f*] *Encephalopathia saturnina.* Orvosi Hetilap. [Encephalopathia.]

[23*a*] 1904. *Adat a Trousseau-tünet újabb magyarázatához.* Orvosi Hetilap. [Contribution to a new explanation of the Trousseau symptom.]

[23*b*] *A tápkészítmények diaetetikus értékéről.* Budapesti Orvosi Ujság. [On the dietetic value of feeding preparations.]

[23*c*] *Tetania-esetek.* Orvosi Hetilap. [Cases of Tetany.]

[23*d*] *Ataxia hereditaria.* Orvosi Hetilap. [Hereditary ataxia.]

[26*a*] 1905. *Az arteriosclerosis okozta ideges zavarokról.* Orvosi Hetilap. [On the nervous disturbances caused by arteriosclerosis.]

[26*b*] *Agyalapi törés ideghüdéssel és arcgörccsel.* Orvosi Hetilap. [Fractured base of the skull with nerve paralysis and facial cramp.]

[26*c*] 1905. *Hozzászólás Schaffer Károly: 'Az agyi érzészavarokról klinikai és anatomiai szempontból' c. elöadásdhoz.* Orvosi Hetilap. [Contribution to the discussion on K. Schaffer's paper on 'Cerebral paræsthesias viewed clinically and anatomically'.]

[26*d*] *Egy anya és hároméves gyermekének tetania-tünetei.* Orvosi Hetilap. [Symptoms of tetany in a mother and her three-year-old child.]

[26*e*] *Részegség megállapítása hullából.* Gyógyászat. [Proof of drunkenness in a corpse.]

[28*a*] 1906. *Polyneuritis ritkább esete.* Orvosi Hetilap. [A rare case of polyneuritis.]

[28*b*] *Jegyzetek Dr. Dunas (Ledignan): 'Levelek az orvosi pályára készülö ifjúhoz' címen a Gyóyyászatban megjelent cikkekhez.* Gyógyászat. [Review of Dr. Dunas (Ledignan): 'Letter to a young man intending to study medicine'.]

[28*c*] *Conjugált szemebénulást utánzó szemizomhüdések.* Orvosi Hetilap. [Conjugate ocular paralysis.]

[28*d*] *Az idegorvoslás recepturájához.* Gyógyászat. [On the psychiatrist's pharmacopœa.]

[33*a*] 1908. *Polyneuritikus sorvadás (felkar és alszár izmainak).* Orvosi Hetilap. [Polyneuritic atrophy in the muscles of the upper arm and of the lower leg.]

[33*b*] *Az ejaculatio praecox jelentöségéröl.* Budapesti Orvosi Ujság. [On the significance of Ejaculatio Præcox.]

[33*c*] *A sexualis paedagogia.* Budapesti Orvosi Ujság. [On sexual education.]

[33*d*] *Baleseti sérülés okozhat-e progressiv paralysist?* Gyógyászat. [Can an accidental injury cause a progressive paralysis?]

[39*a*] 1909. *A balesetbiztosítási intézmény kilátásairól és a balesti idegbántalmakról.* Orvosi Hetilap. [On the prospects of the National Insurance against Industrial Accidents and on the neuroses caused by accidents.]

[61*a*] 1912. *A tudattalan megismerése.* Appeared in 1911 in 'Szabad Gondolat'. [On getting to know the unconscious.]

[61*b*] *Elöszó S. Freud 'Pszichoanalizis'-hez'.* Manó Dick, Budapest. [Foreword to S. Freud's 'Psycho-Analysis'.]

[81*a*] 1913. *A psychoanalysisröl és annak jogi és társadalmi jelentöségéröl.* Gyógyászat. [On psycho-analysis and its judicial and sociological significance.]

[81*b*] *Glaube, Unglaube and Uberzeugung.* A lecture delivered at the Munich Congress. [Belief, Unbelief and Conviction.] Contained in *A Pszichoanalyzis haladása.* [The advance of Psycho-Analysis. Budapest, 1919: Manó Dick.]

[81c] 1913. *Kritik der Jungschen 'Wandlungen and Symbole der Libido'*, 1913. Z. i. 391–403. [Criticism of Jung's 'Transformation and Symbolism of the Libido'.]

[95a] 1914. *Büntények lélekelemzése*. Szabad Gondolat. [Psycho-analysis of criminal acts.]

[111a] 1915. *A veszedalmek jégkorszaka*. Nyugat. [The glacial period of dangers.]

[124a] 1917. *Bardtsdgom Schächter Miksdval.* Gyógyászat. [My friendship with Max Schächter.]

[125a] 1918. '*A mese lélektandról*' (Válasz Lesznai A. cikkére). Nyugat. [On the psychology of fairy-tales.]

[163a] 1923. *Verzeichnis der wissenschaftlichen Arbeiten.* Z. ix. 428–434. [List of scientific works.]

[163b] *Ferenczi-Festschrift der 'Internationalem Zeitschrift für Psychoanalyse'.* Jg. ix.

[163c] *Elöszó Freud 'A Mindenappi Élet Pszichopatholdgidjd'-hoz.* A 'Világirodalom' Könyvk., Budapest. [Foreword to Freud's 'Psychopathology of Everyday Life'.]

[163d] *Elöszó Freud 'A Halalösztön és az Életösztönök'-höz*'. A 'Világirodalom' Könyvk., Budapest. [Foreword to Freud's 'Beyond the Pleasure Principle'.]

[165a] 1924. '*Altató és ébresztö tudomdny*'. Nyugat. [The science which lulls and the science which awakens.]

[165b] '*Ignotus, a megértö*'. Nyugat. [Ignotus, the Understanding.]

[165c] *Versuch einer Genitaltheorie.* Internationaler Psychoanalytischer Verlag, Wien. [Thalassa: A Theory of Genitality.]

[171a] 1926. *Freud's importance for the mental hygiene movement.* Mental Hygiene, x. 673–676.

[171b] *Present day problems in psycho-analysis.* Archives of Psycho-analysis, 1927, i. 522–530.

[171c] *Gulliver-Phantasien.* Read at the Annual Meeting of the New York Society for Clinical Psychiatry. [Gulliver Phantasies, 1928: J. ix. 283–300.]

[174] 1928. *Die Anpassung der Familie an das Kind.* Zeitschrift für psychoanalytische Pädagogik, ii. 239–251. [The Adaptation of the Family to the Child. Brit. J. Med. Psychol., 1928, viii. 1–13.]

[175] *Das Problem der Beendigung der Analysen.* Z. xiv. 1–10. [The Problem of terminating the analysis.]

[176] *Die Elastizität der psychoanalytischen Technik.* Z. xiv. 197–209. [The elasticity of psycho-analytical technique.]

[177] 1929. *Psychoanalysis és constitutio; észrevételek az 1929. 3. szdmban megjelent vezércikkre.* Gyógyászat. [Psycho-analysis and constitution.]

[178] 1929. *Männlich und Weiblich. Psychoanalytische Betrachtungen über die 'Genitaltheorie' sowie über sekundäre und tertiäre Geschlechtsunterschiede.* Psa. Bewegung, i. 41–50. [Male and Female: psychoanalytic reflections on the 'Theory of Genitality' and on secondary and tertiary sex differences. 1936. The Psycho-analytic Quarterly, v. 249–260. Masculine and Feminine. R. 1930, xvii. 105–113.]

[179] *Das unwillkommene Kind and sein Todestrieb.* Z. 1929, xv. 149–153. [The unwelcome child and his death-instinct. J. 1929, x. 125–129.]

[180] *Vorbericht und Schlussbemerkungen zu 'Aus der Kindheit eines Proletariermädchens.* Aufzeichnungen einer 19jährigen Selbstmörderin über ihre ersten zehn Lebensjahre'. Z. für ps-an Pädagogik, iii. 141–171. [Introduction and epilogue to 'On the childhood of a lower class girl. Notes of a 19-year-old suicide during the first ten years of her life'.]

[181] 1930. *A 'psychoanalysis' név illetéktelen haszndlata.* Gyógyászat. [On the unfair use of the designation 'Psycho-Analysis'.]

[182] *'Viszonvdlasz' Dr. Feldmann vdlaszdra.* Gyógyászat. [Counter-plea to the reply of Dr. Feldmann.]

[183] *Relaxationsprinzip und Neokatharsis.* Z. xvi. 149–164. [The Principle of Relaxation and Neocatharsis. J. xi. 428–443.]

[184] 1931. *Kinderanalysen mit Erwachsenen.* Z. xvii. 161–175. [Child Analysis in the Analysis of Adults. J. xii. 468–482.]

[185] 1933. *Freuds Einfluss auf die Medizin.* Psa. Bewegung v. 217–229. [Freud's influence on medicine.]

[186] *Sprachverwirrung zwischen den Erwachsenen und dem Kind.* [Confusion of tongues between the adults and the children.] Z. xix, 5-15. [Translation in J. vol. xxx.]

[187] 'Lélekelemzési tanulmányok.' [Psycho-analytical essays with a foreword by Sigm Freud to mark the 60th birthday of S. Ferenczi.] Béla Somló, Budapest.

POSTHUMOUS PAPERS

Published in Bausteine, Bd. IV

[188] *Gedanken uber das Trauma. I. Zur Psychologie der Erschütterung, II. Zur Revision der Traumdeutung, III. Das Trauma in der Relaxationstechnik.* Z. 1934, xx. 5–12. [Some thoughts on Trauma. I. On the

[188] 1933. psychology of Shock. II. On the Revision of the Interpretation of Dreams. III. The Trauma in the technique of relaxation.] Translations of Parts III and II appeared under the titles ' Relaxation and Education ' and ' On the Revision of the Interpretation of Dreams ' in Indian Journal of Psychology, 1934, ix. 29–38.*

[189] *A Pszichoanalizis Rövid Ismertetése.* Pantheon Kiadás, Budapest, 1936. [A short outline of psycho-analysis.]

[190] *Weiteres zur Homosexualität* (etwa 1909). [Further reflections on homosexuality.]

[191] *Zur Deutung einfallender Melodien* (etwa 1909). [On the interpretation of tunes which run in one's head.]

[192] *Lachen* (etwa 1913). [Laughter.]

[193] *Mathematik* (etwa 1920). [Mathematics.]

[194] *Über den Anfall der Epileptiker* (etwa 1921). [On the fits of epileptics.]

[195] *Beitrag zum Verständnis der Psychoneurosen des Rückbildungsalters* (etwa 1921–22). [Contribution to the understanding of the psychoneuroses of old age.]

[196] *Paranoia* (etwa 1922).

[197] *Psychoanalyse und Kriminologie* (1928). [Psycho-analysis and criminology. Not identical with ' Psychoanalysis and criminology ' (1919) contained in Further Contributions, p. 434.]

[198] *Über den Lehrgang des Psychoanalytikers.* Vortrag in Madrid (1928). [On the training of psycho-analysts.]

[199] *Die psychoanalytische Therapie des Charakters,* Madrid (1928). [The psycho-analytical therapy of character.]

[200] *Fragmentarische Aufzeichnungen aus den Jahren 1920 und 1930–1933.* [Fragmentary notes written during the years 1920 and 1930–1933.]

[201] *Bausteine zur Psychoanalyse,* Bd. III and IV.

BOOK REVIEWS

[1909] Kenyeres Balázs dr.: ' Törvenyszéki Orvostan '. [Medical jurisprudence.]

Gyógyászat 52.

[1910] Farkas, Dr. M.: Über die Kombination von Hydro- und Psychotherapie. [On the Combination of Hydro- and Psychotherapy.]

C. i. 78.

* These publications were an attempt at editing the fragmentary notes. Later it was decided to publish the notes in their original forms with as little editing as possible. Cf. No. 201. *Bausteine zur Psychoanalyse,* Bd. III and IV.

[1910] Jendrassik, Dr. E.: Über den Begriff der Neurasthenie. [On the conception of neurastheny.]
C. i. 114.

Stein, Dr. Ph.: Tatbestandsdiagnostische Versuche bei Untersuchungsgefangenen. [Experiments on the ascertainment of truth with people remanded in custody.]
C. i. 183.

Hitschmann, Dr. E.: Freuds Neurosenlehre. [Freud's Theory of the Neurosis.]
C. i. 601. Gyógyászat 50.

[1911] Dornblüth, Dr. O.: Die Psychoneurosen. [The Psycho-Neuroses.]
C. ii. 281.

[1912] Brenner, Dr. J. (Csáth Géza): Az elmebetegsegek psychikus mechanismusa. [The psychic mechanisms of mental disorders.]
Gyógyászat 1912, No. 24.

Bossi, Prof. Dr. L. M.: Die gynakologische prophylaxe bei Wahnsinn. [Gynæcological prophylaxis in mental illness.]
C. iii. 87.

[1913] Jones, E.: Papers on Psycho-Analysis.
Z. i. 93.

Maeder, A.: Sur le mouvement psychoanalytique. [On the psychoanalytical movement.]
Z. i. 94.

Brill, A. A.: Freud's Theory of Compulsion Neurosis.
Z. i. 180.

—— Psychological Mechanisms of Paranoia.
Z. i. 180.

—— Hysterical Dream States, their psychological mechanisms.
Z. i. 180.

[1914] Allgemeine Neurosenlehre. [General Theory of the Neuroses.]
Jahrbuch für psychoanalytische und psychopathologische Forshungen, vi. 317–328.

Bleuler, E.: Kritik der Freudschen Theorie. [Critics of the Theory of Freud.]
Z. ii. 62.

Jung, C. G.: Contribution to the study of psychological types.
Z. ii. 86.

Steiner, Maxim: The psychic disturbances of masculine potency.
Z. ii. 87.

Flournoy, H.: Epilepsie émotionelle. [Emotional epilepsy.]
Z. ii. 175.

[1914] Weber, R.: Reverie et Images. [Dream and Phantasies.]
Z. ii. 175.

Bjerre, P.: Das Wesen der Hypnose. [The Essentials of Hypnosis.]
Z. ii. 471.

Berguer, G.: Note sur le langage du rêve. [Note on the language of the dream.]
Z. ii. 529.

Partos, E.: Analyse d'une erreur scientific. [Analysis of a scientific error.]
Z. ii. 529.

Meggendorfer, F.: Uber syphilis in der Aszendenz von Dementia præcox Kranken. [On the occurrence of syphilis in the ancestors of patients suffering from dementia præcox.]
Z. ii. 530.

[1915] Kollaritis, Dr. S.: Observations de Psychologie quotidienne. [Observations of everyday Psychology.]
Z. iii. 46.

—— Contributions à l'étude des rêves. [Contributions to the Study of Dreams.]
Z. iii. 49.

Schilder, P. und Weidner, H.: Zur Kenntis symbolähnlicher Bildungen im Rahmen der Schizophrenie. [On symbol-like formations in Schizophrenia.]
Z. iii. 59.

Buchner, Lothar (Pseud.): Klinischer Beitrag zur Lehre vom Verhaltnisblödsin. [A clinical contribution to the theory of pseudo-dementia.]
Z. iii. 60.

Jung, C. G.: Psychologische Abhandlungen. [Psychological Essays.]
Z. iii. 162.

Claparède, Ed.: De la représentation des personnes et des lapsus linguæ. [The occurrence of lapsus linguæ in people.]
Z. iii. 123.

[1917] Décsi, Dr. Imre: 'Ember, Mért vagy ideges?' [Man why are thou nervous?]
Gyógyászat 31.

Adler u. Furtmüller: Heilen und Bilden. [Healing and Forming.]
Z. iv. 119.

Bleuler, E.: Physische und Psychisch in der Pathologie. [Physical and psychical in pathology.]
Z. iv. 119.

[1917] Kaplan, L.: Psychoanalytische Probleme. [Psycho-analytical problems.]
Z. iv. 120.

Putnam, J. J.: The Work of Adler.
Z. iv. 161.

Schultz, J. H.: S. Freud's Sexualpsychoanalyse. [S. Freud's sexual psycho-analysis.]
Z. iv. 270.

Groddeck, G.: Die Psychische Bedingtheit und psychoanalytische Behandlung organiseher Leiden. [Mental determination and psycho-analytical therapy of organic diseases.]
Z. iv. 346.

Claparède, Ed.: Rêve satisfaisant un désir organique. [Dream satisfying an organic desire.]
Z. iv. 345.

[1920] Schaxel, J.: Abhandlungen zur Theoretischen Biologie. [Essays on theoretical biology.]
Z. vi. 82.

Lipschütz, A.: Die Pubertätsdrüse und ihre Wirkungen. [The gland of puberty and its effects.]
Z. vi. 84.

Landau, Prof. E.: Naturwissenschaft und Lebensauffassung. [Science and outlook on life.]
Z. vi. 182.

Strasser, H.: Fragen der Entwicklungsmechanik. [Problems of experimental embryology.]
Z. vi. 183.

Gross, Otto: Drei Aufsätze uber den inneren Konflikt. [Three essays on the internal conflict.]
Z. vi. 364.

[1921] Freud, Sigm.: Drei Abhandlungen zur Sexualtheorie. [Three essays on the theory of Sexuality.]
Z. vii. 496.

Groddeck, G.: Der Seelensucher. Ein psychoanalytischer Roman. [The Soul Seeker. A psycho-analytical novel.]
I. vii. 356.

[1922] Abraham, Karl: Klinische Betrage zur Psychoanalyse. [Clinical Contributions to Psycho-analysis.]
Z. viii. 353.

de Saussure, Dr. R.: La Méthode Psychoanalytique. [Psycho-Analytical Method.]
Z. viii. 379.

INDEX

[In this Index the sub-headings are not arranged in alphabetical order but usually according to the following plan: where a disease is treated the order runs—definition, ætiology, fixation, regression, special form of repression, mechanism, clinical features, clinical varieties, associated disorders, differential diagnosis, treatment; where a mental process is treated the order runs—definition, mechanism, relation to other mechanisms, relation to clinical types; etc.

Page references followed by an * refer to case histories. J. R.]

Abraham: on grandfather complex, 323; on topophobia, 134

Abreaction: original theory of hysterical symptoms, 36, 102; in tic, 153

Abstinence: treatment must be carried out in a, 202, 272; marital, 275

Action: results from unequal inhibition, 381, 405

Actual neuroses: mainly somatic, 16, 32; distinguished from psychoneuroses, Chap. 2

Adler: does not analyse libido, 211, 449

Ætiology of the neuroses: 'degeneration' theory, 24; 'shock'-theory in relation to ætiology, 24, 52, 248; hereditary, 24, 49, 52; unconscious sexual factor never absent, 32, 41, 80; sexual factor alone does not produce illness, 53; non-sexual shocks produce neurosis, 54; blending of ætiologies, 53; women more affected than men, 25

Aggression: (references given under a different topic, viz. Sadism)

Alcoholism: in a case of hysteria, 113*; after cheating at cards, 245*

Amphymixis: of auto-erotisms, 172; of urethral and anal and genital function, 263 ff.

Anæsthesia (psychogenic): in relation to motor disturbances, 98; hysterical distinguished from pathoneurotic, 114*

Anal character (*see also* A. erotism): composite formations, 257* ff.

Anal children: 307*, 408*

Anal erotism: associated with castration complex, 248*; reanimated by bowel complaint, 82; associated with masochism, 47*; and sphincter play, 204*; anal orgasm, 270; and character traits, 257* ff.; stool pedantry, 261; and pseudo-hypochondria, 262; large bowel influenced by complexes, 94*, 270*; shown by silence in analysis, 250*; disguised in dream, 302; and revenge phantasy in a dream, 347; and artistic creations, 420; pecunia olet, 362; and vermin, 328; and eggs, 328; and disgust at foul breath, 362

Analysand: defined as the person being analysed.

Analysis (tuitional): a form of ego-analysis, 220, 291; and active technique, 220

Analytical failures: due to lack of indispensable patience or failure to observe contra-indications, 53; from misapplication of activity, 220

Analytical situation: influences patient all the time, 225; and aim inhibited impulses, 271 ff.

Animism: in Mach's *Mechanik*, 393

Anorexia: at breakfast, 326

Anxiety: genesis of, 161; action-anxiety a reaction to motor over-sensitiveness, 162; and sphincter tension, 268; and pavor nocturnus, 111*, in war neurotics, 134

Anxiety neurosis: found where sexual libido is separated from the psychic, 18, 34, 275; contrasted with neurasthenia, 34; and anxiety-hysteria, 277; and fear of dammed-up libido, 277; and larval onanism, 195; in wife may depend on husband's

impotence, 35; symptoms, 33, 300; virginal anxiety, 35; in war neurotics, 134; treatment, 277
Art: autoplastic tricks of hysterics the prototypes of artistic creation, 104; necessity the driving force, 389; hysteria is a caricature of, 104; 'nonum prematur in annum', 419
Association experiments (Jung): are 'indicators' for unconscious complexes, 38 ff.; prove disturbing to proper analysis, 40
Associations (free): elementary description of, 29, 426; *utterance* not *thinking out* of an idea, 181, 284; and patient's questions, 183; abused, 177; must not be written down, 182; absence of, 179; and obsessional rumination, 177, 221
Attention: at motor end of psychical apparatus, 232; and inhibition, 381; and induction of hypnosis, 402; thinking and muscle innervation, 230; two types of thinker, 231; analyst's attention to dream elements, 238
Auto-erotism: and genitalization, 173
Automatism: of prayer, 299
Autoplastic reactions: in war neuroses, 138; in catatonia, 164; in hysteria, 97
Autotomia: specialized form of defence, cf. tic, 160, 375
Avarice: 248*, 257*, 266

Bio-analytical hypotheses: faculty of adaptation, 370, 375; of growth, 376, 377
Birth-shock theory: criticized, 223; and anxiety, 354; and sphincter anxiety, 268, 270; and 'termination', 294
BJERRE: on spiritual guidance, 211, 235
BREUER: on psychical traumata, 36; on abreaction and retention, 153
Brooding mania: and infantile sexual curiosity, 49*; active therapy, 228

Case histories: *Hysteria*, 42, 43, 45, 46, 49, 94, 104, 108, 111, 112, 118, 189, 209, 222, 244, 250, 318, 326, 329, 352, 413; *Obsessional Neurosis*, 49, 50, 51, 73, 202, 243, 250, 273, 362, 450; *Manic-depression dis.*, 272; *Paraphrenia*, 78, 105, 118, 282; *Traumatic-pathoneurotic*, 84, 112, 113, 126, 136, 144, 150, 152, 154, 159, 160, 168; *not classified*, 72, 73, 74, 257, 299, 321, 331, 363
Castration complex: penis jealousy, 204*, 320*; from negligible injury, 244*; anxiety and sphincter anxiety, 268; and coitus anxiety, 279, 361; and phantasies of femininity, 80*; and parent's occupation, 418; and obsessional neurosis, 274*; and lust-murder-phantasies, 278; and genital paræsthesia, 312; faced clearly in active therapy, 267; and infantile theory of female genitals, 314; and shuddering at scratching on glass, 313; defects in one's children, 120
Catatonia: libido concentration on ego, 163; and tic, 146 ff.
Catharsis: the forerunner of analytical therapy, 37, 199, 449; distinguished from active therapy, 199, 212, 216
Cathexis (*hypercathexis*): in concentration of attention: 404, 405; (*preconscious*) enforced preconscious cathexis in active technique, 196
Censorship: described, 382; in concentration of attention, 404; and politics and erotic literature, 405
Character abnormalities and traits: compared to psychosis, 212, 215, 291; in relation to erotic traits, Chap. 31; and character regression, 363; and active therapy, 211, 214, 263, 266; in relation to organic illness, 82
Character analysis: reduced to sphincter analysis, 263; and activity, 290, 291
CHARCOT: on tic, 151
Chorea: 18
Circumcision: a kind of active therapy, 228; occasionally pathogenic, 249*
Clitoric eroticism: contrasted with feminine genitality, 89; and masculine productivity with sexual anæsthesia, 206
Coitus: physiology text-books give little enlightenment, 103; 'catastrophe'-theory, 279
Comical, the (*see* Wit)
Comparisons: *mechanism of*, 400, 404, 405; *of psycho-analysis*, 397 ff. (separating poppy from rice seeds, 397; shelling pods, 397; vacuum-cleaner, 397; expulsion of worms,

398; animal in cage, 398; dog on a chain, 398; scorpion surrounded by flames, 398; a difficult birth, 399; a storm stirring up weeds from bottom of the sea, 399; artesian well, 399; breaking a gate, 400); *of neurosis* (a spot on the soul, 398)
Consciousness: passive performance, 380; a state of hypercathexis, 380; and concentration, 404; and selective activity of censorship, 380; and inhibition, 381
Conviction: psycho-analysis offers favourable field for investigation, 437; 'palpable proof', 441; proof depends on intuition (Locke), 442; affective feeble-mindedness, 443; 'feeling is believing', 446; disillusionment about authority, 438, 440, 441; impossible without transference, 229, 438, 442, 445; lacking in obsessional neurosis, 228, 438, 444; lacking till produced by activity, 71, 74*, 220, 228; two motives for disbelief, 438; disbelief and distrust, 439; paranoia, 438
Coprolalia: mechanism, 196; and tic, 146, 157
Coprophagia: 46* ff., 325*, 326*
Cornelia's jewels: 318
Crime: an expression of unconscious impulses, 435; and punishment, 431; and social disorders, 432
Cryptamnesia: and rediscovery, 394*
Cure: its nature, 61

Dancing: 161 n.
Déjà vu: explanation of, 422; and hypochondria, 87
Dementia Præcox: a disease due to withdrawal of libido, 22; tendencies to self-cure, 87
Determinism: and analysis, 57
Dialogues of the unconscious: defined, 109*
Disbelief and disillusionment (*see* Conviction)
Disease-neurosis (*see* Patho-neurosis)
Displacement: of affect in obsessional neurosis, 49*, 50*
Dreams: mechanism of hallucination in, 96, 98; dream hallucination and relation between psychic activity and muscle innervation, 232; anxiety dream in war neuroses, 139; interchange of affect, 345*; occupation dreams, 298*; interpretation of a, exposes the unconscious, 40, 346, 412; dreams of the unsuspecting, 346; to whom does one relate one's dreams? 349; the dream of the 'clever baby', 349
DUBOIS' method: 446

Echolalia: and tic, 146, 157
Echopraxia: 163
Education: presupposes psychic control of sphincters, etc., and establishes 'command-automatisms', 92, 265, 283; and habit-weaning, 265; and parental influence (transference) in habit-weaning, 266; sphincter morality is a semi-physiological morality, 267; impeded by habitual sexual gratification, 271; and active therapy, 215, 267; and the parent-*imago*, 446
Ego (*see also* super-ego): habit tendencies in the *id*, the ego a habit-breaker, 285; behaves to sexual impulses as if they were dangers, 88, 99, 161, 275; whole ego may be identified with a part of the body, 85*, 269, 281*; ego-anxiety, 161, 265, 275; education of ego in active therapy, 200, 218, 220, 228
Ego, development of: and discrimination between ego and environment, 164, 366, 441; and an optimum of sexual traumatism in childhood, 77, 417, 418; related to self-destruction, 377
Ego (*death*) instincts: connected with general biological hypotheses, 380
Ejaculatio præcox: psychogenic disturbances of s. vesicles and sphincters, 277
Ejaculatio retardata: 353*
Embarrassment: due to unconscious phantasies, 202, 315
Emotions, expression of: related to materialization phenomena, 96
Eneuresis: and tic, 171
Eroticism: its essential nature, 265; and everyday activities, 191
Erotogenic zones: injury to, may lead to non-narcissistic disease, 86; if there is ego-identification and injury there may be pathoneurosis, 84; the face a quasi-erotogenic zone, 84;

the foreskin an erotogenic zone, 227; genital primacy, 85
Etymologizing: and origin of children, 318*
Exhibitionism: and penis jealousy, 122*, 204*; and embarrassment, 315; and means of inspiring terror, 329*; and Cornelia's jewels, 318 ff.; in face injury, 85*
Exophthalmic goitre: 18

Family romance: the usual neurotic, 415; of a lowered social position, 413*
FEDERN: on catatonic symptoms, 147
FEINDEL: on tic, 148 ff.
Fellatio: in association with psychogenic voice anomalies, 108*
Feminine genital impulse: the change from active to passive pre-conditioned by injury, 89; the woman who hates her conqueror, 89
Flatus: an adult prerogative, 325; excessive, 284 n.
Flexibilitas cerea: 163
Foreskin: an erotogenic zone, 227 ff.
Forgetting: suppression of unpleasant memories, 20, 37
Free will: an illusion of the ego, 285 n.
FREUD: on instincts, 158, 271; on 'The Three Contributions to the Theory of Sexuality', Chap. 30, and p. 52; on blending of ætiologies, 53; on magical, religious, and scientific stages of development, 373; on testing environment, 370, 371; on negation, Chap. 73; on primary process, 369; on the element of suggestion in analysis, 200; on repeating experiences in memory, not in acts, 217; on 'active technique', 196, 223, 224, 236, 271, 293; on narcissism limiting the influence of analysis, 215; on the free play of the analyst's unconscious, 189, 401; on counter-transference, 180 n.; on obsessional doubt, 274; on stammering, 251; on inheritance of experiences, 287; on pollutions, 298; on wit and the comical, Chap. 54
Frustration: associated with end of treatment, 75, 219; and active therapy, 197, 211, 213, 218, 219, 225

Gait: in war neuroses, 131* ff.
Genital paræsthesia: in impotence, 312
Genital primacy: described, 85; a pre-condition to conversion hysteria, 90, 99; only possible if pregenital eroticism is faced, 265, 270
Genitalization: defined, 85, 102; hysteria genitalizes the bodily parts at which symptoms are manifest, 90; a diseased or injured organ may be genitalized (cf. Hysteria), 82; of parts affected by tic, 171, 172
GILLES DE LA TOURETTE: on tics, 146
Globus hystericus: a genital process displaced, 93; a sphincter tension displaced, 268; fellatio and cunnilinguus, 92; case history, 43*
Grandfather complex: 323
GRASSET: on tic, 166
Grief: *normal*, 61; *pathological* (due to unconscious depressing motives), 61
GRODDECK: on the *id* being intelligent, 375; on analytical situation, 225
Group psychology: and censorship (political and erotic), 405 n.

Habit (*see* Chap. 32): a function of the *id*, 285; repetition compulsion, 285; contrasted with instinct, 286; introjection of external stimuli and habit, 286; relation to super-ego, 286; 'bad habits' are masturbation-equivalents, 282; and weaning from psycho-analysis, 293
Hallucination: mechanism, 95, 98, 99, 369
HEBBEL: on déjà vu, 422
Hereditary predisposition: makes trivial incidents pathogenic, 52, 130
HOLLÓS: active treatment of catatonics, 210
Homosexuality: in relation to castration complex, 247; in case of impotence, 94*, 106*, 108*, 244*; in paranoia, 79*, 105*, 359*; betrayed by position during analysis, 242
Housewife-psychosis: combination of anal erotism and character, 257
Hyperæsthesia: in traumatic cases (mechanism), 138
Hypnosis: two types of, 163, 402, 448; a safe but ineffective therapy, 28; suppresses symptoms, 27; can produce increase of innervation beyond the will of the patient, 91; motives

for hypnotic pliability, 163, 402, 443; and analysis (comparison made by a patient), 397; and affective feeble-mindedness, 443; and Dubois' method, 446
Hypochondria: in paraphrenia, 87; hysterical, Chap. 10; 118, 123, 262; distinguished from patho-neuroses, 83; in homosexual case, 108*; 'superstructures' on, 124; incurable without capacity for transference, 124; face, eyes, and genitals are so often the seat of hypochondriacal sensations, 87
Hysteria: elementary description of, 425; a disease in which symptoms are symbols of repressed thoughts, 21, 114; contrasted with actual neuroses, 34; contrasted with obsessional neurosis, 48, 444 n.; contrasted with patho-neurosis, 86, 88, 172; and displacement of libido on to an organ, 82, 99; achieves strengths of innervation impossible to normal, 91; in war neurotics, 131* ff.
Hysterical conversion: definition, 90; unconscious phantasies in bodily terms, 89, 101, 173; genital primacy a pre-condition, 89; of genito-sexual impulses, 102; globus hystericus, 92; vomitus gravidarum, 93; giddiness (special type of), 241; rare symptom found on genital itself, 270*

Identification: in pregenital stage, 265, 267; of whole self with genital, 269; of self with non-genital bodily part, 85; in mimicry, 165; in positivism, 229; of self with child, 122; hysterical, 45*
Illusion: mechanism, 96
Impotence: and birth anxiety, 354; and active therapy, 214, 261; and homosexuality, 94*, 106*, 108*, 244*
Infantile sexual theories: getting a child by eating, 93; on anal and urethral birth, 307*; of the female genitals, 50*, 314*, 317*; on coprophagia, 325*; a cause of reserve, 327*
Inheritance: of experience, 287
'Instance': defined, 197
Instincts (*see also* Ego I.): defusion of, 370, 377, 379; aim-inhibited instincts weakened by gratification, 271; only when attenuated can be used for 'social' ends, 19, 382; the 'capitalists' in psychical 'business', 382
Introjection: introjection stage of development, 373, 406; of external stimuli in habit formation, 286
Itching; pruritus ani and active therapy, 269

JONES: on Janet, 236; on giving advice, 236 ff.; on phonation, 251; on grandfather complex, 323
JUNG: on turning away from past, 211, 258, 449; on laziness, 421

KAPP: on machinery, 389
KOLNAI: on social aspect of analytical therapy, 216
v. KOVÁCS: on tic, 271

Laughter: mechanism of motor discharge, 232
Laziness: not cause of neurosis, 421*
Libido distribution (*see also* Genitalization): disturbed by injury, 81, 376; thinking and motility, 230 ff.; and wit, 403
LINDER: on sucking pleasure, 170
LOCKE: on proof depending on intuition, 442

MACH: on psychogenesis of machinery, 393
Machinery: psychogenesis of, Chap. 75; some are not projections but introjections (organ prolongations), 389, 390; others are pure projections (self-acting machines), 390; intellectual refinement of infantile sensational experiences, 387 ff.; the product of necessity, 389; friction machines, 388; plough, 386 n.; pumps, 388; screw, 388; turning lathe, 388
Mad: fear of going mad in an onanist, 311*
Magical gestures and words: revived by activity, 217
Mania: flight of ideas, 403
Masochism: surrendering a part of the body to algolagnia in order to preserve the genitals, 280; associated with anal erotism, 47*, 280; seated in the cutaneous envelope, 88; m. due to castration threat is secondary, 88 n.; and adaptation to reality, 376;

and exact amount of injury needed, 280; cf. scratching the place that itches, 87; and tic, 160

Masturbation: in ætiology of neurasthenia, 32; why it is exhausting, 33; m. of necessity is relatively harmless, 194; toleration of libidinal tension, 75; larval onanism is not harmless, 195; placed in the series of object-relationship-development, 171; in relation to castration complex, 247; m. equivalents defined, 192; larval forms, 190*, 193; types of larval onanism, 195, 317; m. 'without phantasies', 298; and washing-compulsion, 311*; and nail-biting, 170; and embarrassment, 315; and 'monasterism', 170; and prayer, 299; in relation to tics, 160

Materialization: defined, 96, 104; compared to dreams, 97; distinguished from hallucination, 95; amount of repression required to effect materialization, 97; in globus hystericus, Chap. 7; and conversion, 173

Mechanism: the basis for nosology, 21; displacement of affect in obsessional neurosis, 21, 43*; conversion of affect in hysteria, 21, 43*; projection in paranoia, 22; hypochondria, 123; withdrawal of libido in dementia præcox, 22; in war neuroses, 128; repressed libido turns to anxiety, 331; dream hallucination, 96; identification, 45*; necessary for sense of reality, 379; inhibitory m. in psychical apparatus, 379

Megalomania: in dementia præcox (1908), 22; in combined neurosis and paranoia, 105*; in G.P.I., 368

MEIGE: on tic, 148 ff.

Mimicry: regression, 164

Mnems: 287

Monasterism: and onanism, 170

Morality: double code and incidence of neurosis, 25

Motor type of thinker: 230

Musical faculty: and introversion, 378

Mutism: in catatonia alternating with logorrhœa, 165

Myxœdema: 18

Narcissism: and the erotic primacy of the genital, 85; and castration complex, 248*; and flight from situations which might wound self-love, 239; and exhibitionism, 330*; localized physical symptom in tic and catatonia, 172, 282; in case of face injury, 84*; in patho-neuroses, 81, 248; in paranoia, 81; and psychic assimilation, 406; and artistic production, 420; and stage fright, 421

Negation (Chap. 73): only occurs when there is a repressed unconscious, 374; and provisional acceptance, 367, 376, 379; and transference, 368; and neurosis compared, 369

Negativism: 'stage of negation', 367; in relation to catatonia and tic, 159

Neurasthenia: symptoms and ætiology, 18, 32 ff.; contrasted with anxiety neurosis, 34; and obsessional neurosis, 35; relation of ego to libidinal exhaustion, 275; and psychic attitude to 'losses', 277; treatment palliative, 276

Neuroses: perspective view of, 16 ff.; classification according to method of dealing with return of the repressed, 21 ff.; are screen-symptoms of an abnormal vita sexualis, 32; actual-neuroses, 32; psycho-neuroses, 35; symptoms of various neuroses usually found in same patient, 52 ff.; Sunday neuroses, Chap. 13

Neuroses, *Sunday*: definition, 174; characteristic feature, 174; symptoms, 175; ætiology, 175; mechanism, 176

Nosology: on a basis of mechanisms, 21

NUNBERG: on catatonia, 173

Obscene words: express deepest repressed anal and Oedipus wishes, 403; ignorance of o.w. a symptom of repression, 73*; in free associations, 182; uttered during coitus, 227; and speech and sphincter culture, 226, 251; and tics and catatonia, 161, 165, 171, 226

Obsessional neurosis: a disease which displaces affective values, 21, 444; example of typical displacement, 23, 50*, 243*; cure impossible without psycho-analysis, 48; contrasted with hysteria, 48, 444 n.; obs. acts are protective measures, 51; philosophical brooding and withdrawal from everything sensual, 49*; substituting thought for action (the reverse of laughter), 232; obs. ceremonials have origin in childish games, 284; and postponing working projects, 419; and taboo (elementary description), 430; and religion, 450

Obstinacy: an anal character-trait, 258; overcome by active therapy, 262

Oedipus complex: 111*; Oedipus gratifications concealed behind larval onanism, 214; reactivated by active therapy, 73, 267; and grandfather complex, 323; and myths, 428

Omnipotence: magical gestures, 440; gradual surrender, 373, 441

Onto- and phylogenetic aspects of psychology: in relation to sex, 254; in relation to the 'levels' of the mind, 374; compared to progressive adaptation of animals, 375; 'autoplastic stage', 97; and the polarity brain-genital, 99

Oral character-traits: and active therapy, 271

Oral eroticism: and ptyalism, 315*

Organ libido: stagnation in hypochondria, 124

Organ speech: 'detached instinctive energy', 166

Paræsthesias: of genitals, 74*, 246, 312; of teeth in relation to onanistic phantasies, 101; in hysteric, 45*; of non-genital bodily parts, 87

Paranoia: definition, 81; a disease of projection, 22, 53, 438; and homosexuality, 79*, 359*; combined with neurosis, 105*; and distrust, 438; 'traumatic paranoia', 81; precipitated by anal irritation, 80

Paraphrenia (*see also under* Paranoia *and* Dementia præcox): 403; relation to puerperium, 86

Parapraxes: utilized in analysis, 40; 'supposed mistakes', 407*; 'supposed mistakes' occur most frequently in automatic acts, 411 n.

Patho-hysteria (disease hysteria), 82

Patho-neuroses (*see* Chap. 5): hypercathexis of injured organ, 81; depends on amount of ego identification with the diseased organ plus repression, 83, 88; three possible determinants, 83; preserves libidinal object-relationship but disturbs libido distribution, 82; distinguished from hypochondria by *presence* of organic injury, 83; distinguished from traumatic neurosis, 83; relation to tic, 147; relation to 'castration', 247

Pavor nocturnus: 111*

Pcs.: symbol defined, 304 n.

Pedantry: an anal character, 258, 261

Penance: for unconscious evil thoughts, 51*

Penis jealousy (*see* Castration complex)

Perversion: and conflict, 42 ; neurosis the negative of perversion, 47*

PFEIFER: on necrophilia, 279

PFISTER: on cryptographia, 404

Phantasies: on forced phantasies, Chap. 4; of the transference actively evoked, 72*; of seduction, 73*, 74*; animation and torpidity of p. life due to childhood's experiences, 76; during larval onanism, 191

Phobia: of mice, 109*

Phylogenetic aspects of psychology (*see* Ontogenetic . . .)

Physiology: the 'p. of utility' needs to be supplemented by the 'p. of pleasure', 103

Piety: and obsessional neurosis, 450

Pleasure - principle: 'controller - in - chief' of our actions, 19, 366; in sphincter activity, 265; and negation, 379

Polarity in psychical systems: a division of labour, 99; life- and death-instincts, 367

Pollutions: a phenomenon of materialization, 103; a masturbatory act exiled to dream life, 276; with non-sensual dreams (3 types), 297-300; with sensual dreams, 298; p. dream unaccompanied by orgasm, 297*, 301*; occupation-p., 298*, 300

Polycratism: defined, 423

Pompadour phantasies: 351

Positivism (*Freudian*): and transference, 229

Potency: hyperpotency masking infantile weakness, 264

'Primary process': in wit, 336; in negativism, 367; transformation into 'secondary process', 369

Professions which use cutting instruments (knives, scissors, etc.): traumatic significance of, 248*, 353,* 418

Projection: a stage in development of a sense of reality, 439, 441; in paranoia, 80
Prophylaxis (in neuroses): 30
'Protopsyche': in relation to materialization, 97
Pruritus ani (*see* Itching)
'Psychical systems': Freud's memory systems, 155, 158, 173
Psycho-analysis: described, 29; early history of, 36; began by renouncing hypnosis, 37; a long-drawn-out fight against thought habits, 284, 286
Psycho-physical parallelism, 16 ff.
Psychology: and introversion, 378; and psycho-pathology, 19
Ptyalism: in a case of hysteria, 42*; in an oral erotic, 315*
Puerperal psychoses: due to injury of central erotic organ, 86
Punishment (need for): in masochism, 280
Pyromania: and urethral erotism, 258

RANK: and the birth shock theory, 223, 279, 294, 296; on analytical situation, 225; and the 'termination', 221, 296; on vagina dentata, 279; on 'orgasm' in every dream, 301; on material from different 'levels' in dreams, 302; on the family romance, 416
Reaction formation: against primitive impulses leads to the 'urge towards perfection', 382, 417
Reality (*see also* Conviction, Ego, Development of Ego, Negation): hysteria and autoplastic stage of development, 90; stages in development of capacity for objectivity, 373, 439, 440, 441; stage of negation in development of sense of reality, 367; affirmation a twofold act, 368; erotic reality, 371 n.; reality-recognition and its auxiliary organs, 378, 379; and sacrifice of narcissism, 377; and the well-brought-up child, 76
Reflex arc (applied to psychology): dreams and materialization, 97
Regression: in dreams, 98; in paranoia, 81; in war neuroses, 137; in 'motor type' of thinker, 232
REICH: on invariable disturbance of genital function in neuroses, 264; on onanism, 276
Religion: waning power of, to-day, 444 n.; and obsessional neurosis, 450
Repetition compulsion: and active therapy, 72, 217
Repression: must be graduated to infantile experience if self-composure is not to be lost, 417; and weakening of phantasy-life, 77; and sense of reality, 443; in tic, 156; and symptoms, 114*, 120*
Resistance: to new ideas, 54; by falling asleep, 249; by silence, 179; by talkativeness, 252*; transference-resistance, 45; by generalizations, 184
Restlessness: due to inhibition of larval onanism, 191; while thinking, 230-232; at end of hour, 238
'Return of the repressed': basis of classification of psycho-neuroses, 21; and symptom formation, 20; in normal person, 22; in hysteria, 21; in obsessional neurosis, 21; in paranoia, 22; in dementia præcox, 22
Rigidity of posture: revealing a mental attitude (transference), 281
ROHEIM: on foreskin erotism, 228 n.

SACHS: on poetic expression, 403
SADGER: on giving advice, 236
Sadism: in analyst, 220; sublimated in surgery, 428; and obscene words, 226; and coitus anxiety, 279; lust-murder phantasies in analysis, 278, 279; and killing vermin (children), 328*; and tic, 160
Sanatorium-disease: described, 28
Screen-memories: replace the memories of childhood, 38
Self-destruction: a 'cause of being', 377; and failure to direct sadism to outer world, 376
Self-mutilation: in paraphrenia a means of self-cure, 87
Self-observation: and stage-fright, 421
SILBERER: on functional symbolism, 355; on lecanomancy, 402
SIMMEL: on war hysteria treated with activity, 210
Smelling and sniffing: a prototype of intellectual activity, 267, 370
Smoking: dreaded because of erotic element, 318
SOKOLNICKA: on active treatment of an obsessional, 210

Solipsism: 229, 374
Spectrophobia: 365
SPENCER: on organ prolongations (machinery), 389
SPERBER's sexual origin of speech: 318
Spermatorrhœa: case showing it to be a genital price for an anal pleasure, 270
Sphincter (*education of*, *psychology of s. control*, *s. ego*, *s. morality*, *etc.*): anal erotism, 204*, 250*, 259 ff. 284 n.; s. tensions, 226, 267, 279; s. tensions and emotion, 93; exercises, 226, 263, 266, 268, 274, 277, 289; over action of external s. compensates for weakness of internal s., 263, 277; amphimixis theory, 263; sphincter morality, 267; education, 92, 264, 274; and active therapy, 215, 261, 266, 274*; atypical sphincters, 268; and speech, 250*; and obscene words, 161, 226
Stage-fright: narcissistic self-observation, 421
Stereotypy: (*see* Tic) Chap. 12.
Stigmata: historical, 110; defined, 117; attempted explanation of, Chap. 9; are not *pithiatisms*, 117; though psychogenic are not of ideational origin, 115; permanent change in sensitive end of psychical system in cases of, 98; concentric narrowing of visual fields, 116; of throat, 116
'Stretching': and erection, 269
Substitution: in mechanism of obsessional neurosis, 49
Suggestion: defined, 55, 70, 443, 447; drawbacks to its use, 28, 56, 444, 447; only palliative, 61; and psycho-analysis, Chap. 3 and p. 62 ff., 200, 448; recognition of an evil is a pre-condition of its remedy, herein suggestion fails, 60, 448; effect on consciousness, 57; to be distinguished from the interference with free associations in the 'forced phantasy' technique, 69; to be distinguished from active technique, 200, 212, 224, 266, 291; differs from analysis in that (1) the analyst is more sceptical than the suggestionist, 70, 447; (2) the analyst does not offer advice, 184, 197, 235, 237; (3) the analyst works *against* resistances, 63 ff.
Super-ego: identification with parent, 266, 286; gradual surrender of omnipotence, 373, 440; and habit formation and habit breaking, 286; and social advancement, 417
Symbols: their nature discussed, 100, 352, 355, 403, 407; physiological basis, 101, 355; and *re*-discovery, 407; in paraphrenia, 403; auto-symbolic or functional interpretation, 355; bed-linen, 359; bridge, 352 ff.; child, 320; defæcation, 101; egg, 328; eye, 84, 317; face, 170; fan, 361; head, 170; head splitting open, 123; infection, 305; jewels, 320; kite, 359; *left*-hand side, 111 ff.; luggage, 79; Medusa's head, 360; mice, 109, 111; nose, 101; œsophagus, 101; over-eating, 101; rumpled paper, 359; shoe, 347, 358; sun, 246, 365; teeth, 101; throat, 101; vermin, 327, 361
Symmetrical touching: 242-244
Symptomatic acts: intensively charged with libido, 195; and distraction of attention, 401; and larval onanism, 192*, 195; and tic convulsif, 195; position during treatment, 242
Symptoms: localization of, by bodily predisposition, 42; represent unconscious sexual wish, 95*; are incapable of being relieved, they can be cured or can be substituted, 61; s. cease when libido has found a normal channel, 197; passagère s., 179, 181, 282; symmetrical touching, 242
Synæsthesia: in pollution dreams without orgasm, 300

Taboo: explanation offered by analysis, 430
TAUSK: on occupation delirium, 170, 298; on compensation as a means of discounting repression, 369
Technique (*active*): indications, 70, 198, 208 ff., 270, 289, 292, 294; theoretical, 213; distinguished from suggestion, 69; indications for forced phantasy method, 70, 75*, 207; to be initiated by analyst, not patient, 289, 295; issuing commands and prohibitions, 68, 75*, 206, 220, 221, 236, 261 ff., 266 n.; Freud's use of a.t. in anxiety hysteria, 196, 236, 260; an extension of the principle of abstinence, 201, 202, 206, 260; prohibiting

larval masturbation, 191, 214; works against the pleasure principle, 211, 218; exacerbates symptoms, 213; produces a new distribution of psychical forces, 213, 266; increases capacity to tolerate 'pain', 280, 287; depends on strength of transference, 208, 219, 237, 272, 289; illustrative cases, 70* ff., 121*, 204*, 222*, 273*; an experimental method, 197, 261, metapsychology, 287, 292; repetition compulsion, 217, 224; in character analyses, 215, 220, 291; in psychopathic cases, 291; specially useful in obsessionals, 209, 228; speeds up analytical work, 213, 289; danger of 'curing' too quickly, 213, 220; timing of active measures, 220; sphincter exercises, 226, 266, 274*, 282; activation of sublimated activities, 206; interpretation, 199, 224; rare cases where analyst is active, 75, 291; cathartic technique, 199, 212; 'sexual anagogy', 274*; 'termination', 189*, 209, 221, 223, 293; contra-indications, 69, 208, 217 ff.

Technique (*classical*): general description, 199; *saying*, not *doing*, 181; passagère symptoms, 181; associations must not be written down, 182; patients' questions, 183; dealing with the patients' generalizations, 184; speed of initiation, 180 n.; decisions during treatment, 183; discontinuous analysis, 233; danger of neglecting technique, 219; alternate free play of analyst's phantasy and critical scrutiny, 189; passivity of doctor, 182, 224, 238, 290, 401; the effect of the doctor's silence, 179, 290; augmented by activity, 288; free association abused, 69, 177, 207; absence of associations, 179; patient falls asleep, 179

Therapy (in neuroses, psycho-neuroses, and psychoses): by diet, etc., 27; by electricity, 28; by hypnotism and suggestion (*q.v.*), 28, 235, 447; by moralizing, 27, 235, 446, 449; by sanatorium, 28, 36; by occupational guidance, 28; by anti-neurotic medicaments, 28; recognition of an evil is a pre-condition to its remedy, 60; analysis and confession contrasted, 216

Tic: general ætiological view, 171, 173, 283; age in ætiology (*i.e.* sexual development), 171; infantile character, 152; anal erotism, 171; constitutional narcissism, 145, 151, 161; fixation of libido, 145, 147, 172; mechanism of displacement, 150; special kind of repression, 156, 158; hypersensitiveness, 145, 152, 417; onanism, 144*, 160*, 170, 173, 271*; stereotypy, 144, 153, with other symptoms, 143, 146; 'motor type' of individual, 150, 152, 161; motor discharge, 160, 165, 172; eneuresis, 171; contagious, 165; and injury to bodily parts, 147; pathoneurotic tics, 156, 158; attitude tics, 162, 168; *maladie des tics*, 146; tics and psychoses, 161, 162, 163, 165, distinguished from obsessional neurosis, 169, 170, 173, 174; treatment with 'activity', 282

Ticklishness (*see also* Itching): a hint as to mechanism of, 113; and shuddering, 113*

Time: attacks of a feeling of 'eternity' (delayed evacuation), 270

Torticollis: and tic, 162*

Totemism: explanation offered by analysis, 429

Transference: described, 63 ff.; adds a 'social' aspect to analytical therapy, 216; necessary for conviction about anything, 229; and negation, 368; handling of, 121*, 216, 291, and active therapy, 208, 219; t. resistance (a last effort to avoid an insight into the unconscious), 45; in prison analysis, 436

Transference (*counter-transference*): analyst must be analysed, 187; 'wild' analysts, 188; resistance against c.t., 188; sadism in analyst, 220; analyst must graduate his sympathy, 186; analyst begins to doze, 180 n.

Traumata: originally thought to be important, 52, 80; their dependence on hereditary predisposition in the ætiology of neuroses, 52, 115*, 130, 156; a little sexual traumatism in infancy promotes normal active phantasy, 77; causing regression, 137; 'traumatophilia', 139; and ego injury, 141; caused by sudden affect that cannot be psychically

controlled, 129, 247; and absence of self-confidence, 134; and tic, 147, 156; wounds may help in cure of, 156; and memory traces, 158, 377; of sexual nature in childhood followed by a too cultured life, 417
Tremor: in war neurosis, 125* ff.

Ucs: symbols defined, 304 n.
Urethral children: 307*
Urethral erotism: in relation to castration complex, 122*; analysis of urethral habits, 260, 269*; need to urinate increased when larval masturbation was prohibited, 192*; pyromania, 258; micturition a sedative, 317; phantasies of teasing, 75*; cases, 49*
'Utraquism': defined, 373

Vermin: symbol of children, 327, 361
Voice production: psychogenic anomalies of, Chap. 8*; lady imitators, 109*
Vomiting: in pregnancy, 93, 95; and coitus, 326*; coprophilia, 326*

War neuroses: types of, Chap. 11; conversion mechanism in, 129; neurotic regression, 137*; self-love in, 136; loss of libido sexualis, 141; injuries to narcissism, 141; psychoneuroses, 127, 134; active therapy, 210; cases, 112*, 126* ff.
Washing-compulsion: and masturbation, 311
Will (and will power): and inhibition, 405
Wit: Freud asked himself why people laughed at his 'Interpretation of Dreams', 336; infantile character, 344; economy of inhibition, 334, 344; motor abreaction, 334; condensation, 334; and 'primary process', 336; and the censor, 335; and dream, 335, 337; and puns, 337; technique, 338 ff., 342, 403, 406; aggressive, 339 ff.; obscene, 339 ff.; a social phenomenon, 340; irony, 343; humour, 344; humour and megalomania, 344; automatism and the comical, 343; size in relation to the comical, 343; in the comical only two persons are needed, 342
Words: treated as objects, 442
Working through: symptoms must be 'worked through', 220, 290